AF540696

AN INTRODUCTION TO LEGAL THEORIES

An Introduction to
LEGAL THEORIES

DR. GOKULESH SHARMA
Judge, Civil Court, Lucknow

DEEP & DEEP PUBLICATIONS PVT. LTD.
F-159, Rajouri Garden, New Delhi-110027

An Introduction to
LEGAL THEORIES

ISBN 978-81-8450-048-6

Typeset by **S.S. COMPOSERS**
3190, Mohindra Park, Shakur Basti, Delhi-110034.

Printed in India at **NEW ELEGANT PRINTERS**
A-49/1, Maya Puri, Phase-I, New Delhi-110064.

Published by **DEEP & DEEP PUBLICATIONS PVT. LTD.**
F-159, Rajouri Garden, New Delhi-110027.
Phones: 25435369, 25440916
E-mail: ddpbooks@yahoo.co.in • ddpubs@gmail.com
Showroom:
2/13, Ansari Road, Daryaganj, New Delhi-110002 • Telefax: 23245122

CONTENTS

Preface vii

PART I

INTRODUCTORY REFLECTIONS

1. Greek Philosophy 3
2. Law, Justice, Ethics and Social Morality 12
3. Science and Legal Theory 37
4. Legal Theory and Social Evolution 53

PART II

SURVEY OF LEGAL THEORIES

5. Analytical Theory (Positivism) 65
6. The Pure Theory 91
7. Historical and Anthropological Approaches 108
8. Economic Approaches 129
9. Sociological Approaches 154
10. Realism 182
11. Philosophical and Natural Law Theories 205
12. Oriental and Continental Approaches 244
13. Critical Legal Studies 308

14.	Feminist Theory	318
15.	Post-Modernist Jurisprudence	331
16.	Current Trends in Jurisprudence	337
	Index	341

PREFACE

No specific book has been written which deals about Legal theories particularly touching Indian oriental philosophy. I have tried in this book to present a comparative legal philosophy, on one had, of the Hindu, Muslim and Chinese thought relating to the eastern world and communist philosophy of Russia, and on the other hand, western philosophy of Greek, Roman, British and American thinkers. Although brief role of German, Australian and other thinkers of various other nations have also been taken up for consideration. I have tried to give a complete picture of various faces and theories of law, justice and jurisprudence. The book will also suggest a proper guideline for the future.

The book is divided into two parts and have sixteen chapters. The first part of the book has four chapters. The first chapter deals with a brief outlook of the whole subject. It gives a description of the Greek Theories. Second chapter describes the meaning of Law, Justice, and Ethics. A good discussion of thought of available philosophers of law has been taken up along with a new approach to existing law and future trends. Third chapter deals with Science and Legal Theories. Fourth chapter is about Legal Theory and Social Evolution. It also provides discussion how legal theories effect social evolution. Second part of this book deals with survey of various legal theories whether Oriental, Continental, European, American and what so ever.

The second part of the book has twelve chapters. Fifth chapter deals with Analytical Theories which are also called positive theories. Sixth chapter deals with Pure Theory of law, it is a abstract chapter of legal theories. Chapter seven describes Historical and Anthropological Approaches. Chapter eight provides Economic Approaches. Chapter nine likewise details about Sociological Theories. Chapter ten provide real view of Realistic Theories. Chapter eleven describes Philosophical and Natural Law Theories. Further chapter twelve provides Oriental and Continental Approaches which is a unique feature of this book. Chapter thirteen discloses various kinds of Critical Legal Studies likewise chapter fourteen provides a good work for weaker section of society under Feminian Theories. Chapter fifteen and sixteen are very latest and of recent origin. These descirbes Post-modern Theories and Current available Trends of Legal Theories.

The book is dedicated to my elder brother, late Pandit Sunder Lal Sharma, whose high inspirations have always guided me to work for all possible legal reforms in the society.

I am highly indebted to my wife Smt. Neeta Sharma and my closely associated cousin Sanju and my three kids Sakshi, Kriti & Vasistha and other friends who have cooperated with me in the preparation of the book and helped me a lot, which is unforgettable. My daughter Sakshi is a distinguished law student, She has prepared the manuscript of this book in fool proof manner. All issues have been considered in depth. All have been analyzed minutely with due care and attention even if any provision has been left with or any mistake is discovered or if any kind of omission of any provision is brought to knowledge, then I tender due apologies for the same in advance and I call for suggestions from readers for correction in future.

Lastly I am personally obliged to Shri G.S. Bhatia of Deep & Deep Publications Pvt. Ltd., New Delhi, who has published the book in a very short time. I think the book will be useful for Judges, Advocates and not only to legal experts but also to each and everyone who is interested in the legal field or have a specific interest in law and justice.

Lucknow GOKULESH SHARMA

PART I

INTRODUCTORY REFLECTIONS

1

GREEK PHILOSOPHY

All Systematic thinking about legal theory is linked at one end with philosophy and, at the other end, with political theory. Sometimes the starting-point is philosophy, and political ideology plays a secondary part as in the theories of the German classical metaphysicians or the Neo-Kantians. Sometimes the starting-point is political ideology, as in the legal theories of Socialism and Fascism. Sometimes theory of knowledge and political ideology are welded into one coherent system, where the respective shares of the two are not easy to disentangle, as in the scholastic system or in Hegel's philosophic system. But all legal theories must contain elements of philosophy—man's reflections on his position in the universe and gain its colour and specific content from political theory—the ideas entertained on the best form of society. For all thinking about the end of law is based on conceptions of man both as a thinking individual and as a political being.

This dual aspect will facilitate an understanding of the development of legal thought, as tranced in this book. Some legal philosophers have been philosophers first and foremost, and jurists because they felt the need to express their political thought in legal form. A third group—mainly in recent times—has been driven to consider the ultimate ends of law, by the professional study and practice of the law. They have been nonetheless compelled to accept one or the other philosophical or political premiss.

This may account, to some extent, for the difficulty of assigning to legal theory a place of its own. It must, however, gain such a place; for, as will be apparent throughout this book, the lawyer, whether as legislator or magistrate, whether as citizen or as professional craftsman, is always consciously or unconsciously guided by the principles which legal theory formulates for him in professional form, from the precepts of philosophy and political theory. In Radbruch's formulation, its task is "the clarification of legal values and postulates up their ultimate philosophical foundations."

To the further question of the relation of law to religion, ethics, economics and science, on general answer can be given. These are the sources from which a particular legal theory may be nourished. Religion determines the philosophical and political outlook of the scholastics, ethical principles determine the legal philosophy of Kant, economics underlie the legal thought of Marxism, scientific fact study inspires the functional approach of the realist movement. The answer to these questions must therefore be given in conjunction with any particular legal theory, which is discussed. But all these sources contribute though in varying strength and combination, to form the philosophical and political valuations from which a legal theory is built up.

The present book cannot attempt to give a full analysis to these philosophical, political and other non-juristic premises of legal theory. It must be content to point them out in general terms. This should suffice, however, not only to link a legal theory with the religious or ethical principles, the political philosophy, the economic theory by which it is inspired; the political philosophy, the economic theory by which it is inspired; it should also help to bring out a significant shift in the development of legal thought.

Before the nineteenth century, legal theory was essentially a by-product of philosophy, religion, ethics of politics. The grant legal thinkers were primarily philosophers, churchmen, politicians. The decisive shift from the philosopher's of politician's to the lawyer's legal philosophy is of fairly recent date. It follows a period of great developments in juristic research, technique and professional training. The new era of legal philosophy arises mainly from the confrontation of the professional lawyer, in his legal work, with problems of social justice.

It is, therefore, inevitable that analysis of earlier legal theories must lean more heavily on general philosophical and political theory, while modern legal theories can be more adequately discussed in the lawyer's own idiom and system of thought. The difference is, however, one of method and emphasis. The modern jurist's legal theory, on less than the scholastic philosophers is based on ultimate beliefs whose inspiration comes from outside the law itself.

GREEK PHILOSOPHY

All the main issues of legal theory were formulated by Greek thinkers, from Homer to the Stoics. The rise and development of the Police, the Greek city state, was the persistent background of Greek speculative thought on law and government, from the descriptions of life in a city state on the shield of Achilles—in Homer's Iliad—to the reflections of Plato and Aristotle. But only the combination of two factors could produce the abundance of mature thought on the function and problems of law in a community. The social disorders, internal conflicts, the frequent changes of government, the many periods of tyranny and arbitrariness, provided the external stimulus to speculation about the relation of higher justice to positive law. But only a unique gift of speculative insight and intellectual perception, a sense of tragedy and human conflict which is apparent in Greek philosophy and poetry, made possible the Greek contribution to legal philosophy, and in particular to the problem of eternal justice and positive law.

FROM HOMER TO PERICLES

In Homer's work law has an essential but unproblematical place. Law is embodied in the Themistes which the kings receive from Zeus as the divine source of all earthly justice and which are based on custom and tradition. Justice is still identical with order and authority. An awareness of the conflict between positive law and justice becomes more and more pronounced from the eighth century onwards. It arises against a background of social trouble, of discontent with the rule of aristocracy and frequent abuse of power. The problem of justice (Sikn) becomes articulate in the poems of Hesiod and of Solon, the great Athenian law-givers. Both appeal to Dike, the daughter of Zeus, as a guarantor of justice against earthly tyranny, violation of rights and social injustice. Solon sees Dike as rewarding civil unrest and injustice with social evils while she rewards just communities with peace and prosperity.

The problem of the relation between justice and positive law dominated Greek thinking, as indeed all legal thought ever since. The nature philosophers of the Milesian school turned to external nature as a source of law more permanent than human laws. The process by which Heraclitus found the law of nature in the rhythm of events and subsequent thinkers came to conceive of nature as opposed to reason is described in the following chapter. This development led Greek thinkers to a contemplation of the relation between the outer world of the universe and the inner world of man. In the first phase the main theme is the tragic antithesis between the need to obey the positive law of the state and the higher moral claims of the unwritten and unaltering divine law. The classical expression of this is found in the tragedies of Aeschylus and Sophocles: both Aeschylus' Eumenides and Sophocles' Antigone end in the appeal to the respect for law as the main guardian of order, peace and harmony in the state. Both are still dominated by the sense of accomplishment which preceded the decline of Athenian democracy, a belief in the progress which a civilised and ordered community dominated by wise laws had made over the anarchy and tyranny of earlier days. The last classical expression of this phase of Greek legal thought is Pericles' Funeral Oration.

Greek Philosophy

If we look to the laws, they afford equal justice to all in their private differences; if no social standing, advancement in public life falls to requtation for capacity, class considerations not being allowed to interfere with merit; nor again does poverty bar the way; if a man is able to serve the state he is not hindered by the obscurity of his condition. The freedom which we enjoy in our government extends also to our ordinary life. There, far from exercising a jealous surveillance over each other, we do not feel called upon to be angry with our neighbour for doing what he likes, or even to indulge in those injurious looks which cannot fail to be offensive, although they inflict no positive penalty. But all this ease in our private relations does not make us lawless as citizens. Against this fear is our chief safeguard, teaching us to obey the magistrates and the laws, particularly such as regard the protection of the injured, whether they are actually on the regard the protection of the injured, whether they are actually on the Statute Book, or belong to that code which, although unwritten, yet cannot be broken without acknowledged disgrace.

PLATO'S APPROACH TO LAW

It is the subsequent decline of Athenian democracy, in the Peloponnesian war and after, which provided the background for the preoccupation with justice that dominates the legal philosophy of Plato and Aristotle. As in our own time, the decline in the standards of government and society stimulated the yearning for justice. Faced with the disintegration of Athenian society and the disruption of the very values and accomplishments which Pericles had praised, both devoted a considerable part of their work to a more concrete definition of justice and to the relation between justice and positive law. But as Kelsen has pointed out, they approached the problem from two different angles, contrasted by him as the metaphysical and the rationalistic approach. Plato attempted to derive his conception of justice from inspiration; Aristotle developed it from a scientific analysis of rational principles developed against a background of existing types of political communities and laws. The connecting link between them is concept of virtue, the all-embracing idea of which justice is a necessary part and aspect. From this flows the conception of balanced and harmony as the test of a just commonwealth and a just individual. But here the ways part. Harmony for Plato is a state of inner balance of mind not capable of retional analysis. To Aristotle it is the mean between extremes, deduced by quasi-mathematical principles from a blend of government and human relations.

In his attitude towards from a blend of extremes in government and human relations.

In his attitude towards the necessity and importance of law for the community, Plato's later message differs from that of his earlier work. In the commonwealth pictured in the Republic, the law as an organised and formulated system of rules binding upon the community has no place. That work is mainly devoted to an analysis of the functions of the different classes in the state and in particular to the philosopher-king who are to control the state. The execution of justice is entirely entrusted to these rulers whose education and inspired wisdom are a guarantee of just government. It is the task of the rulers to see to it "that man should to his work in the station of life to which he is called by his capacities."

Plato's later work is, on the contrary, dominated by the problem of law as a formulated system of positive rules governing the whole of the state. If the Republic was a reflection of Plato's ideal state, experience and disillusionment—particularly his work as adviser to the Sicilian tyrant Dionysius—had brought him to consider the necessity of a "second best state." Plato's great work of his old age, The Laws, is entirely devoted to a discussion between an Athenian, a Spartan and a Cretan on the principles and subject-matter of laws in a state. There are few activities which the later Plato did not consider as in need of legal regulation. In The Laws he discusses, through the mouth of the Athenian, in minute detail, such divers matters as marketing regulations, community meals and the legal aspects of every kind of agricultural activity. But the law is meant of regulate further the most intimate personal relations, the emotions of infants, conduct in marriage, and divorce, no less than the types of funerals or the scale of earnings if different occupations. A detailed scale of sanctions—both civil and criminal—cements these laws. There are still state-appointed supervisors, but now take their knowledge and guidance from the written law. As Cairns has pointed out,. Plato anticipates Bentham in his faith in the omniscient legislator. But his philosophy resembles the philosophy of the modern authoritarian welfare state—communist or Fascist—in the extent to which it subjects individual life and administrative control of the state.

Law now appears as a golden stream, the embodiment of "right reasoning". As to the content and sources of this right reasoning, Plato is, however, silent, his conception of justice is still essentially the same as in the Republic.

Justice, namely, virtue in the sense of inner harmony and balance, is not knowable or explicable by rational argument. In several of his Letters Plato has in fact made this observation, on the knowledge of the good, that is of justice, there are no writings of his, "for it does not at all admit of verbal expression like other branches of knowledge." The progress from the Republic to The Laws lies in the insight that a class of aristocratic philosopher-kings, wise enough to apply justice without written laws, cannot be hoped for, but the knowledge of justice which directs the laws of the state is still a matter of mystical inspiration.

The nearest approach to an explicit formulation of the conflict between justice and legality is contained in a short dialogue which, if it cannot be ascribed with certainty to Plato himself, certainly emanates from one of his disciples. In Minos Socrates and a pupil discuss the definition of law and move from the original definition of law as something stipulated in proper form the original definition of law as something stipulated in proper form by the proper authority, to the necessity of relating law to the revelation of truth and good. While the problem is stated with dialectic pungency, the dialogue ends inconclusively with a discourse by Socrates on "Minos" who, as a wise law-giver, received his inspiration from Zeus himself. This does not lead beyond the Platonic conception of justice, as the revelation of good received by the select few and communicated by them to the community in the form of laws.

ARISTOTLE'S CONTRIBUTION TO LEGAL THEORY

Aristotle's contribution to legal theory, inspired as it was by an encyclopedical study of existing laws and constitutions, is a more definite one.

The most fundamental of Aristotle's doctrines is that which has since inspired not only legal theory but Western philosophy in general, i.e., the dual character of man as part and master of nature. Subject, as part of the universe, to the laws of matter and all creation, man, at the same time, dominates nature by his spirit which enables him to will freely, to distinguish between good and evil. This, the mature consolidation of Greek philosophy, underlies the legal thought of scholastic as of rationalist natural law philosophy; of Kant as of Hegel; of John Stuart Mill and Herbert Spencer as of Del Vecchio and Kohler.

The second great contribution of Aristotle to legal thought is his formulation of the problem of justice. His distinction between "distributive" and "corrective" or "remedial" justice still forms a basis of all theoretical discussions on the subject. The first directs the distribution of good and honours to each according to his place in the community; it orders the equal treatment of those equal before the law. This stresses the fundamental fact, always true, but so often ignored by legal philosophers eager to prove the truth of their political conviction, that no ideal of justice can be at once theoretically valid and have a specific content. It is for positive law, based on specific ethical and political principles, to say who is equal before the law.

The second form of justice is essentially the measure of the technical principles, which govern the administration of law. In regulating legal relations a general standard of redressing the consequences of actions must be found, without regard to the person, and for that purpose actions and objects must be measured by an objective standard. Punishment must redress crime, reparation must redress civil wrong, damaged must restore wrongful gain. The conception of Themis, the goddess, who balances the scales without regard to the person, underlies this form of justice. But it must be understood subject to distributive justice.

Aristotle's third major contribution is the distinction between legal and natural justice, or, as we would put it, between positive and natural law. The former derives its force from being laid down as law. Whether just or unjust; it explains the diversity of positive laws; the latter derives its force from what is based on human nature everywhere and at all times.

Aristotle's fourth great contribution is the distinction between abstract justice and equity. The law is necessarily general and often harsh in application to the individual case. Equity mitigates and corrects its harshness by considering the individual case. All discussions of the problem of equity, of the proper interpretation of statute or precedent are derived from this fundamental statement of the problem.

Aristotle's fifth great contribution is his definition of laws as a body of rules binding upon the magistrates as well as the people:

> Laws are something different from what regulates and expresses the form of the Constitution; it is their office to direct the conduct of the magistrate in the execution of his office and the punishment of offenders.

It is to this definition that some modern jurists appeal in opposing unfettered administrative discretion.

Much of Aristotle's work is devoted to the definition and study of the state. In his definition, the continuity of the state is linked with the type of constitution which governs it:

> For if a city is a community, it is a community of citizens; but if the mode of government should alter and become of another sort it would seem a necessary consequence that the city is not the same; as we regard the tragic chorus as different from the comic, though it may probably consist of the same performers.

While Aristotle's particular views on the state were fashioned by his political views and the social conditions of his time, largely formulated in controversy with his master Plato, some general formulations underlie all subsequent discussions of principles of government. In developing Plato's thoughts Aristotle classified the principal forms of government into: (1) Monarchy, (2) Aristocracy, and (3) Polity. Each of these degenerates when they are no longer exercised for the common good but for the selfish interest of him or them who govern. The forms of degeneration are in this order: (1) Tyranny, (2) Oligarchy, and (3) Democracy.

Aristotle also developed the theory of the "mixed state," originally anumbrated by Plato, in which stability is attained by a balancing of diverse forces and tendencies, of the oligarchical element in particular, arising from wealth, birth, education, and the democratic element based on weight of numbers. This principle foreshadows the modern theory of the Separation of Powers.

If Aristotle thus gave classical expression to the great and abiding issues of legal thought, he also showed the limitations of speculation on the ideas of justice and he is not altogether free from the widespread fault of legal philosophers, namely concealing the lack of fundamental solutions by ambitious-sounding formulas. Aristotle's formula for distributive justice was the model for the classical Roman formula: "honeste vivere, neminem laedere, suum cuique tribuere." But if failed to give any direction as to what is just or unjust.

Aristotle's formula of distributive justice says only, that if rights are allotted, and if two individuals are equal, equal rights shall be allotted to them. According to this formula, a capitalistic as well as a communistic legal order is just, and a legal order which confers political rights only to men who have a certain income, or who belong to a certain race or are of noble birth is as just as a legal order which without regard to other differences. Any privilege whatever is covered by this formula. When a legal order reserves all possible rights to one single individual, the ruler, so that all the others—the ruled—have only duties, such a legal order, too, is just, since the difference between the ruler and the ruled is considered to bad so decisive that the ruled cannot be considered as equal to the ruler.

Nor is Aristotle's attitude towards the respective authority of natural justice and positive law unambiguous. In his Rhetoric, which is mainly a manual of the art of litigation, he advises the parties to appeal to universal law if the written law tells against them, but to urge the superiority of positive law over any unwritten law where it is a positive law that supports a party. In his Politics, probably a more reliable indication of Aristotle's own beliefs, he seems to identify justice and positive law. "For justice is a political virtue, by the rules of it the state is regulated and these rules are the criterion of what is right." In other words, Aristotle seems to stress the justice of legality or positivity in preference to any eternal principles of good.

Aristotle's work thus anticipates all the major themes and conflicts of modern Western legal thought: the conflict between the search for absolute values and the necessity to strengthen the authority of laws even if they are unjust; the conflict between the definition of law by reference to ideals, and by reference to the source of authority; the need to supplement any system of written laws however comprehensive, by flexible and creative individual justice, that is, by equity.

In nearly two and a half thousand years of subsequent controversy the scope and the social setting as well as the technical elaboration of these issues have developed and expanded together with the evolution of society. But the fundamental issues have not changed nor has their solution greatly advanced beyond the problems and conflicts as the Greek thinkers stated them.

2

LAW, JUSTICE, ETHICS AND SOCIAL MORALITY

The concept of Justice will be surveyed in its dual relationship to Law and Ethics. A distinction will be made between Ethics, as a system of values governing individual conduct, and Social Morality, as a system of norms which governs the social conduct of a community.

THE CONCEPT OF LAW

All definitions or characterizations of law veer between two extreme positions: One extreme emphasizes its coercive character; the other lays stress on the social acceptance, the actual observance of law by the community to which it is addressed. The coercive aspects of the legal norm rest both on the source of authority (sovereign command, hierachical order) and on the enforceability by sanctions which may be civil, criminal, or administrative. Both elements are pivotal to the theories of Austin and Kelsen, which will be analysed in some detail latter in this book. Whether the "ought" aspects of the legal norm are conceived as an actual command flowing from a sovereign (Austin) or as a hierarchical structure of norms attributed to an ultimate "depersonalized" sovereign (Kelsen), it is the authoritative aspects of the legal norm that are singled out as its essential characteristics. By contrast, the concept of law as reflected by the theories of Savigny and Ehrlich emphasizes the actual observance, the growth of customs, the "living law" of groups and communities, as the decisive element. Such law may receive authoritative confirmation from the sovereign, but it is not created by him. However, the differences between these two approaches are relative rather than absolute; they are essentially matters of emphasis. The "positivist" definition cannot dispense with the acceptance of the legal norm by the community, as shown by the inclusion, in Austin's definition, of "habitual obedience," and, in Kelsen's analysis, of the "minimum effectiveness." On the other hand, at least in the context of a modern legal system, no social behaviour, however steady and supported by conviction on the part of the observing group, can dispense with the recognition bestowed upon it by the legislator, the administrator, or the judiciary, or a combination of all these organs of the modern state.

A third essential element in the concept of law is a degree of generality. The first desideratum of a system for subjecting human conduct to the governance of rules in an obvious one: there must be rules. This may be stated as a requirement of generality. Here, as in so many other fields, John Austin's distinction was basically right, but too rigidly drawn: "where it obliges generally to acts or forbearances of a class, a command is a law or rule, but where it obliges to a specific act or forbearance, or to acts or forbearances which determine specifically or individually, a command is occasional or particular. In the legal systems of modern societies, legal norms, resulting from a constant interplay of legislative, executive, and judicial pronouncements, cover the whole spectrum from extreme generality to great particularity. They range from Constitutional Bills of Rights to orders prohibiting the sale of a particular commodity in a specific district on certain days. The relativity and even elusiveness of the distinction between general and particular command is brought out clearly in the doctrine of the "Stufentheorie". On the other hand, it is equally obvious that a community which had no general prescription at all, but only an infinite multitude of individual commands, would not be regarded as having a legal order. It would dissolve into millions of individual relationships. Taking these three essential elements into consideration, we may say, without an attempt at "definition" of the term, that the concept of law means a norm of conduct set for a given community—and accepted by it is binding—by an authority equipped with the power to lay down norms of a degree of general application and to enforce them by a variety of sanctions.

THE CONCEPT OF A LEGAL SYSTEM

Modern jurists have paid increasing attention to the general concept and minimum requirements of a "legal system" as distinct from the individual legal norm. A legal system "constitutes an individual system determined by 'an inner coherence of meaning,' . . . an integrated body of rules . . ." A multitude of individual legal norms may not amount to a legal system unless they are linked with each other in an integrated structure. An analysis of the minimum requirements of the legal system, which greatly preoccupies contemporary jurists, such as Kelsen, Ross, Hart, and fuller, has therefore a very different perspective from the attempt to define or characterize a legal norm in isolation. The awareness of a legal system as a structure in which the different organs, participants, and substantive prescriptions of the legal order react upon each other, is essentially the corollary to the increasing complexity of modern society, in which millions of individuals depend on the functioning of a complicated network of legal rules of many different types, and the interplay of public authorities of many different levels. In primitive societies the reach of law is generally weaker, and the institutionalization of the legal structure much less developed than in a more advanced and complex society. Not as a matter of conceptual definition, but as a basis for meaningful inquiry into the nature of a legal system, we may accept the suggestion of Graham Hughes that "for many purposes it will be useful to reserve the description 'legal system' for those types of social order characterized by a high degree of institutionalization in the creation of general prescriptions, in the apparatus for adjudicating disputes, and in ordering the disposition of force." A similar conception underlies H.A.L. Hart's rationalization of the differences between primitive and advanced legal systems through the distinction between "primary rules of obligation" and "secondary rules of recognition." Hart's "primary rules of obligation" correspond very closely to what are usually described as "customary" rules. Such rules, which generally are concerned with restrictions on the free use of violence, and other elementary forms of co-existence, are adequate for primitive communities, but inadequate for a more developed society because they are uncertain, static, and inefficient. Hart's "secondary rules of recognition" are in effect a shorthand description for the major aspects of a modern institutionalized legal system, which develops machinery for the formulation of legal rules, for orderly change, and for adjudication.

It is a concept of stratified legal order which forms the model of Kelsen's legal analysis, and a particular of the "Stufentheorie." This analysis reflects a mature legal system in which there is a definite relationship between constitution-maker, legislator, administrator, judge, and private legal subjects. But the analysis of a modern legal system will also include that of other institutions such as the family, the church, or the trade union, which enjoys law-making and sanctioning powers in varying degree (e.g., through the very powerful sanction of expulsion of union members by union procedures which, until recently, have been almost entirely immune from control by the courts, i.e. the state).

The range of a legal system in a modern state—which he prefers to call "legal order"—is aptly summarized by Julius Stone in the following four requisites:

> First, a legal order arises in the general range of modern states, unitary or federal and regardless of its particular ideology; second, a legal order must somehow be distinguishable from a moral and social order; third, the concept of law is a class concept, i.e., it must apply to the members of a given class; and fourth, a legal order is an "experienced single entity," something distinct from the "individual norms which are a part of it."

All the above-mentioned descriptions and analyses of a legal order or legal system have abstained from linking the essence or existence or basic structure of a legal system with certain minimum requirements of justice or morality. An exception is the recent attempt of Professor Fuller to deduce eight requirements of "inner morality" of law from the very nature of a legal system. These eight principles are not conceived as maxims of substantive natural law, i.e., as a summary of the ideals inspiring a particular society as worthy of attainment. They are instead seen as a kind of "procedural natural law." The eight principles are: (1) generality; (2) promulgation; (3) prospective legal operation, i.e., generally prohibition of retroactive legal operation, i.e., generally prohibition of retroactive laws; (4) intelligibility and clarity; (5) avoidance of contradictions; (6) avoidance of impossible demands; (7) constancy of the law through time, i.e., avoidance of frequent changes; (8) congruence between official action and declared rule.

It is difficult to see in what respect these eight requirements do more than spell out the minimum components of an efficiently functioning modern legal system. As such they are applicable to any legal system, regardless of ideology, whether totalitarian or democratic. Even the one requirement that might be thought of as expressing a particular-liberal-philosophy, i.e., the general—though not absolute—prohibition of retroactivity, is essential to the functioning of any legal system. No totalitarian legal order could survive for any length of time if all or a great majority of its laws were made retroactive; legal order would break down in confusion. On the other hand, as Fuller himself says, democratic legal systems may sometimes have to admit retrospective legislation. In this context, Fuller mentions the difference between, e.g., *ex-post facto* criminal statutes (unjustifiable) and retroactive tax laws that impose taxes on earnings received before the date of their enactment (justifiable). The Nazi system, at the height of its effectiveness, complied with all the eight requirements, except, to some extent, that of promulgation.

The Nazi extermination decrees, for example, whose "orderly" and systematic brutality has more than anything else inspired the many post-war discussions on the invalidity of the Nazi legal system as incompatible with basic principles of humanity—were certainly general, insofar as they were made known to them with cynical brutality; they were prospective, clear, and free from contradictions; and they were, unfortunately, far from being impossible of execution. Nor was there any lack of congruence between the law and official action, because the exterminations took place within a hierarchic structure derived from the supreme legislative authority of the Fuehere. It is only by means of a petitio principii, namely that barbarous "laws" should not be qualified as such, that we can circumvent this conclusion. In the earlier debate which clearly inspired Fuller's book, he maintains "that a dictatorship which clothes itself with a tinsel of legal form can so far depart from the morality of order, from the inner morality of law itself, that if ceases to be a legal system." The illustration given by Fuller, and also earlier by Gustavg Radbruch, in his moving attempt to find some criterion of illegality with regard to the greatest enormities of the Nazi system, referred to the chaotic features of the final Nazi period, a period when the shouts of Hitler, pronounced in epileptic fits, could be taken as overruling previously published legal orders. Such a state of affairs is "anarchy" in the strictest sense. It will collapse simply because it can no longer maintain minimum legal order in a complex society. Use of the term "morality" in connection with this galaxy of requirements is misleading. They are "essentially principles of good craftsmanship."

Nor do they offend against the characterization of law as a "purposeful enterprise dependent for its success on the energy, insight, intelligence, and conscientiousness of those who conduct it," and which "displays structural constancies." The legal system of the Nazi period, dominated by the ideology of racial discrimination, was extremely successful, in terms of its stated purpose: the degradation and extermination of "inferior" races, especially of the Jews. No order in human memory has achieved its purpose more swiftly and efficiently; none achieved a greater result in so little time, with comparable economy (including the utilization of the remains of the victims for the production of fertilizers). The use of the term "morality," however qualified, instead of the term "structure," which characterizes the anatomy of a legal system as a purposeful enterprise implies a degree of morality, is his conviction that humanity is progressing in moral insight through growing "participation in institutional procedures" through "human beings confronting one another in some social context, adjusting their relations reciprocally, negotiating, voting, arguing before some arbiter. ..." But this is a picture of pluralistic society, in which groups and individuals can argue and bargain freely, not of a society in which there is no such give and take, at least in the major conditions of political and social life. There is also ambiguity in Fuller's use of the term "conscientiousness" with regard of the administration of legal institutions and precepts. An Eichmann applied the norm set for him, i.e., the efficient disposal of the greatest possible number of Jews, with supreme conscientiousness. Hence his failure to understand why he should be prosecuted. The conscience of a Nazi differs from that of a christian or a pacifist. He is directed by the basic values of the order he seeks to obey and administer.

The structural analysis of a "legal system" is indeed more complex than that of a primitive legal order. It denotes any cohesive order of norms that purports to govern a community through the use of "posited" authority, whether oppressive or liberal, socialist or capitalistic in character. The structural requirements of a legal system must be accepted by the analytical positivist as much as by the advocate of a natural law philosophy. It is only by a consideration of the related but distinct concepts of "Justice", "Ethics" and "Morality" that we can elucidate the relation of the legal order to the values of life.

THE RELATION OF JUSTICE TO LAW AND ETHICS

Every legal system is oriented towards certain purposes, which it seeks to implement. In this sense, every legal system is of necessity a "purposeful enterprise." But in this universal sense the concept of justice is also of necessity devoid of ideological content. The "justice" of a given legal system may be a *laissez-faire* economy, or the public ownership of all productive enterprises; it may be a parliamentary multi-party system or a one-party state; the system may be built upon the ideology of separation of powers, or on the subordination of administration and the judiciary to the will of the legislator. It may aspire to the equality of all citizens, or to a hierarchical structure of superior and inferior citizens; it may implement the supremacy of international over national law or—as is the case with almost all contemporary legal systems—the inverse.

The classical definition of "distributive justice" is that of Aristotle: "Injustice arises when equals are treated unequally, and also when unequals are treated equally." Does this mean anything beyond the proposition, stated earlier, that every legal order is directed toward some ideal of justice? Certainly it cannot lead to any specific political philosophy of equality. It is compatible with legal systems that discriminate between free men and slaves, between blacks and whites, between "Aryans" and Jews, between nationals and foreigners, between rich and poor, between men and women. For all of these are "class concepts," groups which the legal order may consider as being equal or unequal in relation to each other. Some legal philosophers have attempted to extract substantive meaning from the very idea of justice, notably Stammler and Del Vecchio. The failure of both in their attempts to extract from Kants' "practical reason" substantive ideals of justice is analysed later in this book.

The difficulty of extracting any substantive principle from Aristotle's "distributive justice" is increased by the fact that the number and types of classes which a legal order can establish for purposes of differential treatment is almost infinite. For this or that purpose property owners may be distinguished from tenants, local residents from out-of-town residents, high school graduates from elementary school graduates, and so forth. It is common sense and the practical needs of administration rather that principles that tend to limit class distinctions. Yet, there is a procedural residuum in the notion of "equality for equals" which makes it more than a meaningless formula. It implies a minimum machinery of justice, some procedure for the determination of treatment as equal or unequal in a particular case. This carries the implication of a third party procedure, and thus some minimum concept of "due process." Thus Ginsberg is right in deducing from the concept of "general" justice "the control of power relations and more particularly the exclusion of arbitrary power." Some concept of impartiality is inherent in the very process of determination of equality, even in the most hierarchical society. But since there are no theoretical limits to the ways in which a particular legal order chooses to determine and subdivide classes of "equals," "arbitrariness" can become a very elusive criterion. When Ginsberg deduces that because "differential treatment requires justification in terms of relevant differences," arbitrary discriminations, "such as those based on race, colour, religion, sex," must disappear and "equality in political rights is extended to equality in social and economic rights," he slides from a formal and procedural notion of equality to a substantive and political one. To one legal order differences of race, colour, religion, sex, or wealth may appear "relevant" and far from "arbitrary," whereas to another they may not. Nor has history shown a continuous evolution in the sense indicated by Ginsberg. While the belief in steady progress towards democracy and equality was popular in the nineteenth century, the twentieth century has shown, in the most brutal manner, how powerful the philosophies of racial, national, and religious discriminations are. Concepts of justice contrary to the democratic idea of equality govern the majority of the world's states, while in the relations between nations equality has barely begun to compete with the ideologies of nationalism, racialism, and power politics. Another attempt—similar in result, thought not in method, to that of Finsberg—to demonstrate the possiblity of rational justification of values of justice, is that of Chaim Perelman. In his Idea of justice Perelman had demonstrated that the only factor common to various conceptions of justice was "formal justice." This consists in equality of treatment for all the members of one and the same essential category. "The only requirement we can formulate in respect of a rule is that it should not be arbitrary, but should justify itself, should flow from a normative system. But, "the only claim one could right full make would consist in eliminating everything arbitrary save what is implied in affirming the values at the base of the system." In other words, no values and aspirations can be rationally deduced, the ultimate values and aspirations themselves are non-rational. This approach is essentially similar to Aristotle's concept of distributive justice, and to the more modern philosophy of relativism as developed by Max Weber, Gustav Radbruch, Kelsen and others. More recently, Perelman has, however, attempted to find some rational justification for values and norms.

In a work devoted to the theory of argument Perelman took the topics of Aristotle as a starting point for the use of dialectical, in contrast to analytical, proof of legal argument. Juristic argument aims at justification, not demonstration, of truth. The justification of an action, a kind of behaviour or decision is not concerned with truth or falsehood. Justification can deal only with debatable things. It is concerned with arguments of morality, legality, regularity, usefulness or opportuneness. It follows that "assertions which represent the systematic formulation of an ideal cannot be judged the way we judge factual judgment. Their role is not to conform to experience, but to furnish criteria for evaluating and judging experience and, if necessary, for disqualifying certain aspects of it." How can legal argumentation be made "rational"? Perelman's answer is that, in conformity with Kant's "Categorical Imperative," the characteristic of rational argumentation is "the aim for universality"; its postulates must be "valid" for the whole of the human community. This does not mean that the criteria and values of rational argumentation constitute "absolute and impersonal values and truths." This does not mean that the criteria and values of rational argumentation constitute "absolute and impersonal values and truths." Rather do they express "the convictions and aspirations of a free but reasonable man, engaged in a creative, personal and historically situated effort: that of proposing to the universal as he sees it, a number of acceptable theses."

The difficulty with this approach is that we must assume there is a "universal audience" which shares common values. This is possible on the basis of the philosophy of the Stoics, which appeals to universal reason, or the scholastics who deduce the rightness of human institutions from the will and reason of God. On any other assumption, the universality of the audience dissolves itself into a number of conflcting values, ideas and policies.

The impossibility of deriving specific legal ideals from the "sense of justice" is expressed by another contemporary jurist in the distinction between "justice" and "justness." Varied as these judgments on justness will "always be, they respond to emotion which, insofar as language permits a verification, . . . flows from a sense of morality" or "justice" or "values." Ehrenzweig, basing himself on the work of Bienenfeld, looks to psychoanalysis for the answer to the various concepts of justice, which "follow the youth through adolescence to adulthood when their conflict will determine and threaten the very coexistence of families, communities and nations. Yet they coexist. If in need he leans towards communism; if efficient to socialism; if attacked to conservatism, and if attacking to liberalism [and] if in the nationalist dogma of the nursery that is exhibited in the instinctive presentation of a united front against the outsider.

The conflict of values is here transferred from the outside world to the psyche of the individual.

We conclude that "justice," as a generally valid concept, is formal, in the sense that it is the goal to which every legal order aspires as a "purposeful enterprise," and procedural, in the sense that the Aristotelian notion of "equality for equals" implies a minimum machinery of justice and third party determination.

Beyond this, it is necessary to turn to the field of ethics and morality for a determination of the values that may give the idea of justice a specific substantive content.

ETHICS AND SOCIAL MORALITY

The great majority of writers use the terms "ethical" and "moral" interchangeably. Although the choice of terms is largely a matter of preference, it is submitted that the distinction recently suggested by P.F. Strawson between social morality and ethics is more than a matter of terminology, because it clarifies the relationship of individual values to those of the social and, from there, the legal order. In an article entitled "Social Morality and Individual Ideal," Strawson suggests that "the region of the ethical . . . is a region of diverse, certainly incompatible and possibly practically conflicting ideal images or pictures of human life. . ." Ethics is thus the sphere of ideal forms of life set by individuals for themselves.

It is further implicit in his suggestion that these ideal images of man's life—generally called values—conflict, and that "the multiplicity of conflicting pictures is itself the essential element of one's picture of man." By contrast, the sphere of morality denotes "rules or principles governing human behaviour which apply universally within a community or class." A "minimal conception of morality" limits itself to those rules which are "a condition of the existence of society," whereas a more comprehensive conception of morality would embrace the entire body of rules governing a community or class.

The merit of this approach is that it illuminates the tripartite relation between (a) the values that individuals, as conscientious and responsible human beings, set to themselves, (b) the moral norms governing a society which reflects a social balance and choice between conflicting individual values, and (c) the legal order, which must relfect the current social morality but is far from identical with it. In the completely master-minded and conditioned society depicted in Huxley's Brave New World or Orwell's 1984, the distinction between social morality and individual ethics, and ultimately that between law, morality and ethics, might altogether disappear. The norms of social behaviour would be set by "Big Brother," who exercises complete legislative authority, and whose law-making power is used to direct and control every aspect and corner of social behaviour. The individual in turn is conditioned to accept the socio-legal norms as controlling his entire life and precluding the formation of individual values—which in Orwell's terminology would be "ungood."

In contemporary societies the relative spheres of law, morality, and ethics, as defined here, differ, of course, considerably. But in every contemporary society there is some tension between these three orders of conduct. In the pluralistic and relatively individualistic society which characterizes the value system of modern democracy, the tension between these spheres is and must be considerable. There is liberty left for the individual to form and live by one of the many conflicting "pictures of life"; this is limited by the many constraints of social morality, which flow from the necessities of social life, as well as ideological restraints imposed necessities of social life, as well as ideological restraints imposed by society on the individuals living within it. Finally, there is an increasingly active reciprocal interrelationship between the legal and the moral order. On the one hand, moral values press upon the legal system, and on the other, the modern law-maker can to an increasing extent influence and modify the social habits of the community.

Another advantage of the tripartite classification would appear to be that it by-passes the ancient and rather age-worn characterization of law as being concerned with external conduct, and morals as concerned with internal conduct. This is, of course, the classical distinction drawn by Kant in the Critique of Practical Reason, which has been adopted by many moral and legal philosophers. Clearly such a distinction, even if generally valid, is greatly dependent upon the reach of law in society, which is vastly greater in the fairly concentrated and manipulated modern society that it is in primitive communites. A legal system that makes punishment or civil obligation dependent upon malicious intention or capacity to control one's actions reaches into the inner mind of man, and modern psychology has refined and enlarged the interrelationship between the inner workings of the mind and external conduct. Even more barren is the converse proposition that morality is only concerned with internal conduct. The distinction between ethical, i.e., individual value judgments, and social conduct, i.e., morality, helps to clarify this matter. Instead of the watertight and artificial division into three distinct spheres, we should think of a fluid interrelationship, variable with regard to the separation and interpenetration of the three spheres according to the character of the society in question.

ETHICAL THEORIES AND VALUATIONS

There have been innumerable classifications of ethical theories. The most important and recurrent division in that according to the sources of knowledge of ethical values, into naturalistic, intuitionistic, and non-cognitive. Very briefly, naturalism (a term coined by G.E. Moore in his Principia Ethica, 1903) denotes any view that holds that ethical properties can be analysed into or defined in terms of natural ones." Intuitionism holds that ethics is an autonomous discipline with its own peculiar subject matter. In contrast to the naturalists, "Intuitionists" believe that the basic propositions of normative ethics are intutive or self-evident insights of a unique kind, which cannot be inferred from any other discipline.

The link between these two types of ethical theory—which can be almost infinitely subdivided—is that they hold ethical values to be capable of objective determination. By contrast, the "non-cognitive" theories regard ethical values as incapable of any objective analysis, because they are purely emotive, or at least not verifiable."

ETHICAL AND LEGAL THEORY

As will be apparent from the following observations, all three types of theory have had considerable influence on legal theory and correspond to distinct types of jurisprudential thinking. The perspective from which ethical theories are best considered in the light of legal theory is that of "validity." As a convenient point of departure we may take a definition of "validity" that embraces both formal and substantive theories, by abstracting the validity of a legal system from the content of its basic norms. According to Kelsen "a legal norm is valid . . . because it is created in a specific manner, ultimately determined by a presupposed (vorausgesetzt) basic norm." In the formulation of Alf Ross, "a system of norms is 'valid' if it is able to serve as a scheme of interpretation for a corresponding set of social actions, in such a way that it becomes possible for us to comprehend the set of actions as a coherent whole of meaning and motivation, and within certain limits to predict them." From this perspective it may be convenient to divide ethical theories into those that postulate the objective validity of the ethical postulates and those that deny such objective validity. In the former category there are:

The type of ethical theory that is based on metapositive values, either of a religious or a non-religious order. In legal theory this type of ethical approach is reflected in the main body of natural law philosophy, whether of a theological or a rationalistic character.

Those that postulate ethical values of an objective, and therefore compelling, but instinctively felt character. To this approach there corresponds, in legal philosophy, the type of theory that bases postulates of justice on a Rechtsgefuhl (Krabbe), or a sentimento giuridico (Del Vecchio), or "intuitive" law (petrazhitsky). A more rationalized version of this approach in Edmond Cahn's "sense of injustice." In this category there is also Geny's "creative intuition" as a source of legal evolution through juristic action. The philosophical godfather of most of these theories is the French philosopher, Henri Bergson, whose work Evolution Creatrice has been one of the most influential of the present century.

EMPIRICAL THEORIES

A contemporary American philosopher has described empiricism in the following terms:

> It is characteristic of "empiricism," as a philosophical tradition, to assume that we have certain criteria of evidence, or that we can identify a certain "source" of our knowledge, and then to apply these criteria, or a refer to this source, and thus determine what it is that we can know.

In this wide sense, "empiricism" is contrasted with all theories that derive principles of ethical conduct from *a priori* metaphysical premises. In a broad way, "empiricism" corresponds, in legal theory, to "positivism," and metaphysical edthical theories are reflected in legal idealism. In ethical theory, empiricism, to a large extent, coincides with naturalism, since one of the fundamental theses of the latter is that "the truth or falsehood of ethical sentences is established by methods of experimentation and observation characteristic of the natural sciences."

From the perspective of relevance to corresponding legal theories, we may distinguish three major types of ethical empiricism: First, the approach that derives ethical maxims from historical and social experience. Second, the approach that tests ethical values in the light of social facts and realities. This type of empiricism, commonly known as "pragmatism," is a specifically American contribution to modern philosophy and ethics. It is linked with the names of Charles Saunders Peirce and John Dewey. Third, there is "logical positivism," i.e., the approach to philosophical statements which excludes from scientific study anything that in no "verifiable," by either logical deduction or experimental observation. In ethical theory this approach leads to "non-cognitivism," on which some further observations will be made below. Non-cognitivists exclude ethical maxims from scientific enquiry as being essentially "emotive" and not subject to scientific verification.

LEGAL THEORIES BASED ON OBJECTIVE ETHICAL CRITERIA

In jurisprudence, the first approach is represented by those theories that regard certain basic principles of conduct as essential to a satisfactory legal order, not as a matter of *a priori* postulates set by God or reason (natural law) but as a matter of social experience. Generally we can group under this approach all the "social contract" theories, which are predicated on the assumption that men need to restrain their appetites for violence, greed, and domination, in order to achieve a minimum of mutual protection and security. A logical continuation of the "social contract" approach could be Kant's Categorical Imperative and its derivative definition of law as "the aggregate of the conditions under which the arbitrary will of one individual may be combined with that of another under a general inclusive law of freedom." But in Kant's philosophical scheme these principles are not empirical; they are given *a priori,* as an essential basis of man's volition as a free and rational being.

Similar or even identical ethical postulates can thus be derived either from *a priori* judgments or from empirical observations. A corcllary to this duality of approaches in ethical theory can be found in legal philosophy. Thus, throughout the long history of natural law philosophy, many postulates such as the absolute integrity of private property, the supremacy of the law-making authority of the Church over the State, or *vice versa,* the equality or inequality of men, nations, or races, and many more, have been deduced from metaphysical principles of a God-given universe or universal reason. But a contemporary jurist has formulated five principles of what he describes as "the minimum content of natural law" not as *a priori* principles but as necessary to "the minimum purpose of survival which men have in associating with each other." They are thus essentially a continuation and modernization of the "social contract" philosophy. The five principles are: (1) human vulnerability, which makes it necessary for a legal order to restrict the use of violence; (2) approximate equality, which makes it necessary for a legal system to develop rules of mutual forbearance and compromise; (3) limited altruism, which makes necessary some provisions to restrain tendencies to aggression; (4) limited resources, which makes necessary some system of exchange or joint planning of services and goods; and (5) limited understanding and strength of will, from which follows the need for a system of voluntary cooperation in a coercive system. Thus, maxims of conduct which many of the older natural law philosophers have presented as flowing from the immutable natural law philosophers have presented as flowing from the immutable nature of man, are here presented as having been shown by experience and history to be necessary to the survival of man in civilization.

PRAGMATISM IN ETHICS AND LAW

Pragmatism, as a particular type of empirical philosophy, has had a direct and traceable influence on modern jurisprudence, in the American realist movement, of which a detailed account is given below. Its intellectual fathers are William James and John Dewey. The characteristic feature of Dewey's pragmatism, as applied in the realist movement, is the method of enquiry. An enquiry into an ethical proposition may start with the formulation of a value hypothesis; but this value postulate is only provisional, and has to be tested by the means of its possible realization. A study of such means—which include the legal, social, and economic environment of a society-may influence and modify the value postulate. A convenient illustration of this approach might be the question of prohibition of alcohol, which deeply influenced American legal, economic, and social life for more than a decade after the First World War. Absolute prohibition could be stated as a value goal. Means of its execution consist in the appropriate Constitutional amendments, statutory prohibitions, administrative regulations, and the policing of the legal prohibitions. An enquiry into the means of execution may show that the purported enforcement of prohibition leads—as in fact it did—to a vast increase in the consumption of illegal and often lethal alcohol, bootlegging, gang warfare, murder, and a general increase in criminality. The results of such enquiries may lead to an abandonment or the modification of the original value postulate. Abandonment of the ethical postulate, in the light of practical experience, is expressed in the repeal of the Constitutional amendment in the U.S. Constitution. An alternative solution is that of the institution of state-controlled liquor boards, which prevails in Canada.

ETHICAL AND LEGAL THEORIES DENYING OBJECTIVE VALIDITY

Whereas all the previously mentioned types of theory assert that ethical values can be objectively ascertained—whether they be deduced from natural law foundations, from *a priori* principles predicated on the rationality of man, from empirical data based on history, from generally accepted principles of good and right, or from pragmatic enquiry, the "non-objective" theories of ethics deny that ethical values can be objectively ascertained. To them, ethical values are a matter of conviction. They must be believed in but cannot be proved.

RELATIVISM IN ETHICS AND LEGAL PHILOSOPHY

There are, however, two major types of this kind of approach to ethical norms. One trend of thought is best described, in ethics as in jurisprudence, as "relativism'; the other is "non-cognitivism." While both agree on the non-probability of values, the relativists believe that rational argument can and must support the choice of a particular value, by comparison with, and often in opposition to, another value. The non-cognitivists reject all study of ethical values as purely emotive, and therefore not within the realm of science. Probably the most influential of the relativists in modern times is Max Weber, to whose celebrated essay on "Der Sinn der wertfreiheit der soziologischen und okonomischen Wissenschaften" reference is made later in this book. His most important disciple in the field of legal theory is Gustav Radbruch, whose legal philosophy—which in recent years has become the subject of attention far beyond the borders of Germany and Europe—is a profound and important application of the relativistic, whose of attention far beyond the borders of Germany and Europe is a profound and important application of the relativistic approach. For it is not content to state the antinomies of legal ideas, but follows the major antithetic values of legal philosophy into particular legal institutions and concepts.

Among contemporary ethical philosophers, we may list as relativists Dewey, Russell, and Ginsberg. Dewey's entire work is permeated by the thought that value statements are prescriptions or recommendations for action based on alternative convictions, but that "it is morally necessary to state grounds or reasons for the course advised and recommended. These consist of matter-of-fact sentences reporting what has been and now is, as conditions, and of estimates of consequences that would ensue if certain of them are used as means."

Bertrand Russell has, in his many writings, veered from the conviction that ethical statements are purely emotive to one that holds that truth can be discovered by the use of reason. The former view is expressed, for example, in his Science and Religion, where he says that: "Since no way can even be imagined for deciding a difference as to value, the conclusion is forced upon us that the difference in one of tastes, not one as to any objective truths." But in his more recent work in Human Society in Ethics and Politics of 1954, Russel stresses the role of reason.

Reason has a perfectly clear and precise meaning. It signifies a choice of the right means to an end that you wish to achieve. It has nothing whatever to do with a choice of ends. But opponents of reason do not realize this, and think that advocates of rationality want reason to dictate ends as well as means.

The essence of his reasoning is that a concept such as "good" has an intrinsic value of its own. Intrinsic value is "the property of being a state of mind desired by the person who experience it." "Good" is the property of arousing an emotion of approval, "bad" that which arouses disapproval. Thus "good" is linked with pleasure community. "Right" conduct is that which is likely to produce "good" effects. This position is very close to that of Henry Sidgwick, who in his methods of Ethics argued that generally recognized moral rules can be deduced from the principle that we ought to aim at maximizing pleasure. Russell's later theory thus comes close to that of the "naturalists."

Like the former, and like that of the utilitarian legal philosophers—of which an account is given later in this book this approach is full of ambiguities. Even if we accept that the "good" is the end desired by an individual, the test of "approval" is highly ambivalent. Does it mean approval by the entire community, by a select avant-garde, approval by the greatest number or by the wise? Is not the highest ethical conduct sometimes that which is in revolt against the majority and therefore arouses intense disapproval? Ethical pioneers, like the early Christians, the early fighters for women's rights or labour organizations, or pacifists, have had to pursue their values in intense opposition to the overwhelming majority to their fellow contrymen. A similar criticism can be raised against the essay by S.E. Toulmin, which accords with Sidgwick and Russell in the assertion that "to say that X is right is to say that X is worthy of approval." For Toulmin, to be "worthy of approval" means that "there is a valid reason for approving X." It is not the fact of acceptance but the worthiness of acceptance which gives an argument validity. But here the same question arises, namely, what the criteria for worthiness of approval are. One answer given by Toulmin is that there is a valid reason for doing something when it can be shown to be in accordance with rules or maxims accepted in our society. Where there is conflict between rules or norms within a society, it is reasonable to apppeal to an "overall" principple, that "preventable suffering shall be averted." "The notions of 'obligation', 'right', 'justice', 'duty' and 'ethics' apply in the first place when our actions and institutions may lead to avoidable misery for others; but it is a natural and familiar extension to use them also when the issue concerns a chance of deeper happiness for others and even for ourselves." This appears to gloss over the deep conflicts which may rise between confliction values, and in particular between the ethics of an individual and the prevalent morality of a society. Here we can see again the value of the distinction between individual ethics and social morality which has been adopted at the outset of this section. There simply is no necessary equivalence between the avoidance of misery, happiness for others, and happiness for oneself. These emotions or purposes may coincide, but they may also starkly conflict with each other.

The value of the aforementioned attempts does not lie in their somewhat simple version of utilitarianism, but rather in the emphasis on the use of reason and rational argument in the clarification of ends. This appears to be the position of Morris Ginsberg, who describes the task of ethics as being: "(a) to bring out what is implied in the notion of a norm or principle of action, and (b) to survey the major or dominant goods or values and the norms or injuctions they entail." Ginsberg accepts that there is a plurality of values and of conflicting ways of life. He does, however, assert that "there is . . . in every society a general framework, the maintenance or furtherance of which comes to be conceived as an overriding obligation, though this may come into conflict with the demands of particular ideals." It is in an attempt to spell out the principal legal values of a contemporary Western-type society rather that absolute values that Ginsberg, in subsequent chapters, elaborates such matters as economic and political rights, the modern status of association and contract, the ethics of punishment, and freedom of thought. How important rational arguments can be, not in the determination of ends, but in the clarification and concretization of given values, as applied in the legal life of a community, may be illustrated by the problem of freedom of contract. A general catalogue of basic rights and values in a democratic society is likely to enumerate both "freedom of contract" and "equality," as values to be protected by the law. As long as these values remain abstract and general, there appears to be no contradiction. But when we follow the implications of freedom and equality of contract, in the context of modern industrial society, such conflicts and tensions become readily apparent and may compel the subordination of one end to another. In the earlier stages of industrial capitalism, freedom of contract led to an increasing inequality between the entrepreneur and the unorganized worker, due to stark differences in their economic power. This led to a counter-move by the organization of trade unions, which increasingly, through collective organization, compensated for the weakness of the individual worker. In contemporary industrial society, unions tend to face employers as equals, but at the expense of the freedom of bargaining of the individual worker, who has surrendered it for the sake of equality, expressed in better terms and the improvement of his standard of living. Individual freedom of contract here gives way to the more important goal of economic equality. The two values cannot be implemented simultaneously.

It is thus only by following basic ethical values into their implementation in a given social content that their true meaning and ranking can be ascertained. This is indeed a matter of reasoning, supported by factual data. It is only which this qualification that we may accept the attempts of such writers as Russell, Dewey, Perelman, Ginsberg and Toulmin, to emphasize the place of rational argument in the ascertainment of values.

NON-COGNITIVIST ETHICAL THEORIES

David Hume is generally regarded as the father of ethical non-cognitivism. His celebrated statement that reason "is and ought only to be the slave of the passions and can never pretend to any other office than to serve and obey them" not only undermined the foundations of natural law but also implied that reason is essentially the servant of emotions, which latter set the goals of action. But Hume may also be cited in support of the relativist position since, in his Enquiry Concerning the Principles of Marals, he says:

The hypothesis which we embrace is plain. It maintains that morality is maintained by sentiment. It defines virtue to be whatever mental action or quality gives to a spectator a pleasing sentiment of approbation; and vice the contrary. We then proceed to examine a plain matter of fact, to wit, what actions have his influence; we consider all the circumstances, in which these actions agree; and thence endeavour to extract some general observations with regard to these sentiments.

Be that as it may, modern ethical non-cognitivists have asserted emphatically that normative concepts are purely emotive. For the most radical of the non-congnitivists, A.J. Ayer, all normative words are "pseudo-concepts," all genuine concepts must be either empirical or logical. The empirically verifiable and the logically certifiable exhaust the cognitive dimensions of meaning. Everything else, such as a simple command, a blush, a yawn, but also words like "good," "bad," "ought" "worthy," are purely emotive, and there cannot be such a thing as ethical or moral science.

An important modification of this position is Charles L. Stevenson's influential Ethics and Language (1944). Whereas Ayer argues that "what we do not and cannot argue about is the validity of these moral principles. We merely praise or condemn them in the light of our own feelings." Stevenson distinguishes between attitudes and beliefs. Only disagreements in attitude—which comprise the basic values— are genuine and irreducible. You cannot argue about purposes or preferencs. But a value judgment such as that a certain person is "good" has a complex meaning which is partly emotive and partly cognitive. A full picture of ethics must recognize both factors. To illustrate his position, Stevenson gives as an example the choice before trustees for the estate of a philanthropist who have been instructed to forward any charitable cause that seems to them worthy. They argue as to whether to provide hospital facilities for the poor or a endow universities. The choice between these alternatives is an irreducible choice between different "attitudes." But "the discussion is almost certain to involve disagreement in belief. Perhaps the men will disagree. . . about the present state of the poor, and the extent to which hospital facilities are already provided for them. Perhaps they will disagree about the financial state of the universities, or the effects of education on private and social life." On the latter type of question, agreement can be reached through the investigation of facts, which may confirm the one or other position.

In essence, this position is very close to that of Dewey's pragmatic "logic of enquiry." The need to test legal values in the light of reality, by factual evidence, would be regarded by contemporary lawyers as almost too trivial to require demonstration. In part this is due to the efforts of the Americal legal realists, who themselves are strongly influenced by Dewey. But it is today—and has been for some time—part and parcel of the administration of justice in modern society. An outstanding and familiar example is the socalled "Brande is Brief" to which reference is made elsewhere. This brief consisted of a short "value statement," i.e., the proposition that an Oregon statute fixing a ten-hour maximum day for women was in accordance with the Constitutional values embodied in the Fourteenth Amendment, and a very elaborate factual brief as to the conditions actually prevailing in the relevant industries, and their relevance to the state of women's health, safety; and morals.

Among contemporary legal theorists, Alf Ross is clearly a "non-cognitivist." For Ross such terms a "just" or "unjust" are entirely devoid of meaning. They are merely expressions of like or dislike. "To invoke justice is the same thing as banging on the table, an emotional expression which turns one's demand into an absolute postulate. . . . It is impossible to have a rational discussion with a man who mobilizes 'justice,' because he say nothing that can be argued for or against." It seems that this position differs sharply from that of relativists like Radbruch or Ginsberg, for whom there is very much to argue about in respect to conflicting values, even though they accept that the ultimate ends cannot be described as a "non-cognitivist" for the purposes of legal science, insofar as he denies that the prescription of values of any kind, including ethical ideals, can be the proper subject of legal science, he regards the cognition (Erkenntnis) and description (Beschreibung) of the law as a system of norms constituting legal values as the proper realm of legal science. But such values are, for Kelsen as for Radbruch relative not absolute.

The influential contemporary school of Oxford "ordinary language philosophers" is sometimes linked with the ethical non-cognitivists. But it would appear that the Oxford philosophers' emphasis on the analysis of the meaning of language has no particular ethical connotation, positive or negative. It seeks to elucidate the meaning of legal terms and concepts in the context of legal language. An illustration is H.A.L. Hart's "Definition and Theory in jurisprudence", where he investigates the meaning of such concepts as a legal right or corporate personality in the legal context in which they are used. By contrast, Hart's principles of "minimum natural law" are, as shown earlier, not connected with the "ordinary language philosophy" but state an ethical philosophy of an essentially empiric character.

ETHICAL THEORIES AND THE SOLUTION OF LEGAL PROBLEMS: AN ILLUSTRATION

It may be useful to test both the relevance of various ethical theories and the differences between them by applying them to the solution of a legal problem with deep ethical implications. No contemporary problem has shaken the conscience of lawyers more deeply, and revealed more pungently the tension between conscience and legal order, than the problem of disobedience to Nazi laws—a problem that could be transposed to other, comparable situations of conflict between an inhuman legal order and the ethica conscience of the individual. This problem has been at the heart of the revival of natural law thinking after the Second World War, it has inspired the post-war thinking of Gustav Radbruch, and it has been the main subject of a now famous debate between Professors Hart and Fuller.

How would the different ethical theories approach the problem posed for an officer or a civil servant by an order to draft one of the Nazi extermination decrees or to organize a transport of Jews to an extermination camp? How would they react to the problem of the "informer wife" who, utilizing a wartime decree authorizing—or perhaps commanding—the denunciation of family members for utterances hostile to the regime, volunteered information to a special tribunal about anit-Hitler utterance made by her husband within the four walls of the home, refusing the even then existing privileges of the wife not to testify against her husband, because she welcomed this opportunity do dispose, under the cover of legal authority, of her husband and to carry on her own love affairs?

The first possible approach is that of transcendental or "supernatural" ethics, which corresponds to the orthodox natural law of respect for human dignity, as an emanation either of the law of God or of universal reason. It would conclude that a law clearly offending against these elementary principles was void and therefore not binding. From this premise flows the right to punish those who offended the higher law by obeying the positive law. In technical terms, this means that a subsequent legal order such as that expressed by the Nuremberg Charter or by postwar German legislation is made applicable retroactively.

A second approach would be that of the intuitionist ethics. The rightness or wrongness of a conduct would be determined by an objectively but intuitively known feeling of right or wrong, a Rechtsgefuhl or a sentimento giuridico. The difficulty with this approach is that an intuitive evaluation can lead the individual concerned to very different decisions. He may intuitively feel the wrongness of an extermination decree, and derive from this his duty to disobey it, or he may on the contrary accept the injunction of the Nazi law of 1935 which empowered judges to inflict punishment "in accordance with the sound instincts of the people," interpreting such sound instincts as dictating the persecution and even extermination of Jews, Slave, and other inferior races. Or he may be inspired by the feeling: 'Right or wrong, my Country." Intuition may help to inspire marginal decisions in the sense indicated by Gteny, but if asked to guide in the basic choice of values it yields nothing.

Third, there are the various relativistic approaches. One of these, that of Dewey, would be based on a pragmatic "logic of enquiry, directed to the exploration of a given value." Such an approach would tentatively appraise the Nazi laws that "legalized" racial oppression, degradation of the human personality, and mass murder, as evil. It would, however, study the question of subsequent punishment of those who obeyed the Nazi laws in the light of feasibility. Such a study might show that a complete implementation of the goal of punishing everybody who participated in the making and execution of such laws was simply not feasible. The result of such a pragmatic enquiry might be that a more modest goal, i.e., the selection for punishment or other sanctions of those prominently associated with the Nazi regime through their high position or known deeds, would implement more adequately the objective of disapproval of the Nazi values, and of treating equals equally.

While pragmatic ethics are compatible with a relativistic approach, the basic attitude of relativistic ethics would be that whether to obey attitude of relativistic ethics would be that whether to obey or disobey the Nazi laws was essentially a question of choice between the religious, humanistic, hedonistic, and other values relevant to the problem. One possible value—which indeed was chosen by the great majority of Germans—was that obeying the positive authority of the State, at the expense of the principles of human dignity, compassion, and charity. The rationalistic ethics that is usually combined with the relativistic approach would demand a careful study of the means by which the different values would have to be implemented. It would show, for example, that the necessary implication of legal discrimination between "Aryans" and Jews would lead not only to the undermining of the family but also to a profound modification of the principles of equality, in contract, in criminal law, and in other fields. Such clarification of the goals might at least articulate and underline the severity of the choice between values.

"Non-cognitivist" ethics dismiss the entire problem as beyond the reach of rational discussion. It would regard the punishment of Nazi criminals, or their non-punishment, as expressions of conflicting emotions, by the retribution imposed by an outraged humanity, a sophisticated version of the raditional exercise of the rights of victors over vanquished, or on the other hand a sceptical or even cynical acquiescence in the man's cowardice.

SOCIAL MORALITY AND THE LEGAL ORDER

Although, following Strawson, we have distinguished individual ethics from social morality, it is obvious that there is no complete separation between the two. The social morality of a community will be determined by the balance of the thousands or millions of individual ethical "pictures of life" within it. This will not, of course, be necessarily an arithmetical median. The will not, of course, be necessarily an arithmetical median. The relative impact of the multitude of individual ethics upon social morality—and in turn the impact of social morality upon the legal order—will greatly depend on the character of the society. In the pre-democratic age, the ethical values of a greater or smaller group of leaders had infinitely greater impact that of the inarticulate masses. The evolution of many societies, from a stage of kingly or aristocratic leadership to the rise of the middle class, and from there to the participation of the "common man," clearly produces a progressive widening of the basis for the impact of individual ethics upon social morality. But whatever the relative weight of the different groups within a society may be, the social morality of a community at any given time will be the composite of a multitude of ethical values. The variety of the latter depends in turn upon the degree of moral freedom. A liberal and pluralistic society will more easily reflect a variety of ethical values than an authoritarian one. The same number of pacifists may, in one society, produce a legal procedure for exemption of conscientious objectors from military service, while in another they may have no impact at all upon the social morality and the legal order. Ultimately, a completely conditioned society may reduce or eliminate this fear of individual ethics. It, as a now no longer a fantasy, the increasing control over reproduction, through the selected implantation or substitution of certain genes, will be under the control of the masters of a society, individual values—as forecast in Huxley's Brave New World—will become an automatic and standardized reflection of officially controlled genetic. The cultural counterpart is the all pervasive control by "Big Brother" over the individual movements and actions of all individuals. All that we have said so far on the impact of ethics, and the variety of ethical theories, is conditioned upon the survival of social conditions in which individuals can still be produced, grow, and develop with a degree of uniqueness.

In any society there is a close connection between social morality and the legal order. There cannot be—and there never has been—a complete separation of law and morality. Historical and ideological differences concern the extent to which the norms of the social order are absorbed into the legal order. And while, in the traditional, more or less custom-bound society, the flow was essentially in one direction, the gradual transformation of social behaviour into legal custom, and from custom into legislative prescription, in the contemporary, highly articulate and organized society, the law becomes in turn increasingly a major factor in the formation of social morality.

This inter-relationship cannot be by-passed by any legal theory which maintains that law is a self-contained order of enforceable prescriptions. The difference between certain "positivist" theories, such as those of Austin or Kelsen, and others which in one way or another incorporate ethical postulates into the concept of law and the legal order, lies mainly in the question whether the metalegal foundations of a legal order should be sought inside it or outside it. The "habitual obedience" which forms part of Austin's definition of law, or the "minimum of effectiveness" which is the condition of the continuing validity of a legal system in Kelsen's theory, but also "rules which contain patterns of conduct for the exercise of force" (Olivecrona), or the "peaceful co-existence of masses of individuals in social groups and their cooperation for other ends than mere existence and propagation" (Lundstedt)—all incorporate into the law a certain body of social norms, whether the latter be stated as hypotheses or "facts" or parts of the legal definition itself. In the words of one of the most strongly anti-idealistic be a study of social phenomena, the life of a human community; and jurisprudence must have as its task the interpretation of the 'validity' of the law in terms of social effectivity, that is, a certain correspondence between a normative idea content and social phenomena."

LAW, MORALITY AND SOCIAL CHANGE

Unless in minimum of conformity between legal order and social effectiveness is maintained by the various processes of legal evolution, a revolution will ultimately destroy the existing legal order and substitute a new one. When the feudal order that tied peasant serfs to the land was no longer acceptable, the peasants fled to the free cities and eventually the feudal order collapsed. When a majority of Negroes no longer accepts legal, economic, or social inferiority to a white minority within a legal order, and the change of the legal system through legislative, administrative, and judicial reforms fails to keep pace with the change of moral pressure, a revolution will ultimately displace the former order. Sometimes the revolution will come from outside, as in the destruction of the Nazi order by the majority of nations that were willing to fight against it.

The normal process of interrelation between social morality and legal order is one of evolution, i.e., the use of the instrumentalities of legal change for the reduction of tension between the two types of normative order. The intensity of this process of interaction is decisively determined by the degree of organization of a society. Generally in primitive societies the reach of authority, and therefore of law, is limited by physical conditions and social tradition. Most of the social life moves beyond the law, which is concerned with minimum order—defence, a rudimentary system of justice and police, and a minimal revenue system sufficient to maintain government. It is only against this beakground of undeveloped and slow moving societies that the theories of Savigny, Ehrlich, and other advocates of custom as against law-making can be understood. In contemporary society, the reach of the law is far greater, and there are correspondingly closer relations between the legal order and social morality. The transition can, in our time, be closely observed as the many new states of the post-war world seek to transform themselves from traditional static and agricultural societies into societies that aspire at economic development, diversification, and social change. The legal machinery becomes the paramount instrument of social change. In the process it often becomes necessary for the law to impose new patterns of social behaviour upon the society.

Thus it may become necessary for the state that seeks economic and social development to destroy existing patterns of land ownership, especially where they are linked with tribal custom and family tenure. In order to become a modern society, India found it necessary to legislate the abolition of the caste system and of the polygamous marriage. The fact that the legislation has hitherto been far from effective, especially with regard to the abolition of the caste system as a continuing pattern of social life, shows that the power of the law to influence and change social morality is as yet far from unlimited.

The majority of legal systems move between what Strawson has called "maximum" and "minimum" morality, i.e., they vacillate between the incorporation into law of those moral conditions which are crucial to the survival of the legal structure, and the transformation of all or most of the social norms of the community into legal norms. The question will often arise: What in fact are the minimum moral conditions essential for the survival of society and therefore requiring their hardening into legal norms?

LAW AND THE ENFORCEMENT OF MORALS

This question has been the subject of sharp controversy in recent years, against the background of two important aspects of the relation between law and morality, one contained in a decision of the House of Lords, the other in the report of the Wolfenden Committee published in 1957. In Shaw's case, the defendant had composed and procured the publication of a magazine called The Ladies' Directory which gave the names and addresses, as well as nude photographs, of prostitutes, supplemented by a coded indication of the sexual practices. Although Shaw was clearly guilty of two statutory offences, i.e., publishing as obscene libel and living on the earnings of prostitutes, the House of Lords, with only one dissent, also convicted him of a "conspiracy to corrupt public morals." The House of Lords here emphatically asserted "a residual power, where no statute has yet intervened to supersede the common law, to superintend those offences which are prejudicial to the public welfare" (Lord Simmonds). The subsequent discussion, to which the most prominent contributions are Professor Hart's Law, Liberty and Morality (1963) and Lord Devlin's, The Enforcement of Morals (1965), centred around the question of how far the law should go in legislating on morality, beyond was raised, in a socially more serious context, by the report of the Wolfenden Committee which recommended, by a majority of twelve to one, that homosexual behaviour between consenting adults in private should no longer be treated as a criminal offence. The crucial issue of the relation between law and social morality is put in the words of the report itself:

> Unless a deliberate attempt is made by society acting through the agency of the law and equate this fear of crime with that of sin, there must remian a realm of private morality and immorality which is, in brief and crude terms, not the law's business.

The question what the proper sphere of law is, in relation to morality, was the main subject of the debate between professor Hart and Lord Devlin. The former based himself essentially on John Stuart Mill's essay, On Liberty, in which Mill said that "the only purpose for which power can rightfully be exercised over any member of a civilized community against his will is to prevent harm to others." By contrast, Lord Devlin maintained that the State may claim on two grounds to legislate on matters of morals. It could function to promote virtue among its citizens—the Platonic ideal—and therefore claim "the right and duty to declare what standards of morality are to be observed as virtuous and must ascertain them as it thinks best." This conception of the State, which invests it with the power of determination between good and evil, destroys freedom of conscience and paves the road to tyranny, is unacceptable to Anglo-American thought. Alternatively, "society may legislate to preserve itself." In Lord Devlin's judgment, the House of Lords in Shaw's case had done just this when in sought to indict the defendant, inter alia, for corruption of the moral welfare of the State. And it was a jury of twelve reasonable men, expressing the moral values of the common man rather that the educated elite, that best represented the moral standards of a society.

While this debate is highly relevant to the question whether and to what extent a law should, in contemporary British society, interfere with actions that, however contrary to predominant sexual morality and practice, are carried on in private and therefore do not directly affect the public, it does not elucidate the theoretical question of the relation between law and social morality. As we have seen, the dimensions of public order vary greatly from one type of society to another, both historically and ideologically. In a theocratic or totalitarian society, the regulation of sexual practices or of freedom of discussion, even in private, may be eminently a matter of "public order," whereas in a liberal contemporary democracy, influenced by modern psychological, criminological, and sociological studies, male homosexuality carried on in private may be regarded as being of no concern to public order. The Spartans approved of homosexuality because they believed that it promoted courage in battle. A Spartan type society might well legislate for the promotion of homosexuality, private or public, as being an important aspect of "public order."

The essential theoretical lesson of the discussion that has arisen from Shaw's case and the Wolfenden Committee report is that modern, articulate, and highly organized society, equipped with a multitude of media of communication and information, has the means and the power to transform preferred moral standards into law, but that the question how much of social morality should be regulated and promoted by law is a question deeply dependent upon differing social ideologies and ethical valuations.

The only general conclusion to be drawn is that, in any society that preserves a modicum of individual responsibility, there is a tension between individual ethics and social morality on the one part, and social morality and the legal order on the other. How much these three spheres of normative order influence and modify each other is a question that cannot be answered in absolute terms.

3

SCIENCE AND LEGAL THEORY

The nature of scientific inquiry has been described by an eminent contemporary philosopher of science as being "a systematic explanation of facts, by ascertaining the conditions and consequences of events, by exhibiting the logical relations of propositions to one another. . . ." Further, "The conclusion of science are the fruits of an institutionalized system of inquiry which plays an increasingly important role in the lives of men."

For the student of the theory of a social science—law—the first question is whether the same system in inquiry can be applied to the natural science—namely, to the study of matter and its behaviour in the would around us—and to the social science, which are concerned with the patterns of human behaviour, and their interactions, in society. The scope and complexity of this question have been immensely widened by the enormous expansion of the objects and processes of inquiry in both areas in our time. From the relatively simply study of the behaviour of visible objects and clearly ascertainable forms of energy, on the earth and—since the birth of modern astronomy—in the solar system, the objects of study by the natural science now extend, on the one hand, to the nature, movements and interactions of immeasurably minute sub-particles of the atom. This has produced not only a greatly widened area of study, but also many new, different and constantly changing methods of inquiry. On the other hand, the field of the social science has widened, from the study of the relatively simple and static patterns of rural and earlier urban societies, to the enormously larger, more complex and constantly changing structures of modern industrialized societies. These societies are not only vastly greater in area and density of population, but formed by an ever more complex interaction of factors that mould the shape and structure of such societies. "Those who are engaged in a course of decision-making soon become aware that each decision is conditioned not only by the concrete situation in which it is taken but also by the sequence of past decisions and that their new decisions in their turn will influence future decision not only by their effect on the history of events but also by the precedents which they set and the changes which they make in the way decision-makers in the future will see, interpret and respond to events. . . . " That there is a fundamental difference between the scientific methods of the natural science and the social science has been a basic tenet of the various neo-Kantian schools of thought. Kant had made a general distinction between man as part of nature—and to that extent subject to the laws of causation—and man as a reasonable being which regulates conduct by imperatives. But whereas Kant himself had confined this distinction to the theory of knowledge, the neo-Kantians applied it construe a basic difference in the methods and purposes of natural and social sciences. This is a reflection—particularly strong in the nineteenth century—of the growing belief in the accessibility of all human phenomena to scientific knowledge. Neo-Kantian philosophers, such as Dilthey, Rickert and Windelband, apply scientific method not just to the theory of knowledge, i.e., to the perception and the ordering of phenomena outside the human individual, but to the whole of human nature in its different manifestations, thinking, feeling and willing. The chief result of this is the methodological separation of the natural and cultural science. The formen and concerned with the perception of the phenomena of natural science. The latter are concerned with the manifestation of human volition in man's social organization expressing itself in ethics, law and history. These sciences, different in their object, require different principles of approach, and the one which is paramount in neo-Kantian legal theory is the contrast between causality as dominating natural science, and of volition (or purpose) as dominating social science.

METHODS OF INQUIRY

The dichotomy of the methods of inquiry governing the natural and social science, respectively, has been applied to legal theory by modern neo-Kantian legal philosophers, notably Stammler, Del Vecchio and Kelsen. The differences between the theories of these jurists are analysed elsewhere in this book. They share the basic assumption that law is a normative, not a natural, science, concerned with *sollen,* not with *sein.*

Doubts have been cast upon the validity—or at least the absoluteness—of this methodological distinction by both natural and social scientists. For more than a generation, leading scientists and philosophers of science have questioned the purely causal and deterministic character of the natural scientists. Thus, in Science and hypothesis, Henri Poincare has shown that the choice between alternative hypotheses in the natural sciences is choice between alternative hypotheses in the natural sciences is often one of convenience and that the same conclusions may be derived from different premises. It is impossible to make experiments without preconceived ideas, and no experiment gives scientific results without generalizations which serve as prediction for other experiments. Since then, continuous inquiries and changing theories about the structure of the atom, the theory of relativity, the interchangeability of matter and energy according to Einstein's celebrated formula $e=mc^2$, the dual "wave" and "corpuscular" character of the electron, and in particular the quantum theory have led to an interaction between speculative assumptions and experiments in physics. Modern quantum mechanics, and in particular the uncertainty formula of Heisenberg, are the chief bases for assertions of indeterminism in contemporary physical theories, implying at least a partial abandonment of the deterministic principle of causality in the natural sciences. Heisenberg's uncertainty formula asserts that, in the sub-atomic world, owing to the growing precision of the instruments of observation, the relation between the "momentum" and the "position" of a given sub-atomic particle at any given moment cannot be precisely determined. The unpredictable variations in the momentum and position of sub-atomic particles are produced by the interaction of the latter with the instruments used in measuring these features. ". . . [I]n general, every experiment performed to determine some numerical quantity renders a knowledge of others illusory, since the uncontrollable perturbations of the observed system alter the value of previously determined quantities." The principle of causality—so it is maintained—can be retained in the sub-atomic world only by ignoring the ware-particle duality of electrons. If, on the other hand, the traditional notions of space and time are preserved for sub-atomic particles, a deterministic, causal explanation of their movements and interactions is not possible.

To the doubts cast by modern physical theory on the principles of causality and determinism, there corresponds, in the social sciences, an increasing emphasis on certainty and measurability. Behavioural research, i.e., in particular the use of quantitative techniques in the analysis of factual data, as utilized in mathematical equations, is held by a growing number of contemporary sociologists, political scientists and jurists, to provide a far greater degree of certainty of analysis of legal phenomena, especially of the judicial processes. Thus, the question—highly relevant for interpretation of the Constitution by the U.S. Supreme Court—Whether Negroes have been discriminated by precise statistical inquiries and mathematical computation. The probability calculus is said to permit the determination whether and to what extent the exclusion of Negroes is due to chance or to intentional policy, a vital factor in the legal decision. Even before the recent revolutionary expansion in the categorization and analysis of complex factual data made possible by the advent of the computer, the realist movement in legal theory, a generation ago, drew attention to the importance of fact research and analysis in the process of legal decision. Modern behaviourists accept the same premise but use modern computer programming to obtain more precise predictions of legal behaviour. They seek "to obtain a precise and exhaustive distinction between combinations of facts that lead to decisions in favour of one party and combinations of facts that lead to decisions in favour of the opposing party. This distinction can be obtained with the aid of mathematical models."

There has thus been a considerable softening of the once rigid distinctions between the methods of enquiry in the natural and social sciences. By stressing the importance of hypotheses, of uncertainty, and the possibility of articulated or unarticulated value assumptions, the natural scientists let in an element of indeterminism. The social sciences have widened the area of causality, by extending the uses of fact research, statistic and mathematical computations in the determination of legal decisions.

But is doubtful whether the contemporary approaches to the relation of the natural and social sciences indicate a change in substance rather than a growth in self-consciousness about methods of enquiry. Natural scientists have always started from hypotheses which they have sought to verify by experiment. These hypotheses may have been caused by chance observation—like the fall of an apple or the movement of the water in a pail that is swung around—or by a sudden inspiration or by a philosophical speculation on God and Nature. It is the articulation of hypotheses and value premises that has grown. On the other hand, it is doubtful whether such theories as the "uncertainty" principle, however important in physics, represent more than another phase in the unending interplay of theory and experiment in the observation of physical phenomena. They do not affect the basic difference between the objectives or natural and social sciences. The former are exclusively concerned with the study of matter, the latter with the purposive behaviour of human beings. Modern sciences—anthropology, blood chemistry, genetics, psychology—have greatly widened the material component, and therefore the deterministic factors in human behaviour. But there remains an indeterministic element in the human decision, which is not of the same order and the indeterminism of the movements of sub-atomic particles. As long as men do not become purely chemically and genetically predetermined conglomerations of chemical substances—as pictured in Aldous Huxley's Brave New World—they will differ in their ideas, their goals, their conceptions of good and bad which direct their objectives. The arbitrariness or inarticulateness of the choice between competing and conflicting values can be significantly reduced by behavioural research, and the utilization of behavioural data has been immensely advanced by modern computer programming which can handle data of infinitely greater quantity and complexity that the human brain.

As long as man does not become a mere product of chemical

compounds, but retains a uniqueness of mind which enables him to be an individual, to distinguish between good and evil, to choose between alternative courses of action, the main use of modern scientific, technical, mathematical advances must be to widen the area of rationalization in the choice between alternative values. This means not only the articulation of values and interests cardinal to a given legal decision—as it has been attempted in the work and the philosophy of Holmes, Pound, Radbruch, Scheler and others—but also a greatly extended use of modern methods of fact research, as a basis for value decisions. Thus, the vast area of value choices described by the general term of "public policy" can be made far more precise by modern opinion research and statistical inquiries, on such vaital issues of public policy as the legitimacy of birth control or the criminality of homosexual practices. There are beginnings of a theory of rational decision in which the respective roles of values and quantitative factors are sorted out. On the other hand, modern statistical-computer-aided-research methods can be used and may be essential to implement a legal policy decision.

FACTS, VALUES AND JUDGMENT IN THE SOCIAL SCIENCES

While, with regard to the recognition of the interdependence of value hypotheses and empirical evidence, the natural and the social science have come closer together, a basic distinction between values and facts remains. Such a view is, however, challenged by many outstanding social scientists. Ernest Nagel has summarized the principal types of critique as follows:

The first, and most prominent, critique is that which holds that a "value orientation" is inherent in the very choice of material for investigation by the social scientist. The best known exponent of this view is max Weber. A variant of this approach is, second, the view, that, since the social scientist is himself affected by considerations of right and wrong, of his own notions of a satisfactory social order, these personal standards enter into the analysis of social phenomena (e.g., into the appraisal of the physical and psychological "needs" of a particular culture).

A third approach maintains that the distinction between fact and value is untenable with regard to the analysis of purposive human behaviour, since value judgments inextricably inter into what appear to be descriptive of facutal statements. A prominent exponent of this approach is the Swedish economist and social philosopher Gunnar Myrdal. Myrdal distinguishes between "beliefs," i.e., a person's knowledge, to be objectively judged as true or false, and "valuations," i.e., a social situation or relation adjudged to be "just, right fair, desirable, or the opposite, in some degree of intensity or other. . . ." "Opinions" are usually composite of beliefs and valuations. The difficulty, according to Myrdal, is that, in an appraisal of any particular social problem, beliefs tend to be biased, i.e., twisted in the direction of a person's desired hierarchy of valuations.

Valuations are seldom overtly expressed except with they emerge in the course of a person's attempts to formulate his beliefs concerning the facts and their implications in relation to some section of social reality. Beliefs concerning the facts are the building stones for the logical hierarchies of valuations into which a person tries to shape his opinions. When the valuations are conflicting, as they normally are, beliefs serve the function of bridging illogicalities. The beliefs are thus not only determined by available scientific knowledge in society and the efficacy of the means of its communication to various population groups but are regularly 'biased,' by which we mean that they are systematically twisted in the one direction which fits them best for purposes of rationalizations.

From Myrdal, who has written a classical study on "An American Dilemma: The Negro Problem and Modern Democracy," this twisting of beliefs is principally illustrated in the "systems of popular beliefs concerning the Negro and his relations to the larger society."

There is an emotional lead of valuation conflict pressing for retionalization, creating certain blind spots- and also creating a desire for knowledge in other spots-and in general causing conceptions of reality to deviate from truth in determined directions.

In the field of jurisprudence, Professor Fuller appears to be of this persuasion:

> When we are dealing with purposive action projected through time, the structure that we observe, recall, and report lies, not in any instantaneous state of affairs, but in a course of happening, which can be understood only if we participate in a process of evaluation by which the bad is rejected and the good retained.

The movements of a boy digging in the sand cannot be understood until we know that he is searching for clams. In this action "descriptive and evaluative efforts cannot at the outset be considered as being carried on simultaneously because we do not at first know what the boy is trying to do. Transferring this to the wider framework of legal inquiry, Professor directives we may operate within a framework of purposes which conditions our decisions, even though only certain of these purposes are called into consciousness by the facts of the case at hand." The legal process is "the collaborative articulation of shared purposes."

A fourth critique maintains that a value-free social science is impossible, because value commitments enter into the very assessment of evidence by social scientists. Thus, the modern science of theoretical statistics seeks to rationalize the evidence for so-called "statistical hypotheses," i.e., hypotheses concerning the probabilities of random events. To take an example given by Nagel, tests may have to be performed to determine whether a new medicine has toxic effects because of certain impurities in its manufacture. The medicine is tested by being introduced into the diet of 100 pigs, and only three of the animals become gravely ill as a result. The experimenter must decide between two alternative hypotheses: one, that the drug is toxic; and the other, that it is not toxic. The decision between these two alternative hypotheses cannot be made according to strictly mathematical-statistical principles; it involves certain judgments of value, such as a decision of preference on the respective importance of preservation of human lives that might possible be endangered by the drug proving to be dangerous, as against the financial loss incurred by the manufacturer through the abandonment of the product. Statistical theory appears to support the thesis that value commitments enter into the rules for assessing the evidence of statistical hypotheses.

Some social philosophers go further and maintain that the connection between the social perspective of a student of human affairs and his standards of competent social inquiry is not merely contingent but necessary. This is based on the assumption that social institutions and their cultural products are constantly changing, and that the intellectual apparatus required to understand them must change correspondingly.

With regard to all these critical approaches, it may be readily admitted that the element of valuation, and of other uncertainties, in the selection and appraisal of evidence of social phenomena is generally for greater than in the natural science. Yet, "these admissions do not entail the conclusion that, in a manner unique to the study of purposive human behaviour, fact and value are fused beyond the possibility of distinguishing between them." A distinction must be made between "value judgments" as expressing estimates of the degree to which certain types of action, objects, or institutions are contained in a given process of assessment, and "value judgements" as expressing approval or disapproval of a certain moral or social or legal ideal. In all types of science the attempt must be made to distinguish between the characterizing and the appraising aspects. It is generally more difficult to do so in the social science, but not inherently impossible, and much of the difficulty lies in the relatively undeveloped character of complex fact analysis in the social sciences.

POLICY DECISIONS AND THE ART OF JUDGMENT

The growing complexity of modern social and legal planning processes has made the simple distinction between facts and values insufficient. In industrialized, and in developing societies, any decision of major social significance, such as the planning of a road system in a densely settled area, or a government grant for the construction and staffing of a number of new universities, entails a multitude of complex and inter-related factors. Some of these are constants, such as the size of a given area of land, or—at least within a limited period—the rate of growth and composition of the population within a given community.

The great majority of the relevant factors are variables, such as the density rate of traffic influenced by many different factors such as the rate of production of motor vehicles, urban zoning legislation, farming subsidies, technological changes as well as changes in social habits, which may deeply influence patterns of life, or national and local tax policy.

The complexity of the policy judgments involved in such major planning projection may be illustrated by the Buchanan Report of 1963. The terms of reference of the Buchanan Committee were "to study the long-term development of road and traffic in urban begins with a general factual estimate of the expected increase in the number of motor vehicles in Britain over the next few decades, and the more obvious consequences of such increase in various aspects of social life. It assumes that at a certain point Englishmen will react negatively against a state of affairs, which will bring motor traffic itself to a standstill and at the same time drastically impair other basic amenities of life. As against this assessment of a value judgment by citizens, the report also assumes that they will continue to value and desire motor traffic rather than to abolish it in what would be a kind of Erewhonian revolution.

Most of the report is devoted to an analysis of the quantitative and qualitative aspects, and the interaction of the different variables relevant to the situation. This implies an analysis of the types of traffic, moving from buildings to buildings, the minimum accessibility to buildings required in any environment, the functional nature of streets in towns-still multi-purpose streets used for traffic, trade, personal intercourse and parking—and the relation between the minimum of environmental value and the upper limit accessibility. The report also analyses traffic flows with relation to the needs and habits of people as they move from home to work and back.

In a pioneer study on *"The Art of Judgment,"* in which the Buchanan Report figures as one of the principal illustrations of the complexity of factors involved in policy judgments, Sir Geoffrey Vickers analyses the various aspects of this, and of other reports, in terms of: (a) reality judgments; (b) value judgments; and (c) instrumental judgments. Reality judgments are concerned with the appreciation of the reality factor, which have a relatively high degree of certainty—although one generally lower than empirical observations in the natural science. They include such elements as the number, size and projected development of towns, of arable land, the use of streets, and the proportion of the national product invested in motorcar production.

The second factor is the value judgment, which concerns the hierarchy of values and priorities, such as the relative weight attached to good environment as against the conveniences of travel in motor vehicles. The later is a variable in so far as an increase of motor traffic beyond a certain point will defeat the objective of fast and convenient movement from place to place—as is already apparent in the movement of traffic in and out of major towns in most Western countries. Value judgments are also deeply influenced by the economic and social philosophy prevailing in the community. In a centrally directed system, the choices for the individual will be rigidly limited by the planners, whereas in a liberal society the choice between the different values is, to a far greater extent, left to individuals and groups.

There is, third the "instrumental" judgment. This is the judgement which assesses a problem in its full complexity. It is shaped by what Kenneth E. Boulding has called "the image."

. . . As we proceed from lower to higher levels of organization the concept of the image becomes an increasingly important part of any theoretical model, and the image itself becomes increasingly complex. . . . A rudimentary image is exhibited in simple control mechanisms. It is clearly present even at the very earliest stage of life. It grown in importance and complexity as we ascend the biological ladder. It is of overwhelming importance in the interpretation of human behaviour and of the dynamics of society.

The instrumental judgment is based on the skill "which produces apt solutions to the problems set by such surveys of 'reality,' calculated to change the pattern of expected relationships by responses perhaps never tried before."

It is the combination of reality, value, and instrumental judgments which is involved in the process of "appreciation." These processes of appreciation are not confined to public policy and planning decisions. They also occur in private business where, in an age of rapidly changing technology, a new chemical invention may produce a revolution in needs affecting manufacturing equipment and causing a change from on line of production to another. The larger the enterprise involved, the closer the analogy of the policy judgment to that of public authorities.

It is obvious that the complexity of the various types of appraisal involved, and of their interdependence, will involve close integration between scientific methods of inquiry and policy judgments. Because of the dynamics of changing societies, "reality" judgments will to a large extent be estimates of probability in which the mathematician, the statistician and the economist, aided by computer techniques, will have to supply many of the reality estimates—such as of the increase in the population over a given period expected to seek university education, or the interaction between social stratification, income distribution, local taxation, urban amenities and traffic density in a given are, or the estimated effect of slum clearance and provision of community facilities on juvenile criminality and the consequent need for the building of prisons as against reform institutions.

It follows from the above—highly tentative and condensed—observations that there will have to be developed a science as well as an art of policy judgment, and that the two will be closely interlocked. The estimate of probabilities, and of the interrelation of different variables is a given social planning process, will to a large extent be a matter of scientific computation, but subject to the uncertainties that—as we have already seen—are inherent in any probability calculus involving human and social behaviour. But there will remain value judgments, as between technological process and aesthetic factors, between cultural values and economic progress, between the degree of individual choice and the degree of public control, which will deeply affect the total picture. Ultimately the decisional process will be deeply affected by the "image" of the kind of society that will be shaped by all these factors.

SOCIAL AND LEGAL RESPONSIBILITY

Our enquiry so far has been concerned with the extent to which scientific enquiry—by it by the use of natural science processes of enquiry for the purposes of social science, or by the use of scientific methods specific to the social science—can help to clarify and implement social (including legal) value goals.

The present section will be concerned with the more fundamental question to what extent the enormous progress and broadening of the psychological, physiological and genetic analysis may affect established distinctions between right and wrong, and therefore the elements of legal responsibility. In philosophical terms, the question is whether the increasing knowledge of the causes of human behaviour—through the analysis of mind, through the study of social environment by which the behaviour of an individual is conditioned, or through the knowledge of the genetic makeup of a given individual—makes human behaviour predetermined and thus diminishes or excludes the freedom of choice on which moral and legal responsibility is founded.

PSYCHOLOGY AND CRIMINAL RESPONSIBILITY

Modern psychology has dissolved the formerly somewhat simple-assumptions about the capacity of an individual to choose between right and wrong, into a multitude of factors. Until recently, legal theory generally assumed that a person was free to choose and act, unless his freedom was excluded by certain conditions of physical or mental compulsion. "The individual if at the time of his doing what would otherwise be a punishable act he is, say, unconscious, mistaken about the physical consequences of his bodily movements or the nature or qualities of the doing or persons affected by them, or in some cases, if he is subjected to threats or other gross forms of coercion or is the victim of certain types of mental disease." Mental disease was generally defined narrowly, as insanity, and the test of insanity was, in the classical formulation of the M'Naghten rules, "that, to establish a defence on the ground of insanity, it must be clearly proved that, at the time of the committing of the act, the party accused was labouring under such a defect of reason, from disease of the mind, as not to know the nature and quality of the act he was doing, or, if he did know it that he did not know he was doing what was wrong."

This test assumes that a person who intellectually apprehends the distinction between the right and wrong of a given conduct must be held criminally responsible. This identification of knowledge and the power to control one's action was attacked as early as 1883 by the great British criminal lawyer Sir Fitzjames Stephen, and although the M'Naghten test was adopted throughout the British Commonwealth and almost universally in the United States, contemporary psychiatry and criminology have almost universally rejected it as scientifically untenable. The gravemen of the criticism is that knowledge is not the sole guide of conduct and "that the capacity of knowing right from wrong can be completely intact and functioning perfectly even though a defendant is otherwise demonstrable of disordered mind."

Since all contemporary societies continue to have in their midst a considerable number of individuals whose propensities and actions are so dangerous that society must be protected from them, they can only have two alternative responses to the challenge posed by modern scientific analysis of the human mind. First, they can abandon any test of guilt and moral responsibility in favour of a purely utilitarian and socially determined elimination or confinement of persons dangerous to society.

The suggestion has sometimes been made that the insane murderer should be punished equally with the sane, or that, although he ought not to be executed as a punishment, he should be painlessly exterminated as a measure of social hygiene.

Such a philosophy can lead to the exposure of weakling children—as in ancient Sparts—or to the extermination, confinement or sterilization of entire nations, races or other groups of people as hostile or obnoxious to society—a philosophy largely practised in National Socialist Germany.

The second alternative—adopted by the overwhelming majority of modern legal systems—is to modify the concepts of guilt, fault and the moralistic basis of criminal law, in the light of modern science. One such modification if the test of "irresistible impulse." But this is now generally rejected, on the ground that a criminal act of an emotionally or mentally disturbed person may be coolly and carefully prepared, and yet be the act of a madman. Another test, adopted in a much discussed decision of the United States Court of Appeals for the District of Columbia, is "that an accused is not criminally responsible if his unlawful act was a product of mental disease or mental defect." The majority report of the Royal Commission on Capital Punishment adopted a similar test. The Model Penal Code of the American Law Institute holds a person not responsible for criminal conduct "if at the time of such conduct as a result of mental disease or defect he lacks substantial capacity either to appreciate the criminality of his conduct or to conform his conduct to the requirements of law." The Penal Code of Switzerland, the law of Scotland, and more recently the British Homicide Act of 1957 have adopted the test of "diminished responsibility" as justifying a modification of punishment for a criminal act, including detention, treatment or confinement to hospital as possible alternatives.

The importance of all these different responses to modern psychiatry is that, as against the simple antithesis of sanity and insanity, they recognize of whole spectrum of mental disturbances, including in particular psychopathic disturbances, that they consequently distinguish between intellectual apprehension and emotional control, and, as a result, correlate the degree of legal—in particular, criminal-responsibility to the degree of emotional control of which the individual is capable.

But the findings of modern psychiatry and neurology are only part of the widening process of inquiry into the circumstances, which make an individual behave in a particular way. Where these modern branches of medical science inquire into the structure of the individual human mind, modern sociology investigates the social antecedents the social antecedents of anti-social and illegal behaviour. The two join hands where, for example, psychopathic behaviour or abnormal sexual proclivities can be traced to social conditions, such as deeply disturbed domestic circumstances, or upbringing in a social environment conducive to criminal behaviour. Generally, urbanization and industrialization, with all the social disruption they entail, have a demonstrated effect on the rate of crime. The wider the range of inquiry, the more difficult does the simple equation of right and wrong with sin and innocence, good and evil become. A consequence, in the modern science of criminology, as the reaction to crime—which is more and more seen as a particularly grave form of unsocial behaviour. This has gone furthest in the treatment of juvenile offenders. In all the advanced countries of our time, the juvenile offender is now subjected to a special procedure, before separate tribunals, and such measures as probation, approved schools, or supervision by welfare authorities have increasingly replaced punishment as the normal sanction for juvenile crimes. This process has, in some states, (e.g. California) been extended to the adult offender.

MORAL GUILT, DETERMINISM AND LEGAL RESPONSIBILITY

The widening challenge of both natural and social science to traditional notions of the causes of criminal behaviour poses grave problems for legal theory. Does it altogether destroy the moral basis of criminal law? Some distinguished contemporary jurists emphatically deny that anything but the moral wrongness of an act can form the basis of criminal law. Among them are Jerome Hall, who asserts that *mens rea* is "the ultimate summation of the moral judgments expressed in the voluntary commission of numerous social harms" and Lord Denning, who, in his evidence before the Royal Commission on Capital punishment, said that

> ". . . The ultimate justification of any punishment is not that it is a deterrent, but that it is the emphatic denunciation by the community of a crime. . . . "

A similar conception is that of Thurman Arnold, who, in two important decisions rendered during his brief membership in the U.S. Court of Appeals for the District of Columbia, expressed the view that the M'Naghten test should be retained because

> "In the determination of guilt, age-old conceptions of individual moral responsibility cannot be abandoned without creating a laxity of enforcement that undermines the whole administration of criminal law."

But the major trend of contemporary legal theory, in particular with reference to the reaction of the law to the defence of insanity in the light of modern science, appears to point towards a utilitarian approach. This is essentially a modernization of Bentham's philosophy, according to which the sanctions of the criminal law are to be measured in terms of their efficiency in securing the maintenance of law at the least cost in pain. Among the contemporary exponents of this theory are Professors Glanville Williams and H.L.A. Hart. The former has stated that:

Normal people may be punished for the sake of general or particular deterrence, and mentally ill or sub-normal persons may perhaps be given some punishment if it is thought that this may have an effect upon their future conduct. . . . Mentally ill or sub-normal persons whose conduct is unlikely to be influenced by the treat of punishment must be cared for; to punish them for the sake of general deterrence is unnecessary, because normal persons are not influenced by what happens to the insane.

H.L.A. Hart has criticized the doctrine of criminal responsibility based on the "economy of threats" as misrepresenting "the character of our moral preference for a legal system that requires mental conditions of responsibility over a system of total strict liability or entirely different methods of social control such as hypnosis, propaganda, or conditioning." Hart accepts the utilitarian criterion of the cost to an individual "of obeying the law—and of sacrificing some satisfaction in order to obey—against obtaining that satisfaction at the cost of paying 'the penalty.'" But he suggests that the purpose of a system of criminal law not totally based on strict liability, and the freedom of the choice of the individual, can be preserved by a system of "excusing conditions to criminal responsibility." These include the usual defence against criminal responsibility, such as wills, contracts or marriages. In the light of a knowledge of these excusing conditions, an individual can determine his choice. The difference between this and the Benthamite approach is that, in Hart's view, "Excusing conditions are accepted as something that may conflict with the social utility of the law's threat; they are regarded as of moral importance because they provide for all individuals alike the satisfactions of a costing system."

Above discussion underlines the fundamental dilemma with which legal theory is faced, as a result of modern scientific inquiry into the conditions of both individuals and society. Once the assumption of the human being as one who is either moral or immoral and chooses freely between lawful and illegal action is undermined, there is no theoretical limit to the tracing of causes of human behaviour to an infinite chain of antecedent causes. The emotional disorders of a sex criminal may be traced to the slum conditions under which he grew up, or to exposure to the brutality on his father. But the latter is in turn the result of his genetic make up, or of the conditions in which he grew up. And to it goes no in infinite regression. In philosophical theory, the analysis of the increasingly complex interweaving of physical and social factors which determine a given individual is incompatible with "freedom of will," since the actions of murderers as well as of the most selfless and law-abiding members of society are determined by preexisting—physical, mental or social—conditions. Yet the great majority of modern legal systems and of legal philosophers reject the total abandonment of individual responsibility as a criterion of criminal—and to a lesser extent of civil-liability. Modern utilitarians like Hart and Williams agree with "moralists" like Hall or Denning, and with most psychiatrists, on the continuing necessity of retaining some form of punishment related to responsibility, Philosophers appear to agree that the philosophical question of freedom of will must be kept separate from the criteria of responsibility essential to law as a social discipline. In a recent symposium on the subject of "determinism and Freedom," one discussant suggested that "when we judge a person morally responsible for a certain action, we do indeed presuppose that he was a free agent at the time of the action. But the freedom presupposed . . . is nothing more that . . . the ability to act according to one's choices or desires." Another suggestion is that the degree of moral responsibility is dependent on the level of "reflectiveness" achieved by a particular person. The simplest, and also the most convincing, answer to the dilemma is the admission that "we have to recognize clearly that there are two levels of operation. There is the level of daily life and social interaction, i.e., the level of 'free will,' and there is the deterministic level. So far as the deterministic level has concrete reference beyond the purely verbal, it is the level of scientific activity. At this level . . . determinism has the status merely of a programme to direct inquiry, a programme applicable to the overwhelming majority of the phenomena of the world about us. . . . The other level is the common sense level of everyday life, the level of 'free will,' . . . On this level we have to devise a practical method of dealing with situations in which we cannot control or predict."

A legal system must assume freedom of choice between alternative courses of action and direct its sanctions accordingly. It is concerned with the practical ordering of social life in a given community. It does not purport to answer the philosophical question of "free will." And insofar as a legal system must reflect the general attitudes of the society, which it regulates, it must accept that the torturers of children or the killers are not regarded with moral indifference. This is reflected in the views of such experienced trial judges as Lords Devlin and Denning.

What modern scientific analysis can teach us is two things: First, that the simple dichotomy of good and evil, of moral reprehensibility and innocence, must give way to a much subtler gradation of shades of responsibility. This has, as we have seen, already deeply influenced modern criminal law and criminology. Second, the growing knowledge of the biological and social complexities that determine a person's behaviour should teach humility and a sense of perspective. The men who, as legislators, judges or administrators, lay down the conditions of legal responsibility can and should do so, not from a posture of moral superiority, but as executants of a social and legal order which has not yet found any alternative to the criterion of free choice between right and wrong as a basis of legal sanctions. And it is at least possible that, at some time in the future, such insights may modify the collective relations between nations, which still operate in their mutual intercourse on a psychological level that civilized societies have long abandoned in their internal affairs, and that mature individuals would feel ashamed to apply in their personal relations.

GENETICE AND RESPONSIBILITY

The entire discussion of legal theory in the present book assumes a human society based on individuals different from each other in a multitude of ways but all capable, to a greater or lesser extent, of reasoning, and of choosing between different courses of action. The borderline between freedom and necessity must always be somewhat arbitrary, and for the purposes of legal science it is, as suggested here, determined by social necessity rather that philosophical speculation. But certain developments in modern genetics suggest that a society is now conceivable in which the moral makeup of human beings is predetermined by genetic selection. This was foreshadowed in Aldous Huxley's Brave New World, a generation ago. It is now within the realm of scientific possibility.

A leading geneticist suggested a few years ago that reproductions should be regulated by the fertilization of stored genes collected from outstanding individuals, and that such genes should be substituted for the female genes in the fertilized ovum. In this way, mankind could in the future be increasingly populated by the likes of Beethoven, Lincoln, or Einstein, Shortly after, in a symposium on "Evolution and Mans's Progress" this same geneticist suggested a coordination of cultural and biological evolution, and a general extension of artificial insemination to human reproduction. The fertilization of selected female eggs with chosen sperm, subsequently implanted in selected female hosts, "would permit the multiple distribution of eggs of a highly selected female into diverse recipient females, yet when so desired it would enable the child to be derived on its paternal side from the recipient's husband. Possibly, too, techniques involving mature eggs could be combined with deep freezing to allow indefinitely prolonged storage." Though admitting that it was impossible to "proceed in humans according to principles governing simple Mendelian differences," Professor Muller believes that, through the control of reproduction by selected genes, mankind will progress towards a higher intellectual and moral level. A majority of the commentators—all eminent authorities in the field of biology, zoology, sociology, and paleontology—were sceptical. Underlying their doubts was the uncertainty about the results of man's interference with the concept of the pluralistic society, "in which no one way of life is considered absolutely better than several others." and doubt that certain genes and mutations were in all circumstances good or bad. Above all, we do not know who may do the genetic planning for the future society. As a result of the growing concentration of power in a few hands, "Big Brother" may decide on a genetic selection stressing physical prowess, obedience, and low intellectual capacity. "We may soon find that the doctrine of 'clearly deleterious' is no easier to apply in practice that is Holmes' doctrine of clear and present danger in a realm of free speech." The power of genetic determination by preselection will include the determination of the level of moral responsibility. People will increasingly be made to behave according to certain predetermined patterns of conduct.

4

LEGAL THEORY AND SOCIAL EVOLUTION

LAW AND SOCIAL CHANGE

A crisis of society challenges the law more directly perhaps than any other branch of social activity. The profession of the lawyer, and the values dear to the law, are threatened by an upheaval in the foundations of society. Though the law is obviously concerned with politics, economics, social life and ethics, it is its function to give them form and order. From this relation of law to the matters which it regulates, there develop characteristic features, all sound in principle and indeed fundamental to the idea of law, yet all apt to divorce law from social reality in a time of crisis.

The first of these characteristics is stability. Stability is a paramount object of law, and indeed a vital incentive to its development. But the desire of the lawyer to preserve stability of conditions may, and often does, blind him to social changes and developments, with the result that the law eventually becomes a mere phantom or is defied by forces stronger than itself.

The second character is formalism. Since law is a method of ordering social relations in a specific manner, the form gains paramount importance in the legal system and legal training. One of the principal controversies in legal theory is between those who emphasise form and those who emphasise substance. But there is little doubt that, for the average lawyer, the form of regulating a specific social relation becomes more important that the social relation itself. It is extremely difficult for a lawyer working under any modern legal system no to be overwhelmed by technique.

The distinction of precedents, the interpretation of statutes, the tracing of the historical development of a particular clause or notion, matters of evidence and procedure—all these preoccupations tend to overshadow the social stuff behind them.

Thirdly, and perhaps most important in its effect, there is the desire for security from disorder. This, indeed, is a universal human desire, the more cherished because of the frequency of disturbance. However, for the law, security has assumed an overwhelming importance, heightened by the development of social conditions and legal education in the positivist era of the nineteenth century. Under the protection of settled conditions, a steadily growing power of state organisation and an increasing prosperity of the middle class, the background of social and political struggle became dimmer and dimmer for the lawyer, while his technical training became more and more complex. Encouraged by the method of legal education, law developed into a skilled craft, a professional technique, pursued with less and less regard for the social matter which it was to regulate.

This world of comparative security, comfort and self-sufficiency is crumbling everywhere, though in many degrees of speed and intensity. Political revolution, social strife and war are laying bare the roots of law, its close and inevitable link with the ethical political and social foundations of the community in which it operates. Communist and Fascist revolutions alike have brought the lawyer face to face with fundamental political issues; but in every country a continuous though less abrupt social revolution affects the law in its principles as well as in its daily routine work. Such matters as the growth of a publicly directed and state controlled economy, from Fascism to Communism, with many intermediate stages; the universal delegation of powers from a legislative assembly to the executive; the standardisation of industry, business and employment; the growing predominance of collective bargaining with different degrees of state supervision; the development of transport in its effects upon the civilian, the standardisation of housing, building, insurance; the increase of "administrative" or "public welfare" offences—these and many other developments permeate not only the fundamental issues of individual liberty, but every technical rule of contract, tort, property. They demand a new legal technique which cannot be developed without reference to, and consciousness of, the political issues involved.

The challenge is particularly evident in the sphere of international law. For, whereas the municipal lawyer can seek delusive protection behind a rigid division of is and ought, the separation of legislation and application of law, the international lawyer lacks even this comfort. The absence of legislative authority and machinery exposes him, without any protective curtain, to the perpetual changes in international society and should compel him to test his rules perpetually in relation to social reality.

Only too often vital social developments have found the lawyer ill-prepared. The abject prostitution of lawyers in Nazi Germany, Fascist Italy and Soviet Russia, the prolonged blocking of social progress by the legal interpreters of the American Constitution, or the predominantly hostile attitude of English judges towards the inevitable predominance of statute in modern law, have had a profound and, on the whole, negative effect on social and political development.

On the other hand, the many important developments in the English common law of the last decade, or in the interpretation of the American Constitution, would have been impossible without a remarkable change in the legal ideology of the judiciary.

What part has legal theory to play in the reshaping of society? In the past, it appears, jurists and legal philosophers have either claimed too much or too little. Some legal philosophies, like that of Hegel, have purported to give a complete solution to all problems; on the other hand, legal positivism, prevalent during the nineteenth century, as well as Marxist thought have denied to the law any constructive function and reduced it to the rule of the obedient servant.

The many different trends of legal thinking can be divided into three principal types: first, there is legal philosophy proper, comprising all those theories which formulate legal ideals as the basis of a system. Second, there is analytical jurisprudence, which is essentially concerned with legal technique. Third, there are sociological theories, which are essentially concerned with the examination of the relations between legal principles and their functioning in society. These three principal trends of legal thinking have usually been in opposition to each other. Both analytical and sociological theories have opposed legal idealism, while also fighting each other. Yet each of these three principal approaches to the law is necessary. Each requires the others in order to give to the law its proper place in society.

Even the non-lawyer cannot fail to be impressed by the vital part played by legal philosophy in political developments. The ideology of natural law is generally considered to be the essential and characteristic basis of Western civilisation. The relations between God, Nature and Man; the conflicting theories of government; the standards which govern the relations between nations-are all formulated in terms of natural law. A number of the most powerful political philosophies have been put forward in the form of legal philosophies. Hobbes, Kant, Fichte and Hegal have developed their doctrines of state and their whole political ideology an legal philosophy. If these are part of a general philosophical system established by thinkers not trained in the law, there are in modern times no less important legal philosophies developed by jurists, as part of their legal teaching. Among them are Savigny's doctrine of the Volksgeist, a vital part of the romantic exaltation of the nation; Gierke's organic theory, a forerunner to modern doctrines which claim the absolute merger of the individual in the state; Ihering's doctrine, which firmly establishes the coercive power of the state as the basis of law; Duguit's doctrine of social solidarity, which forms an essential basis of collectivist economic theory; Hauriou's doctrine of the institution which prepares the way for corporate supremacy in modern France, on a Catholic basis; Pashukanis's doctrine that in socialist society all law becomes merged in administration.

Nor is this vital importance of legal philosophies an accident. The complex structure of modern society and the extending machinery of government makes for organisation and the formulation of principles in terms of law. But it is vital to recognise that no legal philosophy can be anything but a formulation of political ideals through the medium of law. The attempts of so many philosophers, politicians and jurists to give their ideals the appearance of objective truth by clothing them in legal terminology have brought nothing but confusion and hypocrisy into the perpetual struggle of conflicting ideals. Legal theory formulates political ideals in terms of justice. But it cannot give a magic formula of justice which can say once and for all what is just and unjust.

Aristotle said that justice demanded the equal treatment of those equal before the law. But it remains for each political order to determine whom to treat as equal or otherwise. All legal philosophies, which, in one way or another, have attempted to establish absolute ideals, reveal themselves as pure political ideologies. As Radbruch has said:

> All great political changes were prepared or accompanied by legal philosophies. At the beginning there was legal philosophy, at the end revolution.

Having formulated its basic principles, legal idealism can further follow-up the expression of these principles in legal institutions. At the peak, there many be such principles as the inalienable rights of man, or the supremacy of the will of the people, or the will of the working people of the world. Such legal ideals must be translated into more concrete principles, such as separation of powers, freedom of contract, socialisation of the means of production, or political control of the judiciary.

LEGAL IDEALISM AND THE SOCIOLOGICAL APPROACH TO LAW

At this point legal idealism needs the support of the functional or sociological approach of the law. Legal idealism left alone is dangerously theoretical. It falls an easy victim to the political purposes of skilful perverters. It is the lasting merit of the Marxist analysis to have first revealed the discrepancy between legal form and economic reality. On this basis, a number of sociological investigations have shown how the legal ideology of individual freedom and inviolability of private property has been put into the service of a systematic exploitation by the few of the many. The story of the development of natural law ideology in the hands of the American law courts has been told by Pound, Haines, Frankfurter and others. Thurman Arnold has exposed the myth of corporate personality, by which a protection meant for the pioneer colonist was extended to monopolistic corporations. The realist movement has supplemented legal ideology by making use of statistic, psychology, criminology, business practice, administrative practice, etc. in order to demonstrate the working of law in society.

The investigations, by Continental as well as American jurists, of the ways in which judicial discretion has developed, altered or killed legal principles laid down in constitutions or statutes, give a corrective to the abstract approach inherent in the formulation of general principles. The functional method must, in fact, supplement the idealistic approach, by laying bare possible discrepancies between legal ideology and social reality. Thus, Renner's analysis of the change in the function of property has shown how the legal notion of property becomes an empty shell, while the real function of property is exercised by complementary institutions. Modern English and American jurists have pointed out how, under the cover of the rule of law and of constitutional principles, the power of bureaucracy, big business and trade unions develops and alters the bureaucracy, big business and trade unions develops and alters the structure of the constitution. Students of banking, insurance, transport or housing law have shown how little the principle of autonomy of will and of freedom of contract comes to mean in the modern standard contract, in which equality of bargaining is a mere fiction, while the terms of the contract are fixed once and for all millions of people by the more powerfully organised side. A decision by Denning J. (as he then was) supplies an excellent—though unfortunately rare—example of the sociological interpretation of a legal concept. A firm of builders had challenged a compulsory purchase order made by the city of Bristol under the Housing Act of 1936 for a municipal housing scheme. The challenge was on the ground that the Act used the formula "Houses for the Working Classes," whereas the proposed houses were open to members of all classes, including doctors, engineers and salesmen. Denning J. refused to quash the order and his reasoning included the following characteristic passage:

> "working classes" fifty years ago denoted a class which included men working in the fields or the factories, in the docks or the mines, on the railways or the roads, at a weekly wage. The wages of people of that class were lower than of the other members of the community, and they were looked upon as a lower class. That has now all disappeared. The social revolution in the last fifty years has made the words "working class" quite inappropriate today. There is no such separate class as the working class. . . . Nor is there any social distinction between one or the other. No one of them is of a higher or lower class.

To resolve this tension between legal ideal and social reality is a matter of legal policy. Functional analysis only prepares the way for a political decision to be made by the legislator. He may attempt to come to the rescue of the exploited individual, by abolishing abuses, for example, by anti-trust legislation. He may, on the other hand, decide to attack the power of the "over-mighty subject" may choose to protect equality of bargaining and liberty of contract by means of restrictive covenants, or by an official recognition of collective bargaining. He may decide to fight the power of administrative authorities by rigid judicial supervision (English and American system) or by a system of adminstrative tribunals (French system) or by the complete merger of all law in administration (totalitarian system). Whatever the jurist may have to say of this he does so as a politician, not as a lawyer, though legal experience and knowledge may lend weight to the argument.

Once the choice is made, legal ideology must once more ask for the support of functional analysis, in order to ensure the adequacy of the means chosen to realise the ideal. Many legislative ideals have failed through inadequacy of means. The noble ideals of the German Republican Constitution of 1991 were frustrated, because the basis of economic, administrative, judicial and military power remained unaffected. A modern charter of the rights of men would be futile without the provision of conditions of society, which make their realisation possible. In the light of conditions of society which make their realisation possible. In the light of experience gained by legal developments of the past, for example, the development of fundamental rights in the legal interpretation of the American, German or Soviet Constitutions, the legislator will have to consider how far an ideal such as individual liberty of contract may demand a machinery of collective bargaining, compulsory powers of state arbitration or even a socialisation of all industry. Again, the results of sociological analysis help the legislator to decide how far judicial supervision and administrative discretion are likely to help or hinder the furtherance of the principle adopted. The degree of latitude given to the judge in infliction a greater or smaller penalty may be a small point in the ideology underlying a particular reform of criminal law, but it may be a decisive factor in practice. Unsympathetic magistrates may completely foil, by trifling fines, the best enactment designed to fight food profiteering. This again points to the importance of the personal elements in administration of law, to the methods of choosing judges, administrators or juries.

The legal experience of the period of the industrial revolution has taught us not the futility of ideology in the shaping of the law and thus of the conditions of society—the ultimate direction given to the law must depend on the underlying political ideology—but the fatal consequences of an ideology left unsupported by solid social foundations.

Analytical jurisprudence plays, on the whole, the part of a servant. Any modern legal system, whatever its ideology, depends for servant.

Any modern legal system, whatever its ideology, depends for certainty, clarity and efficiency on an adequate legal technique, provided by a coherent system of concepts and classifications. Yet analytical jurisprudence has no mean part in the clarification of some vital political issues of our time. One of the principal problems before mankind is the alternative between international order and international chaos. In terms of law, it means the clarification of the hierarchical relation between national sovereignty and international legal order. The choice is a political one, but legal theory can do much to help or hinder it, by a clear and consistent definition of law. The definitions of law vary according to the philosophy of their authors. Some emphasise the element of coercion, others that of usage and popular conviction. But no one will dispute that a definition, once chosen, must be consistently used. That indeed is the principal function of the analytical science of law: to develop a system logically and clearly from its foundations. A grave, and sometimes not unintended, confusion has been created by the use of the identical concept of "law" for the type of rule ordering the conduct of individuals within the modern state on one hand and that regulating the relations between the states on the other. While the former is characterised by a central law-making authority and the sanction of enforcement, the latter lacks both. The analytical distinction has been developed by Austin with exemplary clarity. But many important tasks remain for contemporary analytical jurisprudence. The weaknesses of the compromises between national and international sovereignty attempted in the Covenant of the League of Nations and the United Nations Charter, the implications of the partial transfer of sovereignty attempted in the European Communities Treaties, the problem of the division of sovereignty envisaged by the federal form of government, these, among others, are vital preliminaries to a reconstruction of international life.

A particularly important part in the development of future international society will have to be played by comparative jurisprudence. Whether a new international society will develop as a world-wide community, or center round groups of nations closely linked by military, economic and political ties, the assimilation of legal institutions is a necessary part of closer association. The intensity of legal relations expresses the degree of social cohesion achieved between different nations. It is indeed possible and necessary to classify international relations according to the extent to which they depend upon a community of social values. The preparatory work must be done by comparative jurisprudence, combining the ideological, the functional and the analytical approach. A comparison of legal ideals must form the foundation. It will reveal, for example, the impossibility of any but the most superficial relations between legal systems based on rights of man and those based on unrestricted omnipotence of the state. This was illustrated long before the war, by the withdrawal of Germany, Japan and Italy from the International Labour Conventions, their refusal to join the International Broadcasting Convention of 1937 and, in general, their refusal to submit to decisions of international tribunals. Similar difficulties have arisen, more recently, over the tripartite representation in the ILO of the U.S.S.R. and Yugoslavia, because of the alleged identity of state, employers and workers in these states. An understanding of the dependence of law on community of values leads, in contemporary international law, to a general distinction between the international law of coexistence—regulating the essentially formal diplomatic and jurisdictional relations between states—and therefore independent of their political and social structure—and the international law of cooperation, dependent upon community of values and interests, and therefore much more sensitive to internal structure. The science of comparative law has hitherto been chiefly concentrated on an analytical comparison of different legal institutions, such as commercial law, family institutions or criminal law. But a comparison of codes, statutes, decisions may give a misleading impression of either affinity or diversity unless it is checked by a functional comparison.

Legal theory cannot provide a magic escape from the need for decision between alternative ideals and ways of life. But it is not condemned to the purely passive and subordinate function which both analytical positivism and early marxist theories ascribe to it.

To formulate political ideals in terms of justice and to ascertain the means by which these ideals can be translated into social reality, through the agency of a legal order, is the vital function which legal theory must fulfil.

The reasons why the lawyer must open his eyes to the issues of legal theory may be summed up in the following four propositions:

(1) There is no escape for the law from the struggles of life. Each legal philosophy, each legal system, each judgment is necessarily related, though possible remotely, to a political ideology. The self-sufficiency of law is an illusion. It is, to use a well-know phrase by Moltke, "a dream, but not even a beautiful one."

(2) Legal technique is always subordinate to social ideals. The technically most divergent legal system can attain similar social ends if inspired by similar purposes; on the other hand, the closest affinity of legal technique gives no basis for harmony and co-operation where the purposes differ.

(3) The study and practice of law provides one avenue to a diagnosis of social crisis, no less so than any other social science. Consequently the lawyer, not only the legislator, is just as much concerned with social change as the politician, the economist, the sociologist, or the preacher. It follows that there is no reason why the lawyer should not play a leading part in social reform. Among the great social reformers of

history there have not been many lawyers (although exasperated lawyers, like Bentham, have sometimes turned into ardent reformers). But only a misunderstanding of the function of the law can disable the lawyer from taking his part in the evolution of society. In the first place, the lawyer may discover that the law as it stands is inadequate to fulfil the legislative or social ideals which inspire it. Thus, both English and American law of today are inspired by the ideal of freedom of contract. A minority of American judges saw that the transformation of the United States from a state of pioneer farmers to a state of large-scale industry meant a re-interpretation of this ideal in contracts, executive and legislative measures. English judges have seen that at some point freedom of contract may become a travesty of freedom and have accordingly adjusted the law of restraint of trade and of the employer's duties towards employees; but they have not yet adapted freedom of contract to the standardised conditions of modern mass employment, and a legal doctrine of collective bargaining hardly yet exists. In the second place, the lawyer has ample opportunity to assist social progress by developing and interpreting a widely framed legal principle in accordance with changing conditions. Thus, "a reasonable and fair price," or a "fair and equitable" restitution means nothing, except, except in conjunction with the social conditions of the time. Finally, the lawyer, whether as legislator, judge, advocate or administrator, may discover, through his particular way of contact with social reality, that a law fails to achieve its ostensible social purposes and brings misery instead of welfare. It may be the law of blackmail, or of defamation, or of divorce. When that happens the lawyer can and often does draw the legislator's attention to the need for a change in the law. An even wider function devolves on the lawyer in the planning and regulation of the process of transition from static and primitive, to evolving and diversified economies that characterises the many new developing societies.

(4) The respective shares of legislator and practical lawyer in the evolution of society through law are, however, determined both by the political structure of society and by the extent to which the legislative machinery can satisfy the need for social change. Recent developments in Great Britain for example indicate that the courts vacillate between a desire to take an active share in social evolution, through an elastic interpretation of precedent, a socially conscious and helpful interpretation of precedent, a socially conscious and helpful interpretation of statutes, or the use of general principles of

> equity and public policy, and a tendency to judicial aloofness from social reform, as a reaction to increased legislative activity. Differences in judicial temperament add another element of uncertainty. There remains, beside, the increasingly vast and complex task of statutory interpretation, through law courts, administrative tribunals and other agencies. The interaction of legislator and the various laws applying agencies is even more complex in federal systems. In such countries as Australia, Canada, India, West Germany and the United States, the highest constitutional court has an arbitral function which is also to a high degree law-making. As the years go by, the constitutions of these states are less and less understandable in terms of the text rather than states are less and less understandable in terms of the text rather than of successive interpretations. Almost any political issue becomes also a legal issue, and *vice versa*, the lawyer has, through his interpretation, a major influence on the balance of power between federation and states, and on the very structure of the federal system.

The share of the law in social evolution is thus a matter for constant re-examination, in the light of changing political, social and legislative conditions. But two general conclusions emerge:

First, the creative function of the lawyer in the social process shifts from a primary, law-making, to an ancillary, supporting role, as modern states develop from mainly passive and protective into active instruments of social service, and legislative articulateness increases accordingly.

Secondly, the lawyer cannot afford to isolate himself from the social process. His independence can never be more than relative, and it is only a clear awareness of the political, social and constitutional foundations of his function in general as well as of particular legal problems that enables him to find the proper balance between stability and progress.

PART II

SURVEY OF LEGAL THEORIES

5

ANALYTICAL THEORY (POSITIVISM)

The start of the nineteenth century might be taken as marking the beginnings of the positivist movement. It represented a reaction against the *a priori* methods of thinking that characterised the preceding age. Prevailing theories of natural law shared law in order to discover in nature or reason principles of universal validity. Actual laws were then explained or condemned according to these canons. Unverified hypotheses of this sort failed to satisfy the intelligence of an age nurtured in the critical spirit of new scientific learning. Such scrutiny of natural law postulates had damaging results, for they were shown to be without foundation or else the product of false inference.

The term "positivism" his many meanings, which were tabulated by Professor Hart as follows: (1) Laws are commands. This meaning is associated with the two founders of British positivism, meaning is associated with the two founders of British positivism, Bentham and his disciple Austin, whose views will be considered later in this chapter. (2) The analysis of legal concepts is (a) worth pursuing, (b) distinct from sociological and historical inquiries, (c) distinct from critical evaluation. (3) Decisions can be deduced logically from predetermined rules without recourse to social aims, policy or morality. (4) Moral judgments cannot be established or defended by rational argument, evidence proof. (5) The law as it is actually laid down, positum, has to be kept separate from the law that ought to be. Whatever meanings are ascribed to positivism, it is contrasted with natural law, which also has different meanings. In view of these various differences one needs to be chary of classifying any particular writer as positivist or naturalist.

The fifth meaning given above seems to be the one currently associated with positivism. It may spring from a love of order, which aims at the clarification of legal conceptions and their orderly presentation. To insist that "what the law is" is one question, "what the law ought to be" is another, looks neat and tidy. Precision may be elusive but striving towards to whenever possible is commendable and profitable. Positivism flourishes best in stable social conditions. The difficulties of maintaining a rigid separation between the "is" and the "ought" are only projected to the forefront when conditions are in turmoil. It is here worth remarking, perhaps that neither Bentham nor Austin should be thought of as writing in periods of particular stability. What they represent is the intellectual reaction against naturalism and a love or order and precision. Bentham was a tireless campaigner for reform, and both he and Austin insisted that prior to reform there has to be a thorough-going clarification of the law as it is. The significance of stable conditions might conceivably be seen in the fact that the Austinian theory made no headway until after his death, until after the Chartist movement had collapsed, and it then rapidly reached the zenith of its influence in the serene atmosphere of Victorian England.

Whether a separation between the "is" and the "ought" is tenable or not is a debateable issue to which allusion will be made on several occasions. It is necessary, therefore, to try and clarify what that issue is in a jurisprudential context. The preceding portions of this book, especially the crucial analysis of Duty, will have shown that a large part of law consists of prescriptive patterns of behaviour, i.e., models of conduct to which their actual behaviour is judged. Therefore, the "is", which positivists are so anxious to preserve inviolate, is largely composed of "oughts". So far most positivists would agree, but they would add that only those "oughts" acquire the character of "law" which have filtered through certain accepted criteria of validity. In English law these are precedent, legislation and immemorial custom. The distinction in other words, between an "ought" proposition that "is" law and an "ought" proposition that "ought to become" law lies solely in the fact that the former has passed through one or other of the media which alone regulate the use of the label "law". It follows from this that positivists need not deny that judges make law; indeed, the majority admit it. They also acknowledge the influence of ethical considerations on judges and legislators, and that generally it is because a proposition was thought to be moral and just that a judge or legislator adopted it. What they do say is that it is only incorporation in precedent, statute or custom that imparts to a precept the quality of "law". This quality follows automatically from such incorporation were embodied in precedent or statute, it would be "law" none the less because it would exhibit the formal stamp of validity. Therefore, they maintain, every proposition which passes through one or other of the accepted media is "law" irrespective of all other consideration which go towards saying that it should be, or should not be, law. It is this contention which touches the heart of the modern controversy to which some anticipatory reference is necessary. Modern natural lawyers would assert that a proposition is "law" not merely because it satisfies some formal requirement, but by virtue of an additional minimum moral content. According by virtue of an additional minimum moral content. According to them an immoral rule would not be "law" however much it may satisfy formal requirements.

It is also thought to follow from the positivist obsession with the "is" that they distinguish between formal analysis on the one hand, and historical and functional analysis on the other. It is important once more to note that those who assert this do not deny the value of the latter, but contend that they should be kept apart from the former. Any such attempt, however, suffers from an inherent difficulty. Seldom is it possible to study institutions as they are except in the light of their history and function. Many can only be understood in the light of their origins and past influences, which is especially the case with common law institutions, reaching back as they do unbroken for centuries. The suggested division between "analytical" and "functional" study is unhappier still. The preceding chapters should have demonstrated the legal conceptions are shaped by the way in which they are used and the ends which they serve, all of which import social, moral and other value considerations. This leads to a more general objection. If the analysis of legal conceptions as they are inevitably brings in a consideration of their function, which in turn as inevitably bring in considerations of what ought to be law, what then becomes of the alleged distinction between formal and functional analysis?

Some further objections to the "is"/"ought" distinction may also be mentioned at this juncture. It is said that a law is what its maker thought it ought to be, whether it be moral or immoral, as with Herod's decree for the massacre of the innocents. In so far as this assertion relates to the content of a law, no positivist need disagree. But the real thrust of the objections becomes apparent when one consider the structure of concepts, which are shaped by the ends which they serve. This is not a mere matter of content, but of the texture of the law itself. The point is also apparent in the judicial process which, as pointed out, is guided by values. In a situation uncovered by authority, for instance, a judge will enunciate as law an appropriate rule, which will lead to the desired decision; but the point is that he states the rule to be what he feels it ought to be. As far as he is concerned he accepts it as law already because it appeals to his sense of right and before it is made into a precedent. As Sir Garfield Barwick, C.J., said, "the common law is what the court, so informed, decides that it should be . . . for where no authority binds or current of acceptable decision compels, it is not enough, nor indeed apposite, to say that the function of the court in general is to declare what the law is and not to decide what it ought to be." As has been suggested, the same sentiment may underlie the converse situation: what ought not to be law cannot be law, and this may be the explanation of the retrospective effect of overruling. Another point is that principles and doctrines operate differently from rules in that they exert pressure as to the direction in which rules ought to develop. No one disputes that they, too, are part of law, so what "is" law here are statements as to what it ought to be. If, then, for these reasons a total separation of the "is" and the "ought" cannot be maintained, any assertion that they are separate cannot itself represent the position that "is", but only what positivists think ought to be; which makes positivism itself an ideology.

When considering this debate two questions have to be asked: How far is there a separation? And, is it desirable that there should be separation? With regard to the first, the relationship between the "is" and the "ought" is undoubtedly close, as both sides will agree. It is submitted that if the matter is viewed in a temporal perspective a reconciliation may be found. There is no separation is continuum, since the continuity of law, their application and even their criteria of validity are in the long-run dependent on conformity with moral and other such dictates. In this time-frame the naturalists can make out a case. On the other hand, in the present time-frame positivists can likewise make out a case for at least some degree of separation for the practical purposes of here and now. They themselves must concede that total separation is difficult to maintain in the day-to-day business of applying rules. So their contention narrows itself to the means of indentifying "law" at any given point of time, in short to the criteria of validity. When the matter is reduced in this way, the two questions can be re-stated as follows: Are the criteria of validity purely formal and separate from moral considerations? And, should they incorporate a minimum moral criterion? Identification of that which is "law" is very much the concern of lawyers here and now, and in this context the answer to the first question is clearly on the side of the positivists. Even so, it may be possible to draw a slight distinction between precedent and statute as criteria of identification. A lower court is bound to apply an undistinguishable precedent of a superior court, however wrong it may be, so that, with regard to such court, there is a distinction between what "is" and what "ought to be" law. A superior court, however, when overruling the unjust precedent declares that it never was law notwithstanding the formal stamp of validity which it had borne until then. With regard to such a court the "is"/"ought" separation in precedent as a criterion of identification breaks down at that point. Repeal of a statute, on the other hand, takes effect only from the date of repeal, and even when the effect of repeal is expressly made retroactive, there is no denial that the repealed statute was law until it was repealed. Summing up, therefore, one may say that the answer to the first question is that, within the limits of here and now and for the purpose of identifying laws, there is a separation in the criteria of identification (subject to the suggestion to the contrary with regard to precedent).

The second question is whether such a separation is desirable. The arguments that it is undesirable have been considered and need not be rehearsed. Valid laws are what those charged with administering laws identify as such, and the principal reason for keeping the means of identification as clear-cut as possible is convenience. For otherwise no one could know how to regulate his or her daily actions. The task of lawyers, for instance, when advising clients, law-teachers instructing pupils, businessmen conducting their affairs, etc. will be impossible. The importance of being able to tell as clearly and simply as possible whether this is, or is not, a "law" at any given point of time is unarguable obvious. The introduction of morality into the criterion of identification presents considerable difficulties. Morality is a diffuse idea and no one, not even a naturalist, maintains that everything which is moral is "law". Since the area of "law" is bound to be narrower than that of morality, its boundary should be made as clear as possible. There is a difference in the application of formal and moral criteria. Testing the validity of a precept by means of a formal test and a moral test involve different processes. Courts have neither the time nor the training to undertake the latter. A separation between the "is" and the "ought" is useful in providing a standard by which positive law can be evaluated and criticised. Even naturalists concede that there will always be some discrepancy between law as it is and as it ought to be, and as long as this is so the latter can be used to evaluate the former. This argument is thus not conclusive.

The above is an attempt to clarify what is perhaps the most important contention of contemporary positivism. In considering positivist theories it should not be forgotten that although there is much value in being able to identify laws clearly for practical purposes, there is far more to law besides that; but these are matters which will have to be dealt with in due course.

BENTHAM

Analytical positivism in Britain will be associated to posterity with the names of Jeremy Bentham (1748-1832) and John Austin (1790-1859). The latter used to be styled until recently the "Father of English Jurisprudence", but it is now clear from a work of Bentham first published in 1945 that it is he, if anyone, who deserves such a title. Bentham was a fervent champion of codified law and of reforming English law, which to him was in utter chaos. He saw, however, that there could be no reform of substantive law without reform of its structure: so analysis of structure became an essential prelude to reform. Accordingly, he distinguished between what he termed "expositorial" jurisprudence (what the law is) and "censorial" jurisprudence, or the art of legislation (what law ought to be). In the course of writing An Introduction to the Principles of Morals and Legislation he was moved to ask: "What is a penal code of laws? What is a civil code?" In seeking the answer he had to investigate the nature of "a law", which led him into a maze through which he mapped out a path in Of Laws in General.

Thus, what was originally conceived as a kind of substantial appendix developed into a major contribution on its own and which was finished more or less in 1782. It remained unpublished and was only disinterred from the vaults of University College, London, by Professor C.W. Everett in 1939 and published under the title The Limits of Jurisprudence Defined in 1945. A revised edition was published as of Laws in General in 1970 under the editorship of Professor Hart.

Bentham's analysis of a law has to be approached through his Theory of Fictions, which in modern terminology would be styled semantics. There is a tendency to believe that each would corresponds to some object. Indeed, some words do: "real entities". Other words stand for "fictional entities". These have to be understood in terms of real entities by a process called "paraphrasis", a new method of elucidation with a new name made necessary by the inapplicability of the traditional per genus et differentiam technique. Parenthetically it might be remarked here the Bentham anticipated modern linguistic philosophy in a most remarkable way be his insight that the meaning of words depends on how they are used in statements in which they occur. "A law", as distinct from "law", was to him a real entity, and so was an "act"; rights and duties, on the other hand, were fictional. "Law" is fictional entity made up of an aggregate of individual laws. At this point a comment has to be made. As pointed out earlier, "law" in the sense of "legal system" in much more than the sum-total of laws, just as a railway system is more than the sum-total of laws, just as a railway system is more than the sum-total of tracks and rolling stock; it is the pattern of their linkage and a good deal more besides. But assuming that the clue to "law" lies in the nature of "a law", it would seem that Bentham overlooked a significant and different set of phenomena.

"A law may be defined", said Bentham, "as an assemblage of signs, declarative of a volition, conceived or adopted by the sovereign in a state, concerning the conduct to be observed in a certain case by a certain person or class of persons, who in the case in question are or are supposed to be subject to his power". Bentham's concept of a law is thus an imperative one, for which he himself preferred the term "mandate". This definition is flexible enough to cover "a set of objects so intimately allied and to which there would be such continual occasion to apply the same propositions", e.g., not only laws made by legislators, but also judicial, administrative, domestic orders as well as declaratory laws.

It also isolates a unit in terms of which more complex phenomena may be analysed. An important point is that permissions are included; but this so waters down the idea of mandate that it seems inappropriate to rank Bentham among the imperative jurists. Indeed, the imperative aspect of his theory, such as it is, is the least pappy part of it, as will appear. Finally, every law may be considered in eight different respects: source, subjects, objects, extent, aspects, force, remedial appendages and expression.

I. Source

The source of a law is the will of sovereign, who may conceive laws which he personally issues, or adopt laws previously issued by former sovereigns or subordiante authorities ("susception"), or he may adopt laws to be issued in future by subordinate authorities ("pre-adoption"). Pre-adoption may take the form of (a) permission given to the subordinate in the negative sense of his "not being made the subject of a law commanding him not to issue the subordinate mandate which is in question"; or (b) a more positive permission to issue the mandate (which may be reinforced by permission to punish offenders, and by commands to others to assist); or (c) a mandate issued to the subjects of the subordinate of obey. Pre-adoption in senses (b) and (c) can be accommodated within Bentham's broad version of an imperative theory. The difficulty is with susception and preadoption in sense (a). Where a sovereign consciously allows a prior law to continue, or a subordinate to continue issuing laws, he may be said to exercise his will not to interfere; but where such continuance goes by default, this can hardly be said to be an exercise of will, except possible by way of an exceedingly tenuous fiction. Bentham's sovereign is "any person or assemblage of persons to whose will a whole political community are (no matter on what account) supposed to be in a disposition to pay obedience: and that in preference to the will of any other person". There is a difficulty about this because "political community" is defined elsewhere as follows: "Where a number of persons (whom we may style subjects) are supposed to be in the habit of paying obedience to a person, or assemblage of persons of a known and certain description (whom we may call governor or governors), such persons altogether (subjects and governors) are said to be in a state of political society". The result is partly circular: "sovereign" is defined partly in terms of "political society" and the latter is defined partly in terms of the former. Also, it is not clear what exactly is meant by "supposed".

The attributes of sovereignty are interesting. Such power is indefinite unless limited by express convention or by religious or political motivations, The sovereign may consist of more than one body, each of which is obeyed in different respects. Habitual obedience may thus be divided and partial, i.e., owed in certain areas of conduct. When divided in this way the power of each is limited by the other and each has a limited power to prescribe for the other. These laws are of a special kind: "The business of the ordinary sort of laws is prescribe to the people what they shall do: the business of this transcendental class of laws is to prescribe to the sovereign what he shall do". Thus, there is created a form of self-bindingness which has legal quality. This fascinating piece of analysis seems to have been lost on Bentham's disciple Austin, whose rigid simplification in this and other respects long stultified British jurisprudence by providing nothing better than an arid basis for exploration and criticism.

2. Subjects

These may be persons or things. Each of these may be "agible" (active) or "passible" (passive) subjects, i.e., the agent with which an act commences or terminates. Thus, a person may be the striker or the party struck, a thing may be the instrument of destruction or the things destroyed. They may be direct or indirect, the latter constituting the circumstances of an act.

3. Objects

It is crucial in understanding Bentham's analysis to appreciate that each class of acts (including forbearances) is the objects of an individual law. An act originates in persons, but may end in a person or things. (He might perhaps have amplified the part played by forbearances in this respect.) All laws regulate conduct positively or negatively, by imposing duties or granting permissions, "imperatively" or "de-imperatively". To classify act-situations would be too cumbrous a task, but it is possible to classify the sovereign's reactions of them so that they become offences or not. These reactions are the "aspects" of the sovereign's will, which will be considered presently.

4. Extent

Direct extent means that a law covers a portion of land on which acts have their termination; indirect extent refers to the relation of an actor to a thing, e.g. being in a certain place at the time of the act, in short the circumstances. Bentham also alluded in passing to extent in point of time, or duration of a law. He was thinking of time only as a way of determining the subjects of a law. It has been pointed out that time is significant in another way. Whatever the intended duration, the very concept of duration is dependent on certain moral and social factors, which, following Bentham's own line of thought, could be regarded as a part of every law. At this point Bentham seems casually to have opened a door without pausing to peer at the vistas that it reveals.

5. Aspects

Every law has a "directive" and a "sanctional" or "incitative" part. The former concerns the aspects of the sovereign's will towards an act-situation; the latter concerns the force of a law. Command is only one of four aspects of the sovereign's will, permutations of which comprehend the whole range of laws. These four are related by "opposition" (incompatibility) and "concomitancy" (compatibility); and Bentham evolved a "deontic logic" with which to demonstrate the relationship between command, prohibition and permission.

The logic of imperation is as follows:

(i) C ("Do X")

(a) can co-exist with NP ("Permission to do X")—an

obligative duty is not cancelled (de-obligated) by an unobligative liberty to do same thing;

(b) cannot co-exist with P ("Do not do X")—an obligative duty is cancelled (de-obligated) by an obligative duty to do the opposite:

(c) cannot co-exist with NC ("Permission not to do X")—an obligative duty cancels (de-obligates) the unobligative liberty to do the opposite.

(ii) P ("Do not do X")

(a) can co-exist with NC ("Permission not to do X")—for the same reason as in (I) (a);

(b) cannot co-exist with C ("Do X")—for the same reason as in (I) (b);

(c) cannot co-exist with NP ("Permission to do X")—for the same reason as in (I)(c).

(iii) NC ("Permission not to do X")

(a) cannot co-exist with C ("Do X")—an obligative liberty is cancelled (de-obligated) by an obligative duty to the opposite;

(b) can co-exist with ("Do not do X")—an unobligative liberty is not cancelled (de-obligated) by an obligative duty to do the same thing; or

(c) with NP ("Permission to do X")—an unobligative liberty is not cancelled (de-obligated) by an unobligative liberty to do the opposite: but not both together, since (b) and (c) cannot co-exist.

(iv) NP ("Permission to do X")

(a) cannot co-exist with P ("Do not do X)—for the same reason as in (iii) (a);

(b) can co-exist with C ("Do X")—for the same reason as in (iii) (b); or

(c) with NC ("Permission not to do X")—for the same reason as in (iii) (c); but not both together, since (b) and (c) cannot co-exist.

The difficulty of reconciling permissions with an imperative theory, even in the extended sense of mandate, has been mentioned. But this weakness is a minor blemish when set against the depth and incisiveness of this demonstration of jural oppositiiton and contradiction, which is infinitely more acute than Hohfeld's depiction later.

6. Force of a Law, Sanctional or Incitative Part

A law is dependent upon motivations of obedience. The sovereign's wish in respect of a class of acts is a law as long as it supported by a sanction, even if this is not explicit, though usually, of course, it would be. It includes physical, political, religious and moral motivations, comprising threats of punishment (commination, coercion) and rewards (invitations, allurements). There is, however, an important difference which appears to be glossed over. The failure to do, or not do, what a law supported by punishment requires is illegal; but it is not illegal to do, or not do, what a law supported by reward requires.

Regulation of conduct and stipulation of sanction govern different act-situations, so they require separate laws: one saying "You shall not murder", and the other "if you do, you shall be punished". Non-prohibitions and non-commands are unobligative aspects of the sovereign's will and are supported by sanctions affecting, not the subjects of the laws, but other who are subjects of "corroborative" laws not to interfere. From the legislator's point of view, actual punishment is a prediction, since it is outside his province to carry out the threat. Accordingly, he issues subsidiary laws, e.g., that a judge must verify that the accused did murder. The judge in turn is assisted by various officials all of whom are likewise under subsidiary laws. If no one obeys these subsidiary laws, the principal law becomes a dead letter. Now, even though it is true to say, in Bentham's view, that all these subsidiary laws are expressions of sovereign wishes, the inescapable fact is that they add up to no more than a prediction, dependent on probability, of punishment as prescribed in the santional part of the principal law. In other words, the functioning of a law is implicitly a part of Bentham's own concept of a law, and this imports many considerations of a social and psychological character. This further dilutes the imperative character of a law. Nevertheless, he should be given credit for an illuminating hint. For yet again he anticipated the twentieth century to a remarkable degree. His analysis of sanction resembles that of Kelsen and the implication that sanction is a prediction based on probabilities foreshadows the views of the American Realists. On the other hand, he differed from both these in separating the regulation of conduct and the stipulation of sanction into two distinct laws. It is a matter of opinion which view is preferable, but it will be submitted in due course that Bentham's is better.

7. Remedial Appendages

Sanctions are provided by subsidiary laws. But sanctions themselves require a further set of subsidiary laws, "remedial appendages", addressed to judges with a view to curing the evil (compensation), stopping the evil or preventing future evil.

8. Expression

The ways in which the sovereign's will may be expressed are various. The connection with will immediately raises the problem of discovering the will from the expression, which is a root difficulty encountered by any imperative theory. Expression may be "complete", i.e., the matter to be regulated coincides with one law. In all such cases a judge should adopt a literal interpretation. Only where expression is incomplete may he adopt a liberal interpretation. Bentham, the relentless enemy of judge-made law, sought to minimise judicial discretion by trying to ensure that laws were complete, not only in expression, but also in "connection" and "design", and this feature of his analysis needs to be considered separately.

Individuality of a Law

What, then is a "complete law", i.e., "complete" in a jurisprudential sense? A statutory precept, for instance, is made up of parts of laws just as, to use Bentham's own "coarse allusion", a slice of meat cut by a butcher is a cross-section of muscle, bone, tendons, nerves, etc. The jurisprudential isolation of a complete law corresponds with an anatomist's dissection which seeks to reveal the whole muscle, tendon, etc. The individuality of a law, he say, "results from the integrality and the unity of it laid together"; and the purpose of individuation "is to ascertain what a portion of legislative matter must amount to in order on the one hand not to contain less, on the other hand not to contain more than one whole law."

Integrality

This means that a law should be complete in expression, in connection and in design. With regard to the first, the standard of reference is whether the actual will of the legislation has been completely expressed. Every law contains an imperative provision which may be qualified or unqualified, further expounded or unexpounded. It is unqualified and unexpounded, it is complete in expression in itself; if it requires qualification or exposition, it is incomplete without these. Qualifications and expositions cannot, of course, be complete in themselves without the principal provision.

With regard to completeness in connection, Bentham said that more often than not parts of a law "lie scattered up and down at random, some under one head, some under another, with little or no motive taken of their mutual relations and dependencies". Moreover, these parts may have been brought into existence by different bodies and different times. Thus, a statutory prohibition of driving while under the influence of liquor includes, *inter alia*, a police force, courts, judges, breathalysers, procedures, etc. each of which has been brought into existence by different laws at different times. They need to be co-ordinated before a law can be said to be complete in point of connection. One implication of this is that the individuation of every law imports a temporal dimension.

If the legislator's general idea of the mischief deviates from that which, in the light of the particular case, he should and might have formed, the law in question is incomplete in design. The deviation may be that it does not go far enough, in which case it is incomplete in point of amplitude; or it may go too far, in which case it is incomplete in point of discrimination. All exceptions must therefore be set down.

Judicial interpretation of laws is made to depend on their completeness. Interpretation is strict when the will attributed to the legislator is that which he really entertained. Interpretation is liberal when the will attributed by a court is that which he inadvertently failed to entertain, but which he would have entertained had the particular case been presented to him, i.e., when the law is incomplete in point of design. When it is incomplete in point of amplitude, liberal interpretation has to be "extensive"; when it is incomplete in point of discrimination, interpretation has to be "restrictive". In all such cases incompleteness results from the legislator's inadvertence. If, however, incompleteness is only supposed, i.e., when what is thought to be a shortcoming or an overstatement was intended, then liberal interpretation ceases to be interpretation and amounts to overruling the legislator. The weakness of all this lies in the assumption that the wish which the legislator "really" entertained is somehow knowable independently of its expression. To start on the basis that the mode of expression has to be interpreted according of the legislator's will, and then to discover that it is often impossible to discover what this is apart from the mode of expression frustrates the whole exercise. Such is the consequence of any imperative approach, requiring as it does the "ascertaining of the intention of the legislator".

Unity

"The unity of a law", said Bentham, "will depend upon the unity of the species of the act which is the object of it". The way in which different species of acts are designated is largely a matter of wording dictated by convenience. His great point was that each act-situation is the object of a separate law. Here lies the difference between the unity of a law and its integrality. Also, nowhere did he assert that one species of act could give rise to only one offence. Two different laws can create two separate offences out of the same act, as where criminal offences are also torts.

If an act-situation is the object of every law, what of the "laws" of contract or property, which deal with the requirements of a contract and title to property? These neither impose duties nor grant permissions. Bentham's answer was to say that they are not laws in themselves, but parts of laws. Laws forbid breaches of contracts and interferences with property. Statements as to what a contract is and those determining title to property are "expositary" (amplifying and limiting the acts and sanctions) and "qualificatory" (limiting the scope of the laws forbidding interference). Such "parts of laws" are often very complex and pertain to different laws, which is why they are set out on their own for convenience. Ingenious as this explanation is, it is unsatisfying. The point that it completely cuts across traditional usage and habits of thought might be countered to some extent by the reply that he was trying to straighten out the mess resulting from traditional thought and that divergences from accepted terminology is only to be expected. Nevertheless, the divergence should not be too great; indeed, Bentham himself at various points did make concessions to convenience. The point is whether such wholesale divergence oversteps the limits of convenience. More serious is the objection that this classification only follows from squeezing the concept of a law into the straight-jacket of an imperative theory: all laws have to be either commands or permissions. It takes no account of powers, e.g., powers to make contract, create title, etc.

Customary law received short shrift at Bentham's hands. In his view it could never be complete.

At the end of his intricate analysis he returned to the question with which he began: "What is a penal code of laws? What is a civil code?" He concluded that the former consists of laws creating "offence" (those composed of directive and sanctional or incitative parts), while the latter consists of expositary and qualificatory matter. "Offences" in this context are wider than crimes. The characteristic of criminal offences, as distinct from civil offences, lies not in their intrinsic nature, but in the degree of mischief they occasion, the degree of displeasure they evoke and the degree of punishment meted out. To the category of civil offences belong "such offences as it is not judged necessary to punish with any extraordinary degree or species of punishment: to the criminal, such offences as it is judged necessary to punish with some extraordinary degree or species of punishment". It may be asked how such a distinction is applicable to the gradations of treatment, penal, reformative and curative, meted out to criminals. It also breaks down in the case of a tort which is visited by exemplary damages, whereas pulling the communication cord in a train needlessly can only be visited by a £ 25 payment. Why is the former civil and the latter criminal? Or are they both "civil"? The proposed distinction will lead to a formidable re-structuring, which seems scarcely worth the price.

Bentham's ultimate objective was an ideal code. His analysis of a law led him to conclude that such a code should consist of laws analysable jurisprudentially, and its penal and civil branches should be separated. Its advantages would be to minimise the risk of incompleteness of laws and consequently what he termed "licentiousness" of interpretation; to exhibit a common standard by which different the method of teaching the art of legislation. Whether, in the light of the difficulties that have been pointed out, this kind of code would indeed be ideal is a matter of opinion. So strong were his feelings as to the merits of a code that he remained a life-long enemy of judge-made law, which the hoped would be largely eliminated, thereby reducing the judicial function. The likelihood of his hopes being realised in present-day Western-type societies may be doubted; but should these be replaced by forms of totalitarianism, in which the judiciary only reflects governmental values, those hopes may well become a reality.

An assessment of his work is not easy. His main interest lay in advocating reforms, but he also examined problems of international law. In fact, it was he who coined that name. The current resurgence of interest in his work is leading to a great deal of re-evaluation, while his remarkable anticipations of modern thought in so many directions make one wonder whether a final judgment is yet possible. Even as it is, the breadth and depth of his analyses and brilliant insights are such that it does not seem too extravagant to say that had all his writings been known, he could well have been the greatest single contributor to European jurisprudence; which makes it all the more regrettable that the world of scholarship lost so much for so long.

AUSTIN

Throughout the nineteenth century Bentham's Of Laws in General remained hidden in London University; so British positivism came to be dominated by the views of his disciple John Austin (1790-1859) until virtually the outbreak of World War II. As will appear, his work is largely derivative and far less satisfying than Bentham's. The first six lectures, the most influential part of his work, were published in 1832 under the title of The Province of Jurisprudence Determined, and the rest were published posthumously in 1861.

Austin, in sympathy with Bentham as to law reform, conceived his initial task to be a critical analysis of the law as it is. The time he had spent in Germany preparing for his lectures and his study of Roman law brought home to him the contrast between the orderliness of Roman law and the chaos in England. Commentators on Roman law had justinian's codification as their starting point, while their British counterparts were groping amidst a tangle of statutes and diverse and often poor law reports. German lawyers had behind them centuries of exegetical work, while Blackstone's Commentaries was still the only attempt at a systematic arrangement of English law.

Accordingly, Austin set himself the task of making a beginning with the analysis of the principal concepts of English law. Before doing so he felt it necessary to demarcate the province of "law" and to distinguish it from what is ought to be. In his first six lectures he sought to elucidate "law" in the light of which its concepts would then be analysed. Although his fame rests on these preliminary lectures, they were only a prologue to the study of jurisprudence which, to him, meant the analysis of concepts. His concept of law is an imperative one influenced by his preparatory studies, which had impressed upon him the powerful position occupied by the sovereign in municipal law. In Roman law the authority of the Princeps and later of the Emperor was seen to have been unquestionable. European writers had preached in similar vein. Bodin, for instance, said that sovereignty was the absolute and perpetual power within the state and, perhaps most importantly, in the work of Hobbes was to be seen the connection between the law of the state and enforcement by organised power. He had also spoken of law as being grounded in "natural reason", but that is became "law" only by virtue of the command of a sovereign, Bentham's approach, too, was an imperative one based on sovereignty. In the light of these influences Austin's adoption of a similar basis is hardly surprising.

Like Bentham, Austin believed that "law" is only an aggregate of laws, and he defined a law in its most comprehensive signification as "a rule laid down for the guidance of an intelligent being by an intelligent being having power over him". He then distinguished between "laws properly so called" and "laws improperly so called". The former are "general commands" addressed to the community at large and enjoin classes of acts and forbearances; they are also continuing commands. Laws properly so called are sub-divided into laws set by God, Divine law or the law of God, and laws set by men to men, to which he applied the term "positive" to distinguish them from the law of God.

Laws set by men to men also fell into two categories. The first consisted of laws set by political superiors, i.e., by a sovereign person or sovereign body of persons, to a member or members of the independent political society wherein that person or body of persons was sovereign or supreme. This category also included laws set by private persons acting in pursuance of rights conferred upon them by political superiors. This category also included laws set by private persons acting in pursuance of rights conferred upon them by political superiors. All this was termed by Austin "positive law" or "law simple and strictly so called", and was, according to him, the subject-matter of jurisprudence. The second category consisted of laws set by men to men neither as political superiors, nor in pursuance of rights conferred upon them by such superior, e.g., those set by a master to a servant or the rules of a club. They are still laws properly so called, because they are commands, but distinguished them from positive law by giving them the term "positive morality".

Under the general heading of laws improperly so called he placed, first of all, "laws by analogy", i.e., laws set and enforced by mere opinion, such as the laws of fashion, international law and so forth. These also he somewhat confusingly termed "positive morality"—"positive" so as to distinguish them from the laws of God, "morality" so as to distinguish them from positive law or law strictly so called. Laws improperly so called also included a final category, called "laws by metaphor", which covered expression of the uniformaties of Nature.

The first comment to be made on Austin's scheme is that the distinctions which he drew were entirely arbitrary. Not that there is any objection to doing this provided clear indications are given of what they mean. Austin certainly was scrupulous in this respect. He did, however, commit two errors. Although he did not specifically say so, it is clear that he fashioned his concept out of the material of English law with an occasional sprinkling of Roman law, but he proceeded to use it as a criterion of law in general and so excluded, e.g., international law. He was also misguided in applying the either "proper" to what was, after all, his own stipulative definition of "a law".

The key to understanding a law properly so called lies in duty, which is created by the command of a sovereign. A command consists of "the expression or intimation of your wish" that another shall do or forbear, coupled with the power and purpose of inflicting an evil (sanction) in the event of disobedience. A law, therefore, is a command of sovereign backed by a sanction. Duty and sanction are correlative terms, the fear of sanction supplying the motive for obedience.

This simplistic model is open to criticism from many points of view. Austin was seeking to provide a means of identifying a law for the purposes of the moment, but a link this with the means of securing obedience is to confuse identification with functioning. Obedience is a factor relevant to the latter, and in this context, as has been pointed out, fear of sanction is not the sole, or even principal, motive for obedience. Many objections may also be levelled at the association of duty and sanction, which have been developed earlier. Another weakness is the fact that he found himself compelled to treat nullity as a sanction in order to accommodate, e.g., the rule, "You must make a gratuitous promise under seal", within his command-duty-sanction model.

Laws as commands. This idea has encountered the heaviest criticism. Austin's association of duty with command was probably the result of his having been misled by the imperative from in which duties are expressed: "You must, or "You shall". Professor Olivecrona has pointed out that everyone has a store of experiences of actual commands addressed in the imperative form, so that whenever one encounters that form of expression there is an instinctive tendency to suppose that it must have emanated from a command. He points out that duties are "ought" propositions which happen to be phrased imperatively, and it is a non-sequitur to suppose that such phraseology of itself implies command.

With regard to the wider aspects of the command theory, it may well be that the idea at the back of Ausin's mind was, in Buckland's words, "Primarily an English criminal statue". Even so, there is a difference between this sort of law and command. The function of a law is to regulate future conduct indefinitely and to serve as a standard by which to judge deviance; a command is more usually directed to a specified individual or individuals with reference to a particular act or forbearance and does not serve as a general standard of judgement. Apart from this, there are laws which are commands. Austin himself was somewhat exercised by declaratory statutes, repealing statues and "laws of imperfect obligation", which include laws defining, e.g., what a contract is, or a crime, or a law which says that no action shall succeed after the lapse of a limitation period. He concluded that these were exceptions. In this he was perhaps unduly hesitant, for, as Buckland pointed out, declaratory statues could have been treated as repeating earlier commands, while repealing statutes may be said to create fresh claims and duties by their cancellation of earlier ones and so be said to command. Nevertheless, Austin's hesitation and the fact that he was driven to admit exceptions betray some uneasiness with the command thesis. The question of custom troubled him not at all. To him customs were laws when commanded either directly by incorporation in statutes, or indirectly in judicial decisions.

Command presupposes a commander. Austin perceived clearly enough that "no indeterminate party can command expressly or tacitly, or can receive obedience or submission". The question is whether a determinate person, or body of persons, can be discovered who might be regarded as having commanded the whole corpus of the law. Never at any point in history is such a person or groups discoverable. Who, for instance, commanded the whole corpus of the law. Never at any point in history is such a person or group discoverable. Who, for instance, commanded the rule that precedents shall be binding? A sovereign is sovereign within a "state", and "state" is a legally defined organisation consisting of territory, populations, government and a measure of independence in external relations. Who commanded these requirements? Again, it might be thought that the present monarch and members of both Houses of Parliament can command any law they please. But, as Professor Olivecrona has pointed out, the individuals who comprise the sovereign body have attained their position by virtue of rules of law. Who, then, commanded these rules? Whoever commanded them in turn owed their authority to command to the observance of other rules. There is no sense in saying that the rules which brought them to their positions were their own commands. Even if the Crown in Parliament, as a composite entity is taken to be the uncommanded commander, a study of the events of 1688-89 shows that this body in no sense commanded the rule that its command shall be law. It was acceptance of it as the supreme commander, particularly by the judges, that entitled it to command henceforth. Moreover, it is artificial to pretend that any member of Parliament believes that the law of the land has emanated from his commands, for the vast majority of laws existed before he was born. To attribute commands to people, who have neither commanded nor believe that they have done so, is a fantasy.

Although the Crown in Parliament was accepted in 1689 as the Austinian commander, the bulk of the common law and much legislation was already in existence and continued to exist unaffected. Even if it is assumed with Austin that these laws had emanated from earlier commands, the question is why and how commands from earlier commands, the question is why and how commands of a former sovereign continue to be laws under his successor. Austin's reply was that this comes about by virtue of "tacit command" : what the sovereign permits, he commands. This implies that the sovereign both knows of the earlier commands and decides not to interfere. When does he so decide?

It cannot be when their applicability comes before a judge (who, according to Austin, is the sovereign's delegate), since he has no choice in the matter: a previous enactment, however ancient, is always accepted by a judge as being law already. If so, the decision, assuming that there was one, not an interfere with his prior command, and which thereby invests it with fresh authority, can only be that of the sovereign himself. Professor Hart has demolished the whole idea of "tacit command". (i) A sovereign may consciously permit the continuance of a former law, or (ii) such a law may continue by default simply through not being repealed. Tacit command may superficially appear to fit case (i); though it will be noticed that even an actual decision not to repeal is a decision not to command. How, then, can a decision not to repeal impart fresh law-quality to something which never ceased to possess it? Tacit command ceases to be even superficially applicable to case (ii), since non-repeal by default is in no sense "the expression of a wish", which was Austin's own description of command. The continuance of the majority of the laws of a previous sovereign are instance of (ii). In any case, tacit command fails to explain why the laws and system which continue are the same laws and system. If, then, tacit command is rejected, as it must be, what remains is the proposition that laws remain in force until repealed.

Finally, it has been pointed out that even actual commands of a sovereign only acquire the character of laws when certain procedures have been followed. If the Queen, Lords and Commons unanimously assent to a measure at a garden party in Buckingham Palace, it would not become a law, because the appropriate Parliamentary procedures have not been gone through. If these procedures are laws, it is difficult to square them with command (still less with sanction save by way of nullity). If they are not laws, they are indistinguishable from the dictates of etiquette and morals. Yet, distinguished they must be. What all this shows is the inadequacy of the command doctrine.

Sovereignty

Austin's distinction between positive law and positive morality was that the former was set by a political superior. In elaborating this notion he evolved his theory of sovereignty.

Sovereignty has a "positive mark" and a "negative mark". The former is that a determinate human superior should "receive habitual obedience from the bulk of a given society", and the latter is that that superior is "not in the habit of obedience to a like superior". The reference to "habitual obedience" touches obliquely on a valuable point, namely that every legal system is ultimately founded on some social fact for which no legal justification can be adduced. The addition of "the bulk of a given society", however, is arguable, since this is hardly the body that matters. For instance, it was obedience on the part of the judges after 1689 that established the sovereignty of the Crown in parliament. On the other hand, it has been pointed out that Austin confused the *de facto* sovereign, or the body that receives obedience, with the *de jure* sovereign, or the law-making body. In Britain the Crown receives allegiance from its subjects, while the Crown in Parliament is the supreme law-maker. When Austin talked of the uncommanded commander who makes laws, he was referring to the *de jure* sovereign. Another criticism is that the "negative mark" is not so much the concern of municipal lawyers as of international lawyers. For the former the question is whose enactments constitute "laws"? It is a matter of indifference to them that the law-maker obeys some other body in the international sphere as long as it can make laws in the municipal sphere. Finally, it has been questioned whether it is necessary to have a sovereign in a state. The answer depends on the meanings of "necessary" and "state". A sovereign may be "necessary" because definition has made it so. In another sense the question is whether a sovereign is "necessary" as a practical matter. The word "state", too, has shades of meaning into which it is not proposed to enter. The short answer to the question is that there is no need for only law-making body, though in practice this might be convenient.

Austin went on to claim that the sovereign must be illimitable, indivisible and continuous, and he has encountered heavy criticism in each respect. With regard to illimitability, he denied that his sovereign could be limited. Accordingly, substanital areas of constitutional law did not consist of laws but the positive morality. The sovereign cannot be under a duty, since he .cannot command himself. To be under a duty implies that there is another sovereign above the first in not sovereign, Jethro Brown has argued that the sovereign could well be bound by a duty; Buckland, supporting Austin, denies it. As to all this, it is to be observed, in the first place, that Austin overlooked limitations through disabilities rather than duties. Secondly, the exercise of sovereign powers may be limited by special procedures. Thirdly, Bentham showed how sovereignty may be divided in such a way that each component has limited power to prescribe for the other, and how this creates legal self-bindingness on a sovereign. Connected with duties is the question whether the sovereign can have claims. Austin again denied it since, in his view, a claim has to be conferred by a sovereign on someone, therefore to say that one sovereign confers a claim on another is to deny the sovereignty of the latter. It may the thought that the sovereign may confer a claim upon itself, to which Austin replied that this would be to confuse "might with right". Buckland pointed out that this answer is inconsistent with his concept of claims and duties according to which a person is under a duty if he is subject to an evil, which the party with the claim could cause to be inflicted in the event of disobedience. There is no contradiction is saying that the sovereign could fulfil both roles. Accordingly, Buckland himself suggested that since the situation looks like one in which there is a claim-duty relation, there is no point in denying that the sovereign can have a claim. The question may also be asked whether anything of practical moment turns on the issue. It is also to be noted that in most of these discussions there has been a tendency to refer to the Crown as the Austinian sovereign, which it is not; the Crown in Parliament is the sovereign.

The attribute of indivisibility creates other difficulties. The question is whether sovereign authority can be vested in more that one body, not whether it can be exercised by more than one, which Austin would have admitted. Bentham showed how sovereignty could be divided; besides, there are obvious examples, e.g., the old Roman assemblies, the United States of America and the concurrent powers of a colonial legislature and the Westminster Parliament.

Finally, the attribute of continuity may be questioned by asking where sovereignty resides during a dissolution of Parliament. Austin fell into contradiction in trying to anticipate the objection by saying that sovereignty lies with the Queen, Lords and Electorate. This is contrary to his assertion that it lies with the Queen, Lords and Commons, and it also renders the whole concept meaningless. Who, on this view, is the commander, and who the commanded?

In assessing Austin's contribution, it is to be noted that he helped to propagate the positivist doctrine that it is necessary, to some extent at least, to separate the law as it is from what it ought to be. His concept of a law, shorn of its sovereignty, command and sanction attributes, is reducible to a prescription of conduct phrased in imperative form; but this is not a sufficient basis for drawing the distinction he desired between the "is" and the "ought". His method of logical analysis, i.e., of deducing the nature of legal conceptions from his conception of a law, is, as Julius Stone pointed out, no more than the use of a model to reveal the logical consistency of a system. The value of any such model depends on the degree of correspondence between it and the way in which laws and legal conceptions are actually used. Austin presented his scheme in the belief that, notwithstanding some discrepancies, there was a sufficient measure of correspondence with actuality. In this he was mistaken. Also, he did not reveal the reasoning which led him to his concept of a law; he simply made certain assertions and applied them logically. It is always more interesting to probe and test the reasoning behind premises than to follow out their logical implications. The material of his book consists mainly of contemporary English law with occasional bits of Roman law thrown in. The concept of a law which those limits. Unhappily, he extrapolated it into a test of law in general. Even so, what he was doing was, in effect, to give a stipulative definition of how he proposed using the term "a law." But proffering it as "law properly so called" he assumed that "law" has a "proper" meaning and he also utilised the emotive connotation of "proper". His exclusion of international law and portions of constitutional law from "law properly so called" was logical according to his premise; and had he said that the was only doing this because they fell outside the subject as he saw it, it would have been a permissible attitude for him to have adopted. To exclude them, as he did, on the ground that they were not "law properly so called" was needlessly provocative.

Austin paid lip-service to "general jurisprudence", by which he meant "the exposition of the principles, notions and distinctions which are common to system of law; understanding by systems of law, the ampler and maturer systems". This is unhelpful without a criterion for "amplitude and maturity", and some indication as to whether the "common" principles are those which are in fact found to be common, or those which for some reason are "necessarily" common. Nor did he provide evidence that the notions which he did put into his book are in truth shared by "ampler and maturer system", whatever these may be. Indeed, Austin to some externt belied his own thesis by confining his demonstration to English and a little Roman law. Perhaps, he thought that in so far as the legal orders of the Old and New Worlds were based, as far as he knew, on these two systems, they would furnish between them a sufficient basis for general jurisprudence. However, as Buckland observed, Austin and others like him, who profess general jurisprudence, seldom adhere to it.

A comparison of Bentham and Austin must lead to the conclusion that the former provided a deeper and more adaptable theory. His concept of sovereignty was flexible in that it avoided the shackles of indivisibility and illimitability. He was thus able to accommodate the division of authority between organs, as in a federation, or division in certain areas, as well as restrictions of authority and self-bindingness. His concept of a law was broader than Austin's and he avoided the absurdity of "law properly so called". His sanction was both wider and less important than Austin's: laws are still laws even thought supported by moral or religious sanctions, they may even be accompanied by rewards. He thus had no need to resort to "sanction by nullity". The imperative foundation is a weakness in his theory, as has been pointed out, but it was so much broader and less uncompromising than Austin's that he was able to accommodate permissions up to a point; and he certainly avoided the "tacit command" fiction.

Austin's successors in the analytical tradition have abandoned his concept in favour of other formulations. Holland concentrated, not on command, but on "enforcement by sovereign political authority". This suffers from all the difficulties concerning enforcement that were previously examined. Salmond spoke of law as consisting of "the rules recognised and acted on by courts of justice". The reference to justice is not clear. It may be no more than and embellishment of "courts", for nowhere does Salmond appear to make justice a criterion of identification. A minor difficulty is that courts often apply, for example, rules of arithmetic in the course of giving their decisions, but these do not thereby become "law". What is required is the addition of a rider to the effect that the rules are "recognised and acted on" as law by the courts.

H.L.A. HART

Professor Hart (1907-) may be regarded as the leading contemporary representative of British positivism. In his influential book, The Concept of Law, published in 1961, he brought to bear the training of a philosopher, barrister and jurist to the elucidation of jurisprudential problems. As a linguistic philosopher he belongs to the school which sees how words are used rather than what they refer to, and he subscribes to the view that a word possesses, not a "proper meaning", but an inner "core" of agreed applications surrounded by a "fringe" of unsettled applications. As an analytical jurist, he is keenly appreciative, *inter alia,* of Hohfeld's distinctions, the influence of which is evident throughout his many writings.

He approached concept of law as follows. "Where there is law", he says, "there human conduct is made in some sense non-optional or obligatory". Thus, the idea of obligation is at the core of a rule. He commences his book by taking Austin's command theory to task. The idea of command will explain a coercive order addressed to another in special circumstance, but not why a statute applies generally and also applies to its framers. Secondly, there are other varieties of laws, notably powers. Thirdly, the continuance of pre-existing laws cannot be explained on the basis of command; as pointed out, he was able to demolish completely the "tacit command" myth. Fourthly, Austin's "habit of obedience" fails to explain succession to sovereignty because it fails to take account of important difference between "habit" and "rule". Habits only require common behaviour, which is not enough for a rule. A rule has an "internal aspect", i.e., people use it as a standard by which to judge and condemn deviations; habits do not function in this way. Professor Hart maintains that the significance of "rule" has been neglected. Succession to sovereignty occurs by virtue of the acceptance of a rule entitling the successor to succeed, not because of a habit of obedience. He also uses "rule" to distinguish between "being obliged" and "having an obligation". Austin's command-duty-sanction thesis fails to explain why, if a gunman threatens X with "Your money or your life", X may be obliged to hand over his purse, but has no obligation to do so. The reason is that one has an obligation only by virtue of a rule.

Rules of obligation are distinguishable from other rules in that they are supported by great social pressure because they are felt to be necessary to maintain society. How, then, do they acquire the character of "laws"? Regulation of behaviour is by means of what are called "primary rules". Societies which possess only these are in a "pre-legal" condition and suffer from three drawbacks. One is uncertainty as to what these rules are and their scope; but this can be met by having a "secondary rule of recognition" by which to identify primary rules. Secondly, primary rules are static; but this can be met by having secondary rules providing powers to change primary rules. Thirdly, the maintenance of primary rules in inefficient because of the absence of authoritative arbiters of disputes; but this can be met by having secondary rules of adjudication. Thus, primary rules acquire the character of a legal system through their union with secondary rules, i.e., the union of rules creating duties and rules creating powers to create, extinguish, modify and adjudge, as well as a rule of recognition with which to identify primary rules. Thus, "law" for Professor Hart is equivalent to "legal system". Also, the union between primary and secondary rules is more than a plus sign; primary rules acquire the unity of a system through their union with secondary rules. Moreover, there can be primary rules without a rule of recognition, which " is not a necessity, but a luxury, found in advanced social systems". His point is that "in the simpler form of society we must wait and seen whether a rule gets accepted as a rule or not; in a system with a basic rule of recognition we can say before a rule is actually made, that it will be valid if it conforms to the requirements of the rule of recognition". He also attaches much importance here to the "internal aspect" of rules, i.e., their acceptance as standards, since what is crucial is that officials should have the internal point of view.

The volume of discussion which Professor Hart's concept has evoked is comment in itself on the stimulating quality of his contribution. It is unnecessary to marshal all that has been said about different aspects of his work, but some remarks are needed on those relevant to the purposes of this book. In the first place, it is to be observed that a private club prescribes patterns of behaviour for its members and also possesses machinery whereby such prescriptions are added to, modified, abolished, applied and identified. It would seem, than, that the systems which prevail in a club and in a state exhibit the same characteristics. What is needed is some means of identifying the one as the "law of the club" and the other as the "law of the land". It is not enough simply to incorporate identification by officials into the rule of recognition. A club has officials. What has to be answered is the question: Why is one set of officials "officials of the state"? In other words, the system of a club can only exist within, and presupposes, a legal system, and Professor Hart does not appear to give an adequate criterion for distinguishing between them. The difference lies in the nature of the institutions, of which his theory takes no account. A club is an institution, so is law and legal system, and it is at the institutional level that the distinction has to be found.

Next, it is submitted that the distinction between a legal and a pre-legal state of affairs is not at all clear. If, as is alleged, a rule of recognition is not essential to the validity of primary rules in social systems that have not advanced, what precisely is the criterion? According to Professor Hart, in these societies "we must wait and see whether a rule gets accepted as a rule or not"; which then raises the question: When do we know the category of a given society, when do we know that there is a rule of recognition? This rule is not a hypothesis, but a rule of positive law and, therefore, its own validity cannot relate to itself. The answer to the latter question is that "for the most part the rule of recognition is not stated but its existence is shown in the way in which particular rules are identified, either by Courts or other officials or private persons or their advisors." It is not clear why private persons are included. Since the rule of recognition identifies the rules by which the conduct of private persons is to be judged, it would seem that only courts and officials need be included. Comparison with umpires in a game (Professor Hart's own analogy) brings out another difficulty. One can indeed discover what rules umpires recognise, but they, and still less the players, are not in a position to choose which rules to recognise. Professor Hart's officials and private persons seem free to do just this. The result, then, is not very different from Austin's "habitual obedience". If one knows what the rules are in a given legal system, one can discover what its rule of recognition is; the difficulty is to find the rule of recognition *de novo*.

The rule of recognition is grouped under powers as a secondary rule, but it looks more like the acceptance of a special kind of rule than a power. Besides, there appear to be some rules of recognition which are not powers, such as those which indicate the criteria to be applied, e.g., constitutive rules of procedure. It has even been suggested that the rule of recognition is not a power, but a duty addressed to officials.

Professor Hart's concept is based on the distinction between rules creating duties and rules creating powers, since a legal system is constituted by their union. It is questionable whether so sharp a distinction can be draws. It has been pointed out, for example, that the same rule may create a power plus a duty to exercise it, or a power plus a duty not to exercise it. Professor fuller instances a situation where that same rule may confer power and duty, or power or duty according to the circumstances. A trust instrument may give the beneficiary power to transfer is of course entitled to reimbursement out of the estate and has the power to reimburse himself, correlative to the liability in the beneficiary to have the estate reduced in this way. If, however, the beneficiary exercises his power on the occurrence of the condition but before the trustee has reimbursed himself, the beneficiary comes under a duty to reimburse him. Which asks Professor Fuller, is the rule creating the power and which is the rule creating the duty? The distinction lies, not in the rule, but in the circumstances. The Rule in Hedley Byrne is not one rule imposing a duty not to make careless misstatements and another rule conferring a power to disclaim responsibility; on the contrary, it is one rule which is power and duty-conferring—not to inflict pecuniary loss by careless misstatement, except where there is a disclaimer. Some rules abolish one's duty on an event, e.g., a contract discharged by frustration. Such a rule is neither power nor duty-conferring. There may even be rules about secondary rules, which may be power or duty-conferring, e.g., a rule requiring a government to change a law on a referendum, or the duty of a judge to hear a case. It, then, in the light of such examples the distinction between rules creating powers and rules creating duties is as fluid as this, one wonders whether it is a sure enough foundation for Professor Hart's concept. The relation between primary and secondary rules seems to be more complex than would appear from his treatment of it.

Professor Dworkin has pointed out that in unprovided cases what the law is has to be determined with reference to doctrines, standards and principles, which do not derive their law—quality from a rule of recognition. To relegate them to "discretion" is inconsistent with judicial acceptance of them as "legal". Also, at this point it might be appropriate to mention again that in sufficient allowance appears to be made for "institutions", i.e., a legal system consists of particular ways in which rules and clusters of rules operate. These evolve in many ways which cannot be attibuted to a rule of recognition.

Professor Hart's avowed positivism in relation to his concept of law is also open to criticism. He says that the acceptance of a rule of recognition rests on social facts, but he does not concern himself with the reasons why, or the circumstances in which it comes to be accepted. Social and moral considerations way well set limits on a rule of recognition at the time of acceptance so that it may have built-in limitations that provide safeguards against certain abuses of power. A different point arises in the light of the thesis of the present book that when legal phenomena are considered in a continuum, moral and social factors, which are indispensable to continued existence, are an integral part of any concept of them. Professor Hart has spoken elsewhere of "the acceptable proposition that some shared morality is essential to the existence of any society." "Existence of any society" must mean "continued existence", and he does concede that a "minimum morality" is an essential part of every community. This minimum morality is rooted in five facts: human vulnerability, approximate equality, limited altruism, limited resources and limited understanding and strength of will. As a positivist, he excludes morality from his concept of law, for he says that positivists are concerned to promote "clarity and honesty in the formulation of the theoretical and moral issues raised by the existence of particular laws which were morally iniquitous but were enacted in proper form, clear in meaning, and satisfied all the acknowledged criteria of validity of a system. Their view was that, in thinking about such laws, both the theorist and the unfortunate official or private citizen who was called on to apply or obey them, could only be confused by an invitation to refuse the title of 'law' or 'valid' to them. They thought that, to confront these problems, simpler, more candid resources were available, which would bring into focus far better, every relevant intellectual and moral consideration: we should say, 'This is law; but it is too iniquitous to be applied or obeyed'."

It was pointed out that the principal call for a strictly positivist concept of law is to identify laws precisely for the practical purposes of the present and that, for this limited purpose, it is desirable to separate the "is" from the "ought". But to accomplish this no more would appear to be needed than simply those uses of the would "law" by courts; which is akin to Salmond's definition alluded to above. Professor Hart's concept, however, it of "legal system", which is a continuing phenomenon. Indeed, the very union of duties and powers would imply this for, as pointed but earlier, the exercise of a power and the duty created by it can only brought into focus in a temporal perspective. He concedes of society. If a distinction being drawn between the continued existence of society, for which some morality at least is essential, and the continued existence of a legal system? This cannot be, for while a community (a moral system) could exist without a legal system, a legal system presupposes a community. The relation between morals and a legal system is that the latter only develops within and around the morality of a community. It is submitted that underlying all this is a confusion of time-frames. There is no contradiction in saying that an immoral precept is "law" here and now and also that its immoral quality is likely to prove fatal to its continuity. When Professor Hart thinks in a continuum, as he does with society, he has to bring in morality; but in order to defend positivism he shifts ground and takes refuge in the present time-frame, for only in this way can he justify the exclusion of morality for the purpose of identifying laws here and now. There would thus appear to be a greater separation between law and morality. For the limited purpose of identifying "laws" his concept seeks to accomplish more than is necessary; for the purpose of portraying law in a continuum it does not go far enough.

6

THE PURE THEORY

The theory of Hans Kelsen (1881-1973) represents a development in two different directions. On the one hand, it marks the most refined development to data of analytical positivism. On the other hand, it marks a reaction against the welter of different approaches that characterised the opening of the twentieth century. This is not to imply that Kelsen reverted to ideology. Far from it; he sought to expel ideologies of every description and to present a picture of law austere in its abstraction and severe in its logic.

It is necessary to begin by appreciating the premises from which he argued, A theory of law, he said, must deal with law as actually laid down, not as it ought to be. In this, as in some other respects, he agreed with Austin, although he was unaware of Austin's work he first propounded his views. Insistence on this point has earned him the title of "positivist".

A theory of law must be distinguished from the law itself. There is no logic in natural phenomena, but a theory of nature, which purports to take account of them, must be logicilly self-consistent. In the same way, the law itself consists of a mass of heterogeneous rules, and the function of a theory of law is to organise them into a single, ordered pattern. Kelsen obviously did not evolve his theory of law in vacuo, but out of a profound study of legal material as it was actually found. What he did was to proffer it as a way of regarding the entire legal order and to demonstrate the pattern and shape into which it falls when looked at in the way he suggests. But the brilliance and organising power of his concept can best be appreciated after the substance of the law and its problems have been studied.

A theory of law should be uniform, i.e., it should be applicable at all times and in all place. Kelsen thus advocated general jurisprudence. So did Austin, who, as will be remembered, only paid lip-service to it.

Kelsen, however, carried our his analysis on an undoubtedly general basis. Austin's concept of law was derived from limited material, namely, English and Roman law, and ran into trouble outside that sphere. Kelsen, who had the advantage over Austin of profiting from roughly a century of varied developments, was able to arrive at generalisations which hold good over a very wide area.

A theory of law must be free from ethics, politics, sociology, history, etc. it must, in other words, be "pure" (rein). This follows from the last point. If a theory is to be general, it needs to be shorn of all variable factors such as those mentioned. One suspects at this point a measure of reaction against the modernistic introduction of these other influences which has so enormously widened the scope of jurisprudence. It should be emphasised that Kelsen did not in the least deny their value: all he said was that a theory of law must keep clear of such considerations.

Finally, knowledge of law to Kelsen meant a knowledge of "norms"; and a norm is a proposition in hypothetical form: "if X happens, then Y should happen". The science of law, or what in Anglo-American parlance is called "jurisprudence", consists of the examination of the nature and organisation of normative propositions. It includes all norms created in the process of the examination of the nature and organisation of normative propositions. It includes all norms created in the process of applying some general norm to a specific action. According to Kelsn, a dynamic system is one in which fresh norms are constantly being created on the authority of an original, or basic, norm, a Grundnorm; a static system is one which is at rest in that the basic norm determines the content of those derived from it in addition to imparting validity to them.

Arround these points Kelsen unfolded his picture of law. It appears as a hierarchy of norms. One should, in his view, distinguish between propositions of law and propositions of science. In his earlier writings the distinction, adapted from Kant, was drawn in a straightforward manner. Propositions of science relate to events which have been observed to occur and which necessarily do occur. Thus, whenever an apple is parted from its parent tree, in the absence of support it inevitably fall to the ground. If a new fact or event is observed which fails to conform to a scientific "law", then that "law" has to be modified to include it. Propositions of science may thus be described as dealing with what necessarily does happen, i.e., what "is" (sein). Propositions of law are different. They only deal with what ought to occur, e.g., if X commits theft, he ought to be punished. Even though in a given case events may not work out according to the legal "ought", that does not invalidate it or call for modification. X may commit theft but go unpunished, for the may escape detection, he may bribe the officials who administer the law, or he may die. Even though any of these things may happen, the proposition that "if X commits theft, he ought to be punished" remains good. Legal propositions, therefore, deal with what ought to be (sollen). "The principle according to which natural science describes its object is causality", said Kelsen; "the principle according to which the science of law describes its object is normativity". It is true that in modern science, particularly quantum physics, strict causation has been abandoned in favour of the "principle of indeterminacy", a modified version of causation in terms of probabilities. Accordingly, the Kantain distinction between the "is" and the "ought" requires some modification too. However, the laws of science, thought based on probabilities, remain descriptive of behaviour; juristic laws are not concerned with description, but with imputation of responsibility and are prescriptive of what ought to ensue. So put, Kelsen's distinction can be preserved, for it is a cardinal feature of his theory that laws consist of "ought" propositions.

Two observations might be made on all this. In the first place, Kelsen in his early writings expressed this distinction rather misleadingly. He said in one place:

> "The law of nature (meaning causality) runs: If A is, then B must be. The legal rule says: If A is, then B ought to be... It is evident that this connection is not that of cause and effect. Punishment does not follow upon a delict as effect upon a cause. The legislator relates the two circumstances in a fashion wholly different from causality. Wholly different, yet a connection as unshakeable as causality. For in the legal system the punishment follows always and invariable on the delict even in fact, for some reason or other, it fails of execution. Even though is does not so fail, it still does not stand to the delict in the relation of effect to cause."

The Kind of expression is not only misleading, but it can also induce others to do less than justice to his thesis. In more recent works, however, he distinguished between causality and imputation without the disturbing touches as above. "Under certain conditions", he said later, "a certain consequence ought to take place. This is the grammatical form of the principle of imputations".

A second source of misunderstanding is more important. Legal norms are expressions of "oughts". The sense in which this is so will shortly be explained. Such "oughts" should be distinguished from the "oughts" of valuation. The legal "ought" proposition is in the form, "If X happens, then Y ought to happen" ; value "oughts" shape the content of legal propositions, whether or not they are desirable, and with these Kelsen was not concerned. He did not deny that there are such "oughts" a part from the formal "oughts" of the law. What he said was that the latter should be kept separate from these others. Nor did he deny that the "oughts" of the law may have their origin in these other "oughts". To formulate a theory of law account need only be taken of the formal "ought" without reference to origin or content.

Kelsen found the distinction between legal and other "oughts" in that the former are backed by the force of the state, the preoccupation of law being with the prospect of disobedience rather than obedience. Thus, it is the prescription of sanction that imparts law-quality to a norm, or putting it in another way, "Law is the primary norm, which stipulates the sanction". Only in this way does "law arrive at its essential function". While it is true that in the statement, "If a person does X, then Y ought to happen", there is implicit the idea that a person ought not to do X if he wants to avoid Y, yet the law is only invoked when X has been done. What matters in law is what should happen then. In this way a legal norm prescribes conduct by attaching a sanction to contrary behaviour. All this, it is urged, (a) that the "essential function" of law is by no means confined to dealing with wrongdoing, (b) that the form "If X, then Y ought to happen", does not necessarily imply a sanction for the breach of some duty, and (c) that, in any case, sanction is not essential to duty. As to (a), as will be seen presently, Kelsen made the efficacy of the total legal order a condition of the validity of every norm which means that the very existence of a legal system implies that its laws are in the main obeyed rather that disobeyed. This suggests that the main function of laws is to give guidance by prescribing how people ought to behave. Further, prescribing behaviour, even in Kelsen's indirect sense, suggests that moral and social values are indispensable despite his earnest effort to exclude them. The use of force in the event of disobedience becomes very much a secondary function. As to (b), it was pointed out earlier that the form, "If X, then Y ought to happen", would fit the rule that if one earns more than a certain amount, then one ought to be taxed. But taxation is in no sense a sanction, nor is there a duty not to earn more than that amount, then one ought to be taxed. But taxation is in no sense a sanction, nor is there a duty not to earn more than that amount. As to (c), it was also pointed out in some detail why it is erroneous to associate sanction with duty, especially in view of the numerous instances of sanctionless duties. In the light of all this it is submitted that any concept of law which revolves around sanctions cannot be an accurate reflection of law as it actually is.

To the extent that the provision of sanctions is regarded as crucial to law, the theories of Austin and Kelsen agree, but they differ in elaboration. For Austin, law is a command backed by sanction. Kelsen disagreed in two respects. Firstly, he rejected the idea of command, because it introduces a psychological element into a theory of law which should, in his view, be "pure". The most that the conceded was that a law is a

> "de-psychologised command, a command which does not imply a 'will' in a psychological sense of the term. . . a rule expressing the fact that somebody ought to act in a certain way, without implying that anybody really 'wants' the person to act in that way."

Secondly, to Austin the sanction was something outside a law imparting validity to it. To Kelsen such a statement was in adequate and confused. For the operation of the sanction supporting a rule resolves itself into the operation of other rules; and further, the validity of a rule has nothing to do with its sanctions. To illustrate the first of these objections, Austin would have said that the sanction behind the proposition, "you ought not to steal", is that if you do steal, you will be imprisoned. To Kelsen, the operation of the sanction itself depends on the operation of other rules of law. Thus, one rule prescribes that if a man has committed theft, he ought to be arrested; another rule prescribes that the ought to be brought to trial; other rules prescribe how the trial ought to be conducted; another rules prescribe how the trial ought to be conducted; another rule prescribes that if the jury brings in a verdict of "guilty", the judge ought to pass sentence; another rule prescribes that some official should carry that sentence into execution. In this way the contrast between law and sanction in the Austinian sense disappears.

With reference to the validity of a rule, Kelsen asserted that the validity of an "ought" is not to be derived from any "is" of fact outside the law; it derives from some other proposition standing behind it and imparting validity to it. Thus, the validity of each of the rules comprising the sanction depends on some other rule, which in turn rests on another and so on. The rule that some official should imprison a convicted thief derives its validity from the judicial order prescribing imprisonment for theft, and this in turn derives its validity from rules regulating the competence of the court and the rules of substantive law and procedure. In this way there begins to emerge a picture of law, not just as a collection of "ought" propositions, but as a hierarchy of "oughts". The conjecture which this opens up is the end of the progression. Kelsen's solution was that in every legal order, no matter with what proposition of law one begins, a hierarchy of "oughts" is traceable back to some initial, fundamental "ought", on which the validity of all the others ultimately rests. This is the Grundnorm, the basic or fundamental norm. Kelsen recognised that the Grundnorm need not be the same in every legal order, but a Grundnorm of some kind there will always be, whether, e.g., a written constitution or will of a dictator. The Grundnorm is not the constitution, it is simply the presupposition, demanded by theory, that this constitution ought to be obeyed. Therefore, the Grundnorm is always adapted to the prevailing state of affairs. The Grundnorm only impart validity to the constitution and all other norms derived from it, it does not dictate their content. The difference between his positivism and natural law theory is that the latter determines content as well. There is also no reason why there need only be one Grundonrm, not has it to be a written constitution. In Great Britain, for instance, the entire legal order is traceable to the propositions that the enactments of the Crown in Parliament and judicial precedents ought to be treated as "law", with immemorial custom as a possible third. This does not contradict Kelsen's thesis, for what he contended was that a system cannot be founded on two conflicting Grundnormen. In Britain there is no conflict between the authority of the Crown in Parliament and of judicial precedent; the former takes precedence over the latter.

There are several features about the Grundnorm deserving of the closest attention. In the first place, in what sense is the Grundnorm a norm? It does not conform to Kelsen's own formulation of a norm: "If X, then Y ought to happen"; it only empowers and certainly does not impose sanctions. Next, according to Kelsen every rule of law derives its validity from some other rule standing behind it. The Grundnorm has no rule behind it. Its validity has therefore to be assumed for the purpose of theory, which is why it is said to be the "initial hypothesis", "the postulated ultimate rule according to which the norms of this order are established and annulled, receive or lose their validity". Put in another way, one cannot account for the validity of the Grundnorm by pointing to another rule of law. The Gundnorm validates the rest of the legal system; one cannot therefor utilise the system, or any part of it. To validate the Grundnorm. As one writer put it, such an attempt would be like trying to pick oneself up by one's bootlaces. This point has already been considered from another angle, namely, in connection with statue and judicial precedent, where the impossibility of finding a reason in law why these should be able to impart the quality of "English law" was demonstrated.

Kelsen's distinction between the validity of a rule and its effectiveness has only been touched upon. A rule is valid, not because it is, or is likely to be, obeyed by those to whom it is addressed, but by virtue of another rule imparting validity to it. Thus, a legal norm is valid before it is effective, as is the case with a new statute before it has been applied. Yet, the validity of each individual rule does depend on the effectiveness of the legal order as a whole. In Kelsen's won words:

> "It cannot be maintained that, legally, men have to behave in conformity with a certain norm, if the total legal order, of which that norm is an integral part, has lost its efficacy. The principle of legitimacy is restricted by the principle of effectiveness."

He later modified this somewhat to the extent of saying that the legal order has to be "by and large" effective. It will therefore be seen that, with reference to a given rule of law, its validity and its effectiveness have to be kept separate. Effectiveness of the order as a whole is a condition, not a reason, of the validity of the Grundnorm and of any individual norm: "a condition *sine qua non,* but not a condition *per qaem.*" At the legal of the Grundnorm the question, Why is it valid? Is meaningless, but it is of the utmost importance that the Grundnorm should secure for itself a minimum of effectiveness, i.e., a certain number of persons who are willing to abide by it. It is futile to say that the proposition that the will of the Tsar should be accepted as law is the Grundnorm in Russia today. On the other hand, the fact that enactments of the Crown in Parliament are in fact disobeyed quite frequently does not render the proposition that the Crown in Parliament is law constitutive any the less a Grundnorm of English law. There must not be a total disregard of the Grundnorm, but there need not be universal adherence to it. All that is necessary is that it should command a minimum of effectiveness.

When a Grundnorm ceases to derive a minimum of support, it ceases to be the basis of the legal order, and any other proposition which does obtain support will replace it. Such a change in the state of affairs is said to amount to a revolution in law. This is because, as pointed out, the Grundnorm is not itself the constitution, but the assumption that this (effective) state of affairs ought to be obeyed, and because, for the reason, the Grundnorm is adapted to that state of affairs and not *vice versa*. It follows, therefore, that a change in the situation involves a revolution in the theory which is adapted to it. The constitutions of the various Deminions derived their validity from statutes of the Crown in parliament at Westminster, from which it would seem to follow that the Grundnorm of the Commonwealth legal order is that enactments of the Crown in parliament at Westminster are law *ipso jure* for the Commonwealth. But the Dominions having discarded that doctrine, their acquisition of independence has amounted to a revolution in the legal order of the Commonwealth.

The Grundnorm is thus a key concept in Kelsen's theory, but it raises many difficulties. The change effected in the British Grundnorm in 1689 amounted, according to his thesis, to a revolution in the system, buy why did it remain the "same system"? Kelsen would probably have denied that it is the same; which is not the way lawyers and jurists actually regard the position. It would only be a suggestion as to how they ought to regard it. The piont might be illustrated in another way. British courts might abandon stare decisis tomorrow, i.e., the Grundnorm that "precedents ought to be binding", but it would be odd indeed to say that a new system comes into being thereafter. All this, however, harks back to the earlier question: What exactly is the Grundnorm in Britain?

Some writers have pointed out, with a hint of criticism, that in whatever way effectiveness of the Grundnorm is measured, Kelsen's theory has ceased to be "purt" at this point. For, effectiveness would seem to depend on those very sociological factors which he so vehemently excluded from his theory of law. If, then, the Grundnorm upon which the validity of all other norms depends is tainted with impurity, it is arguable that the others are similarly tainted. Another line of attack on the claim to purity is that Kelsen's whole scheme is an *a priori* one dependent on empirical observation for confirmation. He offered it as a "theory of interpretation", which implies that it is not a description but a medel and thus evaluative in function. It is possible to make too much of this, for Kelsen's analysis of the structure of the legal system in no way impaired by these comments. The criticism touches, not the theory, but his claim to its purity. He admits that the Grundnorm is founded on factors outside the law. That being the case, whether his theory is said to be pure only from the Grundnorm onwards, or partially pure because of its initial impurity, is not very material. The fact is, as the words of Kelsen indicate, that the effectiveness of the legal order as a whole is prerequisite to the validity of each single rule in it.

The objection, though verbal, carries more serious implications. If, as seems clear, some inquiry into political and sociological factors has to precede, or at least is implicit in, the adoption of a particular Grundnorm as the criterion of validity, and if the validity of every part of the system is dependent upon the continued effectiveness of the whole, then on his own showing the study of jurisprudence should include the study of the social environment. It might also be pointed out that Kelsen's picture is that of a legal order viewed in the present time-frame, which explains his exclusion of moral, sociological and other considerations from the question of the validity of any rule. Yet, he could not avoid having to make some measure of effectiveness a decisive attribute of the Grundnorm and of the legal order as a whole. The force of this point may be seen when one asks why a particular Grundnorm was accepted, especially if this followed on a revolution? Might it not be that the new criterion of validity was able to command a "minimum of effectiveness" because it was thought to guarantee that measure of justice and morality, which the previous criterion did not? They could it not be argued that the supremacy of the Crown in Parliament was accepted in 1689 in order that tyrannous and arbitrary acts should no longer be valid as they had been by virtue of the supremacy of the prerogative? On this line of argument the Grundnorm is effective, and continues to be effective, in so far as an element of morality is built in as part of the criterion of validity. If so, the continued validity of every proposition of law derived from the validating source has an ethical background and the separation of law from morality would cease to exist. Moreover, apart from the Grundnorm, if, in Kelsen's own thesis, a norm in the form, "If X, then Y ought to happen", is an indirect way of prescribing the behaviour needed to avoid Y (assuming Y to be a sanction), then the values that prompted the prescription in this indirect way must also underlie the form; and the same applies to every other such norm. All this amounts to a formidable argument leveled not merely at Kelsen, but at positivism in general. It is sufficient here to observe that, if sound it would strike at the foundation of his separation of "is" and "ought".

Kelsen gave no criterion by which the minimum of effectiveness is to be measured. All he maintained was that the Grundnorm imparts validity as long as the "total order" remains effective, or, as he later put it, "by and large" effective. As to this it may be asked, in the first place, for how long must effectiveness be maintained for the requirement to be satisfied? In *The State* v. *Dosso* the Supreme Court of Pakistan, expressly on Kelsenian grounds, had held a usurper to be effectively in power and hence lawful (even though, incidentally, he himself was deposed the day after the judgment was published). Later in *Jilani* v. *Government of Punjab,* the Supreme Court declared both the first usurper and the second illegal, repudiated Kelsen in toto and overruled Dosso, which relied on him so heavily and because of which, as one judge quoted approvingly, "a perfectly good country was made into a laughing stock." Secondly, what is the measure of "total" and "by and large." The Rhodesian case, *Madzimbamuto* v. *Lardner-Burke,* exposes the weakness here, for as one judge pointed out, an effective order cannot be said to be totally, or even by and large, effective as long as its judiciary refuses to accept the legality of its basis. Finally, what does "effectiveness, which makes people obliged to obey, and effectiveness which makes them feel under an obligation to do so. A usurper may by force and fear achieve the former, but not the latter, which, as judicially acknowledged, is the kind of effectiveness required by Kelsen. A judge of the Supreme Court of Pakistan, examining the position of the deposed usurper President, said in words reminiscent of Professor Hart, "He obligated the people to obey his behests, but in law they incurred no obligation to obey him".

It is not clear what is connoted by the description of the Grundnorm as a "hypothesis" or "postulate" or "presupposed". There is no analogy here, be it noted, with scientific hypotheses, which are assumptions used to account for the totality of known facts. It is sometimes the case that two alternative scientific hypotheses may be equally apt to explain the phenomena in question. But there is no room for alternative Grundnormen, which may serve as postulates of a given legal system. There must be only one Grundnom, which is supreme and uncontradicted; otherwise there can be no unified theory. As to this, the requirement of effectiveness suggests, on the one hand, that the Grundnorm is a fact and not a pretence or assumption. On the other hand, it is not itself the constitution but the presupposition, required by theory, that this constitution ought to be obeyed. As such it is not a social reality and does not march happily under Kelsen's positivist banner. There is a further difficulty. An effective constitution is a fact upon which the Grundnorm posits an "ought". It has been axiomatic since Hume that an "ought" cannot be derived from an "is" without the interposition of a value judgment that the "is" is desirable and for that reason ought to be. It looks, therefore, as if Kelsen's theory conceals an ideology that might is right and hence ought to be; which is no different after all from the adoption of *a priori* assumptions by naturalists, besides being an open invitation to revolt and crude force. Many of these difficulties would be avoided if what was said earlier is borne in mind. The criterion of validity refers to the medium or media which impart to a rule the quality of "law", "valid" here meaning "legal". The "minimum of effectiveness" refers to the acceptance of such media by those in charge of administering "law". This is all that would have been needed for Kelsen's demonstration, but by using the notion of Grundnorm he seems to have inflated a pedestrian simplicity into something misleadingly large.

The idea of a medium, accepted by courts, which imparts to "laws" this quality, is more useful than that of a Grundnorm enjoying a minimum of effectiveness. For instance, in the lacuna that exists during a revolution, when the old basis has been overthrown and something has still to replace it, there is no longer a Grundnorm, but the tribunals may continue to apply "laws" identified as such by means of some criterion which they still recognise, albeit provisionally. It does not matter that that criterion belongs to the order that has gone; as long as it is accepted by the judges as having imparted the quality of "law" to the proposition in question that is all that is needed. This was endorsed in the test case of *Madzimbamuto* v. *Lardner-Burke,* which was brought during the Rhodesian rebellion. Here the revolutionary 1965 Constitution was acknowledged to by effective, yet for over two years the Rhodesian courts refused, and the Judicial Committee of the Privy Council still refuses, to accept it as "legal". During that period the Rhodesian courts were nonetheless prepared to uphold at least some measures of the illegal regime as "laws", and the displaced 1961 Constitution, which had ceased to be effective, was still held to possess controlling force inasmuch as the laws of the illegal authority had to conform to it. The case is inexplicable on Kelsenian doctrine. It shows, firstly, that effectiveness is not the criterion of the Grundnorm, but what courts are prepared to accept as the fount of validity; and, secondly, that the validity of a law does not necessarily derive from an effective Grundnorm, but that this, too, depends on what courts accept as valid. A third point, which has since emerged, is that a particular Grundnorm may be accepted and rejected by the same court depending upon the time at which, and the conditions under which, it site. In *The State* v. *Dosso,* for example, the Supreme Court of Pakistan accepted the regime, which had usurped power unconstitutionally, as legal on grounds of effectiveness; but later in *Jilani* v. *Government of Punjab,* the Supreme Court declared it illegal, notwithstanding effectiveness, and overruled Dosso. The court was not saying that it was lawful while it lasted, but that it was unlawful ab initio. It is to be noted that by the time of the later decision the usurper had been overthrown, and it may well be that such pronouncements will nearly always be retrospective, since judges actually sitting under the power of a regime have little alternative but to accept it as legal: those who refuse will simply be replaced, or else their judgments will be nullified. Against this Smith regime and also of several Pakistan judges who, even under the illegal regime, not only voiced their doubts but even held particular measures void. All this boils down to the fact that validity is always a matter to be determined in the context of a given point of time and depends on what judges are prepared to accept at that moment.

In the result it would seem that Kelsen's theory does not apply in revolutionary situations, in which case it ceases to be a "general theory"; or, if general, it ceases to be true. In settled conditions it teaches nothing new; in revolutionary conditions, where guidance is needed, it is useless, for the choice of a Grundnorm is not dictated inflexibly by effectiveness but is a political decision, as Kelsen has admitted.

From all this it will be evident that the Grundnorm is a very weak point in the theory. Yet such as it is, it provides the start of Kelsen's demonstration. The rest of the system is pictured as broadening down in gradations from it and becoming progressively more and more detailed and specific. The entire process is one of the gradual concretisation of the basis norm and the focussing of it to specific situations (Stufentheorie). It is a dynamic process, for the application of a higher norm involves the creation of new lower norms. Thus, the practical manifestation of the acceptance of statute as a basis of validity requires the creation by statute of certain general norms, which may be described as propositions of substantive law, as well as the machinery and procedure for the application of these general norms. The application of general norms by this machinery, as represented by a judge or other official, to a particular situation in turn involves a creative elements in so far as the judge by his decision creates a specific norm addressed to one or other of the parties. The final stage is the carrying out of the compulsive act. At the end of the progression, therefore, sanction is a permission to someone to execute the coercive act. This means that "ought" here covers "may" and "can". It is to be noted that in the application of the general norm the judge may be left with an element of discretion, or he may consciously choose between alternative interpretations which the norm permits. The doctrine leaves room for value-judgments in the course of the decisional process. Their exclusion from the theory is not intended to diminish the actual parts they play. Again, the application of a general norm may depend upon the act of the parties, e.g., an agreement or some form of wrongdoing.

Several interesting implications follow from this view of a legal system. In the first place, the traditional distinction between "public" and "private" law is seen to be largely one of degree, while at times it virtually disappears. They are both part of the process of concretisation and are both norm-creating. The distinction between them lies sometimes in the fact that they operate at different levels of the structure, and at others in the organs which apply them. With criminal law, for example, the distinction would seem to disappear altogether. Secondly, in a similar way the distinction between legislative, executive and judicial processes appears in a new light. They are all norm-creating agencies, the executive and judiciary being but steps in the concretisation of norms in particular cases. Thirdly, the distinction between substantive law and procedure is relative, procedure assuming greater importance. It is the organs and process of concretisation that constitute the legal system. Fourthly, the distinction between questions of law and fact also become relative. The "facts" are part of the condition contained in the "if X" part of the formula, "If X, then Y Ought to happen". The application of a norm concretises every part of it, including the "If X" part. Therefore, the finding of fact by a judges is not necessarily what actually happened but what he regards as having happened for the purposes of applying the particular norm.

Fifthly, the legal order is a normative structure which operates so as to culminate in the application of sanctions for certain forms of human behaviour. It follows that the idea of duty is of its essence, which is evident in the "ought". Kelsen made no specific allowance for powers, while liberty, in his view, "is an extra-legal phenomenon". Liberty is the jural opposite of duty, but Kelsen's stand in the matter reflects a wider issue, namely, between an "open" and a "closed" concept of law. The former is one in which law concerns only specific regulation so that anything as yet unregulated falls outside law. The latter is one in which all aspects of behaviour are within law, whether positively through specific regulation or negatively through liberties; in short, liberty and duty are two ides of the same coin. Kelsen's theory is clearly an "open" one. As to this, it is as well to remember that liberty may result (a) from the fact that legislators and judges have not yet pronounced on the matter, e.g., invasion of privacy; or (b) from a deliberate decision not to interfere, as in *Bradford Corporation* v. *Pickles*; or (c) from the deliberate abolition of a preexisting duty, e.g., the statutory abolition of the duty forbidding homosexuality between consenting adults. There is some plausibility in saying with Kelsen that liberty in sense (a) lies outside law; but it seems odd to say that the liberty pronounced by a court in (b) is extra-legal; and order still to say the same of the statutory provision in (c) Analytically, the resulting position in all three cases is the same, namely, no duty not to do the act. There seems to be no justification for distinguishing between any of them, nor does Kelsen himself attempt to do so. Perhaps, one ought instead to question his sweeping exclusion of liberty as such from a concept of law.

On the other hand, when he turned to the concept of claim, he stood on firmer ground. This, he maintained, is not essential. It appears when

> "the putting into effect of the consequence of the disregard of the legal rule is made dependent upon the will of the person who has an interest in the sanction of the law being applied."

Claim is only a by-product, as it were, of the law. Kelsen showed how modern criminal law has for the most part discarded ancient ideas of the law being set in motion by the injured person and is now enforced directly by officials, i.e., the idea of individual claims is no longer the foundation of the criminal law. It is still the basis of the law of property and contract and so on, but in Kelsen's view there is no reason why it need be, and may well be dispensed with in the future.

Sixthly, to Kelsen the concept of "person" was simply a step in the process of concretisation. This has been previously discussed, and it was seen that by "person" he meant only a totality of claims, etc. "person" is a legal conception, and he therefore rejected the traditional distinction between "natural" and "juristic" persons. The former are biological entities, which lie outside the province of legal theory. They are only the concern of the law in so far as they focus duties and claims, etc.

Lastly, the most significant feature of Kelsen's doctrine is that the state is viewed as system of human behaviour and an order of social compulsion. Law is likewise a normative ordering of human behaviour backed by force, which "make the use of force a monopoly of the community". Moreover, a state is constituted by territory, independent government, population and ability to enter into relations with other states, and each of these requirements is legally determined. The inescapable conclusion is that state and law are identical. This is not to say that every legal order is automatically a state, e.g., highly decentralised orders like primitive communities; only relatively centralised legal orders are states. Kelsen further rejected any attempt to set the state apart from law or to say that law is the "will of the state".

Kelsen also applied his theory to the system known commonly as "international law". His earliest work did not touch on this field, and it was only after Verdross, one of his disciples, had started to adapt his approach to international law, that Kelsen himself took an interest in it. But his theory, when applied in this field, does reveal some limitations. However assured his thesis appears when demonstrated with reference to long established and settled municipal systems of law, in the palpitating condition of international relations it has serious limitations. The Pure Theory demands that a Grundnorm be discovered. If there are conflicting possibilities, then, as Kelsen himself admitted, his theory provides no guidance in choosing between them. All he said was that the Gurndnorm should command a minimum of support. In the international sphere there are two possible Grundnormen, the supremacy of each municipal system or the supremacy of international law. The argument based on the former, as pictured by Kelsen, would run as follows. Every national legal order cannot ex hypothesi recognise any norm superior to its own Grundnorm. The English legal order does not apply in France, nor *vice versa*. But the English legal order recognises the validity of the French legal order in France; and if the only Grundnorm known to English law is its own, it follows that the English legal order regards the validity of the French legal order in France as being in some way a delegated normative order from the English Grundnorm. Similarly, approaching the matter from the English Grundnorm. Similarly, approaching the matter from the French side, the French legal order can only recognise the validity of the English legal order in England as being derived from the

French Grundnorm. Such is the outcome of the doctrine of national sovereignty and it tends to a state of anarchy in which each national order recognises only its own Grundnorm and endures other legal orders as subsidiary to it.

Kelsen would have none of this. He argued instead for a monist view of the relationship between international and municipal law, and declared that the Grundnorm of the international system postulates the primacy of international law. Nations in practice, he argued, recognise the equality of each other's legal orders, and the doctrine of equality must mean that they recognise the existence of a Grundnorm superior to the Grundnormen of their own particular legal orders. The equal force of national systems is an impossible notion unless there is some higher authority, which bestows equality. The same conclusion is arrived at in a different way. Much of international law rests on custom; it consists in rationalisations of the actual practice of states. When a description of the conduct of states is transmitted into a prescription of how they ought to behave, it becomes international law. But Kelsen's insistent contention was that the validity of an "ought" can never be derived from an "is", but only from a superior norm. He also maintained that a legal norm is distinguishable from norms of morality, ethics and the like in that it is backed by force. In the international sphere he found the element of force in war and reprisals.

All this is very questionable. The first thing, which his theory requires, is the Grundnorm of the international order. This is by no means clear: it may be the principle pacta sunt sevanda, or "coercion of state against state ought to be exercised under the conditions and in the manner, that conforms with the custom constituted by the actual behaviour of the states"; but other suggestions have been offered by other writers. As Stone has commented,

> "it is difficult to see what the pure theory of law can contribute to a system which it assumes to be law, but which it derives from a basic norm which it cannot find."

It looks as if Kelsen shifted the meaning of Grundnorm. It was pointed our earlier, with reference to municipal law, that the Grundnorm has to possess some basis in fact, namely, a minimum of effectiveness. On the other hand, scientific hypotheses are different in that they are truly suppositions, which are accepted so far as they explain observable phenomena. It would seem that with reference to international law the Grundnorm is a pure supposition, unlike that of municipal law. For, assuming that a monist legal theory has to be offered to account for the present state of international society, then one way of explaining the assertion of equality by states would be by hypothesising a norm superior to that of each national order from which equality might be said to derive. But it is open to doubt whether even an attempt at a monist explanation is worthwhile. (a) One is entitled seriously to question whether there is any Grundnorm which commands the necessary minimum of effectiveness demanded by Kelsen's theory. State recognise such doctrines as pacta sunt servanda or equality only in the sense of paying lip-service to them when it suits their convenience to do so. Indeed, an alternative, and as plausible, a hypothesis to explain equality is that it springs from a sense of mutual forbearance inspired by fear. Indeed, it has been asserted judicially that "in International Law there is no 'legal order' as such". So the hypothesis of a superior norm of the international order is no more than one possible assumption, and an unreal one at that. With reference to municipal law, on the other hand, Kelsen's whole theory would be meaningless unless the Grundnorm commands a minimum of effectiveness in action and not just in words. Post hoc is not propter hoc. (b) It is not easy to reconcile a monist theory does allow, it is true, for limited conflicts within a given order, but those between international and municipal law are too extensive to ignore. The case of *Jalani* v. *Government of Punjab,* is a vivid illustration not just of conflict, but of the categorical rejection by a municipal court of Kelsen's monism. An attempt was made to buttress the effectiveness of a revolutionary regime, and hence its legality, with the fact that it had received recognition at international law. The Supreme Court said that to do this would be to assume the primacy of international law over municipal law, a doctrine which was emphatically repudiated. With reference to the emergence of a new government as well as a new state, it was pointed out that their recognition at international law is irrelevant to their legality at municipal law. "The validity of a new government is governed by the law of the state", said the Chief Justice. Even when a new state comes into being through secession, the courts of the parent state are not bound by international recognition accorded to it. The creation of the State of Bangla Desh out of East Pakistan was precisely in point, and as to this a judge of West Pakistan said: "While under International Law, East Pakistan has become an independent state, the municipal courts of Pakistan will not confer recognition on it or act upon the legal order set-up by the rebel Government"; and he added that Kelsen's monistic theory is "wholly inapplicable to municiapal courts".

In view of the absence of a minimum of effectiveness in support of any one Grundnorm for the international order, there is no reason to prefer a monist explanation law Kelsen was making an assumption as to what ought to be the case rather than what actually is. Lillte wonder that Sir Hersch Lauterpacht, one of Kelsen's own pupils, was moved to question whether he was not here reverting to natural law ideodogy.

These difficulties will be avoided if the idea of a Grundnorm is replaced by that of an indentifying criterion, accepted by courts, which would regulate the use of the label "international law". Propositions concerning the conduct of state would then be "international law" because the appropriate tribunals accept them as such whenever they satisfy the criterion. It is true that different types of tribunals might view the criterion differently, or might even accept different criteria. Notwithstanding this, there might be here a sufficient basis for constructing a more realistic theory of international law than a monist one.

Finally, to treat war and reprisals as providing the element of force would be acceptable only of resort to them was permitted by the international legal order and forbidden as instruments of national policy. It is true that international law does not forbid was and reprisals entirely as instruments of national policy, not even after the Briand-Kellogg Pact, 1928, or the Charter of the United Nations, but the whole object of international law is to try to prevent these. War represents the breakdown of international law.

In the light of all this, as Professor Friedmann observed:

"Logically Kelsen should have been led to deny the character of law to international law in present international society."

In any case, in view of the difference between the connotation and function of the word "law" as applied to international and municipal legal order, it is questionable whether the attempt to construct a unifying theory is feasible.

The conclusion of many writers is that, notwithstanding the logical coherence of Kelsen's structure, he provided no guidance in the actual application of the law. Thus, he showed how, in the process of concretising the general norms it may be necessary to make a choice either in decision or interpretation. The judge or the official concerned is already aware of that necessity; his need is for some guidance as to how he should make his choice. The answer is not to be found in Kelsen's teachings, but in value considerations of one sort or another, which Kelsen sedulously Kelsen, who was most anxious to insist that he was not concerned with that aspect. To criticise him for not having done something which he expressly disclaimed would be unfair. He set out to achieve a limited objective, namely, to present a formal picture of the legal structure, and what he set out to do, he did do. To say that he should have aspired to do more is not a criticism of what he has done, but a criticism of his limited objective.

Another more serious aspect of the above point is that a legal order is not merely the sum total of laws, but includes doctrines, principles and standards all of which are accepted as "legal" and which operate by influencing the application of rules. Their validity is not traceable to the Grundnorm of the order. Are these, then, to be lumped with values and banished from, a theory of law, even though they are admitted to be "legal"? If so, it is a grave weakness in any such theory.

Finally, although Kelsen has been hailed as having provided the outstanding theory of the twentieth century from a positivist point of view. It has be remembered that Bentham's Of Laws in General only saw daylight after Kelsen had made his contribution. Some difference between them, are significant. Kelsen's. The most important of these is that Kelsen's method individuating a norm, "If X, then Y ought to happen", minimises the regulatory function of law. This, as has been pointed out, stems from his obsession with sanctions: conduct is only a condition which brings them into play or avoids them. Bentham took full account of the regulatory function and clearly perceived that one law prescribes behaviour and another prescribes a sanction: they are two different act-situation. Bentham kept them apart, while Kelsen rolled them into one. Kelsen was also driven to the difficult conclusion that laws are ultimately permissions to apply sanctions and that "ought" thus includes "may" and "can"; which Bentham avoided. Bentham gave sanction a much broader meaning than Kelsen. On the other hand, both of them perceived that "constitutional law" is a part of every law as ordinarily formulated, the linkage for Bentham being that such laws are compounded of other laws enacted at other times and in other contexts, while for Kelsen the linkage being their validity traceable through to the Grundnorm.

7

HISTORICAL AND ANTHROPOLOGICAL APPROACHES

The historical outlook will be dealt with in this chapter. It comprises, on the one hand, inquiries into the past and evolution generally with the object of elucidating the position today. The question to be answered is to what extent the "oughts" of contemporary laws have been fashioned by the past. This is what some of the jurist, who belong to what is known as the Historical School, have purported to do. On the other hand, there are inquiries into the past, especially into primitive and undeveloped communities, which are conducted for their own sake in order to discover what "law" might appropriately be taken to mean in them. Such inquiries are distinguishable as the Anthropological approach and will be touched on at the end of the chapter.

HISTORICAL SCHOOL

The Historical School, arose more or less contemporaneously with Analytical positivism at the beginning of the nineteenth century, and should be regarded as another manifestation of the reaction against natural law theories. It did not emerge as something novel in European thought, for it had been germinating long before then. The reaction against natural law theories provided a rich bed in which the seeds of historical scholarship took root and spread.

The prelude to the historical approach to law is the story of the study and reception of Roman law in Europe. The gradual disappearance and decay of Roman law in the ages which followed the dissolution of the Roman empire were arrested by a revival of academic interest in that system in the eleventh century in France and in Italy and principally at the law school in Bologna. This new interest took the form of adding to the texts explanatory glosses and commentaries. The Glossators accepted Justinian's boast that conflicts had been eliminated from his codification, and they devoted their ingenuity to reconciling and explaining away the many conflicts that did undoubtedly exits. There was another more signification side to their work, which was that they endeavored to fit the problems of their feudal society into Roman terminology and thus paved the way for the later reception of Roman law into Europe. The work of the Glossators culminated in the Glossa ordinaria of Accursius in the early twelfth century, which superseded all previous glosses and came to be accepted as the final resolution of the conflicting opinions of individual Glossators. The scholars who followed them were known as the Psot-Glossators or Commentators. The most interesting features of their work is the way in which they attempted to relate the Roman law to contemporary problems, but they used for this purpose, not the original texts, but the Glossa. So it was that when Roman law was eventually received into Europe in the fifteenth and sixteenth centuries it was a diluted version adapted from the Glossa that was received.

The Renaissance kindled fresh interest in the teachings of the Romans themselves. The outstanding name in this connection is that of Cujas, a Frenchman, who resorted to the Roman originals underneath the accumulated silt of commentary and gloss. He is more: he was the first scholar to understand Justinian's Corpus Juris in historical perspective. It is difficult to appreciate nowadays who lacking in historical sense people were in those days. The tendency was to regard the Corpus juris more or less as a simultaneous product, rather than as a collection of materials which had been changing and developing over centuries. More than one hundred years spanned the jurists of the Classical period, whose writings comprise the Digest, while between them and Justinian another three centuries elapsed. This lack of historical sense led to elaborate and fanciful explanations for difference which were easily explicable on historical grounds. The admirable work of Cujas, however, was confined to the academic sphere and failed to penetrate through to practice. For this there was good reason. As long as Roman law remained "the law" in the countries of Europe, inconsistencies had to be reconciled and historical explanations of their origin were of no avail. The living law could not be self-contradictory. Accordingly, there developed a gulf between the academic jurist and the practitioner, which also explains why the historical approach remained for so long in the background.

The position in Germany at the start of the nineteenth century deserves special mention, since this was the cradle of the Historical School. Roman law functioned as the common law subject to canon law, imperial enactment's and customary law, so far as he was still extant. The Roman law was assumed to have been accepted as a whole, not in fragments, in the form of Justinian's codification as found in the works of the Glossators and Commentators. The practical problem which lawyers had to solve had altered with the ages, but the methods of applying the law differed little from that of the Italian courts in the time of the Glossators. Moreover, the panorama of the law as a whole was confusing, for local variations were innumerable. In these circumstances a proposal was made by Thibaut, of Heidelberg, in 1814 for a code on the lines of the Code Napoleon. This was immediately answered by von Savigny (1779-1861) in an essay entitled On the Vocation of our Age for Legislation and Jurisprudence, with which, in the words of Ihering, a new jurisprudence was born. So powerful was his influence that the move towards condification was effectively halted and it was not until 1900, after many years of sustained agitation, that Germany ultimately acquired here code, the Burgerliches Gesetzbuch.

Although Thibaut's proposals were the immediate stimulus for the rise of the Historical School, other factors had combined to prepare the way. The first of these has already been mentioned, namely, the reaction against the unhistorical assumptions of the natural law theorists. As these were exposed as hollow and false, so the need was felt for a more realistic investigation into historical truths. Secondly, the attempt to found legal systems based on reason without reference to past or existing circumstances had proved to be revolutionary, the culmination of this being the French Revolution, with all its attendant brutalities. A reaction set in against the rationalism that promoted such barbarity. This was a factor which weighed heavily with Savigny, a conservative nobleman, who acquired a deep and lasting hatred for the Revolution. Thirdly, the French conquests under Napoleon aroused the nationalism of Europe. Fourthly, the French had spread the idea of codified law, and the reaction against anything French carried with if hostility to codification. Finally, the influence of certain early pioneers in the new way of thinking should not be ignored. Montesquieu had maintained that law was shaped by social, geographical and historical considerations. Burke in England had voiced the same sentiments by pointing to the importance of tradition as a guide to social change. These factors, boosted by the genius of Savigny, started European thought along a new road.

Savigny was born in Frankfurt in 1779, and was nurtured in the natural law discipline. His interest in historical studies was kindled at the universities, first of marburg and then of Gottingen, and was greatly encouraged when he became acquainted with Niebuhr at the University of Berlin. He also acquired a lasting veneration for Roman law. In 1803 appeared his first major work, Das Recht des Bestzes (The Law of Possession), which was considered in Chapter 12, in the last section of which Savigny's distinctive method became apparent. He traced the process by which the original Roman doctrines of possession had developed into the doctrines and actions prevailing in contemporary Europe. Savigny next set himself the task of laying the foundation for future historical labours by producing a basic history of the development of Roman law in mediaeval Europe. It was his thesis that Roman law had been received into Germany so long ago that her legal soul had become a mixture of Roman and local laws. In this great work, The History of Roman Law in the middle ages, which appeared in six volumes between 1815 and 1831, he analysed the Roman element to its roots, and in his other great work. The system of Modern Roman Law, he analysed Roman and local laws. These two together form an imperishable monument to his learning and industry. He was also supremely conscious of his mission, which was not opposed to reform; it was to preach the warning that reforms, which went against the stream of a nation's continuity, were doomed. He emphasised that the muddled and outmoded nature of a legal system was usually due to a failure to comprehend its history and evolution. The essential prerequisite of the reform of German law was, for him, a deep knowledge of its history. Historical research was therefore the indispensable means to the understanding and reform of the present, and he said, somewhat belatedly it is true, but nonetheless clearly:

> "The existing matter will be injurious to us so long as we ignorantly submit to it; but beneficial if we oppose to it a vivid creative energy—obtain the mastery over it by a through grounding in history and thus appropriate to ourselves the whole intellectual wealth of preceding generations."

His warning, then, was that legislators should look before they leap into reform, but he spoilt this wise advice by over-generalisation. The core of Savigny's thesis is to be found in his essay On the Vocation, The nature of any particular system of law, he said, was a reflection of the spirit of the people who evolved it. This was later characterised as the Volksgeist by Puchta, Savigny's most devoted disciple. All law, according to him, is the manifestation of this common consciousness. He wrote,

> "Law grows with the growth, and strengthens with the strength of the people, and finally dies away as the nation loses its nationality."

A nations, to him, meant only a community of people linked together by historical, geographical and cultural ties. The boundaries of some nations may be clearly defined, but not of other nations, and this is reflected in the unity or variety of their respective laws. Even where the unity of a people is clear, there may lie within it "inner circles" of variations, such as cities and guilds. He then went on to elaborate the theory of the volksgest by contending that it is the broad principles of the system that are to be found in the spirit of the people and which become manifest in customary rules. From his initial premise it followed that law is a matter of unconscious growth. Any law-making should therefore follow the course of historical development. Custom not only precedes legislation, but is superior to it, and legislation should always conform to the popular consciousness. Law is thus not of universal application; it varies with peoples and ages. The Volksgeist cannot be criticised for being what it is. It is the standard by which laws, which are the conscious product of the will as distinct from popular conviction, are to be judged. An individual jurist may misapprehend the popular conviction, but that is another matter. In place of the moral authority, which the natural lawyers lawyers of the preceding age had sought to posit behind law, the Historical School substituted social pressure, behind law, the Historical School and that of the Sociological School which succeeded it.

The view of the nature of law dovetailed neatly with Savigny's historical method of work, for if law is s reflection of a people's spirit, then it can only be understood by tracing their history. It is clear, all the same, that in his revolt against the lack of historical sense, which characterised natural law theory, he swung the pendulum of legal thought with unnecessary violence in the opposite direction. But to point out Savigny's exaggerations is not to detract from the very great importance of his contribution.

On the idea of the Volksgeist several comments should be made:

(1) There is undoubtedly an elements of truth in it, for there is a stream of continuity and tradition; the difficulty lies in fixing it with precision. Savigny, however, made too much of it. As with most pioneers, he drew too sweeping an inference from modest premises. The whole idea of the Volksgeist certainly suited the mood of the German people. It was a time of the growing sense of nationhood, a desire for unification, an interest in the dramatic marking the appearance of the Romantic movement. German thinking also, seems somewhat prone to personify the abstract, and to attribute a mystical coherence to ideals. Gierke's personification of corporate existence, was an example; Savigny's Volksgeist is another. The idea of a volksgeist is acceptable in a limited way, but Savigny extrapolated it into a sweeping universal. He treated it as a discoverable thing; but it is common experience that even in a small group, and a fortiori in a nation, people hold different views on different issues. "The" spirit does not exist. So Savigny's whole thesis is probably best treated as the juristic contribution in Romanticism. In this it would appear that his historical sense deserted him, for it amounts, in effect, to the adoption of *a priori* preconception. It will be remembered that in dealing with possession he did much the same thing, namely, to draw and inference from limited date, and then to use it as *a priori* talisman.

(2) The transplanting of Roman law in the alien climate of Europe nearly a thousand years later is inconsistent with Savigny's idea of a Volksgeist. It postulates, if anything, some quality in law other than popular consciousness. His endeavor to establish that the reception of Roman law had taken place so long ago as to make the Germanic Volksgeist an expression if it was unconvincing. Apart from this, a Survey of the contemporary scene shows that the German Civil Code has been adopted in Japan, the Swiss Code in Turkey and the French Code in Egypt without any apparent violence to popular susceptibilities. The French Code was also introduced into Holland during the Napoleonic era, displacing the Roman-Dutch common law, and it is significant that after the overthrow of Napoleno the Dutch never went back. They had, however, taken Roman-Dutch law to their colonies in the Cape of Good Hope and Ceylon with the odd result that it flourishes today in two such dissimilar national climates as southern Africa and Ceylon, although it has long since disappeared in its homeland. The reception of English law in so many parts of the would is also evidence of supra-national adaptability and resilience. Indeed, the great protest in South Africa today is that far too much English law has been allowed to overlay the "national" Roman-Dutch law.

(3) The Volksgeist theory minimises the influence which individuals, somethimes of alien race, have exercised upon legal development. Every man is a product of his time, but occasionally there are men who by their supreme genius are able to give legal development a new direction. The wonderful Classical jurists of Rome, Littleton, Coke, may be cited as examples. This is especially the case in modern times when new doctrines are deliberately introduced by a handful of policy-makers. Ehrlich pointed out that customs are norms of conduct, juristic laws are norms for decision. They are always the creation of jurists.

(4) The last two points lead to the further objection that the influence of the Volksgeist is at most only a limited one. (a) The national character of law seems to manifest itself more strongly in some branches than in others, for example in family law rather than in commercial or criminal law. Thus, the general reception of Roman law in Europe did not include Roman family law. Even more significant is the fact that the successful introduction of alien systems into India and Turkey affected the indigenous family laws least of all. The inference appears to be that very few branches of law, perhaps only family law and succession to some extent, are really "personal" to a nation. (b) A further distinction may have to

be drawn between the creative influence. It is undoubtedly the case that new doctrines have been, and are constantly being, introduced by individuals. The most that indigenous tradition can do is to bring about practical modifications of these gradually and by degrees. Turkey provided a vivid example, where new marriage laws, which were contrary to the existing traditional laws, were introduced as a matter of deliberate policy. The result thereafter, from a juristic point of view, was a fascinating process of action and reaction between the old and new law. It might be thought that this bears out Savigny's contention that legislation should conform to existing traditional law, or it is doomed, in a sense so it does, but an example such as this also reveals something else. It shows that in modern times the function of the Volksgeist is that of modifying and adapting rather than creating, and that, in any case, as just pointed out, even this function manisfests itself only in the very "personal" branches of the law. There is less evidence today of its creative force and none of its influence over the whole body of the law. If one thinks in the time-frame of the moment, the Volksgeist is discernible only in retrospect, but he sought of make it a test of validity, i.e., to use it in the present time-frame where it is irrelevant. This confusion in his frames of reference left his theory open to attack.

(5) Law is sometimes used deliberately to change existing ideas; and it may also be used to further inter-state cooperation in many spheres. Even in Germany one may instance Bismarck's shrewd and successful attempt to cut the ground from under the feet of the socialist movement by introducing the Railway and Factories Accident Law, 1871, well before social conditions were ripe.

(6) Many institutions have originated, not in a Volksgeist, out in the convenience of a ruling oligarchy, e.g., slavery.

(7) Many customs owe their origin to the force of imitation rather than to any innate conviction of their righteousness.

(8) Some rules of cutomary law may not reflect the spirit of the whole population , e.g., local customs. Savigny, it will be remembered, did allow for these by recognising the existence of "inner circles" within a society. But the question remains: if law is the product of a Volksgeist, how is it that only some people and not all have evolved the rule? On the other hand, some coustoms, e.g., the Law Merchant, were cosmopolitan in rogin: they were not the creatures of any particular nation or race. In short, it is not at all clear of any particular nations or race. In short, it is not at all clear who the Volk are whose Geist is said to determine the law.

(9) Important rules of law sometkimes develop as the result of conscious and violent struggle between conflicting interests within the nation, and not as a rusult of imperceptible growth, e.g., the law relating to trade uniouns and industry. Evolution does not follow an inexorably determined part.

(10) A different objection to the volksgeist came from Savigny's opponents. They pointed out that, taken literally, his thesis would thwart the unification of Germany permanently by emphasising the individuality of each separate state and by fostering a parochial sense of nationalism.

(11) An inconsistency in Savigny's work was that, while he was the protagonist of the Volksgeist doctrine, he worked at the same time for the acceptance of a purified Roman law as the law of Germany. There was in Germany in Savigny's day a vigorous school of jurists who strongly advocated the resuscitation of ancient Germanic laws and customs as the foundation of a modernised German system. The leader of this school, Eichorn, was a fellow professor with Savigny at the University of Berlin. Savigny never opposed the work of Eichorn, but he opposed the expulsion of Roman law. The obvious objection to savigny is that his endeavour to preserve Roman law as the law of Germany was inconsistent with his idea of the Volksgeist of the German nation. One explanation lies in his personal devotion to Roman law. Another is that in his earliest work on possession he had been able to expose the misinterpretations of Roman law by later commentators, and this very possible implanted in his mind the idea that the Romans were better craftsmen than incompetent moderns. But the point apparently overlooked by Savigny was that, whatever many have been the case with possession, in other branches of the law these post-Roman interpretations were "adaptation", rather than "perversions", to meet contemporary needs. It might even be argued that the so-called "misinterpretations" were indeed expressions of the Volksgeist of each different country. Another and better reason for the preservation of Roman law might have been that, in view of its long established reception, to dispense with it would have unsettled three centuries of development. In order to account for the original reception of an alien system Savigny argued that at that date the Germanic law was incapable of expressing the Volksgeist. This questionable proposition fails to show how an alien system was better able to express it than the indigenous law. Far from the law being a reflection of the Volksgeist, it would seem that the Volksgeist had been shaped by the law.

Such are the objection to savingy's idea of the Volksgeist. Other aspects of his work of his work also need mention. His veneration for Roman law led him to advance certain dubious propositions. For instanced, there was in Roman law a strict adherence to the doctrine of privity of contract with few exceptions, i.e., no one other than parties to a contract can be entitled or obliged under it. The law of negotiable instruments, of course, is a contradiction of this. Savigny accordingly condemned negotiable instruments as "logically impossible". This reveals one of the more unfortunate results of devotion to a postulate as well as the limitations of the Volksgeist idea. It could hardly be supposed that the populace had any feeling in the matter one way or the other, while the feelings of the commercially minded were strongly in favour of negotiable instruments. Indeed, the whole weakness of Savigny's approach was that he venerated past institutions without regard to their suitability to the present.

The Volksgeist, according to Savigny, only formulates the rudimentary principles of a legal system. He saw clearly enough that it could not provide at the detail that is necessary. He accordingly maintained that as society, and consequently law, becomes more complex, a special body of persons is called into being whose business it is to give technical, detailed expression to the Volksgeist in the various matters with which the law has to deal. These are the lawyers, whose task is to reflect accurately the prevailing Geist. This is nothing but a fictitious assumption, in no way related to reality, to cover up an obvious weakness in his principal contention. As Sir Carleton Allen Said, it is not possible to pretend that the Rule in Shelley's case, for instance, is rooted in the instincts of the British. Savigny's thesis, however, contained another and even more awkward implication. The only persons who talked of the Volksgeist were academic jurists, unversed in the practical problems of legal administration. Therefore, the Volksgeist, resolved itself into what these theorists imagained it to be. On the other hand, it is possible that there is a very limited sense in which Savigny's contention is acceptable, It has already been pointed out that the Volksgeist manifests itself, if at all, only in a few braches of the law and, even in these, by way of modifying and adapting any innovations that may be introduced. So, Savigny's proposition might be taken to mean simply that in these spheres of the law it would be helpful if legislators took account of tradition when framing new laws.

Consistently with this theory, Savigny further maintained that legislation was subordinate to custom. It should at all times conform to the Volksgesit. It has been pointed out that the did not opposes legislation or reform by way of codification at some appropriate time in the future, but his attitude was generally one of pessimism. He certainly opposed the project of immediate codification on several grounds. In the first place, he pointed to the defects of contemporary codes which, to his mind, preserved adventitious, subsidiary and often unsuitable rules of

Roman law, even while they rejected its main principles. Secondly, in matters on which there is no Volksgeist, a code, in his opinion, might introduce new and unadaptable provisions and so add to the prevailing difficulties. Such an argument would appear to have been disposed of by the subsequent experience of many countries. Thirdly, he argued that codification could neven cater exhaustively for all problems that are likely to arise in the future and hence was not a suitable instrument for the development of law. Fourthly, he suggested that an imperfect code would create the worst possible difficulties by perpetuating the follies underlying it. On the other hand, when lawyers were in a position to create a perfect code, no code would then be necessary since the lawyers could adequately cope with the problems that arise. Fifthly, he argued, even more oddly, that codification would highlight the loopholes and weaknesses of the law and so encourage evasion. The short answer to the last two contentions is that they leave out of account the possibility of amendment and alteration. Codification, in Savigny's view, should be preceded by "an organic, progressive, scientific study. Reform should await the results of the historians' work. It is true that reformers should not plunge into legislation without paying some heed to the past as well as to the present. Savigny was over-cautious in this respect, for as Allen observed, his doctrines had the unfortunate tendency "to hang traditions like fetters upon the hands of reformative enterprise". So little in fact did the historians contribute in the years that followed that drastic legislative action became imperative; which it did in 1900.

Savigny's work, on the whole, was a salutary corrective to the methods of the natural lawyers. He did undoubtedly grasp a valuable truth about the nature of law, but ruined it by overemphasis.

Another writer of whom some mention should be made is Gierke (1841-1921). He was profoundly interested in the "association", which has always exercised a peculiar fascination for German thinkers. Associations have significance in law, and are sometimes treated as persons. Gierke denied that the recognition of an association as a person depended on the state. The reality of social control lies in the way in which autonomous groups within society organise themselves. He then proceeded to trace the progress of social and legal development in the form of a history of the law and practice of associations and propounded a classification of associations and propounded a classification on the following lines: firstly, he contrasted groups organised on a territorial basis, such as the state, with those organised on a family or extraterritorial basis: then he contrasted association founded on the idea of fraternal collaboration (Genossenchaften) with those founded on the idea of domination (Herrschaften). In his view legal and social history is most accurately protrayed as a perpetual struggle between the Genossenschaft and the Herrshaft. Thus, in feudal society men were organised in tight hierarchical groups based on the holding of property; this system was opposed in the Middle Ages by the emergence of collaborative groups such as the guild and the city. These degenerated in turn, and with the Renaissance and Reformation the state appeared as the significant factor in social organisation. In his own day Gierke felt that the collaborative in independent collaborative organisations within its own frame-work. The pivot of social control, then, lay not in state organisation, but rather in these collective bodies within the state.

Gierke represented a collectivist, rather than an individualist approach. To this extent his work touched on that of the sociologists. But his interpretation of this development on historical lines entitles him to be ranked among the historians. His doctrines of mass psychology, thought largely fanciful, anticipated modern inquiries. He also never quite succeeded in reconciling the independence of autonomous bodies with the supreme power of the state. He devised a pyramidal structure, which made society consist of a hierarchy of corporate bodies culminating in the state. He wished at the same time to defend the independent existence of the lesser corporate bodies and to limit absolute state power by arguing that the state was the expression of reason and the sense of right. This, of course, was easily brushed aside by those who wished to use Gierke's doctrines as a justification for absolute totalitarian power.

The Dialectic Interpretation

Savigny and his followers did not face the question of how the Volksgeist is formed. His theory therefore appeared to be somewhat incomplete and this opened the way for the reintroduction of a natural law explanation. It became possible to posit again an immutable ideal behind evolution. Variations in historical development emerge in the course of progress towards the realisation of an ideal. If there is some unchanging ideal at the root of it all, then all systems, notwithstanding their evolutionary variations, should share certain common features; which according to this view, they do. This is the explanation of such resemblance, not so much conscious borrowing and analogy. Such an idealised historical interpretation of law is associated with the name of Hegel (1770-1831). It is so abstract as to bear little relation to fact and is far removed from the work of men like Savigny and Gierke.

Hegel distinguished between laws of nature and positive laws. The former are outside human consciousness and can neither be improved nor assisted by men; they have to be accepted because they exist. Positive laws, on the other hand, are man-made and, as such, do not have to be accepted because they exist. This would seem to be approaching the distinction between the "is" and the "ought", but with Hegel that distinction tends to be blurred. He also proceeded to distinguish between the philosophy of law, which concerns the rationality of law, and the study of the positive law itself. Thought is the rational process of synthesising contradictions and of reconciling the general with the particular, the abstract with the concrete. Legal philosophy, being rational, should conceive of law in a rational way. Philosophy is only concerned with reality so far as this is rational, i.e., so far as it is the rational reconciliation of appearance and essence. So, mere factual existence is not "real" in this sense. Since it might be the product of fortuitous (irrational) factors. When therefore Hegel asserted, "The which is rational is real and that which is real is rational", it is important that this remark be understood in the context of his approach and the fact that he was only concerned with ideas.

Hegel sought to explain history on an abstract, evolutionary plane. The idea of evolution as expounded biologically by Darwin was shortly to influence human thinking profoundly. Hegel, however, a little earlier saw it unfolding as a process of action and reaction between opposites, thesis and anti-thesis, which results in their synthesis, the whole broadening slowly towards the realisation of freedom. The "idea", says Hegel, has as it's antithesis the "idea outside itself", which is nature. The synthesis is "spirit" (of which Savigny's Volksgeist is possibly an aspect). The subjective spirit (thought and consciousness) and its synthesised in the absolute spirit. Law comes into the category of objective spirit. Law and other social institutions are the result of free subjective will endeavouring to realise freedom objectively. In this development the starting-point is the idea of freedom, which implies will. Freedom and will are complementary. Personality arises when the will becomes individualised. The idea of freedom has a three-fold sphere of operation. There is, first the freedom of the individual in relation to himself, which concerns his proprietary rights. Secondly, there is the perception of freedom in others in conformity with the common will of all, which brings in contract. Thirdly, the freedom of the individual opposes itself to the common will, which is wrongdoing. Taken in turn, and stated most baldly, the explanations are as follows. As to property, the free will of a person is imposed on a thing, which is unfree and impersonal. A thing has no end in itself and only acquires one from the will of the individual. The right of property is therefore the first manifestation of freedom. Contract is approached from the angle of property. Not only may property be the subject of one person's will, but it may also come within the purview of another person's will. When a thing is held by virtue of the individual's conformity with their mutual will, the matter falls into the sphere of contract. Wrongdoing occurs when the will of the individual is opposed to the general will. The conflict then brings about morality, which is the anti-thesis of freedom. Social ethics is the synthesis between these two. Social ethics starts at the level of the family. When members of the family become independent, society comes into being with its attendant institutions of law, etc. Society is then the anti-thesis of family. The synthesis is the state, which combines freedom and social co-existence. In the state Hegel found the highest achievement of human endeavour, and to be a member of the state was to him the supreme objective. The individual is the product of his culture and age, which are realised only through the state. Law and state are thus concrete manifestations of the national spirit, which together with others are in turn a manifestation of a world spirit.

On all this it might be remarked that one seeks in vain for the facts to which these formidable abstractions relate. For the purpose of his demonstration of conflict Hegel attributed objective existence to values and natural phenomena. But is should be pointed out that the conflict between thesis and anit-thesis is a logical contradiction, whbich is not the case with natural phenomena. If he had confined his attention to the action and reaction of ideas as evidenced by historical fact, he might well have been led to other, though less imposing, conclusions. Besides to treat values as having objective existence is to make an "is" out of "ought". All in all, his highly abstract scheme is nothing but a verbal juggle into which divergent interpretations can be fitted. It is therefore not surprising to find it being utilised in support of two such dissimilar ideologies as Nazism and Marxism.

The Biological Interpretation

A variant of the historical interpretation and one which also sought to find the clue to the nature of contemporary law in evolutionary processes is the so-called Biological approach. The publication of Darwin's On the Origin of Species in 1859 was destined to affect human thought profoundly in many directions. Side by side with this there was the rise of psychology as a new fashion in thinking with a concomitant preoccupation with group psychology. Its effect in legal theory is to be seen in the interpretation. Its effect in legal theory is to be seen in the interpretation of law as the product of evolutionary forces, and in this connection the work of Herbert Spencer (1820-1903) is a characteristic example.

Darwin's broad thesis was that evolution was a struggle for existence in which those creatures that are able to adapt themselves to changing conditions survive. In human beings the survival of the fittest called for the development of the social instinct. Spencer also adopted the idea that a collection of individuals form a community. He promulgated three fundamental laws of society, the principles of persistence of force, the indestructibility of matter, and the continuity of motion. The combination of these principles with other laws results in the process of evolution, which is that process by which an amorphous, homogeneous mass evolves into a series of distinct, orderly bodies. Spencer then proceeded to draw parallels between the social organism and biological organism.

The adaptation of the individual to social conditions is due to heredity. He inherits a social instinct from his ancestors, including ideas of morality, obligation, right and justice. In this way different sociological groups evolve differently and so, too, do their laws and institutions.

There are two stages in the progress of civilisation. In the fists which is primitive, war and compulsion figure prominently; in the second, which is advanced, peace and freedom are prominent. Spencer, however, was a strong individualist with a *laissez faire* approach to government. He denied the complete absorption of the individual in the state and maintained that the duty of government was to secure the greatest possible amount of individual freedom. He abhorred any form of welfare activities by the state. Each person may do what he lies, provided he does not infringe the equal freedom of others. His theory of evolution together with his *laissez faire* idea of government led him to a reactionary position with regard to legislative reform. He held that all conscious legislative attempts to improve social organisations were doomed to failure and that Man must await the working out of evolutionary laws.

Whatever may have been left of Spencer's theory has disappeared with the advent of the welfare state; his biology would now be dismissed as crude. The objections to his theory were epitomised by Mr. Justice Holmes, who said:

> "The liberty of the citizen to do as he likes so long as he does not interfere with the liberty of others to do the same, which has been a shibboleth for some well-known writers, is interfered with by school laws, by the Post Office, by every state and municipal institution which takes his money for purposes thought desirable, whether he likes it or not. The Fourteenth Amendment does not enact Mr. Herbert Spencer's Social Statice."

Spencer's work does represent, however, the transition from the historical approach to the sociological.

The Racial Theory of Law

This was the theory of law that prevailed in National Socialist Germany Under Hitler. It was nothing more than an emotional and militant adaptation of theories and ideas in support of the quest for power. From the biological interpretation was derived the idea that law was inherited by blood. The Historical School was made to lend its support in seeking the roots of the law in the past and for the nationalistic flavour that was imparted to it. The writings of Hegel, who showed how the individual could be integrated into society, were utilised so as to suppress individual rights.

The National Socialist theory of law revolved round two cardinal principle. The application of the first was as follows. The state is a group and a group has no strength or unity without a leader. The leader, therefore, becomes the mystical personification of national unity. Law and state mean the same thing, and since the leader is the embodiment of the state, law is what the leader commands. This had three implications: (a)

Unquestioning obedience was demanded. (b) Law should serve political ends. (c) Nothing, not even reverence for statutes, should stand in the way of implementing the will of the leader. According to the "racial principle" law was inherited by blood. It should (a) serve the ends of the state and its policies. (b) It should help to preserve racial purity, for the state cannot be strong unless it is racially pure. This was the justification for the persecution of the Jews. (c) The Code of 1900 was attacked on the ground that its basis was Justinian's Byzantine version of Roman law. Therefore, besides being an alien system, it was condemned as being "oriental" and "Jewish" in origin. (d) The only international system which could be tolerated was a Nordic one, i.e., one based on a blood tie. The League of Nations could therefore command no respect. Every state has a natural privilege and power to prevail over other states and to take their land as room for its people. Any treaty which attempted to restrict this privilege could rightly be ignored.

It is fortunately not necessary to dwell on the details of this perverted conception of law, nor to enter into a refutation of it. The answer of a sort that did come at the end of a world shattering war was effective enough.

ANTHROPOLOGICAL APPROACH

Anthropological investigations into the nature of primitive and undeveloped systems of law are of modern origin and might be regarded as a product of the Historical School. Pride of place will here be accorded to Sir Henery Maine (1822-1888), who was the first and still remains the greatest representative of the historical movement in England. It is not easy to place Maine's contributions to the theory of law. He began his work with a mass of material already published on the history and development of Roman law by the German Historical School, and he was able to build upon that and also to bring to bear a more balanced view of history than if found in Savigny. Maine, however, went further. He was learned in English, Roman and Hindu laws and also had knowledge of Celtic systems. In this respect he parts company with the German historians. Instead of stressing the uniqueness of national institutions, he brought to bear a scientific urge to unify, classify and generalise the evolution of different legal orders. Thus, he inaugurated both the comparative and anthropological approaches to the study of law, and history in particular, which was destined to bear abundant fruit in the years to come.

Maine set out to discover whether a pattern of legal development could be extracted from a comparative examination of different systems. Especially between Roman law and the common law. What he sought were laws of historical development. He was led to distinguish between what he called "static" and "progressive" societies. The early development of both types is roughly the same and falls, in his thesis, into four stages. The first stage is that of law-making by personal command, believed to be of divine inspiration, e.g., Themistes of ancient Greece, and the dooms of the Anglo-Saxon kings. The second stage occurs when those commands crystallise into custom. In the third stage the ruler is superseded by a minority who obtain control over the law, e.g., the pontiffs in ancient Rome. The fourth stage is the revolt of the majority against this oligarchic monopoly, and the publication of the law in the form of a code, e.g., the XII Tables in Rome.

"Static" societies, according to Maine, do not progress beyond this point. The characteristic Feature of "progressive" societies is that these proceed to develop the law by three methods—fiction, equity, and finally legislation. Ample examples of the use of fiction are to be found in Roman and early English law. The operation of equity and legislation has been considered in the earlier chapters of this book.

As a general inference Maine believed that no human institution was permanent, and that change was not necessarily for the better. Unlike Savigny, he favoured legislation and codification. He recognised that the advance of civilisation demanded an increasing use of legislation, and he often contended that the confused state of English law was due to its pre-eminently judge-made character. Codification is an advanced form of legislative development, and represents the stage at which all the preceding phases of development are woven into a coherent whole. He also did not share Savigny's mystique of the Volksgeist.

Side by side with these doctrines Maine developed another thesis. In early societies, both "static" and "progressive", the legal condition of the individual is determined by status, i.e., his claims, duties, liberties, etc. are determined by law. The march of "progressive" societies witnesses of disintegration of status and the determination of the legal condition of the individual by free negotiation on his part. This was expressed in one of Maine's most famous generalisations:

> "The movement of progressive societies has hitherto been a movement from Status to Contract."

An evaluation of Maine's work must take into account the pioneer character of his comparative investigations. Since his day the study of anthropology has developed into a separate branch of learning. Modern research over a wider field and with better equipment has corrected Maine's work at many points, and departed from it at others. One should be charitable about his errors and marvel at his genius in accomplishing so much. Some comment should, however, be made about the development from status to contract. There was much to support it. In Roman law there was the gradual amelioration of the condition of children, women and slaves, the freeing of adult women from tutelage, and the acquisition of a limited contractual capacity by children, women and slaves, the freeing of adult women from tutelage, and the acquisition of a limited contractual capacity by children and slaves. In English laws the bonds of serfdom were relaxed and eventually abolished. Employment came to be based on a contractual basis between master and servant. Maine's own age was one in which legislation was removing the disabilities of Catholic, Jews, Dissenters and married women. He witnessed the triumph in the American Civil War of the North, a community based on contract, over the feudal and status-regulated South. In the modern age, however, a return to status has been detected. In public affairs, and in industry in particular, the individual is no longer able to negotiate his own terms. This is the age of the standardised contract, and of collective bargaining. Such developments, however, should not be held against Maine. He was not purporting to prophesy and, indeed, he expressly qualified his proposition by saying that the development had "hitherto" been a movement towards contract.

Modern anthropologists have had the advantage of following the trails blazed by Maine and by others after him with the added advantage of being able to profit from the researches of fellow-workers in many directions. It is not surprising, therefore, to find that maine's conclusions about primitive law have now been discredited or modified. The idea that early development passed through the successive stages of personal judgments, oligarchic monopoly and code has been abandoned as drawing too simple a picture. Primitive societies are seen to have been more complex than had been supposed. There have been several forms of such societies, so there is an initial problem of determining what sorts of societies should be classified as "primitive". It is now thought that there were seven grades of them, the First and Second Hunters, the First, Second and Third Agricultural Grades, and the First and Second Pastoral Grades. The agricultural and pastoral grades are to some extent parallel. The degree of development of social institutions does bear some correspondence with the degree of economic development. From all this it will be gathered that primitive societies exhibit a wide range of institutions; there is nothing like a single patterns as Maine had supposed.

There has also been modification of the sequence, as stated by Maine, of later development, namely by means of fiction, equity and legislation. Deliberate legislation is now seen to have been an early method of law-making with fiction and equity coming in at a later stage. The codes, which one finds at the culmination of the primitive period, were chiefly collections of earlier legislation.

Primitive law was by no means as rigid as mains as rigid as Maine had supposed, nor were people inflexibly bound by it. Field-work among "contemporary primitives" has revealed that considerable latitude in inherent in the content of their customary practices. For instance, Malinowski's first-had experience of life among certain Pacific islanders enabled him to demonstrate how, e.g., their practices make allowance for good and bad harvests, or take due account of an excess of generosity on the part of individuals. Observations by Gluckman of the Barotse of Northern Rhodesia have shown that the very indeterminate character of their standards permits a desirable flexibility in application. Rigidity develops at a much later period. Above all, it is generally agreed that even in primitive societies people do control their destinies, that they are by no means blindly subservient to custom. The conscious purpose of achieving some end precedes the adaptation of human behaviour, and the adaptation of behaviour is followed by adaptations of the structure of social organisation.

It used to be accepted that law and religion were indistinguishable in primitive societies. This view has given way to an increased recognition of the secular character of primitive law. The exact extent to which law and religion were associated seems, however, to be in some doubt. Diamond, for example, criticises Maine most strongly for his assertion that they were indistinguishable; the association of the two, in his view, is a comparatively late development. Hoebel, on the other hand, defends Maine on this point. Hocart believed that the dualism between religion and the secular authority (the state) originated in a division of function between a "sky-king", who was the supreme regulator and as such responsible for law, and an "earth-king", who was charged with the task of dealing with evil and wrongdoing; the former was reflective and unimpassioned, the latter quick in decision and violent in action. The role of the "sky-king" would seem to have combined religion and law. Further, if Hocart is right there seems to be implicit in this the distinction between the primary, prescriptive patterns of conduct and the secondary machinery of sanction; which leads on to the next point.

It is likewise agreed among anthropologists that there is, at any rate as far as contemporary primitive societies are concerned, a phenomenon that can be isolated from religious and other social observances and for which the term "law" would be convenient. Bohannan has suggested that law comes into being when customary reciprocal obligations become further institutionalised in a way the society continues to function on the basis of rules. These concern mainly the relations of individuals *inter se* and of groups, i.e., primary patterns of conduct importing an "ought". Gluckman has shown that among the Barotse the laws consist mainly of positive injunctions, "you ought", rather than negative, "you ought not". These "oughts" of primitive law are distinguishable from others by the nature of the obligation to obey them. It was a cardinal point of Malinowski's thesis, supported by Hogbin, that obedience to customs rests on the reciprocity of services. People do unto others what the law bids them do because they depend on some service in return as part of their mutual co-existence. It is spontaneous and incessant goodwill that promotes and preserves social existence. It is possible that Malinowski underestimated the part played by sanctions. It might well be also that the ceremonial with which these services are usually rendered underlines their obligatory character, not disobedience, that is contemplated by law, the primary rule, not sanction. But some mechanism there has to be for dealing with cases of conflict and breach. As long as obedience prevails there is no call for this machinery. Examples of its working are also of interest. For instance, the records kept by Gluckman of the judicial processes among the Barotse show that the main task is reconciliation rather than the ordering of sanctions, which implies that even at the secondary stage an attempt is made to ensure conformity with the primary pattern of conduct. Sanctions apply only when reconciliation has failed or is not possible. One form which these take is to abandon the wrongdoer to the avenger, who has the moral support of the community behind him. In other cases, compensation may be payable to the victim, and it is a matter of dispute whether vengeance preceded compensation or whether they existed side by side. This is why it is difficult to distinguish between civil and criminal wrongdoing in early societies. The question depended on whether the action was thought to affect the society or only the individual. In the result, the conclusion which most anthropologists have reached is that what is called "law" should be described in terms of its function and the attitude of the people towards it rather than in terms of form or enforcement. It would appear to be something compulsorily observed and certainly far from what is commanded or backed by sanction.

Lastly, another point, which has emerged from modern investigations, is the disposal of the belief in communism as the primitive form of society. This may be seen in many ways, particularly in the prevalence of jealously protected private ownership of socially productive weapons and institutions, such as spells, incantations and, above all, ritual.

So far not much has been said, save indirectly, of the organisation of government. In this connection the outstanding contribution of Hocart deserves mention, especially as his name is insufficiently known among jurists. On the evidence collected from a large number of widely separated tribes in many parts of the world. Hocart came to the conclusion that the functions of modern government were gradually fitted into the framework of a machinery that was previously fulfilling other functions. In other words, the framework of government was there before there was any governing to be done. Man does not consciously seek government; he seeks life, and with that end in view he does one thing after another, evolving and adapting special procedures and techniques, till he finds himself governed. The means by which primitive societies sought life was ritual. The lives and well-being of individuals depended on the life and well-being of society. Ritual was therefore a social affair and society had to organise itself for it. The structure of ritual was such that different roles were assigned to different individuals and groups. In all this one may detect the origin of caste; the various castes that one finds, the fisher, the farmer, the launderer, the potter, etc. may not have derived from the trades that the people actually pursued, but from the roles they fulfilled in the ritual. There probably was some connection between trade and a role, for no doubt it was usual to assign to a person the role which he was fitted to fulfil whenever this was possible.

It was the organisation, founded on ritual, that was adapted for purposes of government. Since the king could not play every role simultaneously, he assigned to each chieftain a particular role simultaneously, he assigned to each chieftain a particular role which had a particular objective. The aim of the ritual was the control of nature so as to render it bounteous and abundant. The particular form which the ritual assumed in any given case depended on the aspect of nature which was to be controlled, whether sunshine or rain or harvest or game, etc. To the group that was identified with some aspect of nature was entrusted the ritual concerning it. It follows from this, first, that only the group that exclusively owned a particular ritual was competent to perform it; secondly, every ritual had its leader; thirdly, the performers did not merely imitate nature as it happened to be at the moment, but as they wanted it to behave, e.g., to shed rain at a time of drought—an "ought" not an "is"; fourthly, in order to control nature the performers had to become one with nature and identify themselves with it; and fifthly, such equivalence was accomplished by the "word", which thus acquired special significance.

There was always a tendency for rituals to coalesce in one person or group of persons. The greatest cumulator was the king and this process of cumulation is centralisation. Even after the king had begun to fulfil several roles, his chiefs had to stand ready to lend their assistance if called on to do so. In the role of the sun the king became the supreme regulator of the world, and this regulative function assumed greater and greater importance and eventually became the mark of the king. The aim of the ritual, as has been remarked, was to make nature bounteous. It followed that nature should itself be amply provided before a generous return could be expected of it. The king being identified with nature, the prosperity of the people could only be achieved by making the king prosperous. Revenue and tribute were the means of making him so.

In these and various other ways Hocart discerned the outlines of government, the organs of which were fitted into the existing framework of ritual. It is not possible in this short space to pursue his demonstration further, nor to consider his parallel investigations into the meaning of ceremonial statement, doctrines and courtesies relating to monarchy even today. One thing, which his analysis has endorsed is the prescriptive nature and function or primitive law.

CONCLUSION

To much attention on those factors of the past that have shaped the content of the "oughts" of the law of today should not be allowed to throw other factors out of focus. Historical factors are not nearly so important as those factors of today, for it is not so much what shaped an "ought" in the past that matters as the factors that conspire to keep if alive. It is suggested that historical approaches would find their appropriate setting as part of a general sociological approach. Another weakness is the mystical, nationalistic flavour which it imparted to theories about law, but this has not penetrated through to his country. Again, historical interpretation can so easily be made to lend its support to the particular ideology of the interpreter. Savigny's whole teaching evolved out of his strongly conservative, anti-revolutionary, Civil law bias. Spencer's biological parallels could just as easily have led him to conceive of the state as a unifying organism in which the individual loses his identity; in fact, it was only his individualist outlook that led him to other conclusions. Of the manner in which historical interpretation was used in support of the Nazi ideology it is not necessary to speak.

Against all this, some of the practical contributions of the Historical School, leaving aside its more extreme manifestations, have had lasting effect. It provided the great stimulus to the historical study of law and legal institutions, which has ingrained a sense of historical perspective in the outlook of lawyers. In England it inspired men like Maine, Maitland and Holdsworth and others scarcely less famous. It has demonstrated the perils of over-hasty legislative experiment and has taught the cautionary lesson that development should flow, in some spheres at any rate, within the channels of tradition. As to the nature of law, it has demonstrated the connection between some parts of law and cultural evolution, and the need to delve into the past some times in order to obtain a full understanding of the law as it is at present. Above all, it awakened new confidence in convictions relating to the content of law by insisting that formal criteria of validity are of subordinate importance. In this way it may have had an indirect result in paving the way for the resurgence of natural law in this century, which seeks to base even the validity of law on its moral content.

On the question what kind of a concept of law would be apt for historical investigation, it would seem that so far as the study seeks to uncover the factors that have shaped the institutions of today what is needed is a concept which not only identifies the "oughts" of the law, but also includes the dynamic force that have shaped and developed them. So far as the investigation is anthropological, a formal criterion of identification does not appear to be appropriate or applicable. A broader conception is needed and one that will distinguish institutions the social reaction to them. It is clear from what has been said that anthropological inquiries have given to the "ought" fascinating new interpretations.

8

ECONOMIC APPROACHES

It might be regarded as a variant of the historical approach in so far as it has sought to unfold a pattern of evolution; but it also concerns the part which law has played and is playing in society and, as such, is distinctly sociological. It will be clear, therefore, that this approach, like these others, concerns the content of law, the nature of which is regarded as being but a reflex of an economic substrate. Another point of interest is that the original Marxist interpretation challenged the indispensability of law and foreshadowed its eventual disappearance. "Law" in Marxist theory lumps together laws and their administration, so it is in this sense that the term will be employed herein.

Many factors may be said to have contributed to the rise of the movement now under review. The critical spirit of positivism had accustomed people to challenge existing standards. Advances in contemporary science shed their influence in the same direction. The failure of religious ideals to stand up to critical inquiry led to the substitution of materialist ideals in their place. The new movement had as its object the improvement of the condition of poor and working people, who found in it new hope and encouragement. Formal positivism was largely indifferent to the justice or injustice of existing conditions of life. Although Bentham was more concerned with reform that with formal analysis, his successors in the analytical tradition, notable the Austinians, concerned themselves increasingly with the law as laid down and not with efforts to improve it. In consequence, positivism fell into disfavour with those who were dissatisfied with existing conditions, and was regarded as casting a cloak of legality around injustices. The new movement was iconoclastic and was able to expose some of the injustices concealed behind traditional facades. It accordingly appealed to a certain type of mind, which felt for the first time enlightened and emancipated. Unfortunately, the enthusiasm which it aroused prevented its own assumptions from being subjected to similar iconoclastic scrutiny. It called for action and change and was revolutionary in purpose and so appealed to all who felt inclined to rebel against complacency and monotony.

The interpretation of law as part of an economic interpretation of social evolution is a by-product of the social and political theories of Marx and Engels, which have since been put into practice by Soviet Russia and certain other countries. Russia was the first to do so, and for over twenty years until after the Second World War remained the only one. Other countries have largely copied her, so the ensuing discussion will proceed with reference of Russia. One difficulty in the way of its presentation is the absence of any theory of law worked out on this basis. Neither Marx nor Engles elaborated one for reasons that will shortly become clear. What they say about law is incidental to their views on society generally. Jurists in Russia today, however, are having to work out a theory of law, but as yet none of them has said a great deal that is new: each plays a variation on the basic theme derived from Marx and Engles. It is therefore to their works that attention should first be paid. The practical application of their doctrines since their day has necessitated certain changes and adaptations, which leads to the next difficulty, namely, deciding into what periods the narrative should fall. On this there is no unanimity. For present purposes it is sufficient to adhere to the following scheme. (i) The period of "war communism", including the "theoretical" period from Marx to 1920, i.e., the establishment of the proletarian dictatorship in Russia. (ii) The period form 1921 to 1937, which could be subdivided into the period of the New Economic policy, the N.E.P., from 1921 to 1929; and from 1930 to 1937, the "construction of socialism", during which the N.E.P. was abandoned. (iii) The period from 1938 to the present day, which could be sub-divided into the period from 1938 until the death of Stalin in 1953, which may be called "consolidation of socialism"; and the post-Stalin era, which may be called "construction of communism", at least since 1961.

I. THE PERIOD FROM MARX TO 1920

The views about law of Karl Marx (1818-1883) and of his great friend, Friedrich Engles (1820-1895), are to be gleaned from their various works. Marx was influenced, so Lenin insisted, by developments in contemporary science, in particular the prevalent belief that the physical world was governed by a universal principle of causation. He believed that social phenomena were likewise governed by some universal principle, namely, the economic principle. In this respect he was a social scientist in that he sought descriptive propositions about social evolution. He was also influenced by the dialectic philosophy of Hegel, but differed from him over the Hegelian notion that reality and, indeed, history was the unfolding of an "idea". On the contrary, said Marx, the "idea" is a reflection of reality, otherwise the idea is only a distortion or "ideology"; and this is what he meant when he said of Hegel's dialectics that "with him it is standing on its head. It must be turned right side up again." Marx and Engels insisted on being "scientific". Although, like Hegel, they visualised history as unfolding according to the recurrent conflict between a thesis and an anti-thesis, in place of his ideals they substituted material and economic forces and the determinant factors of development. "Scientific socialism", so they preached, must replace "utopian socialism".

The primitive tribal society, in their view, contained no antithesis within itself as long as there was equal distribution of commodities. It was a communist order, an Eden, before it was perverted through selfishness and greed. When distribution became unequal, the society was destroyed and split into classes patterned by the division of capital and labour. Man became avaricious and self-centred with no thought of the common weal. The value of commodities then came to be governed by the cost of the labour required to produce them. The place of the tribal society was taken by the state, which became the instrument of the stronger class, whether this is described as a slave-owner's state, a feudal state, or bourgeois state. The modern capitalist state necessarily involves the domination of the labouring majority by a minority, who control the economic resources of the country; law is an instrument by which this minority exploit the workers. The tension between capital and labour will eventually break into conflict, a revolt of the majority against the minority, and the majority will gain control of the economic resources and will seek to eliminate the minority. The state thus established is the proletarian dictatorship.

> "After the proletariat has grasped power, the class struggles does not cease. It continues in new forms, and with ever greater frenzy and ferocity, for the reason that the resistance of the exploiters to the fact of socialism in more savage than before."

The dictatorship of the proletariat is said to represent "the highest form of democracy possible in a class society", and is also "substantially the dictatorship of the Party, as the force which effectively guides the proletariat". The term "democracy" is here used in a sense different from that in the West. The proletarian dictatorship is indeed a dictatorship, but in so far as it has been formed by the masses and acts in their interests it is a democracy. The distribution of commodities at this stage of development will follow the maxim, "From each according to his ability, to each according to his work". Inequality inevitably persists and state organisation continues to be necessary.

Out of this conflict will eventually emerge communism or the classless society. Domination will cease, inequalities will vanish, and with them the state and law will disappear as well. It is not altogether clear when Marx and Engels expected the advent of utopia. It may be (a) when production has reached such a point that all people can be supplied with their needs without having to compel them to work, in short, when the maxim, "From each according to his ability, to each according to his needs", can be applied. (b) It may be when crime and other forms of wrongdoing have been eliminated, for as long as these continue the machinery for their repression will continue to be needed. Lenin believed that after the removal of the economic causes of crime, a great part of, if not all, wrongdoing will disappear. (c) More recently Soviet jurists have tended to postpone the disappearance of the state until capitalism disappears in all, or most other countries, in other words, when the danger of capitalist encirclement disappears.

Marx supposed that the defects and inequalities in human society were due to factors that lay in production and economic conditions and outside the nature of Man. This assumes that Man is by nature equal and free, and that only in the communist society would he be able to realise his true self. For, as both Lenin and Stalin asserted, the individual will only be liberated when the mass is liberated. "Everything", said Stalin, "for the mass".

From all this the following doctrines are deducible as to the nature of law.

(1) Doctrine of the Economic Determination of Law

Ideas, according to Marx, are reflections of reality; and in this respect he differed, as pointed out, from Hegel, who maintained that reality was but a reflection of an idea. A false or distorted appreciation of reality was to Marx an "ideology" in a derogatory sense. The bourgeois picture of society if an ideology distorted to suit the situation of those who present it, namely, the ruling class, in whose interest it is to give a false picture and quieten the masses and further their own ends. Law is a superstructure on an economic system; economic facts are independent of and antecedent to law. The notion that law is a reflex of an economic substrate is not an ideology, for it accords with reality. Bourgeois theories of law, however, which present is as something other than this, are distortions. There may be other superstructures and other ideologies, e.g., religion, but they all have their ultimate reality in the economic background.

(2) Doctrine of the Class Character of Law

Law is an instrument used by the economic rulers to keep the masses in subjection. Even after the establishment of the proletarian dictatorship law will continue to be used as the instrument by which the working-class majority can crush and eliminate the capitalist minority. There will still be the need to force people to work, to punish wrongdoing, to stamp out "counter-revolutionary" and other subversive activities, and to maintain some inequality of distribution, which is still unavoidable. Law is thus an instrument of domination.

(3) Doctrine of the Identity of Law and State

The state came into existence as soon as there was unequal distribution of commodities and class distinctions developed. Law was one of the means whereby the capitalist minority sought to preserve and increase their power, while those who had property sought to protect it against those who had not. So law and the state in capitalist societies together form an apparatus of compulsion wielded by the minority to oppress and exploit the working majority. Even in the proletarian dictatorship these will remain as instruments of compulsion and domination. The state, therefore, reflects an essentially unequal condition of affairs. The depiction of it as a just and fair institution is again a distorted ideology. It will be noticed that this doctrine of the identity of law and the state corresponds with that of Kelsen, but for entirely different reasons.

(4) Doctrine of the Withering Away of Law and State

When the communist or classless society arrives, there will no longer by any domination or inequality. Therefore, the instruments of domination, i.e., law and the state, will, in the words of Engels, "wither away" and be replaced by "an administration of things". If it is asked how criminality and wrongdoing will be dealt with, Lenin replied that, in the first place, no special machinery will be needed:

> "this will be done by the armed people itself as simply and readily as any crowd of civilised people, even in modern society, parts a pair of combatants or does not allow a woman to be outraged:" secondly, "we know that the fundamental social cause of excesses which consist in violating the rules of social life is the exploitation of the masses, their wand and their poverty. With the removal of this chief cause, excesses will inevitably begin to 'wither away'."

This doctrine of the withering away of the state is an uncomplimentary comment on the dialectics of Hegel. It is now worth-noticing that, whereas to Hegel the state was the highest achievement of human endeavour, Marx used his method of reasoning to arrive at the extinction of the state. It should also be noted in this connection that what will wither away is the proletarian dictatorship, which is, as it were, a step towards the classless society. The bourgeois state will not wither away; this has to be smashed and destroyed.

The reason why neither Marx nor Engels elaborated a theory of law should now be obvious. Law, in their view, was an instrument of domination, to be done away with, not developed and elaborated. Although they regarded law as reflecting economic conditions, it would not be fair to suggest that they thereby deprived to of all its creative force. It can play, and has played, a creative part, but always conditioned by its economic substrate. In the proletarian dictatorship law should be a means to an end, namely, to prepare the way for the classless society. It is thus an instrument of governmental policy. There is certainly rule by law; there cannot be a rule of law, for reverence of the law for its own sake is a "bourgeois fetish". Since law is but a means to an end, it should on no account hamper the work of the proletarian state. There should be no division between "public" and "private" law, because (a) law being a reflection of an economic substrate, there will be no public and private spheres of interests is the economy, and (b) law being an instruments of domination, only the proletarian government will dominate and there is thus only governmental law. Nor will there by any separation of powers. Judicial independence as traditionally understood must go. Judges are instruments of policy and must give effect to this, to which end they have to be strongly in doctrinated before they can be fit for office. Thus, in the early days of the proletarian dictatorship in Russia Judges had to apply their "socialist consciousness" of justice and such Tsarist laws that were useful guides in the absence of decrees of the Soviet government. Even so, they did not have to apply a provision which they considered unsuited to the new conditions. In criminal cases server penalties were to be inflicted on enemies of the regime than on those who interfered with their fellow citizens from purely personal motives. It was left originally to the judge to decide whether a given act was prejudicial to the regime or was purely personal in character. This was the notorious "principle of analogy" according to which all socially harmful conduct could be treated as criminal. This doctrine went into decline, but it did carry the interesting corollary that conduct which, although technically criminal, was not socially harmful should not be treated as such. Equally drastic was "guilt by association" whereby members of the family of a person convicted of certain offences against the state, who knew of his activities but did not denounce him, were punishable. This, too, has gone. Finally, although it would not be true to aver that individuals should enjoy no liberties other than those expressly conferred upon them, there has to be nevertheless a strict regulation of these, especially in regard to property, according to governmental policy.

The principal difficulty in the way of assessing the doctrines of Marx and Engels lies in sifting the parts that are valuable from irrelevancies. In the first place, causation is now no longer regarded as an inexorable principle governing the material world. This is the same erroneous assumption that was made by the Historical School. In social phenomena Marx and Engels sought to discover in the economic principle the counterpart of causation.

Towards the end of his life, however, Engles admitted that both he and Marx had exaggerated the economic influence and that it was not the sole motivating factor in human society. What they would say, then, is that it is the ultimate or most important factor. That depends on the criterion of "ultimate" and "most important". It ceases to be objective and becomes a matter of personal evaluation. The economic factor is undoubtedly important, but other factors have also to be reckoned with. Traffic law, for example, and large parts of criminal law are not based on economics. Indeed, the law which has to deal with violence to the person has been brought about by weaknesses in human nature. It is a wishful pretence to say that impulses such as anger, lust, revenge and jealousy, to mention but a few, are always rooted in economics. Today, the second generation of Soviet youth, which never knew capitalism, exhibits much the same tendencies as youth elsewhere, and the Russians have started somewhat belatedly to develop criminology. Cupidity is not rooted exclusively in the economics of capitalism, but in human nature; increased availability of the good things of life whets the appetite for more. Furthermore, although Marx foresaw the "managerial revolution", he treated it as part of the dialectic of capitalist development and did not appear to have grasped its full implications. Modern economists have long since abandoned Marx's labour theory of value, which has become inapplicable to conditions of mass production and still more so to "automation". There can be no other conclusion than that an explanation of history in terms of some single determinant factor will inevitable fail, for it is bound to be an over-simplification.

This leads to another point. Both Marx and Engels purported to be "scientific", i.e., they found the cause of existing ills in economic conditions and suggested that the cure lies in a rectification of the economic system. But so far as the economic factor is not the only one underlying law and society, the picture they drew of these in the light of the economic factor alone is incomplete; it is, in other words, a distortion of "ideology" in Marx's own sense of that term. The degree of distortion is proportionate to the importance of the factors omitted. Marx seems to have confused legal theory, which may be described as an "ideology" in his sense of the term in that it reflects "reality", and actual laws, which are an integral part of the economic infrastructure of society, i.e., part of the "reality" itself. The classless society which he envisaged is the end which he wanted to bring about, and in this is a distortion of another kind, the introduction of a teleological consideration, of politics into science, carrying with it a moral obligation consideration, of politics into science, carrying with it a moral obligation to further this end. The ideological character of Marxism is evidenced by the fact that the Soviet authorities dare not admit that there are flaws in the basic thesis. Their attitude has been that the "truth" is there if only the correct interpretation can be found, or else to ignore or minimise awkward facts, thereby making the doctrine a religion.

Marx explained the evolution of society on the basis of the class struggle, the struggle between capitalists and workers. It is undeniable that there has been considerable friction between them, but generalisations should only be made with the utmost circumspection. "The" class struggle, or any class struggle, should always be related to the place where it occurred, the period, the persons involved, and other circumstances. It is a shortcoming in this respect that leaves Marx's handling of historical facts open to doubt. There have been many class struggles in the course of human history, and they have all influenced the development of law and society, e.g., religious struggles and not least between Trotskyists, Leninists and Maoists. It is also not clear why "the class struggle" has to culminate in violence. It may be that human nature being what it is, capitalists will not relinquish their position without force. As against that, Great Britain and the Scandinavian countries have shown a peaceful road to socialism. Although a recurrent pattern of conflict between workers and capitalists can be detected, the danger of erecting it into a principle and of arguing mechanically from it can be seen in the following fact. According to Marx, the tension between workers and capitalists grows more acute with the development of capital. This will tend to become more and more international, and hence the famous call to the workers of the world to unite. This led to the conclusion that the conflict will be precipitated in those countries where capitalism is most developed. Instead, it occurred in Russia, which was at that date semi-feudal and had only the rudiments of capitalism. This was why some orthodox Marxists at the time wondered whether they would not be better engaged in promoting a capitalist revolution instead. For a quarter of a century Russia remained alone, and the next country in which the conflict occurred was China, another very backward state. The countries of Eastern Europe, which have turned over to socialism at the end of the Second World War, are scarcely examples, since, with the possible exception of Yugoslavia, the presence in those countries of the Russian armed forces at the critical time was no small and more international has been fulfilled up to a point. It fails, however, to take account of the strong sentiments of nationalism aroused by two world wars. It will thus be evident that there are dangers in erecting "the class struggle" into a principle for the purpose of drawing the sweeping deductions that Marx sought to make.

Marx and Engles were strictly materialistic and the "scientific method" figured prominently in their discussions and in those of their followers. Yet they themselves could not escape from *a priori* assumptions in their nature as unscientific as those of the "ideologists" whom they condemned. The adoption of Hegelian dialectics is one. Marx would have been better advised not to have linked his "class struggle" with this, since it is no more than an abstract juggle of words into which almost anything might be fitted. Implicit in his adoption of it are the following assumptions: (a) that the dialectic interpretation of history is correct; (b) that the conflict between "thesis" and "anti-thesis" is identifiable with "capital" and "labour"; and (c) that the "synthesis" will be the classless society. All three are open to question. The first two are insufficiently supported by evidence, the third has no evidence at all. Besides, why stop there? Why should not the classless society in turn become a thesis with its own anti-thesis, evolving into some other synthesis? Equally serious is the assumption that primitive society was happy, containing no anti-thesis within itself, communism without state and law; and that Man is so intrinsically nice that once the corrupting influence of economic maladjustment is done away with he will become a paragon of virtue. This looks like a reversion to a natural law theory, and by saying that primitive society had no anti-thesis within itself and that corruption set in with the unequal distribution of commodities, it would seem that the legend of the Fall of Man has been given a new meaning. This view of primitive society, especially its communist character and the absence of private property, is wholly suppositious. Again, there is no doubt some truth in the assumption that the wickedness of men is prompted, at least in large measure, by economic conditions, but it is no justification for the sweeping proposition of Lenin.

Actual legal system usually precede theory. Russian Marxists, however, claim that their philosophical theory came first and that the legal system was modelled on that. While this is true up to a point it should be noted that from the start, and increasingly since about 1920, legislators and judges were forced to proceed according to social needs, and jurists had to struggle to provide theoretical support. So theory could not help having to follow actual law after all.

The characteristic feature of law in the Marxist picture of things is that it is an instrument of domination and exploitation wielded by capitalists against workers. In this there is a further erroneous inference. Whatever truth there might be in the statement that law has been used as an instrument for the repression of one class by another, it does not follow that this is, or need necessarily be, its sole function. For (a) regulation, and even coercion, is unavoidable to enable the intricate concatenation of interests and activities that make up any society to function efficiently. (b) Law is an important agency for the preservation of security and moral standards. Not only is it necessary to set moral standards, but also to maintain them. This remains true in the proletarian dictatorship, which has to educate the masses in the values of communism, and also in the communist society where each new generation needs education. In the execution of so huge a task law in indispensable. Therefore, it is implicit of so huge a task law is indispensable. Therefore, it is implicit even in Marx's own teachings that law possesses an important social function other than exploitation and domination. (c) Law also serves to restrain oppression by classes or individuals. Rule by law inevitably leads to abuses, which could hamper the task of educating The masses by weakening people's respect and confidence in law. On the contrary, the educational task will be greatly aided if people see in law a bulwark. So, even for Marxist purposes, ideas of "rule of law" and "due process" are not so absurd after all. (d) Law gives practical expression to the balance that has to be struck between competing interests; and this is true even in Russia today where there are no classes. Judges no longer simply reflect governmental values, since all values are governmental. Law, then, ceases to be merely an instrument of domination and becomes a means of adjusting interests, and, more important, a measure of judicial independence becomes necessary. Above all, (e) Law satisfies the ineradicable human craving for justice, i.e., like treatment in like cases, and certainty; both of which require rules and precedents. Marx, it would seem, failed to distinguish sufficiently between the various uses to which law can be put and has sometimes been put; and, in any case, his observations should be limited to the purpose which law was being made to serve, as he saw it, in some countries in his day.

When the proletarian dictatorship was established in Russia the repressive use of law reached greater heights than before, but this was explained as a temporary phase and a means of achieving utopia to which this period of travail would give birth. For there was still a capitalist minority, which the working-class majority had to dominate and eventually eliminate. By the mid-1930s, however, there was no longer a minority left, but law continued to flourish even more vigorously. Indeed, it was possible to say in 1935 that all minorities had been eliminated. The continued need for law, then, was (a) to provide the economic organisation for the new society, which is of slow development; and (b) to discipline the social conscience of people. It is easy to lead the ignorant. Education inevitably teaches people to think, and the more they are taught to do this, the harder it is to keep the power of thought within channels. Precisely for these reasons legal enforcement had to become increasingly ruthless. The state cannot wither by degrees, but has to remain strong until communism is achieved. It was also emphasised that state and coercion were necessary as long as the Soviet Union was surrounded by enemies. All this was summed up in the Stalinist dialectic: "The dying out of the State will come not through weakening State authority, but through intensifying that authority to the utmost". (Stalin did not regard himself as bound by any law.) It may be that this aggrandisement of the state also lies behind the oft-stated need for a perpetual state of revolution. But the point is that law is not necessarily bound up with exploitation. What is left is a picture of law as an instrument of coercion, which is no different from the concept familiar to the West. Modern Soviet disquisitions on the subject now seek to draw distinctions between "bourgeois" and "socialist" law and tend, on the whole, to avoid reference to domination and exploitation.

The state, according to Marx, is an engine of compulsion by which the economic rulere keep workers in subjection. So the idea of a "classless state", which developed under Stalin after about 1938 and has become prominent since, undermines the Marxist foundation of state in class conflict. Mr. Krushchev adopted the policy of "peaceful co-existence", which meant that other states were not to be treated as constant enemies. This weakened further the Stalinist justification of the continued existence of the state as a defence mechanism. Mr. Krushchev also took the line that the "classless state" is an intermediate stage, a "state of the whole people", interposed between the proletarian dictatorship and communism, which might even be called the "first stage of communism". The Communist Party has become the "party of the whole people", which, on the face of it, is a Marxist absurdity, since the party is that part of a class which is organised ot serve as its spearhead and guide in the struggle. What was now meant, as explained by Mr. Krushchev, was that the communist Party is one of two "friendly classes" in an "all-people's state". In these circumstances the continued existence of the Party can only be a return to a new ruling class. The contradiction of Marxist dogma that state and class-conflict are synonymous remains glaringly obvious.

It was predicted that with the arrival of the classless society law will "wither away", but that there will remain "an administration of things". This follows from the thesis that law is but the reflection of an oppressive economic system without law. But, as was admitted, there will still have to be some regulation of behaviour, which is what Engels referred to as "an administration of things", and the point has been increasingly recognised in later Programmes of the Soviet Communist Party. According to Mr. Krushchev, "Under communism, too, there will remain certain public functions similar to those now performed by the state, but their nature and the methods by which they will be accomplished will differ from those existing in the present stage". In other words, there will probably be a tendency to deal with more and more areas by ministerial decree than by courts: transfer, not abolition, from the category of private law to public or administrative law. This would appear to be a verbal point: the regulation of conduct which will remain is not to be called "law". For, if "law" is defined with reference to domination and oppression, when these have disappeared what remains will not be "law". There may be a deeper reason. To all Marxists the word "law" carries a strong pejorative connotation, and because it is so associated in their minds with everything unjust and oppressive, they cannot bring themselves to continue to apply so odious a word once perfection has been reached. But it is obvious that a very large sphere of human regulation will have to remain even after the arrival of the classless society. Whether this is to be called "law" or not is immaterial. A similar obsession with the pejorative connotation of "state" led Lenin to deny that the proletarian dictatorship was anything more than a "semi-state" of "commune" state. It has also subsequently been conceded, that there can indeed be "law" without a state, and in this way it was sought to uphold international law. On the other hand, there developed the theory, which Stalin found convenient, that the state is superior to law. All these are not just deviations from Marx, but denials of the class character of law, its identity with state and its use solely as an instrument of exploitation. One should be chary of levelling accusations of contradiction in a philosophy which is rooted in the Hegelian logic of contradictions; but even so there are contradictions and contradictions.

Finally, the maxim, which embodies the goal towards which all this endeavour is directed, namely, "from each according to his capacity, to each according to his needs", suffers from the weakness that it is difficult to see how needs are to be measured and what checks there will be on exorbitant demands. One wonders whether there ever will be abundance, for the more people have the more are their appetites likely to be whetted.

II. THE PERIOD FROM 1921-1937

After the revolution in Russia, the proletarian dictatorship was established along Marxist lines between the years 1918 and 1920. The period from 1921 to 1937, can be divided into two parts. The first part, which lasted till about 1929, may conveniently be described as the period of the New Economic Policy, the N.E.P., while the second part from 1930 onwards, marks a departure from the N.E.P. and the construction of socialism.

The establishment of the proletarian dictatorship required a "revolutionary legality" by means of which the victorious majority could dominate and eventually exterminate the capitalist minority. The period now being considered did not prove to be as short-lived as had been hoped. So codes had to be introduced, and professional judges appointed. Whereas in 1918 and 1920 judges had been enjoined to rely on their "socialist consciousness of justice". they had now to abide by "the general principles of the Soviet legislation and the general policy of the government of the Workers and Peasants". Having won freedom from the power-structure of the Tsars, the revolutionaries set-up an even more ruthless power-structure to prevent opposition to themselves. The cohesion of the state would be wrecked if divisive values were allowed to develop and people were allowed freedom to act in pursuance of them. Accordingly, severe repression was introduced, which included one of the most effective ways of nipping in the bud the growth of unwelcome values, namely, a secret police to inhibit people from expressing views other than orthodox among themselves. Without communication ideas cannot spread.

There was also what Berman felicitously styles the "parental" function of law. The party had to guide the masses to communism by educating the training them rather like children for the part they would have to play in the future. All this was reflected in the administration of law, for it was recognised early that law enforcement had a decisive role to play in this process. The need to educate and train the populace justified virtually unlimited activities by the secret police, trails in secret and the like, and enabled these to flourish notwithstanding constitutional guarantees of free speech and respect for the individual. Side by side with all this was an exclusive and ceaseless propaganda campaign coupled with a jealous exclusion of foreign influence and contact. The latter has only been relaxed slightly in very recent times. The work of educating the people for a communist society would be gravely impaired, if not undone, if they were allowed to see that conditions elsewhere were at least not as bad, and in some respects perhaps better, than in Russia.

The wave of nationalisation that followed in the wake of the initial revolutionary ardour proved to have been premature. The Soviet state was faced with crises of the first magnitude in the spheres of production and distribution. The only way out was to reintroduce private enterprise and capital for, and the New Economic Policy was decided on at the Tenth Communist Party Congress in March 1921.

The feature of the N.E.P. was that it constituted a partial compromise between Marxist ideas and capitalism under the strict supervision of the state. The N.E.P. has been happily described as "state-controlled private enterprise". It was necessary in the interests of the nation to give scope to private enterprise and at the same time to prevent an abuse of it. Private enterprise and private rights were subordinate to the national interest, and were deemed to be forbidden unless expressly permitted. Alongside all this, in the interests of efficiency, Lenin introduced the concept of "one man Management".

Another characteristic of the period was the feeling of tension that pervaded the nation, which had just emerged from the throes of an unprecedented upheaval, and was faced with internal crises and surrounded by enemies. Little wonder that a state of emergency was felt to exist, and an attitude of the utmost severity was adopted towards political deviations.

The meet the new situation a theory of law was evolved. The principal contribution of this period was that of Pashukanis (1891-1937), who was strongly influenced by two German writers, Jellinek and Laband. He developed what is known as the "commodity-exchange theory". All law, he maintained, was built-up of relations between individuals. He followed Marx in believing that law was a reflection of economic conditions, but departed from Marx in supposing it to consist of the exchange of commodities between individuals. Commodity-exchange calls for individual rights and legal relationships. The various aspects of law reflect these relationship. The thesis that commodity-exchange is the basis of law has been challenged by Dr. Schlesinger as being historically untrue. He quotes primitive blood-feuds and the payment of wergild and asks in what sense these relationships reflect commodity-exchange. Pashukanis also maintained that law presupposes theoretical equality, not subjection. Law is the peaceful means of settling conflicting interests of persons, who are treated as being on an equal footing however much they may be unequal in fact. In the ultimate perfect society individual interests will not conflict, for there will then be unity of purpose. Therefore, there will be no need for law. As Dr. Schlesinger points out, Pashukanis's contention leaves unexplained, (a) why there cannot be individual relationships apart from commodity-exchange, and (b) the relationships entered into in the course of production of commodities as distinct from their distribution. Following from the last point, Pashukanis maintained that once the perfect society is reached the national economy will pass wholly into the hands of the state. But law, which presupposes the conflict of individual interests, will come to an end. The implications of this are that law and state are distinct, which is a departure from Marx, and that law will wither away before the state. Finally, Pashukanis asserted that "bourgeois law" had ceased to exist in Russia as far as production was concerned, but that so far as capitalism, and hence the conflict of private interests, was allowed to survive, Russian law still bore characteristics of it.

It is obvious that this theory was adapted only to the peculiar situation that obtained during the N.E.P. By about 1930 the position had altered. The concession made of necessity to private enterprise was withdrawn. The Second Revolution took place to eliminate the capitalists, a "revolution from above" this time, i.e., by those in power to exterminate the minority whom they had hitherto permitted to exist. Private capital and private enterprise now became illegal, and the change was justified on the ground that the ultimate interest of the proletarian dictatorship rose superior to the sanctity of its won prior laws. Moreover, it was clear by 1930 that the long-awaited revolutions in other countries would not materialise and that Russia would have to wait a long time in the midst of her enemies. The state and its apparatus were a guarantee of defence and were necessary until all, or most, other countries had turned socialist. The withering away of the state was postponed until the remote future and less and less was said about it. Finally, in December 1936 a new Constitution was promulgated and acclaimed as the triumph of socialism. Strict observance of laws was insisted on. "We need the stability of laws now more than ever", said Stalin.

Once the special conditions which had brought the N.E.P. into being had passed, the theory of Pashukanis was outdated. His views were subjected to attacks on both fair and unfair. There was, in the first place, its obvious weakness that law was based on exchange and not on production. Marx himself had laid emphasis on production. There was, moreover, another deviation from Marx in that law was represented as regulating conflicting interests of equals and not as an instrument of domination. Secondly, on his doctrine law was destined to wither away before the state. By the 1930s law had become a firmly established institution In Russia, which necessitated there important changes in ideas. (a) The essentially sociological concept of Marx, Engels and Pashukanis, which viewed law as the product of the economic structure of society, was beginning to give way to a normative concept. (b) Since there was no longer a capitalist minority left, the idea of law as an instrument of domination began to be replaced by one that identified it with the wishes of the people themselves. (c) Though law was still viewed as an instrument of policy, it was also the means of providing security for expectations as determined by policy. Although law was still viewed as "a political category... Nevertheless law can no more be reduced simply to policy than cause be identified with effect". So law was seen to have an important task to perform and its withering away was something that should be indefinitely postponed, at best forgotten. Pashukanis's doctrine was attacked on the ground that it encouraged "a nihilistic attitude" towards Soviet law. Some people went so far as to distort what he had said and alleged that he preached the withering away of the state as well, which it was pointed out was dangerous and inexpedient in the face of a hostile world. In view of the fact that law had become an important institution in Russia, it was necessary now to propagate the idea that Soviet law was somehow better and different from capitalist law. It is not surprising in consequence that pashukanis's statement that Soviet law partook of the character of "bourgeois law" grew increasingly unpopular. In the result Pashukanis was impeached and disappeared in 1937.

III. THE PERIOD FROM 1938 TO THE PRESENT

This period falls into two parts, from 1938 until the death of Stalin in 1953 and the post-Stalin era from 1953 onwards.

The first part witnessed the consolidation of socialism in the form of a monolithic state with complete subordination of legal theory to political expediency. This was also the period of the "personality cult", fostered by Stalin. The doctrine of the "classless state", previously mentioned, was propounded, and the state, represented by the Supreme Soviet, was held to be superior to all its laws. A more interesting development was the Yugoslav attack on the Stalinist regime as a counter-revolutionary dictatorship. While differences in the conditions prevailing in different countries must inevitably yield different applications of Marxist doctrines, it was accounted "deviation" to adopt any interpretation of them other than that of the U.S.S.R. In 1948, Yugoslavia, under Marshal Tito, insisted that each country should be left to interpret Marxism in its own way, and denounced the Soviet model under Stalin as a betrayal of Marxist-Leninism. It was alleged to be nothing but a form of capitalism exploited by a new ruling class of bureaucrats, who have merely substituted a bureaucratic state in place of a bourgeoise state. Whereas Russia postponed the decline of state power and law to some distant epoch, Yugoslavia was prepared to phase it into immediate effect as and when it proved feasible. This is the approach which is termed "Titoism". It calls for new methods: for instance, in place of state ownership there should be "social ownership" by free associations of producers; and workers should take as much part as possible in economic management. Such "industrial self-management" is achieved by allowing each enterprise to be run by a workers' council, a measure of overall control and co-ordination being maintained by the appointment of a director by the People's Committee of the Commune. The state as such is still responsible for order and national defence, but its other aspects could well be allowed to wither away.

After the death of Stalin there was a relaxation of centralisation. Stalin had been a firm believer in it. Krushchev introduced decentralisation in his administrative reforms of 1957, which were criticised as too localised and unco-ordinated. Accordingly, in 1965 centralisation was re-introduced with minor modifications towards giving state enterprises wider powers.

At the Twentieth Party Congress the image of Stalin was dethroned by Mr. Krushchev, who denounced him as a criminal and for fostering a "personality cult". This made the Russians rather more inclined to self-criticism than they would otherwise have been and readier to admit, to themselves though not openly, that there might be some truth in the Yugoslav gibes after all. Accordingly, the breach with Yugoslavia was patched up by the admission that there could be "several roads to socialism", although there has been a renewal of differences from time to time. There was also relaxation of some of the other rigid controls. In Russia this had no marked effect, probably because the controls had never been felt to be unduly oppressive by the mass of people, who had no tradition of freedom. In Hungary, on the other hand, the result of de-control was the tragic uprising in 1956, which had to be crushed by massive Russian intervention, and controls were re-imposed. Later in 1968 the doctrine of "several roads to socialism" was forgotten when Czechoslovakia attempted to introduce a relaxed form of "communism with a human face". This, too, was crushed by massive intervention by Russia with somewhat half-hearted support from her Warsaw Pact partners. A different breach has occurred between Russia and Albania, supported by China, and between Russia and China. The Chinese, too insist on their own, the "Maoist", interpretation of Marxism, and accuse the Russians of having betrayed socialism. This clash is more than just ideological; it is a bid for leadership of the communist world, the outcome of which remains to be seen.

It has already been pointed out that Mr. Krushchev emphasised the classless character of Soviet society where there is now a "state of the whole people", that the Communist party is a "party of the whole people" and one of two friendly partners in the "all-people's state". These are all contrary to strict Marxism and only reconcilable with a revised version of it to the effect that a state, differing from the burgeois state, can and should survive under socialism as the "first stage of communism". This is the period of the "construction of communism", for although socialism has won in Russia, the goal of communism is still afar. Three conditions remain to be fulfilled before its removed, which calls for strict protective measures, within and without; (b) the masses need to be completely re-educated; and (c) economic abundance has to be secured, which necessitates experiments was set as a vague, tentative date for the dawn of the New Age. The problem is to know who decides, and on what criteria, that the time has arrived. Unless some clear indication of this is forthcoming, the vision of a state-free and law-free society must remain no more than a vision. After the fall of Krushchev, there was a return to severer treatment, but the doctrine of the state of the whole people remains.

Soviet jurists are now increasingly confronted with problems similar to those that face lawyers in other countries. Socialist legality is openly proclaimed and the need for a theory is increasingly felt. Insofar as laws serve the socialist economy they are just and deserve obedience from all bodies and persons. But they are still only instruments of policy, not objects of veneration in themselves, so they are not binding on the Supreme Soviet. This is why a doctrine such as the "rule of law" is still incomprehensible to Soviet jurists. One danger is that this attitude opens the way for an unscrupulous abuse of power by the rulers, as indeed happened under Stalin; another is that the patent association of law with expediency weakens respect for it and may well hamper the task of re-education. So "due process" now tends to be insisted on. Moreover, it was felt to be expedient to incorporate in the Constitution of 1936, which was hailed as the final victory of socialism in Russia, a bill of fundamental rights although it remained a dead letter for many years.

There are important difference between the structure of the Soviet state and capitalist states, and these have wrought some changes in the Soviet concept of law. The guiding principle of Soviet law has been floridly described as follows:

> "in Soviet law such a single and general principle is that of socialism—the principle of a socialist economic and social system resting on socialist property, annihilation of exploitation and social inequality, distribution in proportion to labour, a guarantee to each member of society of the complete and the manifold development of all his (spiritual and physical) creative forces, and true human freedom and personal independence."

The practical working of this principle has resulted in the following broad characteristics. In the first place, a distinction is drawn between ownership of the means of production and ownership of consumer goods. The former is wholly in the state, and only the latter is open to individuals, "the home garden and a cow". The land belongs to the state, but the individual has title to his house. The resale of consumer goods is subject to strict scrutiny. Some problem remains with producers who employ no labour and with individual artisans. Apart from consumer goods purchased by means of income from labour, there is inheritance. This was forbidden in the Communist Manifesto as a method of perpetuating private ownership in means of production; but inheritance has been increasingly recognised over the years. There is another distinction between state ownership and ownership by co-operatives (kolkhozes), and there is also ownership by public and social organisations, e.g., trade unions.

Ownership by co-operatives facilitates the performance of functions and tasks. For instance, land is nationalised and belongs to the state; kolkhozes have the use of it in perpetuity for the purposes of management and cultivation in strict conformity with state planning. This is a new for of ownership. The promise of abundance requires a centrally directed national economy, which has entailed not only a vast mass of regulations but also severe regimentation of the populace. Whether this helps or hinders the achievement of the ultimate objective is open to argument.

Secondly, in the sphere of production, economic and business relationships, e.g., between transport, producing and manufacturing concerns, are essentially transactions between state organs *inter se*. State organs are of two kinds, those that are subsidised by the state and those that have been made into autonomous bodies known as State Trusts. The latter are legal persons and correspond with the public corporations in other countries. Their property is, as it were, conceded to them by the state. The regulation of relations between these agencies e.g., a manufacturing and a transport concern, is conducted on the basis that they are individual bodies.

Thirdly, there are the relations between the state and the individuals, e.g., between a State Trust and its employees; but these do not present any novel ideas.

Fourthly, industrial contracts are subject to the national economic plan. Sometimes the plan directs that certain "contracts of supply" shall be entered into and outlines the pattern of the nature, scope and timing of the obligations, leaving only details to be arranged by the contracting enterprises, who know best their own particular needs. To meet the situation where they are unable to agree, a system of state arbitration (Gosarbitrazh) has developed, its function being not merely to deal expeditiously with disputes, but also to assist in negotiating the terms of proposed agreements. At other times the plan only posits the goal to be attained and the enterprises are left to decide what contracts, if any, should be entered into and with whom. This leaves greater freedom of contract, though it is bounded by the task fixed by the plan for each enterprise. The freedom to select one's contracting partner promotes competitive efficiency, since an inefficient enterprise will not secure contracts. The achievement of a plan, and not profit, being the basis of contracts, if follows that specific performance, reinforced by penalties, and not compensation, is the accepted remedy. At the other end of the scale, contracts with the consumer public and between private individuals are no different from contracts in Western countries. As consumer good become increasingly available, these kinds of contracts increase too.

Fifthly, the admission of individual ownership in consumer goods involves a recognition of private rights, albeit to a restricted extent.

Sixthly, the regulation of all these relations, and particularly disputes between parties, have of necessity to be entrusted to tribunals, the courts, which have to be impartial and independent. The familiar doctrine of judicial independence and impartiality has thus gained ground. "Judges are independent and subject only to the law": so runs Article 112 of the Constitution. In this connection a tribute should be paid to the Soviet Supreme Court, a conscientious and fair-minded body of men, whose restraint and care have done much to raise the standard of the Soviet administration of justice. If the law is to be administered with firmness, it must be certain and predictable.

Finally, observance of legislation is strictly enforced. Even so, the Constitution is not treated as a fundamental law. Both the Praesidium and the Council of Ministers have legislated contrary to it.

All this introduces new ideas in some respects, but only a redistribution of emphasis in other. Not only are Soviet jurists now facing the same sort of problems as those in other countries, but many laws themselves have approximated more and more to those obtaining elsewhere. Such has been the case with criminal law, family law, private rights and many other branches. Perhaps the biggest retreats have been in criminal law and family law. The abandonment of the idea that crime is only the reflection of capitalist economy has induced a revised approach to the problem of criminality. The vital influence of a stable family background on children has also been recognised. Apart from these the following points may be noted:

(a) The emphasis has shifted from the protection of the interest of the individual in himself and his property to the state's interest in the individual. This does away with the distinction between "public" and "private" law; all law is "public".
(b) The safeguarding of "socialist legality" and protection against abuses and oppression is entrusted to a body known as the Prokuratura, which may be compared with the Ombudsman.
(c) The task of counsel in courts in primarily to further the cause of socialism, and this circumscribes his duty towards his client.
(d) Since law is a superstructure on an economic foundation. Its material source lie in collectivisation and the presence of a People's State. Its formal source is legislation. There is no doctrine of the separation of powers. Interpretation of legislation has to be in accordance with the principles of "socialist legality", i.e., judges are bound to reflect official policy. But this is difficult with the bulk, complexity and technicality of modern statutes. In this climate the question whether judges should adopt a creative attitude or merely

abide by the letter of the law involves a delicate balance of considerations. Since state policy is paramount, it might be said that they are limited to interpreting, not to creating rules. However, this is not possible owing to the very nature of the judicial process. So what happens is that the judicial authorities, especially the Supreme Court, help to develop law by publishing instructions as to how laws should be applied for the guidance of other courts; and the prokuratura is at hand to guard against aberrations of the courts. This is a new form of precedent in its broad sense and it has a creative function.

(e) The educational function is a very important aspect of law. Not only must the parties be made to feel that socialist laws are best and most just, but legal administration of social conscience in preparation for communism. Thus, there tends to be more sermonising in Soviet courts than in Western courts; and criminal courts especially are very much courts of morfals.

(f) At present custom plays a very minor role, as an occasional aid in the interpretation or application of legislation. Perhaps, in the future truly communist society, when people will have been socially re-educated, custom will come into its own as the principal source of socialist conscience.

All these developments, whether approximating to Western ideas or evolving new ones, should show how far the Russians have gone in legal theory. The only way to reconcile them with traditional Marxism is to say that law will have to flourish before it will disappear. From at least one source orthodox Marxists may derive comfort and hope. This is the intervention on behalf of, or against, an accused or suspect person, and the performance of various legalistic and preventive functions by representatives of the group to which he belongs, be it a factory or garage (obschestvennost). The Comrades' (People's) Courts were revived by Mr. Krushchev in 1959 wherever there are at least fifty persons living or employed, e.g., farms, factories, apartment blocks and even schools. They deal with minor matters, such as foul language, drunkenness, lateness for work and some kinds of civil disputes. Use has also been made of the "public meeting" to denounce "parasites", i.e., those living off unearned income. These institutions might be thought to foreshadow a time when law and courts will have vanished and the people themselves deal with problems as they arise. The rationale behind them is that a state advancing towards communism has to start creating institutions for keeping order according to healthy public morality, which are not those of the state.

Despite the claim that Russia has made a revolutionary break with her part, many aspects of the system reflect a stream of continuity. It has been pointed out that the Tsars had repeatedly inaugurated industrial enterprises, which were sold or leased to individuals. Nationalisation, therefore, in effect restored to the state what had been its property. The diversity of ethnic and cultural groups in Russia is connected with their age-old resistance to "Russification". Lenin had encouraged such resistance in order to weaken the Tsarist regime, but later found himself forced to accept them as separate states. Amidst these divergences the Orthodox Church used formerly to function as a unifying spiritual force, and its mantle has now descended on the communist Party. The fact the communism has become a substitute faith would explain why political dissenters are visited with the same sort of repression and ridicule as that which used to be meted out to religious dissenters. The Tsars had inherited the Mogul tradition of absolute autocracy. There never had been a "rule of law"; there always was a tradition of "rule by law". The traditional identification of crime with sin made criminal courts into courts of morals; which remains very much the case. Equality before the law was unknown, and the tradition was continued into the proletarian dictatorship while class distinctions remained. But even after the disappearance of such distinctions, equality before law could not sprout like a mushroom overnight. Offences against the state had always been specially dealt with; and that is still so. Even the Prokuratura is the descendant of an institution of Peter the Great.

In the light of all this it may be asked: How far has the soviet system achieved justice? With regard to justice in the allocation of benefits and burdens, there is undoubtedly a more even distribution than before, and this might be regarded as its greatest achievement. The amounts of burdens and benefits that have been distributed has been strictly controlled by government policy; but the more detailed problem of evaluating different kinds of work and need is no easier in Russia than elsewhere. With regard to justice in preventing the abuse of power, this has not been achieved at all. As pointed out, the removal of Tsarist power was only succeeded by an even more ruthless power-structure. Further, a centrally directed economy entails a vast bureaucracy and red-tape. With regard to justice in preventing the abuse of liberty, it is true to say that this has been achieved, but only at the cost of allowing very few liberties. With regard to justice in deciding disputes, it would appear from what has been said that the Soviet Union is moving more and more towards the position in Western countries. Finally, with regard to justice in adapting to change, there is no difference between the Soviet Union and other countries in adapting to technological advances. Indeed, it might even be easier in Russia where there can be no strikes against the introduction of new methods and machinery. On the other hand, any move which even hints of political change will receive short shrift. The rigid orthodoxy, which the Soviet seeks to impose even on other countries under her wing, makes the possibility of this kind of change within her own territory extremely unlikely.

A word might also be said about the Soviet attitude towards international law. The capitalist threat from abroad is not only an explanation of the severity of the measures adopted internally, but also a clue to Russia's insistence on the sovereignty of states and her policy in international affairs. There was an initial theoretical difficulty as to how the idea of law, which was viewed as the product of an economic structure, could apply as between states with widely differing economic systems. This led at first to confusing attempts to introduce the class concept into international relations, which were replaced by the view that international law is simply an instrument of policy. The result has been a highly eclectic selection of principles and interpretations. Thus, while Russia was still militarily weak she sought to make use of international law for protection. To this end she put forward and persisted in claims that were designed to make denials of them by other states appear as aggression; she rejected the League of Nations as a tool of capitalism, but found no difficulty in joining it in the face of the growing German threat in 1934. After the Second World War, by which time she had achieved a position of power, the continued furtherance of her own interests led to the reversal of attitudes previously adopted. During the Korean War in 1950, for instance, in order to support the North Koreans it was found necessary to reject the very definition of aggression which she herself had insisted on in 1933; nor could she bring herself to support the International Declaration of Human Rights.

Two main developments are worthnoting. The first is that with the establishment of a number of communist states since the Second World War there is increasing talk of a new "socialist international law". The economic structures of these countries being more or less alike, the possibility of an international law, between them at any rate, which is not simply an instrument of policy, is now more real. The invasion of Czechoslovakia in 1968 by the Warsaw Pact countries was prompted by Russian fears of "deviation". The Brezhnev doctrine of the "limited sovereignty" of other communist countries, which was propounded to justify the invasion, raises questions as to what the sovereignty of states now means in the communist world. It is an almost open avowal of the satellite status of these other countries. Moreover, this event, even if it stood alone, makes one wonder what is to be made of the familiar and apparently serious charges continuing to be made of Western "imperialism" and "aggression". Secondly, even in relation to capitalist countries, the policy of "peaceful coexistence", if seriously pursued, should bring about a different attitude towards international law, accentuated perhaps by the realisation of the economic and political inter-dependence of states. Instead of two systems of international law, one for socialist states after all. But the ingrained Marxist dialectic sees this as a kind of synthesis produced by the economic and political competition between all states. Whatever the type of international law, the underlying question is: Does the Soviet Union regard it as binding and, if so, on what basis? The answer that seems to be given is: agreement. This cannot stand up to analysis, but since it is part of a wider question concerning international law in general, it will be postponed until later.

CONCLUSION

When considering the nature of law from an economic point of view two questions have to be distinguished. One is the extent of the economic influence on the content of the law. In so far as it has been demonstrated that a great many rules have been shaped by economic factors, perhaps more than had been suspected, this can be accommodated, within traditional concepts of law. The other question is what kind of a concept of law would be appropriate for Marxism as practised in contemporary Russia. This would have to be a functional concept, but one that would need to be sharpened with reference to the re-education of the people and the ushering in of a better society. As such, it would be an instrument of executive, rather than class, policy and would center on the executive rather than on the courts. A concept focussed on the latter will unfold a far from satisfactory picture of law as it operates in Russia. For the decision of Soviet courts can never be fully understood except in the light of the theoretical and ideological background of the principles that are being applied: all of which are dictated by policy. But at bottom the idea of law still remains very much the expression of an "ought".

Apart from this the contribution of the economic approach is varied. The most significant point that has emerged is the indispensability of law. The marxist approach was a thoroughgoing attempt to do away with it, but the practical experience or Russia has only demonstrated its importance. It may be that the final stage of development, according to Marxist predictions, has not been reached, but it is clear that even if it is reached the prescription of behaviour and a measure of coercion will continue to exist. There is no reason, apart from an emotional one, for refusing to call all this "law". The signification difference from Western societies is that law will not serve as a watch-dog on the government—a rule by law rather than a rule of law. How far an effective safeguard against an abuse of governmental power will be evolved remains to be seen.

Marx and Engels painted a confident picture of evolution, "the" class struggle reaching a point when conflict arises and results in the establishment of the proletarian dictatorship, which in turn develops into communism. Their followers, both in and out of the Soviet Union, have sometimes tried to force the pace of events. These tactics have been somewhat exaggerated by opponents of Marxism, but they do, even in themselves, reflect unfavourably of disciples should not discredit the teachings of the prophets, yet to have to force the occurrence of events, which are supposed to follow an evolutionary plan, can only raise doubts as to its correctness. The policy of "peaceful co-existence", so prominent in Soviet pronouncements in the last two decades, may will be inspired by an appreciation that the events will nevertheless take time.

The Marxist doctrines in their practical content come to this. For reasons good or bad, the existing structure in capitalist countries needs to be altered. In Russia it is a fact that the structure was changed and the Russians are seeking to improve upon it still further. But this great and praiseworthy experiment is quite independent of any question as to the nature of law, as the Russians are beginning to perceive. Unfortunately, questions as to the nature of law were quite unnecessarily dragged into the social experiment at its theoretical stage and were coloured by a strongly emotional element. This intrusion of emotion is nowhere more evident than in the use by Marxists of such words as "law", "state", "bourgeois" and some others. Although they approve of the term "science", it should be realised that there cannot be a "scientific" discussion of any topic until the emotional element has been expelled.

There is no reason to suppose that communism is the universal social panacea. It might well prove to be the answer for some types of societies, but not others. Two points appear to stand out in this connection. The first was well summed up by Dr. Schlesinger, who said:

> "Socialism of the Russian type may be a historical expedient by which nations held back under a capitalist regime may catch up with those more advanced."

Nor is there any reason to suppose that communism will work in the same way, or at all, in countries which have reached a high state of development under a capitalist system. Secondly, the Russian type of communism requires a degree of regimentation of the masses, the success of which inevitably depends on the nature and temper of the people concerned: the more ignorant and traditionally inclined to subservience the better the chance of success, the more educated and independent the greater the difficulty. The Russian peoples throughout their history never knew emancipation in the sense that inhabitants of Western countries have known it. Indeed, the boast of the Revolution was that if freed them from serfdom; which is true. But it is a relative kind of freedom compared with the traditions of certain other countries, which have long been schooled in the pursuit of independence and resistance to dictatorship. Such countries are less likely to embrace a communist regime than those which have long been oppressed or have remained largely ignorant, and they are likely to fare badly for a long time under one. This is one reason why communism succeeds with oppressed peoples; another is the hope which it holds out to them. But even with these an unremitting process of education is needed; how much re-education would be needed for some races of the West can only be guessed. The Hungarians in 1956 and the Czechs in 1968 demonstrated to their cost the reaction of peoples to an uncongenial regime as soon as control was slightly relaxed, while a similar relaxation in Russia evoked no reaction.

The attack on religion and its ideals has only succeeded in substituting one kind of religion for another. It is doubtful if Marx or Engels foresaw, or would have welcomed, the worship they now receive. The adherence to what one wit has described as the "gospel according to St. Marx" has involved Soviet jurists in some strange mental feats in trying to maintain his doctrines as the official creed and at the same time to take account of developments inconsistent with it. The official attitude seems to be that the "truth" is in Marx if only the right interpretation can be found. But if the very nature of things departures from his teachings have proved to be inevitable. As long as these are officially countenanced, they are "interpretations"; when they cease to have official support, they are denounced as "deviations". Even from a Soviet point of view, why should it not be admitted that the teachings of Marx have obvious limitations and have also in some respects become out of date? In 1956, the "personality cult" was denounced with regard to Stalin. Whether its rejection will extend to Marx, Engels and Lenin and if so, to what degree, remains to be seen. Indeed, outside religion the adherence to the belief in the infallibility of one man would be a mark of an immature mentality. One explanation might be that, having erected the whole of their structure on Marx, the Russians are afraid to risk the consequences of admitting the existence of flaws in the foundations. But it is also difficult to escape the suspicion that there is in their attitude elements of immaturity and religious fervour, as borne out, for example, by the genuine desire to convert the whole world, the refusal to see or believe that anyone can be right but themselves, and the faith in the inevitability of a communist triumph. In the face of such sturdy and militant enthusiasm it is not easy to sift what is solid and sound from the emotional admixture of eulogy and abuse. Indeed, in contemporary Marxism is to be seen the twentieth-century version of the Crusades.

9

SOCIOLOGICAL APPROACHES

In the nineteenth century the focus of attention began to swing away from individual rights towards social duties, and carried with it an emphasis on the function which law fulfils in communal existence. The rapid increase in population, inequalities engendered by the industrial revolution on a scale hitherto unprecedented, were factors which, together with others, created new problems in society. The Historical School had shown an essential connection between law and the social environment in which it develops. Prior to the nineteenth century such matters as health, welfare, education, economics, were not the concern of the state. Now, however, the state came increasingly to concern itself with them. This implied regulation through law, which compelled legal theory to readjust itself so as to take account of such preoccupations. Towards the latter half of that century the shortcomings of purely formal analysis were being felt. The increasing number of social activities with which the law had to deal produced a host of new problems for the solution of which guidance was needed. Traditional approaches to law, analytical positivism in particular, were forced into confessions of mental bankruptcy in meeting these demands. Finally, revolutions and social unsettlement not only upset any complacency about social stability, but also provoked anxiety about the shortcomings of law.

The diverse character of the various types of inquiries that are styled "sociological" invites some comment. Sociology means, broadly, the study of society of which law is but a part. The founder of sociology, in a sense, is Comte (1798-1857), because he was the first to employ the term "sociology" to connote an independent discipline, and he also unified the work of earlier men. Comte insisted that advancement of knowledge came only through observation and experiment and proceeded to construct a hierarchical classification of the science, from mathematics, through physics, chemistry and biology to what he called sociology. Even though it was more difficult to apply the scientific method to sociology, it was still, in his view, the most fruitful. Sociology the defined as the science of social order and progress. It includes two compartments, social statics and social dynamics, the former being the theory of social order and the latter the theory of social progress. Society is a developing organism, whose progress is marked by the specialisation of functions within it. Its distinctive feature is its capacity for improvement and development if guided by proper scientific principles. The task of sociology is to discover and work out these principles. Earlier Montesquieu (1689-1755) in his L'Esprit des Lois had endeavoured to trace the effect of social environment on law. He busied himself with legal institutions with the object of offering explanations for them. He stressed the influence of geographical and climatic conditions on law which, in his view, could operate only through the medium of society. He perceived the importance of history as a means of understanding the structure of society and also drew attention to the part played by economic factors. In all this might be seen anticipations of what later developed into the Historical, Economic and Sociological Schools. In his own work, however, the appear as pointers to such studies rather than as studies in themselves.

As a subject, sociology is still young and in search of respecability. One step towards this would be to win for its methods the dignity that comes of being able to invoke the magic word "scientific". The following is a list of the main resemblances between sociological and scientific methods:

(1) Sociology, like science, proceeds from observation to hypothesis, and deductions therefrom are in turn checked back with "reality". In this respect the difference between them is largely one of degree, for sociology is still very much at the stage of observation, which indeed is being conducted on a massive scale with all modern techniques, but with as yet only exploratory hypotheses, classifications, models and tentative laws of probabilities.

(2) It is theoretical and aims at synthesising other disciplines, some of which are long established, such as history, economics, law, etc.

(3) It progresses cumulatively in that new hypotheses are evolved as much out of the correction, extension and refinement of earlier ones as out of new data.

(4) It is non-ethical, i.e., impartial in evaluation. Just as a scientist puts aside his own values when observing his data, so too the sociologist excludes his own preferences and prejudices when observing his data, which include current values and opinions. Put in another way, the values of a sociologist qua sociologist are the same as those of a scientist, namely

neutrality and scrupulousness. There are, however, two qualifications. The social observer cannot avoid being personally involved in the society or group which he is observing, of which he is a part and in which he has a role to play. The scientist is not involved with his data in this way. Secondly, social behaviour has causal as well as purposive explanations, i.e., the questions to be answered are not only "How?", but also "what for?" Sociological explanations are therefore sometimes termed "structural-functional", the structural side being explanatory and descriptive, the functional side being both heuristic and teleological.

(5) It seeks to describe, explain and predict, in short to derive descriptive laws which will predict, as opposed to prescribe, social behaviour: that which "is", not that which "ought to be". The material out of which such descriptive laws are derived include: (a) social morphology: which concerns the form of social structure as affected by such factors as the quantity and distribution of population, geography, climate, etc. (b) Social change: which may in turn inspire conscious or unconscious efforts to resist, adapt to or alter it. So-called "short-term" theories of social change confine themselves to changes that have occurred and the influences behind them without extrapolating these into some general law of change, whereas "long-term" theories aim to do precisely that. (c) Social pathology: which concerns social disturbances and maladjustment. Criminology is a well-know aspect of this. (d) Social controls: which include laws, morals, religion, public opinion, fashions and so on. (e) Group behaviour: which deals with the problems of the interaction between individuals *inter se* and groups.

Law are not the only instruments of control; others, such as morals, religion, etc. are at least as effective, if not more so, with the result that they all figure prominently in sociological study. No less important is the relation between public opinion, its unifying and divisive power, and the various sorts of issues on which opinions are held. The important point is that all forms of control are in their nature "ought" propositions, prescriptive not descriptive. The concern of sociology is not with prescriptive not descriptive. The concern of sociology is not with prescriptions as such, but with the phenomenon that when such prescriptions are regularly followed, they produce uniformities of behaviour which recur with such a degree of probability that they may then be described in terms of the "is", i.e., patterns which do occur as a matter of observation. It might seem from this that sociologists are here deriving "is" from "ought", but this is not so. The point is that the sociologist is primarily concerned with descriptions of social behaviour and only concerned with prescriptions in so far as these happen to produce regularities which can be observed. In no sense is he logically deriving the one from the other.

This reveals a crucial difference between the point of view of the sociologist looking at law as the sum-total of legal administration and as a given phenomenon of society ("legal sociologist"), and that of the lawyer looking at the operation of laws and the conceptual tools of a lawyer's equipment in their social and functional setting ("sociological jurist"). The former regards society as a whole, including the part played by legal administration in bringing about observable patterns of behaviour. He is interested in the fact of the regular application of force and the fact of the regular use of guides for determining disputes (norms of decision), both of which help to shape patterns of social behaviour (norms of conduct). Thus, his concept of law tends to be that of an ideal type, a model of the totality of legal administration, which help to shape patterns of social behaviour (norms of conduct). Thus, his concept of law tends to be that of an ideal type, a model of the totality of legal administration, which can be fitted into a model of society. On the other hand, the sociological jurist is primarily concerned with laws and the tools of a lawyer's trade; he accepts the former as being prescriptive in their nature and considers their function and functioning in society. The present chapter will be concerned mainly with the point of view of the sociological jurist, not of the legal sociologist, though works of the latter type cannot be excluded altogether. Needless to say, the authors, whose works will be dealt with, have not themselves maintained any such rigid distinction and in some cases it is arguable into which category they fall. Whether any further distinctions is to be drawn between "sociology of law" and "sociological jurisprudence" is doubtful. If "sociology of law" is thought to be concerned with the manner in which laws work in society, there is, it is submitted, no difference between it and sociological jurisprudence; if it is concerned with society and how legal administration as a whole fits into it, then it is synonymous with legal sociology.

The social study of laws has assumed four forms. (1) There are inquiries which seek the social origins of laws and legal institutions. They are concerned with the content of the "oughts" and the factors that have and are shaping them. (2) There are also examinations of the impact of laws on various aspects of society. (3) There are other inquiries which deal with the task which laws should perform in society. The results of these studies generally take the form of prescriptions addressed to persons who make and administer laws and not to members of society at large. Such "prescriptions for administration" are in a different category from the "prescriptive oughts" of laws themselves. Lastly, (4) there is the attempt to find some social criterion by which to test the validity of laws. So wide is the field that is covered by these categories that it will be possible to do more than consider the work of some representative writer or writers.

I. SOCIAL ORIGINS OF LAWS AND LEGAL INSTITUTIONS

The theories which deal with origins fall into three categories. Two of these, namely, the Historical interpretation and the Economic interpretation, have been considered in the previous two chapters, where it was pointed out that they are but versions of the sociological approach. Something has still to be said of the theory of Ihering, which sought to explain the origin of laws without resorting to a metaphysical concept like the Volksgeist or a single evolutionary principle as Marx had done.

Ihering

Ihering (1818-1892) passed the early part of his juristic career as an orthodox member of the German Historical School, during which time he intensively studied Roman law and published four volumes of a work, The Spirit of Roman Law. This he left unfinished, for its execution had convinced him that the origin of laws lay in sociological factors, a thesis which he proceeded to urge for the rest of his life. In the third volume of The Spirit he concluded that the basis of a "right" was an interest, and this led him to consider more closely how laws dealt with conflicting interests. His ideas came to fruition in his major work, Der Zweck im Recht ("Purpose in Law"), which has been translated into English as Law as a Means to an End. The dominant notion to be found in the exercise of human will it that of purpose. Causality in the natural world is governed by a "because". A stone falls because, without support, it must fall.

> "The stone does not fall in order to fall, but because it must fall, because its support is taken away; whilst the man who acts does so, not because of anything, but in order to attain to something. This purpose is as indispensable for the will as cause is for the stone. As there can be no motion of the stone without a cause, so can there be no movement of the will without a purpose."

Law is but a part of human conduct, and in the idéa of purpose Ihering found the mainspring of laws, which are only instruments for serving the needs of society. Their purpose is to further and protect the interests of society. Purpose should also guide juridical thinking, of which his analysis of possession was an outstanding example.

The problem of society is to reconcile selfish with unselfish purposes, and to suppress the former when they clash with the latter. Ihering stressed that law does not exist for the individual as an end in himself, but serves his interest with the good of society in view. Man, as a social animal, whether as a member of the state, Church, etc. stands on a superior plane to Man simply as an animal. Property, for example, is both a social and individual institution, which justifies expropriation and Limitation of the individual's rights. In order to reconcile the individual with society, it is necessary to balance various interests, which he grouped into three categories: individual, state and social. The social activities of people need to be encouraged, and this is accomplished by means of the "principle of the levers of social motion". There are for, the first two being the principles of Reward and Coercion. These seek to identify the selfish interest of the individual with some larger social interest. To give an example, since the economic wants of Man need satisfaction trade is instituted to fulfil this need, thus achieving a social purpose by pandering to the selfish profit motive. This is an example of Reward being employed. Coercion is a feature of that part of the social machinery which is called legal administration, namely, coercion organised in a set form by the state. By its side there is also unorganised coercion in the form of social conventions and etiquette. In addition to these there are two altruistic principles, Duty and Love, which also direct men towards social ends.

The significant point which emerges from Ihering's analysis is that laws are only one type of means of achieving an end, namely, social control. There is a distinction between society and state; laws are a feature of the latter. He insisted that laws should be treated from the angle of purpose and convincingly demonstrated the inadequacy of what he called the "jurisprudence of concepts", that is, mechanical deduction from given premises. He insisted also on the interdependence of all factors that obtain in society, which include: (a) extra-legal conditions, i.e., those under the control of nature, such as the climate and the fertility of the soil; (b) mixed legal conditions, those in which laws do not play a prominent part, such as self-preservation, reproduction, commerce and labour; and (c) purely legal conditions, those interests which are secured solely by legal regulation, such as the raising of revenue. Finally, he stressed the coercive character of legal regulation. His analysis led him to a definition in the following terms:

> "Law is the sum of the conditions of social life in the widest sense of the term, as secured by the power of the State through the means of external compulsion."

In his approach Ihering was building upon the work of the English thinkers, Bentham and Mill, whose utilitarianism may be said to have influenced his theory of purpoes. But Ihering insisted on the need to reconcile competing social and individual interests. In this respect he merits the title of "father of modern sociological jurisprudence", for, as will presently be seen, the problem of the harmonisation of interests plays a prominent part in the theories of some modern writes. Ihering himself did not indicate how this was to be resolved. His social utilitarianism, as it is usually called, stops short of this question and only draws attention to it. His concern, as stated at the beginning, was to example the origin of laws, not their application. He was also rightly convinced of the futility of *a priori* theories of justice; a law may be bad today and good tomorrow if the social background has shifted in the meantime.

II. IMPACT OF LAWS ON SOCIETY

Ehrlich

Ehrlich's (1862-1922) thesis was that laws found in formal legal sources, such as statues and decided cases, give only an inadequate picture of what really goes on in a community, for the norms which in fact govern life are only imperfectly and partially reflected in them. He draw a distinction between norms of decision, which correspond to that which is traditionally understood to be laws, and norms of conduct, which govern life in society. There is often a considerable divergence between it and import it into contracts. Eventually it may become embodied in a statute, but by this time modifications of it and fresh usages may have developed. So the process goes on. There will always be an inevitable gap between the norms of formal law and of actual behaviour. The point that Ehrlich was seeking to make was that the "living law" of society has to be sought outside the confines of formal legal material, in other words, in society itself. One learns little of the living law in factories, for example, by reading only the Factory Acts, the enactments and the common law relating to master and servant, trade unions, etc. One needs to go into the factory if one is to observe how far the formal law is followed, modified, ignored and supplemented. Only a minute fraction of social life comes before courts, and even then it usually represents some form of breakdown of social life. The task of formal law-makers is to keep it as nearly abreast of the living law as possible.

The existence of a social order ante-dates formal legal provisions and, moreover, certain facts, according to Ehrlich, underlie all laws. Propositions of law with reference to them arise in three ways, by endeavouring to give effect to the relations they create, by controlling or invalidating them, or by attaching consequences to them. A formal concept of law consists of the synthesis of generalisations constructed from the various propositions of law. If it is asked how the living law, as distinct from the formal law, is to be discovered, Ehrlich's answer was: from (a) judicial decisions, which are only evidentiary; (b) modern business documents against which judicial decisions need to be checked; and above all (c) observation of people, by living among them and noting their behaviour.

It follows from all this that state organisation plays but a subsidiary part. The norms emanating from the state and its organs are only one factor of social control and should be considered in conjunction, with others such as customs, morality and the practices of groups and associations. When looked at in the context of living law, there is no difference between formal legal norms and those of custom, etc. for it is social pressure that ensures obedience to both types in practice. So, to Ehrlich a stature which is habitually disregarded is no part of the living law. Enforcement by the state is not the distinction between formal and living law; the difference resides in social psychology. Some types of rules evoke different feelings from others. So there are many reasons why a person obeys even a legal rule other than fear of state enforced sanction. The characteristic of formal rules lies in the kind of feelings they arouse by virtue of their generality and social significance. It is a fact that different societies, and even the same society at different times, have had different feelings about what is socially important, so the line between legal, on the one hand, and moral and social rules, on the other, has constantly shifted. There is in all this some parallel with the views of Savigny, but Ehrlich's approach is infinitely more practical than Savigny's remote and mystical Volksgeist. Such regard for the living law requires that the scope of jurisprudence should be enlarged. It should concern itself with an observational study of society, since formal laws are only an adjunct of the living law.

Ehrlich's work was a powerful influence in inducing jurists to abandon purely abstract preoccupation and to concern themselves with the problems and facts of social life. While acknowledging his beneficial stimulation in this direction, one should not overlook some drawbacks in his theory. The distinction between formal and living law is necessary and important. But there is some danger of a merely verbal discussion as to whether both should be called "law", or only one, and if so which. He deprived formal law of any creative activity and gave it too much the appearance of trailing in the wake of social developments. It is true that reforming legislation is sometimes the formal expression of a like of public feeling, but it is also true that many norms of behaviour have been given shape and direction by the constant enforcement of laws. Ehrlich's distinction between norms of decision and norms of behaviour is important; but he failed to emphasise sufficiently their mutual interaction. Ehrlich's contentions were also somewhat outmoded even when he propounded them. State organisation is now, and has been for a long time, playing an ever-increasing part in the regulation of social life. It is by no means merely ancillary to the living law; it has come to be of transcendent importance. The picture which Ehrlich drew was truer of the past than of today, but it was ceasing to be true even in his own day. He was ready to admit the increasingly important part that was being played by state organisation, but he failed to absorb its implications into his theory. Finally, Ehrlich's conception of jurisprudence could make it unwieldly and amorphous. To urge that laws should be studied in the context of society is proper and beneficial, but the way in which Ehrlich proposed to conduct the study of society would all but submerge the significance of laws and might very well lead to the death of jurisprudence as a subject.

III. THE TASK OF LAWS IN SOCEITY

No account of the function which laws should perform in society would be complete without some mention of the pioneer contribution of Bentham.

Bentham

Jeremy Bentham's (1748-1832) contribution to analytical jurisprudence has already been dealt with. What will be considered now is his social philosophy. He was without doubt a stout individualist who approached the problems of society on that basis. His moral philosophy, social sense and juristic insight cannot be separated, but if there was one theme which ran through his many writings it was his utilitarian outlook on life. Man, in his view, was governed by pleasure and pain. In this one is tempted to detect the influence of Hobbes, who based his philosophy on the innate selfishness of men. The function of laws, according to Bentham, should be the promotion of the greatest happiness of the greatest number. This was only one application of the Principle of Utility, which approves or disapproves of action according as it increases or diminishes happiness. Bentham, be it noted, did not invent the utility principle; he took if from others, notably Hume, and developed it in the minutest detail. It is also worth remembering that his "pleasure" has a somewhat large signification, including altruistic and obligatory conduct, the "principle of benevolence"; while his idea of "interest" was anything promoting pleasure. The task of laws should be to bring about the maximum happiness of each individual, for the happiness of each will result in happiness for all. There is in this the age-old problem of reconciling interests of the individual with those of the community, but it amounts almost to a contradiction to try to harness a selfish pursuit of pleasure and avoidance of pain to the unselfish service of the common weal. One way of avoiding contradiction would be to suppose that individual pleasure-pain motivations by and large would not run counter to those of the community. Perhaps, Bentham did believe this, at least when he wrote his Introduction to the Principles of Morals and Legislation. It has also been suggested that he may have embraced dual standards, that of community interest in the public and political sphere, and self-interest in private matters. However this may be, as an unremitting reformer, he favoured legislation on a drastic scale to remedy the evils which he saw around him, but once these had been eradicated legislation should aim at providing subsistence, abundance, equality of opportunity and security for all. His individualist leaning manifested itself in his insistence that individual and private property were essential. This was necessary he argued, to ensure the fulfilment of settled expectations.

The utility principle has been subjected to searching examination. In the first place, it is not easy to see how a subjective criterion such as pleasure and pain can be transmuted into an objective one. Pleasure connotes an emotional attitude of approval, pain of disapproval. To judge an action according to the pleasure-pain criterion is to judge it subjectively. To say of a given course of conduct "I prefer it because it is conducive to pleasure" is no more informative than just "I prefer it". For conduct is not leaded with pleasure or pain-giving qualities; these are dependent on individual reaction. The problem then is: whose reaction should be the criterion? It is true that some types of conduct are generally thought of as conducive to pleasure and others to pain, but the problems arise with reference to conduct as to which feelings are equivocal or divided. This leads to another objection. The consequences of pleasure or pain of an action may well be indefinite in time or unforeseeable; it may give rise to immediate pain with a promise of pleasure or *vice versa*. These factors of time and uncertainty render assessment virtually impossible. Nor is it easy to see how the happiness of the majority will embitter the minority to the point of provoking disharmony. The converse proposition has also been advanced, namely, by promoting the happiness of other one promotes one's own happiness as well. As a general proposition this, too, is in need of proof. Apart from all this, the root difficulty of the principle of ensuring the happiness of the greatest number is how can this be used to apportion three houses, for instance, among four people. Above all, the pleasure-pain categories are too simple in themselves. It led Bentham into artificialities in forcing some very complex problems into these two straitjackets. It was also naïve to imagine that Man is motivated simple by reaction to pleasure and pain. Bentham appeared to have assumed that there is such a thing as an "average man". In truth, many actions are done unthinkingly, or from habit; and pleasure and pain come as often as incidents to other actions. It may be that he confused causes of action and reasons for action. He seems also to have assumed that laws could be made to operate on some single principle, which, as is evident in modern times, is an unfounded belief. Lastly, the ignored history and tradition altogether. They should not be exaggerated, but neither should they be excluded.

It is subject to the limitations of the utility principle, which pervaded his thought, that Bentham's jurisprudential contributions should be assessed. His work in the analytical (expositary) field has been examined. This was preliminary to his main interest, which was reform (censorial jurisprudence), and it is to this aspect that the following remarks refer. The utilitarian justification for having laws at all is that they are an important means of ensuring the happiness of the members of the community generally. Hence, the sovereign power of making laws should be wielded, not to guarantee the selfish desires of individuals, but consciously to secure the common good. "The public good", said Bentham, "ought to be the object of the legislator; general utility ought to be the foundation of his reasoning". In order to do this there has to be a balancing of interests was destined to play an important part in more modern theories. Bentham himself did not solve satisfactorily the problem of how such balancing can be achieved. The pleasure-pain motivation, as has been pointed out, is too simple to explain conduct; so any attempt to work out a calculus of interests on that basis was doomed. The "weight" accorded to interests differs according to the values of different individuals, and the policies of different countries will yield different results, e.g., Soviet Russia. Another contribution was his insistence on law-making to achieve social ends. The conscience of the people has to be trained so that they learn to find pleasure in ways that are not anti-social. To this end laws should be made which would make anti-social. To this end laws should be made which would make anti-social. Behaviour unprofitable, in other words, a source of pain to the doer rather than pleasure, and his views are still of absorbing interest. It will be noted that Bentham, although he would not have gone as far as the Soviet Communist Party in mass re-education, seems to have leaned in that direction. Lastly, he preached that laws should be judged by their consequences. For all these reasons it is clear that this aspect of his work entitles him to rank as a pioneer of functional jurisprudence in addition to his many other pioneering contributions. A very great deal of what has been done since is only development along his lines.

The Tubingen School

It was mentioned earlier in this chapter that Ihering had detected the origins of laws in purpose, namely, the resolution of conflicting social and individual interests. He stopped short of the point of suggesting how such reconciliation is to be effected. Bentham, as just indicated, had previously advanced a pleasure-pain criterion and his views had been introduced into Germany by Edward Beneke, though they only came to be well known through Ihering. A number of practitioners, known as the Tubingen School, attempted to evolve a "jurisprudence of interests" on the line suggested by Ihering, but stopped short of Bentham's principle of the greatest happiness of the greatest number. Instead, they were content to say simply that laws protect some, but not all, interests. A legal rule is, therefore, in a sense a decision on a prospective dispute and, as such, contains in itself a balance between competing interests. To understand a rule one has to see which social interests gave rise to it and how they were adjusted by the rule. Its interpretation and application should seek to ensure that those interests, which the law-maker preferred, shall prevail. A number of rules may be unified into a concept and concepts and rules into a system of law. Concepts so unified are useful for the purpose of systematic exposition, but for the purpose of applying and interpreting laws other and different concepts are required. These are "concepts of guidance" for those who have to administer laws. Unhappily, these functional concepts were never evolved. The reason for this lay in the lack of interest on the part of the Tubingen School in the goal which laws should seek to achieve; for the way in which interests are viewed and assessed is dependent on the end to be achieved. Here Bentham might have given them a lead. Despite the disappointing nature of their work, the problem which they failed to resolve is worthy of mention if only as a prelude to the contribution of Roscoe Pound, the American.

Roscoe Pound

Nowhere has the study of laws in society been taken up with such industry and enthusiasm as in America. Here, the law school and the jurist enjoy a status akin to that of jurists on the Continent and superior to that to their counterparts in Great Britain. These factors have combined to produce an American movement in sociological jurisprudence of great importance which draws its exponents both from the faculty and the bench. Outstanding among these is pound (1870-1964), of the Harvard Law School. As with Bentham, his theme was a constant one, maintained in his extensive writings throughout a very long period.

Sociological jurisprudence, according to Pound, should ensure that the making, interpretation and application of laws take account of social facts. Towards achieving this end there should be: (a) a factual study of the social effects of legal administration, (b) social investigations as preliminaries to legislation, (c) a constant study of the means for making laws more effective, which involves, (d) the study, both psychological and philosophical, of the judicial method, (e) a sociological study of legal history, (f) allowance for the possibility of a just and reasonable solution of individual cases, (g) a ministry of justice in English-speaking countries, and (h) the achievement of the purposes of the various laws. This comprehensive programme covers, as is evident, every aspect of the social study of laws. It is not possible to follow Pound's elaboration of each of these aspects, and all that can be done here is to outline his thought.

The common law, he said, still bears the impress of individual rights. So, in order to achieve the purposes of the legal order there has to be: (a) a recognition of certain interests, individual, public and social, (b) a definition of the limits within which such interests will be legally recognised and given effect to, and (c) the securing of those interests within the limits as defined. When determining the scope and subject-matter of the system the following five things require to be done: (i) preparation of an inventory of interests, classifying them; (ii) selection of the interests which should be legally recognised; (iii) demarcation of the limits of securing the interests so selected; (iv) consideration of the means whereby laws might secure the interests when these have been acknowledged and delimited; and (v) evolution of the principles of valuation of the interests.

Pound likened the task of the lawyer to engineering, an analogy which he used repeatedly. The aim of social engineering is to build as efficient a structure of society as possible, which requires the satisfaction of the maximum of wants with the minimum of friction and waste. It involves the balancing of competing interests. For this purpose interests were defined as "claims or wants or desires (or, I would like to say, expectations) which men assert *de facto*, about which the law must do something if organised societies are to endure". It is task of the jurist to assist the courts by classifying and expatiating on the interests protected by law. Pound's arrangement of these, elaborated in detail, was as follows:

A. Individual Interests

These are claims or demands or desires involved in and looked at from the standpoint of the individual life. They concern:

(1) Personality: This includes interests in (a) the physical person, (b) freedom of will, (c) honour and reputation, (d) privacy, and (e) belief and opinion.
(2) Domestic relations: It is important to distinguish between the interest of individuals in domestic relationships and that of society in such institutions as family and marriage. Individual interests include those of (a) parents, (b) children, (c) husbands, and (d) wives.
(3) Interests of substance: This includes interests of (a) property, (b) freedom of industry and contract, (c) promised advantages, (d) advantageous relations with others, (e) freedom of association, and (f) continuity of employment.

B. Public Interests

These are claims or demands or desires asserted by individuals involved in or looked at from the stand-point of political life.

> "The claims asserted in title of a politically organised society; as one might say for convenience, the claims of the state, the political organization of society."

There are two of them:

(1) Interests of the state as a juristic person. These, as pointed out earlier, are not applicable in this country where the position of the Crown has obviated the need for the personification of the state. They include, (a) the integrity, freedom of action and honour of the state's personality, and (b) claims of the politically organised society as a corporation to property acquired and held for corporate purposes.

(2) Interests of the state as guardian of social interests. This seems to overlap with the next major category.

C. Social Interests

These are claims or demands or desires, even some of the foregoing in other aspects, thought of in terms of social life and generalised as claims of the social group. This is much the most important category, since most, if not all, the interests in category A would be statable here from a social, rather than in individual, point of view. Social interests are said to include—

(1) Social Interest in the General Security

"The claim or want or demand, asserted in title of social life in civilised society and through the social group, to be secure against those forms of action and courses of conduct which threaten its existence."

This embraces those branches of the law which relate to (a) general safety, (b) general health, (c) peace and order, (d) security of acquisitions, and (e) security of transactions.

(2) Social Interest in the Security of Social Institutions

"The claim or want or demand involved in life in civilised society that its fundamental institutions be secure from those forms of action and courses of conduct which threaten their existence or impair their efficient functioning."

This comprises: (a) domestic institutions, (b) religious institutions, (c) political institutions, and (d) economic institutions. Divorce legislation might be adduced as an example of the conflict between the social interest in the security of the institution of marriage and the individual interests of the unhappy spouses. Pound pointed out that the law has at times attached disabilities to the children of illegitimate and adulterous unions with the object of illegitimate and adulterous unions with the object of preserving the sanctity of marriage. The example is not altogether fortunate, since the extent of which such vicarious suffering has deterred would-be offenders in minimal. Then again, there is tension between the individual interest in religious freedom and the social interest, at any rate in some countries, in preserving the dominance of an established church.

(3) Social Interest in General Morals

"The claim or want or demand involved in social life in civilised

> society to be secured against acts or courses of conduct offensive to the moral sentiments of the general body of individuals therein for the time being."

This covers a variety of laws, for example, those dealing with prostitution, drunkenness and gambling.

(4) Social Interest in the Conservation of Social Resources

> "The claim or want or demand involved in social life in civilised society that the goods of existence shall not be wasted; that where all human wants may not be satisfied, in view of infinite individual desires and limited natural means of satisfying them, the latter be made to go as far as possible; and, to that end, that acts or courses of conduct which tend needlessly to impair these goods shall be restrained."

Thus, this social interest clashes to some extent with the individual interest in dealing with one's own property as one pleases. It covers: (a) conservation of natural resources, and (b) protection and training of dependents and defectives, i.e., conservation of human resources.

(5) Social Interest in General Progress

> "The claim or want or demand involved in social life in civilised society, that the development of human powers and of human control over nature for the satisfaction of human wants go forward; the demand that social engineering be increasingly and continually improved; as it were, the self-assertion of the social group towards higher and more complete development of human powers."

This has three aspects: (a) Economic progress, which covers—(i) freedom of use and sale of property, (ii) free trade, (iii) free industry, and (iv) encouragement of invention by the grant of patents. Now, (i) and (iii) are less marked today than they used to be. Indeed, it might even be said that progress has been achieved by a reversal of them. The policy of free trade, which has as its corollary the disapproval of monopolies, might appear to have been endorsed by legislation against restrictive practices. While this is true of private monopolies, it should be noted that there is an ever-growing demand for monopolies in the state or state-controlled institutions. The encouragement of invention by the grant of patents, too, in somewhat suspect, for it opens the possibility of acquiring patents in order to suppress inventions. On the whole, therefore, item (a) is the least happy.

The interest in general progress also includes: (b) political progress, which covers: (i) free speech, and (ii) free association; and (c) cultural progress, which covers: (i) free science, (ii) free letters, (iii) free arts, (iv) promotion of education and learning, and (v) aesthetics.

(6) Social Interest in Individual Life

> "The claim or want or demand involved in social life in civilised society that each individual be able to live a human life therein according to the standards of the society."

It involves—(a) self-assertion, (b) opportunity, and (c) conditions of life.

Having listed the interests recognised by law, Pound considered the means by which they are secured. These consist of the device of legal person and the attribution of claims, duties, liberties, powers and immunities. There is also the remedial machinery behind them, which aims sometimes at punishment, sometimes at redress and sometimes at prevention. He also addressed himself to the question of how in any given case the interests involved are to be balanced or weighed. Interests, he insisted, should be weighed "on the same plane", as it social interest, since that very way of stating them may reflect a decision already made. One should transfer the interests involved on to the same "plane", preferable in most cases to that of the social plane, which is the most general. Thus, freedom of the person might be regarded as an individual interest, but it is translateable as an interest of the society that its members should be free. But, assuming that a choice has been made, the extent to which it can be given effect in any given case depends on the texture of the legal institutions that are involved. Some are more flexible than others and permit a freer play for the balancing process. Elsewhere Pound classified the institutions of the law as follows. There are, first, rules, which are precepts attaching definite consequences to definite factual situations. Secondly, there are principles, which are authoritative points of departure for legal reasoning in cases not covered by rules. Thirdly, there are conceptions, which are categories to which types or classes of transactions and situations can be referred and on the basis of which a set of rules, principles or standards becomes applicable. Fourthly, there are doctrines, which are the union of rules, principles and conceptions with regard to particular situations or types of cases in logically interdependent schemes so that reasoning may proceed on the basis of the scheme and its logical implications. Finally, there are standards prescribing the limits of permissible conduct, which are to be applied according to the circumstances of each case.

Such, then, is the substance of Pound's theory. That his contribution is considerable goes without saying. He more than anyone helped to bring home the vital connection between laws, their administration and the life of society. His work also set the seal on prior demonstrations of the responsible and creative task of lawyers, especially the judge. In so far as his theory laid such heavy emphasis on the existence of varied and competing interests and the need for adjustment between them, it will have enduring value. There are, however, some other respects in which his views are open to criticism.

In the first place, Pound's engineering analogy is apt to mislead. What, for instance is the "waste and construction, for relation to the conflict of interests? Further, the construction, for example of a bridge, is guided by a plan of the finished product, and the stresses and strains to be allowed to each part are worked out with a view to producing the best bridge of that kind in that place. But with laws there can be no plan, worked out in detail, of any finished product, for society in constantly developing and changing, and the pressures behind interests are changing too. Therefore, the value or importance to be allotted to each interest cannot be predetermined.

Pound assumed that *de facto* claims pre-exist laws, which are required to "do something" about them. But it can be contended that some claims are consequent on law, e.g., those that have resulted from welfare legislation. Besides, what does "do something" about them mean? It is not enough to say that law has to select those that are to be recognised. "Recognition" has many gradations, which makes it necessary to specify in what sense an interest is recognised as such. Thus, the cult of Scientology is not outlawed, but it has been officially condemned, which makes it difficult to say in what sense the law recognises or does not recognise it.

It is not interests as such, but the yardsticks with reference to which they are measured that matter. It may happen that some interest is treated as an ideal in itself, in which case it is not the interest as an interest, but as an ideal that will determine the relative importance between it and other interests. Thus, whether the proprietary right of a slave-owner is to be upheld or not depends upon whether sanctity of property or sanctity of the person in posited as the ideal. The choice of an ideal, or even a choice between competing ideals, is a matter of decision, not of balancing. And it is with the choice made by judges and the ideals which they adopt that lawyers are concerned.

The balancing metaphor is also misleading. If two interests are to be balanced, that presupposes some "scale" or "yardstick" with reference to which they are measured. One does not weigh interests against one another, even "on the same plane". But with reference to some ideal it is possible to say that the upholding of one interest is more consonant with, or more likely to achieve it than another; which means that with reference to that given ideal the one interest is entitled to preference over the other. This leads to another consideration. The "weight" to be attached to an interest will very according to the ideal that is used. For example, with reference to the ideal of freedom of the individual all interests pertaining to individual self-assertion will carry more weight than social interests; but with reference to the ideal of the welfare of society the reverse might be true. The point is that the whole idea of balancing is subordinate to the ideal that is in view. The march of society is gauged by changes in its ideals and standards for measuring interests.

In any case, all questions of interests and ideals should be considered in the context of particular issues as and when these come up for decision. An interest is not presented to a judge preclassified as part of an overall scheme, but in relation to one or more other interests in a given situation. Each situation has a pattern of its own, and the different types of interests and activities that might be involved are infinitely various. It is for the judge to translate the activity involved in the case before him in terms of an interest and to select the ideal with reference to which the competing interest are to be measured. Therefore, the listing of interests is not as important as the views which particular judge take of given activities and criteria by which they evaluate them.

How does one know when interests exist, how are they made articulate? The answer is: when presented in litigation. Lists of interests can be drawn up, not in advance of but after the various interests have been contended for in successive cases.

The recognition of a new interest is a matter of policy. The mere presence of a list of interests is, therefore, of limited assistance in helping to decide a given dispute. What this and the last paragraph suggest is that interests need only be considered as and when they arise in disputes; the matter that is of importance is the way in which they are viewed and evaluated by the particular judge.

In any case, lists of interests are only the products of personal opinion. Different writers have presented them differently. With reference to Pound's own elaborate scheme, it is to be observed that his distinction between categories B and C, Public and Social interests, is doubtful. Even the distinction between A and C, Individual and Social interests, is of minor significance. As Pound himself says, in most cases it is preferable to transfer individual interests on to the plane of social interests when considering them. On the suggestion previously made, it is the ideal with reference to which any interest is considered that matters, not so much the interest itself, still less the category in which it is placed. None of these remarks is intended to detract from the value of Pound's analyses of the interests themselves. All that is urged is that as a guide to the administration of laws the listing of interests is unhelpful.

It is difficult to see how the balancing of interests will produce a cohesive society where there are minorities whose interests are irreconcilable with those of the majority. How does one "balance" such interests? Whichever interest is favoured, the decision will be resented by those espousing the other; a compromise will most likely the resented by both. There is a different problem where a substantial proportion of the populace is parochially minded and have little or no sense of nationhood. The prime task is such countries are the creation of interests and the emphasis is, once more, on the need for ideals. Pound's theory cannot be accepted too generally.

It is worthwhile repeating that the criticism here is not that Pound ignored ideals of guidance, but that he seems to have devoted too little attention to them. His awareness of them is evident, for example in his own distinction between "natural natural law" and "positive natural law". The former, according to him, is "a rationally conceived picture of justice as an ideal relation among men, of the legal order as a rationally conceived means of promoting and maintaining that relation, and of legal precepts as rationally conceived ideal instruments of making the legal order effective for its ideal end." The latter is "a system of logically derived universal legal precepts shaped to the experience of the past, postulated as capable of formulation to the exigencies of universal validity." As early as 1919 Pound did offer a set of postulates as underlying contemporary society. But these are far from sufficient today and they have, both in Great Britain and America, been outmoded by the march of events. It is submitted with respect that it would have been preferable had he enlarged on the criteria of evaluating interests instead of developing particular interests. It is possible that his work has not had the practical impact that it ought to have had because of this somewhat sterile preoccupation with interests and too little attention to the criteria of evaluation.

IV. SOCIAL CRITERION OF THE VALIDITY OF LAW

Duguit

Duguit (1859-1928) was a professor of Constitutional Law in the University of Bordeaux. He attacked traditional conceptions of state, sovereignty and law and sought to fashion a new approach to these matters from the angle of society.

Social life should be viewed, he insisted, as it is lived, so as to be able to extract the most accurate generalisations. The outstanding fact of society is the interdependence of men. This has always existed and becomes more and more widespread as life grows more complex and as Man's mastery of the world increases. People have common needs, which require concerted effort; they have also dissimilar needs, which require mutual adjustment and accommodation. No one can live at the present time without depending on a far-reaching web of service provided by his fellow-men. Water, food, housing, clothing, recreation, entertainment and so on are dependent on other people. This social interdependence is not a conjecture, but a stark, inescapable fact of human existence. All organisation, therefore, should be directed towards smoother and fuller co-operation between people. This Duguit called the principle of Social Solidarity.

From this platform he launched his assault on traditional conceptions of the state, sovereignty and law. All institutions are to be judged according to how they contribute towards social solidarity. The state can therefore claim no special position or privilege. It is not some mystical entity, but an organisation of men, which can only be justified so far as it furthers social solidarity. When it ceases to do this there is a duty to revolt against it. It is worth pointing out that at no stage did Duguit deny the existence of an organised unity known as the state. This is very much a fact and to deny it would be unreal. What he said was that it is not essential nor entitled to special reverence.

The doctrine of sovereignty has likewise become meaningless. It used to be the personal attribute of a monarch, so such ideas as "sovereignty of the people" and the like are inappropriate and empty. The idea is, moreover, inadequate for composite and heterogeneous unities of delegation does not alter the fact that parts of sovereignty have been ceded. Nor can sovereignty be reconciled with the increasing responsibilities attaching to the state. For these reasons sovereignty fails to explain the kind of authority that governors now wield over the governed. A better way of looking at it is that all power and organisation are subject to the test of social solidarity. Their existence is functional and does not extend beyond the functions they perform in society. At this point, however, it might be noted that sovereignty is a term with many meanings, and cannot be wholly expelled in this way. There has to be some ultimate source of authority in every society.

In Duguit's view, with the disappearance of sovereignty there disappears also the authority traditionally ascribed to laws, for the basis on which these were thought to rest is then sapped of vitality. If sovereignty is mythical, so too are the notions that a law is: (a) the command of a sovereign, single and indivisible, (b) unchallengeable, and (c) the product of a single creative act.

Such is the core of Duguit's thesis. It contains some interesting implications. This first and most obvious is that the state is not indispensable. He drew particular attention to the move towards decentralisation and away from a central machinery of authority in view of the increasingly complex structure of modern society. A vague parallel might here be detected with the Marxist conception of the "withering away of the state", though Duguit's approach was different. Against this, it can be argued that totalitarian states of recent times have shown how power can be vested in decentralised groups in such a way as to enhance that power of the central authority.

The state is a useful, though not an essential, organisation, but its power is restricted by social solidarity. Whether such a state of affairs is achieved through a constitution or a judiciary, it is akin to the advocacy of a rule of law. The objection is simply that this is far from being the state of affairs in all countries. It will be remembered that Duguit's own initial contention was that life in society should be viewed as it actually is, so it would seem that his argument is only a plea for what is ought to be. Duguit proceeded to assert that when the state ceased to promote social solidarity there is a duty to revolt against it. Apart form the unreality of basing so drastic an action on a matter of personal evaluation, the point at which disobedience becomes justified is by no means as simple as this.

The interdependence of men is a fact, but "social solidarity" is an ideal. For, in the first place, in practice it becomes a matter of personal evaluation when the question to be decided is whether a given course of conduct is conducive to social solidarity or not. Does a law imposing or forbidding racial segregation promote social solidarity? It is difficult to see how this can be answered objectively and otherwise than in the light of political, religious and moral evaluations. Secondly, whose evaluation of social solidarity is to prevail? There is evidence that the forces of social disruption are as potent as those of solidarity. It would appear that Duguit has unfortunately fallen into the error of enlarging a limited truth into an absolute.

The most significant feature is the way in which Duguit used social solidarity as a criterion of the validity of laws. He asserted that a precept which does not further social solidarity is not law, and denied that statutes and decisions make law in themselves. There are three formative laws, namely, respect for property, freedom of contract, and liability only for fault. The precepts of positive law should conform to these formative laws and they only achieve validity when received and approved by the mass of public opinion. "A rule of law exists whenever the mass of individuals composing the group understands and admits that a reaction against the violation of the rule can be socially organised." Public opinion is thus the expression of the social solidarity principle, by which the validity of laws should be judged. But this is open to serious objection. What is this mass opinion? Its vagueness and unsatisfactory nature are obvious. By what means is it discoverable? Situations very frequently arise as to which no particular feeling exists and others as to which opinion is divided. It is unrealistic to suggest that a court will, or will be allowed to, decline to receive an enactment as "law" because it can be shown that public opinion does not subscribe to it. Once more, it is clear that this is no more than what, in Duguit's opinion, should be the position.

Duguit avoided all imagery of the state as a person with organs and will of its own. The state is nothing more than an organisation of individuals and it is they who issue commands and carry out decisions. He likewise denied the personality of corporations and similar groups. The coherence of all such associations lies, not in some mystic personality, but in social solidarity. It is ironic that Duguit, who foresaw how personification of the state could lead to totalitarianism, which he abhorred, should have had his own theory used for that very end. Thus, national socialist jurists seized on his minimisation of conflict within society as a justification for the suppression of trade unions and strikes. Employers and workers were pictured as comrades united in their own particular factory or local organisation, which in turn was absorbed in the unity of the state. This created a romantic bond of loyalty to the state and any act against it was treachery. Such a perversion of his doctrines to support the aggrandisement of the state would have horrified Duguit.

His view of the function of government led Duguit to deny the distinction between public and private law. All laws are only means of serving the end of social solidarity and should be judged by that criterion. It the distinction between public and private law Duguit suspected a method of elevating the state above the rest of society and, as such, he had none of it.

Duguit also denied the existence of rights, "natural rights" he treated as myths, since modern research has shown that Man has always lived in society and was never entirely independent. The core of the law lies in duty, which is the means of securing that each one fulfils his part in the furtherance of social solidarity. The only right which any man can possess, he said, "is the right always to do his duty". What are commonly called "rights" are only incidental to the relations with other people which arise in the course of performing one's social duty. The reality is thus not the right, but the duty. This aspect of Duguit's theory is not only unnecessary, but also verbalistic. He admits, as indeed could hardly avoid doing, that relationships do arise between individuals. These are commonly described in the language of duties as well as of rights. His objection is merely to the use of the word "right".

Finally, Duguit would banish the ethical element from law. But all he did, it would seem, was to substitute one ideal in place of others.

Duguit's views have had considerable influence. Their adaptation by Nazi and Fascist jurists has already been alluded to. Soviet jurists, too, found parts of his work congenial. His functional approach to laws, his denial of the distinction between public and private law and his advocacy of a form of the "withering away" of centralised authority and its replacement by a decentralised "administration of things" had some attraction to the early Marxist interpreters. His work had influence in another direction as well. The emphasis that he placed on the importance of the group, coupled with advance in later sociological thought, shifted the focus of attention to group behaviour, about which something must now be said.

V. GROUPS AND INSTITUTIONS

Modern society presents a confusing pattern of different values, which exert different pressures of greater or lesser intensity and of varying application and concern. It is relevant in this connection to have some idea of the influence of groups, roles and institutions.

All groups have some sort of unity. For a start, some attention should be paid to the phenomenon known as stratification, which refers to the divisions and cross-division of people into degrees of compactness, fluidity, distinctness and separability. They may be temporary or permanent, closed or open (depending upon the ease with which people can pass in and out), occupational (e.g., teachers, miners), functional (e.g., income groups), feature (e.g., racial, religious, casts), and so forth. Stratification influences the social set-up, as where statue differences structured feudal society, and racial, religious, or functional differences shape modern societies. It also facilitates social control, as when classifications according to income, race, religion or caste become decisive in the moulding and application of certain types of laws. Other kinds of groups result from co-operative effort on the part of a number of persons to achieve a common purpose, coupled with a sense of belonging to that group. These range from giant, permanent organisations to *ad hoc* and localised bodies, such as a union of residents in a town to oppose a threatened invasion of some amenity.

Groups and Values

A point of jurisprudential interest lies in the intimate connection between group phenomena and values and moral pressures. The values of society are closely connected with large power-groups. The aims and ideals of such a group are in the first instance matters of evaluation by its members, but the degree of pressure brought to bear behind the aims and ideals depends on the strength of the groups. The stronger the group, the more likely is it that what is stands for will in time begin to prevail outside itself. Powerful economic groups, for instance, have had decisive influence throughout the whole of society, as Marx demonstrated. Once the aims and ideals of a group have become socially accepted in due course of time they cease to be dependent on power, and acquire a life of their own. They in their turn become supports for power and factors sine quibus non in the continuance of power or the establishment of new power. Governments, for instance, are generally anxious to associate themselves with accepted values of certain groups, especially those of religion, because they transcend the present power-wielders; and this is no doubt why the regime in South Africa is anxious to justify apartheid by pointing to the support of the influential Dutch Reformed Church. The close association between power-structures and values is also to be seen in the fact that rebellion against one is so often rebellion against the other. Another point is that values evolve slowly and are changed as slowly. In this way they can serve as a brake on the exercise of power. This may be illustrated once more with reference to South Africa where the government has found that convictions about apartheid now run so deep that they hamper the introduction about apartheid now run so deep that they hamper the introduction of any policy which smacks of liberalism.

The pressure on an individual to submit to a group derives, among other things, from his knowledge that others also submit. This generates the feeling of being bound, which the individual either accepts or rejects. Among those who accept, there is the further feeling that there has to be some measure of discipline to preserve the group; while even among those who glory in rejecting it, there is the feeling that non-conformity is rebellion.

Roles

Whenever a person's conduct towards others has some measure of permanence his behaviour becomes, as it were, institutionalised, i.e., a "role". Roles evolve as solutions to problems of interaction between individuals and groups and have been described as "recognised and established usages governing the relations between individuals and groups". What becomes institutionalised is a way of going about things and it is, thus, an idea. Not only human beings, but ideas also count, said Renard. The institution may take the form of a role, such as that of chairman, which results from the fact the every group has to have someone to control proceedings; or even a place occupied by a person, such as "father's place" at table, which may simple be the most convenient place to seat him so that he will not be in the way of those serving the meal. These are very simple examples, but what is common to all forms of institutionalised behaviour is that there has to be general and continuous acceptance of a way of doing things, which comes to serve as a standard of behaviour. This is because roles exert pressure to act in certain ways and carry directions for behaviour. A role may involve a number of relationships ("role-set"), and different roles may overlap. Both social roles and strata tend to have built-in values, so that they are more than just factual situations. Hume illustrated this with an example of the difference between a sapling, which destroys the parent tree, and parricide. In both situations, he said, the factual position is the same, namely, destruction of the parent by its offspring. The difference lies in the disapproval attaching to the one and not to the other, and this comes through regarding the human relationship as a role. Roles exert pressure on the performers in various ways. One is the pressure to conform to the traditions and standards of the given role, e.g., of judge or legal adviser. Likewise certain types of strata influence people to live up to the values, which are part of them, in order to win acceptance or retain acceptability and prestige in them.

While it is true that an "ought" cannot be derived from an "is", behaviour-patterns do become so interlocked and inter-dependent that if one person fails to conform, he disrupts the whole to a greater or lesser extent. The structure of society consists of interrelationships between numberless roles and groupings, which are often more durable than human beings. The "ought" behind "you ought to conform" to these roles does not express an emotional attitude towards the conduct in question, so much as a condition *sine qua non* of social existence; things being as they are, conformity is the effective way of carrying on together. At this point language takes a hand. Conformity tends to be labelled "right", "proper", or "correct" because it fulfils expectations and is convenient; non-conformity tends to be labelled "wrong", "improper", or "incorrect" because it frustrates other people's expectations and is inconvenient. These words already have powerful moral connotations, and so it comes about that through language there occurs a shift in the meaning of "right" or "wrong" behaviour in the sense of being effective or ineffective in achieving an end to such behaviour being effective or ineffective in achieving an end to such behaviour being thought to be "morally right" or "morally wrong". It should not be forgotten that it is through language that people learn huge numbers of values, which are inherited and propagated by means of verbal symbols. To take an example, in the present social structure in Southern Africa apartheid, in the opinion of the white races, in the "right" (i.e., the only effective) way to preserve stability, since integration with Africans is likely to prove very unsettling; but this has generated the conviction that it must also mean that apartheid is "morally right". In primitive societies the roles performed in religious ritual patterned social structure. The effective way of achieving certain ends (inducting intervention or non-intervention of the gods) was by performing certain ritual actions. So, as Hocart taught, society was organised on the basis of ritual, and the various roles were assigned to different individuals, usually heads of important families. Here, too, the "ought" behind conformity was that this was a condition *sine qua non* of achieving the desired ends rather that that of obligation. The latter evolved out of the former.

Groups as Institutions

Society abounds in institutions of many kinds. An important distinction is that between organised institutions, groupings of people, e.g., Church, family, etc. and conceptual institutions, e.g., property, ownership, etc. Institutions, such as courts, police and the like, perform legal functions, but they consist of persons. Group institutions evolve slowly, for however they come into being, perhaps even by force initially, it takes time for them to become into being, perhaps even by force initially, it takes time for them to become accepted. Such evolution is a social, not a juridical, phenomenon. A sociological theory of institutions is one which explains such data as found in society and is, in effect, an analysis of society; a sociological theory of the law of institutions is concerned with the manner in which laws take account of them.

The pioneer institutionalist was Hauriou (1856-1929), who spoke of an institution as "an idea of an undertaking which is realised and which persists in a social environment". To achieve this an authority with organs is called into being; and manifestations of a communion among the members of the social group, who are interested in realizing the idea, are directed by the organs and regulated by procedures. Hauriou distinguished between institutions-personnes, groups of human beings, and institutions-choses, "institution-things" (e.g., rules of law, marriage); but the latter he largely ignored. One feature about his theory is that he only look account of those ideas which are innate in men as social animals and in the very nature of social life, i.e., principles of constitution and regulation without which no kind of group activity would be possible. He further limited his treatment to groups, which have achieved a certain degree of development. These features, coupled with an avowed Catholic orientation, gave his theory a natural law thins, which has been noted by several writers. An Italian, Romano, adopted a more positivist approach and paid attention to "institution-thins". There are, he said, many more *de facto* institutions is society than enter into Hauriou's analysis. In so far he tried in this way to take account of all institutions as facts found in any given society, his theory may be said to be empirical and more truly sociological that Hauriou's.

Hauriou's theory is not a theory of group personality, but rather a theory of groups i.e., of their social reality; and it is also to be noticed that institutionalism does require the subordination of the individual, to some extent at least, to the institution. There is in this a danger that such a theory may easily be utilised so as to demand unquestioning obedience to a totalitarian regime in the same way as Duguit's theory was used.

Conceptual Institutions

Interest has recently grown in legal concepts and even law itself as institutions. Professor Mac-Cormick has drawn attention to the distinction between an "institution of law", e.g., contract, and a particular contract, which is an instance of it. An "institution of law", according to him, depends on whether there is (a) A set of institutive rules, namely, those specifying what constitutes, e.g., a contract. Such rules include, but are not co-extensive with, power-conferring rules, since an event may bring a conceptual institution into play. (b) Consequential rules, which specify that when a particular institution exists, then certain jural relations follow in consequence. (c) Terminative rules, which specify how institutions shall end. These, too, include, but are not co-extensive with, power-conferring rules. The important point about institutive rules is that they only indicate the conditions which are "ordinarily necessary and presumptively sufficient" for the existence or creation of a particular instance of the institution. The qualification leaves flexibility and room for value considerations to play their part. In this way it would seem that there is a return to a study of legal concepts via the treatment of them as institutions.

The institutional nature of laws has been approached by Professor Honor'e through the group. To say that something is law is to strike an attitude towards disobedience, and a theory of law is, among other things, a theory about such attitudes. To understand laws one has to begin with a group, since all laws are laws of a group. There must be a shared understanding about certain prescriptions of behaviour which curtail liberties of action. Such prescriptions need to be effective, which requires the interlocking of different kinds of rules, initial and remedial. These need to become institutionalised in the sense that they apply to all members of the group, or in specified circumstances, and there must be group understanding about a rule determining how the group officers are to be appointed and how they function. When, therefore, "we find prescriptions which are reinforced by genetic or remedial rules of an institutional character (i.e., supported by group understandings as to the jurisdiction and appointment of the relevant officials) we can speak of the prescriptions and rules that support them as laws".

The above description would fit the arrangements of different kinds of groups, e.g., Church, clubs, etc. Professor Honor'e such as the state, to derive from the fact that such groups are able to institutionalise to a greater extent than other groups, the use of force in remedial situations. A different analysis of a legal system as an institution comes from Dr. Raz. According to him, the distinctive feature lies in the working of courts. Their decisions are binding even when wrong; but they themselves are bound to apply certain norms prescribing the behaviour of individuals when giving decisions as to whether actual behaviour complies with those norms. So far, the description would fit the institution of a private club as well as the legal system of a state. The distinctive features of the latter are that it is comprehensive, in that it claims authority to regulate every type of behaviour; it is supreme, in that it claims authority over all institutions and organisations; and it is "open", in that it provides binding force to certain norms which are not part of it, e.g., private agreements or foreign laws.

CONCLUSION

Summing up, one might say that the greatest practical contribution of various sociological approaches has been field-work in examining the interaction between law and its social milieu. In this respect the position in Great Britain still lags behind that in other countries, but a good deal is now being done. Another far reaching outcome is likely to be a pointer to the evolution of ideals on an empirical basis. It has been abundanty demonstrated that laws play a significant and creative role in society, and such a dynamic function presupposes the existence of ideals, even unavowed, which provide directing force. The transcendental idealism of the past suffered a blow at the hands of positivism from which it could never hope to recover; positivism in turn faltered in the face of the problems that confronted it. The rise of sociological study has made possible a synthesis between the two by restoring ideals in a way that could satisfy and give life to the exacting positivist discipline. It is no coincidence that the functional approach has heralded the revival of natural law in this century; it was, indeed, a necessary precursor.

What is it that lawyers, who engage in a social study of their subject, seek to accomplish? To answer this the previous distinction between sociological jurists and legal sociologists is cerned with laws in their social context. They inquire: (a) into the circumstance in which laws arise and become differentiated from morality and the like; (b) how the administration of laws is related to justice; and (c) what influences are mutually exerted by laws and other types of social phenomena and changes in them. The first of these is essentially a historical type of inquiry and nothing need be added to what has previously been said. The emphasis is very much on the prescriptive content of law. The second question, (b), has two aspects. There is, on the one hand, the question of the criteria which should govern the application of laws. What is needed is a theory for the guidance of administrators. Laws are means for achieving certain ends, ant there are thus two sets of "oughts" : those of laws themselves which prescribe the conduct of people in society and by which their actions are judged, and a functional set which prescribes how judges and other administrators should apply the general prescriptive norms so as to achieve certain ends, whatever these might be. In additions to this, there is the question of the social criteria which are thought to govern the very validity of the general prescriptive norms. In connection with the third question, (c), Ehrlich's distinction between norms of decision, which correspond to prescriptive rules by which conduct is judged, and norms of conduct according to which people actually behave, is of signal importance. The latter are shaped by the gradual acceptance of the former, but there is also the reverse process whereby the behaviour of people brings about changes in prescriptive rules.

In contrast to all this, the term "legal sociologist" has been used to refer to those whose main interest is the analysis of society and who seek to fit legal administration as a whole into a concept of society. In this enterprise the differentiation of legal administration from the operation of other forms of social control becomes necessary. It brings in at once the distinctive character of legal enforcement, namely, the machinery of sanction, as an important social fact. A caution which must be uttered is that no inferences should be drawn from any such concept of law outside its frame of reference. In brief, one should be wary of deducing from it the nature of laws and legal concepts. It has been pointed out, for example, that the provision of sanctions is part of a concept of "law in society", but that a misleading picture is presented when inferences are drawn from this as to the nature of the concept of legal duty. The sociologist is concerned with what "is", i.e., the totality of legal administration as an observable social phenomenon; but from such an "is" cannot be derived assertions about the prescriptive "oughts" behind laws, for the two spheres of discourse are distinct. It would be as erroneous as trying to deduce propositions about actual social behaviour from the prescriptive content of laws. These points may seem obvious enough, but there is an occasional tendency to overlook them.

10

REALISM

Realism ought not to be left out of account, for it is a procrustean tern covering various kings of inquiry which have provided interesting, novel and vigorous stimuli in contemporary legal thought. These are of two kinds which are as follows.

AMERICAN REALISTS

A preliminary warning is needed against the tendency to imagine that there is anything like a "school" of American Realists. A difficulty in the way of a coherent presentation of their views is that there are varying versions of realism as well as changes of front; positions formerly defended with zest have since been forgotten or abandoned. Although the descriptions "realism" and "legal realists" are commonly used, this terminology is abandoned in more recent writings. Judge Jerome Frank (1889-1957), a leading exponent, preferred the phrases "experimentalists" or "constructive skeptics", and has described his own attitude as one of "constructive skepticism". He repudiated the charge that "the 'realist school' embraced fantastically inconsistent ideas" by pointing out that "actually no such 'school' existed". The common bond is, in his words,

> "skepticism as to some of the conventional legal theories, a skepticism stimulated by a zeal to reform, in the interests of justice, some court-house ways."

All that will be attempted in these pages is to outline the theses of two outstanding exponents. American Realism is a combination of the analytical positivist and sociological approaches. It is positivist in that it first considers the law at it is. Reform is the ultimate aim, but a prerequisite to reform is, in positivist thinking, a true understanding of law as it is. On the other hands, the laws as is stands is the product of many factors. Inasmuch as the realists are interested in sociological and other factors that influence the law, their approach may fairly be described as being in part sociological. Their concern, however, is with law rather than with society. They share with sociologists an interest in the effects of social conditions on law as well as the effect of law on society. But they emphasise the need for a prior revelation of the actual behaviour of lawyers. Julius Stone calls the realist movement a "gloss" on the sociological approach. It is part of that aspect of sociology, dealt with in the last chapter, which treats law as a given social phenomenon. Its distinctive feature is the stress that it lays on factual studies of the behaviour of lawyers.

"Theory" is a means towards understanding, and the test of scientific theory lies in predictability. To understand what "law" is, one should be able to predict how judges decide cases. Many factors contributed to this spot-lighting of the American judiciary. One is the check imposed upon legislative power by the American Constitution. The judges interpret the Constitution and have power to quash legislation in conflict with it. It is also a regrettable fact that American judges have not enjoyed quite that degree of trust and confidence as their British counterparts. A possible reason is that American judges in the lower courts are elected, which opens the door to political influence. Again, American legal institutions are young compared with those in Great Britain. The days when judges were consciously building up the law are still fresh in the minds of American jurists. It is therefore less easy for them than for British jurists ever to have thought of the judicial function as being a mechanical application of rules. Also, the divergent and separate common law systems that obtain in the different States are evidence of the creative function of the judges. How could these systems have developed along different lines from a common starting point were it not for the creative faculties of judges?

At one time there was a tendency to regard the movement as a thorough-going attempt of dispense with the "oughts" of the law. Only the "reality" of law matters in fact, and "reality" is what actually happens and no more. Ideas of "ought" and such like were not allowed to distort the perception of clear, simple fact.

The realist approach is highly empirical. Law, i.e., the decisions of judges, is the product of ascertainable factors. Included among these are their personalities, their social environment, the economic conditions in which they have been brought up, business interests, trends and movements of thought, emotions, psychology and so forth. The importance of the personal element was not new, and attention has previously been drawn to the part played by such factors as these. The realists gave them decisive significance.

The seeds of the movement were sown in a famous paper of Mr. Justice Holmes (1841-1935) in 1897, in which this great judge put forward a novel way of looking at law. If one wishes to know what law is, he said, one should view if through the eyes of a bad man, who is only concerned with what will happen to him if he does certain things. The traditional description of law is that it consists of rules from which deductions are made.

> "But if we take the view of our friend, the bad man, we shall find that he does not care two straws for the actions or deduction, but that he does want to know what Massachusetts or English courts are likely to do in fact. I am much of his mind. The prophecies of what the courts will do in fact and nothing more pretentious are what I mean by the law."

Mr. Justice Holmes was in no sense purporting to give a final definition of law, or do more than give a description suitable for the context in which he was writing. The statement that law is only what courts do is iconoclastic, and suggests that ethics, ideals and even rules should be put on one side. Holmes himself had no such intention, for in the same paper he proceeded to insist on the need to restrict the area of uncertainty and no the need for more theory. "We have too little theory in the law," he said, "rather than too much". Nor did he, at the time when he wrote, have any suspicion that he would be hailed as the prophet of a new faith. Yet such has been his fate. Another pioneer of the new fashion in thinking was Gray (1839-1915), who drew a distinction between law and sources of law. The former is what the judges decide. Everything else, including statute, are only sources of law until interpreted by a court. Pushed to its logical conclusion, the obvious implication of this is that even a judicial decision is "law" only for the parties in the instant dispute and thereafter becomes a "source of law", since everything will depend on the interpretation that is put upon it in a later decision.

Among the techniques, which opened up a new vista in the study of law, the following are the most important: (a) The realists introduced studies of case-law from a point of view which distinguished between rationalisation by a judge in conventional legal terminology of a decision itself. Unfortunately, the way in which in their early writings they expressed their interest in what judges actually do (decisions), rather than in what they say they do (reasoning), did create the impression that they were stressing the latter to the exclusion of the former. (b) The inquiry into the motivation behind decisions opened up further lines of investigation. So, the study of the personalities, upbringing and psychology of judges and jurymen assumed significance. (c) The realists also study the different results reached by courts within the framework of the same rule or concept in relation to variations in the facts of the cases, and the extent to which courts are influenced in their application of rules by the procedural machinery which exists for the administration of the law. (d) Too much attention has traditionally been devoted to the processes in appellate courts to the neglect of lower courts. Accordingly, some realists have urged that research be broadened so as to include the activities of lower courts and the relation between their work and those of upper courts. Knowledge of what goes on in the lower courts in needed in order to know what law "means to persons in the lower income brackets". Jerome Frank thought that there is as much of a contrast between the picture of the law that one gets by studying the work of appellate courts to the exclusion of a study of trial courts as there is between an account of manners in Buckingham Palace and in a New York subway. His comment on Cardozo's account of the nature of the judicial process is:

> "Cardozo most of his days an appellate court lawyer or appellate court judge, suffered from a sort of occupational disease, appellate-court-it is."

Frank's Law and the modern Mind (1930) is perhaps as typical of early realism as any other work of that period. His main attack was originally directed at the myth of achieving certainty through legal rules. The traditional picture of a legal order is that rules impart to it at least some measure of certainty and uniformity. There is a difference, pointed out by Beale, a great American jurist, between rules and judicial decisions. The "law" consists of rules; a judicial decision is in no sense the only law, because it is given by virtue of a rule. Frank was vehement in attacking this notion. In the first place, if judgments were so easy to forecast, no one but litigious maniacs would ever go to court. It is quite untrue to suggest that uncertainty stems from uncertainly in rules. In the majority of cases, even where there is some rule which can be applied, two opposite conclusions are perfectly possible. He gave two examples to contradict Beale's thesis that law is distinct from judicial decisions. The Supreme Court in 1917 was equally divided on the question of the validity of a certain statute. In 1923 the Court by a majority declared it to be invalid. In the meantime the personnel of the Court had varied several times, and had the matter come up between November 1921 and June 1922 the decision would have gone the other way. What, then, was the law during the period from 1917 to 1923? The answer would surely have varied according to the date when the question was asked, and according to guesses as to the personnel of the Supreme Court. His other example was where the Kentucky State Court took one view of the law of Kentucky on a particular point, while the Supreme Court took a different view of the law of Kentucky on the same point. The question, what was the law? Depended on whether it was asked of the Supreme Court or the Court of Kentucky. Law, therefore, cannot be divorced from judicial decisions; it is not, in the words of Holmes, "a brooding omnipresence in the sky". Frank rejected such objectifications of the law, which he despised as "Bealism".

From this point onwards Frank divided realists into two camps, described as "rule skeptics" and "fact skeptics". The "rule skeptics" rejected legal rules as providing uniformity in law, and tried instead to find uniformity in rules evolved out of psychology, anthropology, sociology, economics, politics, etc. Kelsen, it will be remembered, maintained that it not possible to derive an "ought" from an "is". The "rule skeptics" avoided that criticism by saying that they were not deriving purposive "oughts", but only predictions of judicial behaviour analogous to the laws of science. Frank called this brand of realism the left-wing adherents of a right-wing tradition, namely, the tradition of trying to find uniformity in rules. They, too, had to account for uncertainty in the law on the basis of rule-uncertainty. The "fact skeptics", among them Frank, rejected even this aspiration towards uniformity. It savoured of "Bealism". So he abandoned all attempts to seek rule-certainty and pointed to the uncertainty of establishing even the facts in trial courts. These have to be established largely by witnesses, who are fallible and who may be lying. It is impossible to predict with any degree of certainty how fallible a particular witness is likely to be, or how persuasively he will lie. All persons, judges and jurymen alike, from different impressions of the dramas subconscious predilictions, varied idiosyncracies and prejudices. Eternal verities are not to be erected on such a basis. Frank alleged that all those who write on legal certainty, not excepting the "rule skeptics", overlook these difficulties.

> "They often call their writings 'jurisprudence'; but, as they almost never consider juries and jury trials, one might chide them for forgetting 'jurisprudence'."

Frank suggested that this craving for certainty and guidance, which men seek in the law, may stem, in part at any rate, from the yearning for security and safety which is an inescapable legacy of childhood. The child puts his trust in the power and wisdom of his father to provide an atmosphere of security. In the adult the counterpart of this feeling is the trust reposed in the stability and immutability of human institutions. Frank suggested that the quest for certainty in law is in effect a search for a "Father-symbol" to provide an aura of security, and although he attributed great prominance to this factor, he offered it only as a "partial explanation" of what he called the "basic myth", and listed fourteen other explanations as well. He called on lawyers to outgrow these childish longings for a "father controlled world", and to follow the example of Mr. Justice Holmes, the "completely adult jurist".

Rules, then, are merely word-formulae. If they are to have any meaning at all, such meaning has to be sought in the facts or real life to which they correspond. Frank adopted a quotation from Holmes:

> "We must think things not words, or at least, we must constantly translate our words into the facts for which they stand if we are to keep to the real and the true."

If the "facts" in the world which correspond to talk about law are actual decisions this yields a very simple picture of law. Frank's original view was that "law on any point is either (a) actual law, i.e., a specific past decision as to that situation, or (b) probable law, i.e., a guess as to a specific future decision". Later he showed a reluctance to use the word "law".

> "instead," he said, "I would state directly—without an intervening definition of that term—what I was writing about, namely (1) specific court decisions, (2) how little they are predictable and uniform, (3) the process by which they are made, and (4) how far, in the interest of justice to citizens that process can and should be improved."

The above passage, taken from the Preface added nineteen years after the original version, represents a modification of Frank's position, or, alternatively, an attempt to dispel misconceptions about it. Shortly after the first publication, however, statements such as the distinction between "actual" and "probable" law not unnaturally created a certain impression, which touched off considerable controversy. In reply to Roscoe Pound's attack Llewellyn protested that his criticism was beside the point as it was not founded on what the realists had actually said, but on what they were supposed to have said. The realists were at least guilty of over-statement; and whether misconceived or not, the polemic is a fact of history, which had the merit of inducing some healthy re-thinking and clarification by both sides. Much of the heaviest fire was brought to bear in defence of rules against a real or imagined onslaught on their existence.

How far did the realists reject rules? Indeed, it is clear that they did not all do so. The importance of rules may be questioned, but that is a matter of degree. To assert even that a judge's "hunch" determines the way in which he manipulates and applies a rule is unexceptionable. But if anyone were to assert or imply that rules are illusory and that the "hunch" reigns supreme, this would be too strong a statement. In many cases judges are largely bound by rules and have little choice, whatever their sympathies; and even when they circumvent rules, they do so in a manner which conceals the fact that they are doing so. In other words, the "hunch" can operate only within the framework of the rules. In another sense, the assertion that the "hunch" is supreme goes scarcely far enough, for the "hunch" is itself the product of standards, patterns of behaviour, concepts and rules. Suppose that X rides off on the first bicycle, which he finds parked in the street and which Y had placed there a short while before. There can be no doubt that in an action by Y against X the "hunch" would comedown in favour of Y, because it is born of ideas about ownership, rights of possession and so on. The importance of rules can be demonstrated in another way by asking, How does one know who is a "judge"? The point is that the position of a judge, and, indeed, of every other official is defined by rules. The realists properly drew attention to the many factors that influence the judges apart from rules. They rightly indicated that it is fallacious to regard what the judges say as an infallible guide to what they do. Yet, it is equally fallacious to assert that what judges say can never be a guide to what they do; they sometimes say that they are bound by rules because their decisions have in fact been so governed. The point is that the reasons which particular judges give for doing certain things are very much a part of what they do. So, to be realist in the full sense of the word would require that allowance be made for the way in which non-realist judges behave, which includes their adherence to rules. So, if anyone, were to reject rules, he would be more unrealistic than most "traditionalists". Much of the trouble seems to stem from misleading impressions created by the way in which some realists expressed themselves.

Preoccupation with the hunches of individual judges tended to obscure the fact that judges do agree by and large on certain yardsticks of evaluation, and also the fact that they consciously strive to put aside personal considerations. Shared values produce an extensive and impersonal background against which instances of purely personal prediliction are very few. Again, a quirk may manifest itself on some occasions and not others and it would be misleading to exaggerate its significance. The point is that the realists succeeded in filling but a minute fraction of the picture of judicial action by looking only at personal and environmental factors; the pressure of rules and other impersonal factors play a much more decisive part.

A rule is certainly more abstract than a judicial decision and to that extent may be thought to be farther from "reality". But both are the concern of the lawyer. In cases which never come before the courts lawyers have to advise their clients as to the law. It is true that here, too, much of what is stated to be law has been the subject of previous judicial decisions. But immediately after a new statute comes into force, and before it comes before the courts, it would be possible for a lawyer to advise his client that a new rule of law has superseded the old rule. To argue that such a statement would only be a statement as to "probable law" is quite unrealistic. A great many daily transactions go forward and are governed by what everyone takes to be "law" even though few of them ever reach the tribunals.

The contention that "laws" are only what judges and officials do is a somewhat unusual meaning of the word. Statutes and precedents are followed because they are "laws" already. When it is stated that statutes are accepted by the courts as capable of imparting to propositions the quality of "law". Gray and Frank appeared to say that the stamp of "law" is only applicable after the judge has actually decided; which is not the accepted usage. The fact the judges interpret statutes and precedents and keep shaping and re-shaping their contents does not mean that they are not "laws" until interpreted. Clay is clay before, during and after it has been moulded. Moreover, why is it "realistic" to apply the word "law" at the point of interpretation and no other? A decision is no more "real" in providing the damages, property, or whatever else is sought, than a rule. For the decision has still to be carried out and the officials charged with that task may be bribed, the defendant may be bankrupt, etc. Another difficulty is that it may be abundantly clear in advance that because of the insufficiency of evidence the court is certain to acquit, for example, a thief, and in fact does acquit him. If law is what a court does, or prediction of what it will do in fact, would it be said in a case such as this that there is no law forbidding theft? If it is said that a court might have convicted had there been sufficient evidence, that immediately implies the presence of some rule, independent of the decision, on the basis of which a conviction might have been obtained. To say that the actual decision alone becomes "law" necessarily means that it forthwith ceases to be "law" for the future, since it will in its turn be subjected to interpretation and be embodied in another decision. "Law" then, in the words of one critic, "never is, but is always about to be. It is realised only when embodied in a judgement, and in being realised expires."

Any interpretation based only on things which have come before tribunals overlooks the point that law is very much concerned with regulating future behaviour. Such regulation is guided by policies formulated in prescriptive propositions, accepted as "laws" by courts. This being the case, the expulsion of the "ought" from a concept of law is impossible. As pointed out, even the idea of law as what judges do should include the reasons for their action, which would bring in their acceptance of prescriptive rule. It may be that some realists, at any rate, were seeking to derive descriptive rules of judicial behaviour, in which case they and the "traditionalists" were talking about different things.

Whatever merit there was in Frank's assertion that devotion to rules in a manifestation of a childish craving for certainty and fixity, it would seem that it was only he who seemed anxious to pin the word "law" to something definite and fixed, namely, actual decisions. Few, if any, "traditionalists" ever asserted that rules can guarantee absolute certainty; on the contrary, they avow the unavoidability and indeed necessity for some measure of flexibility and discretion. To say that law should aspire towards economy of thought and precision is one thing; to say that nothing is law which is not fixed and precise has no basis whatever. A denial that certainty in law can be achieved through rules is no reason why these may not be called "law". The point would not be worth mentioning were it not for another misleading impression. Frank's statement, quoted earlier and echoing Gray, that until a court has pronounced on a matter there is only "probable law", suggested that even a statutory rule is not "actual law" until it has been the subject of a judicial decision. But to change the accepted meaning of the word "law" in this way would involve re-writing textbooks and reports to no purpose. For rules would still remain, though not called "law". In one place Frank was driven to admit the existence of rules, though he deemed it is mistake to call them "law", thereby reducing the whole matter to a verbal level. In fairness to Frank, it must be pointed out that this was, at worst, a misleading way of expressing himself. In his later thoughts he forcibly reaffirmed the importance of rules, and in his own words, "backed our of the silly word battle" which is an admission that he had created a misleading impression.

To look at law solely from the point of view of one who is concerned with predicting judicial reactions is too narrow. If, e.g., one were to regard law as a judge, it would be futile to say that it consists of predictions as to how he himself will decide and, moreover, his own past decisions and those of other judges would only comprise a fraction of the law in his view. From the point of view of a legislator law will appear, not so much as what judges do, but what they are made to do. Further, the realist viewpoint is helpful in a system which leaves considerable independence to the judiciary. In a system in which judges are strictly controlled and in which their discretion is greatly reduced, the focus of attention will inevitable shift away from the judges to those who do wield power and discretion.

From all this it should be clear that up to this point the realists said nothing about law which would be denied by "traditionalists". That might have been able to expel the "ought" or rules from the law, but they did not succeed in doing either. They denied that certainty can ever be completely achieved through rule, which no "traditionalist" will controvert.

Once the rule controversy is put on one side, there is a better chance of assessing the solid contribution of the realists, which was to furnish a valuable extension to the work of sociologists. The latter investigate the values and forces that provide the motive power for the working of rules as instruments of social regulation. But a study of values alone will not explain the view which particular judges are likely to take of them, nor the degree of importance they may individually attach to one value or another. It is here that the realists were able to uncover innumerable personal and other factors that on occasions determine judicial choice. The "fact skeptic" went further and revealed how these factors affect even findings of fact. Frank, in his later writings, notably Courts on Trial, summed up his objective as being the demonstration, not of the nature of law, but of the difficulties and problems that beset trial judges rather than appellate judges, and of the inadequacy of existing methods of trial. Not only have the realists given a penetrating insight into the judicial process, but they have encouraged and enlisted the aid of significant statistical inquiries. By all means let the illusion, if indeed it presists, that rules can secure certainty be dispelled, and let day-light be shed on those factors that make for flexibility and variation with a view to the removal of caprice and prejudice. But nothing in all this should impair the prestige of rules or the prescriptive function of law.

No account of realism can be complete without some mention of Karl N. Llewellyn (1893-1962), whose work spanned the movement from its beginnings in the 1930s until his death in 1962. Some of his early writings, too, lent themselves to misinterpretation, but these should be viewed as part of the whole development of his thought. He outlined the principal features of the realist approach as follows:

(1) There has to be a conception of law in flux and of the judicial creation of law.

(2) Law is a means to social ends; and every part of it has constantly to be examined for its purpose and effect, and to be judged in the light of both and their relation to each other.

(3) Society changes faster than law, and so there is a constant need to examine how law meets contemporary social problems.

(4) There has to be a temporary divorce of "is" and "ought" for purposes of study. By this Llewellyn meant, not that ideas of justice and teleology are to be expelled altogether, but that they are to be put on one side while investigation what the law is and how it works. By this divorce both processes will be improved. The realists are vitally interested in the aims and ends of the law, and it was precisely a desire to improve the law that brought the movement into being. Adequate reform, however, has to be preceded by an examination of how the law in fact operates. Such an investigation will be imperfect and clouded if done with "an intrusion of ought-spectacles during the investigation of the facts".

(5) The realists distrust the sufficiency of legal rules and concepts as descriptive of what courts do. This was always a cardinal point in their approach to law.

(6) Coupled with this is a distrust of the traditional theory that rules of law are the principal factors in deciding cases. The realists have drawn attention to many other influences which, in their view, play a decisive part. To define law solely in terms of legal rules is therefore absurd.

(7) The realists believe in studying the law in narrower categories than has been the practice in the past. They feel that part of

the distortion produced by viewing the law in terms of legal rules in that rules cover hosts of dissimilar situations, where in practice utterly different considerations apply. So, in the law of contract, topics such as mistake and frustration must be studied in small fields according to their application in different types of transactions. Possession would be another good example.

(8) They also insist on the "evaluation of any part of the law in terms of its effects" and on "the worthwhileness of trying to find these effects".

(9) Finally, there must be a sustained and programmatic attack on the problem of the law along the lines indicated above.

As Llewellyn admitted, these nine points were not new. The first three furnished an obvious foundation for any sociological approach to jurisprudence. Perhaps, the main characteristics of realism lay first, in the peculiar prominence ascribed to the fourth, fifth, sixth, seventh and eighth points; and, secondly, in the amalgamation of all nine points into a working programme and the actual carrying out of research along these lines.

A decisive stage in the development of Llewellyn's though came with his notable anthropological investigation in collaboration with Hoebel into the "law-ways" of the Cheyenne Indians, which broke fresh ground in anthropology by introducing the case-method of approach. The direction of field-work for this undertaking grew out of his early realism, while his later realism was much influenced by the conclusions that were reached. In particular the "law-jobs" theory was evolved side by side with this project. It can be explained as follows. Certain needs have to be met if a group is to survive and achieve its purpose, namely, (a) adjustment of trouble-cases, which gives off new material for doing other law jobs. This job is comparable to running "garagerepair" work. (b) Preventive channelling of conduct and expectations so as to avoid trouble. (c) Preventive re-channelling of conduct and expectations so as to adjust to change. The importance of both these is to be seen in the resistance to certain types of new legislation, e.g., racial integration. Such legislation introduces "law" by which trouble-cases are to be decided, but it may fail to channel conduct in advance in accordance with it and so prevent future trouble-cases. (d) Allocation of authority and arranging procedures, i.e., arranging the "say" and the manner of its saying (authorities and procedures for decision-making). (e) Providing incentive and direction within the group, i.e., the "whither" of the group as a whole. (f) Ways of handling legal tools in these various law-jobs and their upkeep and improvement—the job of juristic method. There can never be one hundred per cent fulfilment of each job, so one difficulty is in knowing at what point shortcoming amounts to failure. Does "groupness" cease if there is failure in any one or more of the jobs, and, if not, at what point does it cease?

Llewellyn became increasingly preoccupied with the problem of method and never ceased to reiterate that realism was not a "philosophy", but a "technology" ("see it fresh, see it as it works"). He stressed the concept of "institution", which is "in the first instance an organised activity build around the doing of a job, or cluster of jobs". Law-jobs are done by institutions. This makes behaviour the focal point of his jurisprudence, and he probable meant no more than this when he said early on:

> "This doing of something about disputes, this doing of it reasonably, is the business of law. And the people who have the doing in charge, whether they be judges or sheriffs or clerks or jailers or lawyers, are officials of the law. What these officials do about disputes is, to my mind the law itself."

Thus, an institution always has a job to do and to do it well. There is, he says, a leeway to be wrong or right, but a leeway to do right is never a leeway to do wrong. Performance of law-jobs is one aspect of the task of law-government in society. There must then be some distinction between law and other social institutions. This lies in the fact that law requires specialists and procedure, supremacy within the group, effectiveness and regularity.

Towards the end Llewellyn was concerned with what be saw as a growing loss of confidence in appellate courts because of the unpredictability of their decisions. This, he thought, was unjustified, so in the Common Law Tradition. Deciding Appeals, he sought to restore confidence by showing that there is a "reckonable" quality about appellate court work. He agreed with Frank to the extent of distinguishing between work in train courts and appellate courts, but whereas Frank scorned the latter he concentrated on them. Craftsmanship, he maintained, is possible in litigation. "A craft is a minor institution. A major institution differs in that its job-cluster is fundamental to the continuance of the society (or group) with typical resulting complexities". Crafts evolve around such major institutions. Craftsmanship in law includes not only the various skills of lawyers, but also tradition, ethos, training, etc.; and the way in which legal craftsmen use their skills determines their "style". There are various ways of dealing with precedents—following, distinguishing, expanding and re-directing. A judge's handling of them is not capricious or arbitrary, but is guided by his "situation-sense", which is a key-concept as well as being the most obscure. It is more than just "the view taken of the facts". It seems to include stating the facts in categories which are as close to the actual facts giving rise to the dispute, together with an understanding of the whole background, i.e., the trade, standard practices, etc. and the prevailing opinions and values. The doubt about this is that, whatever it means, a situation-sense may by forthcoming in some types of disputes, but not in others. Apart from situation-sense, a check on arbitrariness and caprice is also maintained by fourteen steadying factors, relating to the whole ethos of the profession, tradition, training and techniques. "Reckonability" is said to depend on three laws, of which the first is the "Law of Compatibility", where the application of an appropriate rule is compatible with sense. This increases "reckonability" of the decision and the direction of its ratio. Secondly, there is the "Law of Incompatibility", where the above does not obtain and where the ground of decision lies outside the rule. Thirdly, there is the "Law of Singing Reason", where there is a rule with a right "situation-sense" and clear scope and thus gives maximum "reckonability". The judicial craft which results from a right situation-sense, reason and justice is called the "Grand Style", which is overtly functional and purpose orientated, as opposed to "Formal Style", which is overtly concerned only with the logical application of "paper" rules. The "Grand Style" is one of the fourteen major steadying factors alluded to above, and Llewellyn relied heavily on it to produce "reckonability".

From all this it will be evident that Llewellyn's position was far removed from that of people like Frank. It has been doubted whether there was in fact a crisis of confidence, and if so, whether he succeeded in restoring confidence by re-establishing the "reckonability" of appellate decisions. The case-law material used in the book consists of a small percentage of appeals. It has been estimated that 70-90 per cent of appeals are "foredoomed" and "not worth appealing". This fact alone, it has been pointed out, "would have disposed more satisfactorily of the alleged crisis of confidence than his attempts to show that the Grand Style promotes reckonability". Further, the "situation-sense", which appears to be basic to his thesis, is too vague, being in every case the product of a shifting balance. Be that as it may, long before the publication of this work, Llewellyn had given practical demonstration of his jurisprudence in the great and successful Uniform Commercial Code of which he was one of the chief architects from 1937 to 1952. His biographer points out that in it may be seen how "Grand Style" thinking can be utilised, not only in judicial opinions, but also in legislation. Perhaps, one may best sum up by saying that the Common Law Tradition is Llewellyn's magnum opus, but that the Uniform Commercial Code is his monument.

In recent years attempts to predict judicial behaviour have taken a mechanical turn for which the term "jurimetrics" has been invented. It takes the form of different kinds of investigations into legal phenomena by using symbolic logic, behavioural models and mechanical aids. Boolean algebra is used to analyse complex sets of facts, prediction of behaviour has moved away from that of the individual to that of groups, and the use of computers is being explored increasingly. These new directions are not necessarily dependent on realism, but may be regarded as developments along its line.

THE GROUP APPROACH

A group, e.g., the American Supreme Court, has group reactions. It is difficult to predict the behaviour of an individual, but that of a mass of people is easier. Student groups have been used as models of actual social groups. It is not enough merely to take account of the wav in which the members of a group vote; it is necessary to consider the influence of personalities and of reasoned argument. In this connection two types of leadership are thought to be significant: task-leadership, which is directed towards solving a given problem efficiently, and social-leadership, which provides a friendly atmosphere conducive to solving it.

This kind of inquiry can only work so long as there is a constant membership within the group. If this varies, as with the Court of Appeal or House of Lords, and there is no knowledge in advance of the precise composition of the group in a given case, there is no basis for prediction. There is also the difficulty of obtaining adequate information about the inner workings of a group. What is available tends to be fragmentary at most, e.g., memories and biographies, and these, in any case, are not available until after death. Even if it can be discovered who is the task-or social-leader, it is not clear how one could tell whether these tasks have in fact been preformed as well as they should, or performed at all. The use of models could be misleading. When using scientific models, which are simplified abstractions of fixed phenomena, the corrections that have to be made are fixed too. Where, however, the phenomena fluctuate, as with human beings and social phenomena generally, it is impossible to know what corrections need to be made. For this purpose models are useless.

COMPUTER PREDICTION

It has also been suggested that in so far as there is consistency in decision and attitude, the prediction of judicial opinions by computers becomes possible. Computer techniques in this connection have been of fact studies (correlation between the circumstances in particular cases and decisions given in them) and attitude studies (correlation between personal attitudes to policies and decisions given). With regard to the former, it is said that the acceptance of a fact by an appellate court rests on identifiable conditions surrounding the way in which it was presented to the trial court. Further, if the accepted facts are combined in certain ways, the decisions will go one way. Personal attitudes are also said to be capable of being scaled by means of scalogram analysis. The basis of this is that a person who reacts positively to a weak stimulus will react similarly to any stronger stimulus, while a person who react negatively to a strong stimulus will react similarly to any weaker stimulus. If a line of cases can be made to scale in this way, this would show that a set of values is shared by members of that court. The future behaviour of that court then becomes predictable, as well as the probable effects of a change in composition.

It is submitted that such attempts at prediction seem destined to fail. The personal element just cannot be eliminated from judicial decisions: (a) Everything depends on how facts are viewed and stated. The same set of facts can be stated in different combinations and at different levels of generality. No mechanical aid can predict which combination or level is likely to be chosen. (b) Different ratios can be extracted from a decision depending on whether the later court wishes to see resemblances or differences. It is known which way a judge is going to regard a rule, a computer is not needed; if it is not known, a computer is useless. Another important consideration is that the predictability of judicial decisions depends upon consistency in judges' attitudes to values; but people's attitudes change with age and experience.

Moreover, computer prediction can only work on the basis of reported decisions, the majority of which, especially those of lower courts, are unreported. This means that the bulk of a judge's early decisions are unlikely to be available, so the basis for predicting his reactions is woefully inadequate. Prediction also requires constant working material; it cannot operate when new matter is being introduced, whether by legislation or creative decisions. Computers are of on help here. Finally, even if computer prediction were possible, a by-product may well be what is known as the "Heisenburg feed-back effect". Where computer analysis has indicated that a judge's decision will be such and such in a particular case, or type of case, that very fact could induce him either to dicide accordingly as if in submission to fate, or else to decide the opposite deliberately so as not to be dictated to by a machine. To produce either reaction detracts from the judicial function.

Even the possibility of trial by computer has been canvassed, the choice being given to the defendant. All that needs to be said on this is that the data programmed into a computer will reflect the personal quirks of the programmer, which will be substituted for the quirks of the judge. At least, the judge works in the open, whereas the programmer works behind the scenes.

SCANDINAVIAN REALISTS

The American Realists were practising lawyers or law teachers, who sought to approximate legal theory to legal practice. In Scandinavia the group of jurists known as realists approached their tasks on a more abstract plane and with the training of philosophers.

HAGERSTROM

Hagerstrom (1868-1939), who may be regarded as the founder of the movement in Sweden, has written at length, especially on Roman law, but much of his work is not available in English. His basic position was as follows. He denied the existence of objective values. There are no such things as "goodness" and "badness". In the world. The words represent simply emotional attitudes of approval and disapproval respectively towards certain facts and situations. It is only language form that has erected them into absolutes and has created an illusion of objectivity. So, too, the word "duty" only expresses an idea, the association of a feeling of compulsion with regard to a desired course of conduct. Language form again gives objectivity, e.g., "it is my duty to do so and so". Similarly, the idea of "right" has no factual basis, but derives from a feeling of power associated with it, which has a psychological explanation. This led Hagerstrom to deny the possibility of any science of the "ought". All questions of justice, aims and purposes of law are matters of personal evaluation and not susceptible to any scientific process of examination. In this way many of the traditional problems of legal philosophy become illusory, and must be replaced by an examination of the actual use of legal terms and a psychological analysis of the mental attitudes involved.

Hagerstrom applied this technique to the study of Roman law. He examined the concepts of Classical Roman law and set forth the thesis that they were rooted in magical beliefs, i.e., that they were developments of the primitive belief in the power of words to affect happenings in the world of fact. The conception of obligation was, he said, a magical bond, the "vinculum juris", giving power to the creditor over the debtor. This power could only be created in special ways, by the use of magic recitations, such as stipulation and the debtor could free himself from it by performance or by uttering with the creditor's consent another magic formula. Power over property, dominimum or ownership, was also a magic power. The archaic mode of conveyance, mancipation, with its formal acts and formula asserting title before its acquisition was a ceremony based on magic. Law starts in religion, e.g., Mosaic Law, and the monopoly enjoyed by the priestly class, the pontiffs, in early law is also evidence of this idea that law is based on magic.

It is possible that Hagerstrom was making too much of a point which has some substance. It is probably true that adherence to form and ritual is rooted in word-magic, but how far Roman law in the Classical period should be interpreted along such lines is a matter on which opinion should be reserved. Wordfetishism is a habit that is easily formed. The natural reaction of a baby in its earliest days to discomfort, for instance, is to utter a sound. When sound is uttered, in the majority of cases the offending situation is rectified. The baby's limited appreciation of cause and effect can only register the broad fact that sound succeeded in bringing about an alteration in the world of fact. Food appears, discomforts disappear and persons materialise. As the child grows older it is made to realise that not every time it makes a noise is it going to get its own way. Deep down, however, there remains that unshakeble conviction that sound does have power; obviously, it cannot be any and every sound, but only certain special (magic) sounds. The ground for belief in word-magic is thus prepared very early and during the most receptive period of consciousness. In so far as law gives a person power to control property as well as the actions of other persons, it is not surprising that it should have become associated with word-magic from the earliest times. To put the machinery of the law into operation the proper incantations have to be uttered. This was not peculiar to Roman law; it is to be found in every system and traces remain today. People outgrow is and find ways and means of circumventing it. New uses are found for the original forms and this, together with an element of conservatism, combine to keep formality and ritual alive long after the inner belief in word-magic drops out. It is true that in Classical Roman law some of the early forms of law survived, but whatever their origin, the interpretation of Classical law on the basis purely of word-magic is questionable. Professor Olivecrona, a follower of Hagerstrom, accepts his leader's explanations of Roman law, but he does say a propose of modern law generally that people still retain the outer form of word-magic although the inner belief in it disappeared long ago. That remark might well be applied to Classical Roman law.

As with the American Realists, there is hardly a "school" of Scandinavian realism. Individuals, who are thought to belong to the group, exhibit important differences among themselves. Notwithstanding these, however, they would in the main agree in denying the possibility of a science of justice or values. To them, these are purely subjective reactions, or else reflective of class or political ideology, and it is not possible to construct a science on such a basis.

LUNDSTEDT

Vilhelm Lundstedt (1882-1955) might be regarded as the most extreme of the Scandinavians. Law is simply the fact of social existence in organised groups and the conditions which make possible the co-existence of masses of people. He attacked metaphysical ideas in every form. Nothing exists which cannot be proved as fact, and he was particularly ruthless in dismissing traditional concepts as being emotive responses or mirages of language. To say that a person is under a duty "is only a feeling or sentiment that he ought to conduct himself in a certain manner, consequently something quite subjective. This subjective element legal writers have been forced to turn into the exact opposite, into the monstrous contradiction: an objective duty!" To say that a person has broken a duty is a farrago of words for the plain fact that he is likely to be punished, or made to pay a sum of money. Similarly, a "right" is a term for the favourable position enjoyed by a person in consequence of the functioning of legal machinery. Law simply consists of rules about the application of organised force.

The whole idea of law as a means of achieving justice is chimerical. It is not founded on justice, but on social needs and pressures. Indeed, "the feelings of justice are guided and directed by the laws as enforced, i.e., as maintained". In place of justice Lundstedt substituted the method of "social welfare", which is "a guiding motive for legal activities", namely, "the encouragement in the best possible way of that . . . which people in general actually strive to attain". Judges should think in terms of social aims, not "rights". He insisted that these are not aims for which people ought to strive, but those, which they are observed to be seeking. They include decent food, clothing, shelter, security of life, limb and property, freedom of action and protection of spiritual interests. The method of social welfare strives to attain the best balance between these and other competing interests without the intrusion of values.

Lundstedt's iconoclasm is extreme. However true it may be that concepts such as duty and right have no verifiable content, they are convenient tools of thought and are used in deciding cases. The wholesale rejection of them, as he advocated, would only distort what actually goes on. Thus, as answer to his view that a person in consequence of the functioning of legal machinery is that everything depends on why a court viewed his position favourably. This is because success in the action depended on the idea of a right. It happens, too, that a person may enjoy a favourable position by virtue of a right even though it is socially undesirable that he should do so.

If, as he so vehemently insisted, all conceptual thought is non-sensical, the same must apply to his own concept of "social welfare". However, leaving that aside, it is not clear how far the method of social welfare represents the observable pattern of administration and how far it is what Lundstedt himself would have liked to see. Nor does this method seem very different from what other writers have said. In any case, as has been pointed out, balancing interests is just not possible except with reference to yardsticks of evaluation. The very concept of social welfare is a product of political or socio-moral evaluation. If the actual interests of people are allowed to proliferate to the point of complete social fragmentation and anarchy, that would spell the end of legal activity and, indeed, of social welfare. If this is not to be allowed, then the point at which legal activity has to step in is a matter for decision as to where the line should be drawn, not of observation. Moreover, is a small, but enlightened minority, agitating for reform, to remain outside the endeavour of the social welfare method until, presumably, it attains large enough proportions?

Other Scandinavians have not gone as far as Lundstedt. Even Professor Olivecrona, who perhaps came nearest to his views, does not do so. Indeed, some have reacted sharply against his uncompromising condemnation of any appeal of justice and morality.

OLIVECRONA

A less extreme and more acceptable form of scepticism comes from Professor Olivecrona (1897-1980). He expressly refrains from defining law. "I do not regard it as necessary to formulate a definition of law", he says.

"A description and an analysis of the facts is all that will be attempted". If one seeks to investigate the nature of law, it begs the question to begin by assuming what it is, and he insists that the facts must be examined first. The method of identifying these "will be simply to take up such facts as are covered by the expression rules of law".

The question of the validity of law is a matter of much concern to the Scandivavians. Olivecrona approaches it from the angle of bindingness. Law has "binding force" in so far as it is valid; an invalid law is not binding. This question of the binding force behind law has been a perennial puzzle and is, expressly or impliedly, the foundation of many theories. There is no such thing, says he, as "the" binding force behind law. Many attempts have been made to find where it resides. Natural lawyers have asserted that it lies in natural law; but if asked why natural law is binding, the answer is a confession of faith. Natural law, whether conceived as an expression of the will of God or as a set of principles based on reason, is said to be binding *per se*. Morality cannot be substituted in place of natural law, for law is treated as binding whether or not it is consistent with morality.

Others have tried to discover the binding force of law in the consent of the governed. This is not wholly true because at no time are the subjects of a system of law asked whether they consent to be bound. Also, it would follow that once consent is withdrawn law ceases to bind, which obviously is not the case.

Another attempt to unravel the binding force is to attribute it to the "will of the state". This, too, is imaginary since the "will of the state" as distinct from the wills of individuals is a myth. The question is whether any individual, or group of individuals, is discoverable in whose will the binding force of law may be said to reside. The answer must be in the negative because, in the first place, there never has been and never will be any person or group of persons who can be regarded as having "willed" the whole law, let alone its binding force. Secondly, it is equally fictitious to imagine that the binding force rests in the wills of legislators or citizens collectively. Such persons have other matters to think of than willing laws or their binding force.

Nor again is it meaningful to say that the binding force of law is derived from unpleasant consequences ensue in a host of situations which have nothing to do with law. A person gets burnt if he puts his hands in the fire. Conversely, there are occasions when law is treated as binding although unpleasant consequences do not ensue. A person may commit a breach of the law and go undetected, but no one would say that the law is therefore not binding on him. Nor is it satisfactory to say that the binding force is derived from the unpleasant consequences that ought to ensue, for, as kelsen has shown, the reality of "ought to ensue" consists of the operation of other rules of law and the binding force of these will in turn have to be sought.

Professor Olivecrona accordingly rejects the idea of "the" binding force of law as illusory and meaningless. It is not an observable fact in the milieu of society. "The" binding force of law is a mirage of language; it "exists" only as an idea in individual minds. Laws, too, "exist" in the form of printed or written words or else in memory. Their importance lies, not in where or how they are stored, but in the fact that they produce behaviour. This results from the fact that most people have a feeling of being bound by law, which is quite different from saying that there is some impalpable binding force existing somewhere outside the mind. It is feeling of being bound that has to be explained.

Olivecrona accordingly approaches his inquiry by examining the idea of duty, which has been dealt with and need not be repeated. His conclusion, in substance, is that duty involves the idea of action and an imperative mode of expression, and that the feeling of being bound stems from the psychological associations connected with this mode of expression by certain agencies. The picture of law which emerges is or patterns of conduct in imperative form, which are distinguishable from other imperatives by virtue of the nature of the feeling of being bound that is associated with them. This feeling is not the same with regard to any other kind of imperative, e.g., that one must wear black at funerals. The feeling of being bound by "law" is psychologically associated with certain agencies when they follow certain procedures, together with the publication of law-texts through certain media, which are assumed to give a true account of them. Law, therefore, is a set of "independent imperatives" prescribed by these agencies. It is thought, however, that Olivecrona would admit that law prescribes models of conduct. He would, therefore, not deny that it consists of "ought" propositions.

Nor does he dismiss the idea of rights altogether. He emphasises that it does not correspond with an ascertainable "thing", that it is, in short, a "hollow" word. A court could pronounce on a factual situation without calling "right" in aid. Thus, proof of a right is accomplished by proving certain facts or events whose effects are determined by law. These facts are called "title". In a court nothing stands between proof of the facts and judgment; the one is the direct courts, as soon as the facts constituting the title are in existence, the person concerned may do certain things and other persons must not and cannot do certain other things with regard to him. Yet, between the facts and the judgment and between the facts and the behaviour the idea of a "right" is invariably interposed, and it is said that the favourable decision or the behaviour proceeds from the right, which has been created by the title. In truth, the idea of a "right" connotes a multitude of other ideas relating to behaviour patterns, not only for the "possessor of the right", but also of other persons. It implies directives as to how the right-bearer and others can and should act, it informs people about legal situations, it is purposive in achieving or maintaining a state of affairs, and it is a means of harnessing the force of the state. This analysis, together with that of duty and the feeling of being bound, leads him to conclude that "law is nothing but a set of social facts" based on the application of organised force.

By way of a general observation, it might be remarked that some people are left with a feeling of dissatisfaction after reading Olivecrona's exposition. Its very simplicity raises a doubt as to whether he may have overlooked some deeper and more profound truth. It is submitted, however, that the common sense which he brings to bear in his discussions is the best feature of his work. Obscurity has passed for profundity too often. It is a useful working rule that clarity of expression is an index to clarity of thought Obscurantist jargon earns much unmerited respect from those who hesitate to condemn as nonsense that which they cannot understand. The clear pages of Olivecrona's presentation are preferable to the turgid complexities of many others. Apart from that, however, one who searches his book for guidance in the solution of legal problems will search in vain. Nowhere is there a hint of values or other such considerations from which the law draws its vitality. It would be unfair to level this as a criticism, for a person should not be criticised for not having said something which he never set out to say and which, in any case, he would not have denied. Olivecrona's object, like Kelsen's, was limited to a formal analysis of law as it is. The picture of law which emerges is that is consists largely of propositions phrased in an imperative form and emanating from certain agencies. It might be said that there is nothing very new in that. Finally, although he repeatedly insists that law is nothing but a set of social facts, nowhere in his book does he explain what he means by "fact". Law also provides a model of behaviour which, too, presumably is a social fact. Perhaps, an explanation of the crucial term "fact" would have been instructive.

The chief merit of his work may perhaps be summed up as follows. He destroyed many traditional myths concerning law, e.g., "binding force" and command. He has given a moderate, sane and commonsense approach to some highly abstract problems of legal philosophy. His approach should not be regarded as self-sufficient, but it is an invaluable corrective to some others.

ROSS

The Danish jurist, ALF Ross (1899-1985), also admits the normative character of law (as did Kelsen by whom he was influenced). He distinguished between laws, which are normative, and statements about laws in books, which are descriptive. Unlike Kelsen, however, he confines his attention to particular legal order. Like Olivecrona, he maintains that laws need to be interpreted in the light of social facts and he, too, is concerned with the problem of validity. Like the American Realists he tends to highlight the position of courts.

"A norm", say Ross, "is a directive which stands in a relation of correspondence to social facts". To say that a norm exists means that a certain social fact exists; and this in turn means that the directive is followed in the majority of cases by people who feel bound to do so. The principal feature of legal norms is that they are directives addressed to courts. A norm may derive from a past decision, but is follows from this view that all norms, including those of legislation, should be viewed as directives to courts. The judgment or order of the court then forms the basis for action by the state, which is a "monopoly of the exercise of force". It follows from this point of view that norms directed at individuals with regard to behaviour are only "derived and figurative". In his later work, however, he concedes that "from a psychological points of view" there is another set of norms directed to individuals, which are followed by them and felt to be binding. Strictly speaking, he adds, there is no need for the latter: to know the former "is to know everything about the existence and content of the law." Norms of the law may be further divided into "norms of conduct", which deal with behaviour, and "norms of competence or procedure", which deal with behaviour, and "norms of competence or procedure", which direct that norms brought into existence according to a declared mode of procedure shall be regarded as norms of conduct. Thus, norms of competence are indirectly expressed norms of conduct.

The crucial concept is "valid law". Ross approaches this from the point of view of an observer, i.e., validity as a describable phenomenon. It can be established in terms of social facts by employing has to show that a rule is effectively followed, and that rule has also to be felt to be binding by those who follow it, just as the validity of the rules of chess is established by showing that they are adhered to by players, who feel bound to do so. Legal norms consist of past decisions and other normative propositions followed by courts and by which they feel bound. The test of their validity is the predictability of decisions.

"'Valid law'," he says, "means the abstract set of normative ideas which serve as a scheme of interpretation for the phenomena of law in action, which again means that these norms are effectively followed, and followed because they are experienced and felt to be socially binding by the judge and other legal authorities applying the law. . . . The test of validity is that on this hypothesis—that is, accepting the system of norms as a scheme of interpretation—we can comprehend the actions of the judge (the decisions of the courts) as meaningful responses to given conditions and within certain limits predict them."

Norms are thus operative "because they are felt by (the judge) to be socially binding and therefore obeyed". A norm, then, is "valid" if a prediction can be made that a court will apply it. At this point Ross puts forward an interesting contention. Validity is not an "all or nothing" concepts as it is with other writers; the degree of predictability that a norm will be applied determines the degree of its validity. "This degree of probability depends on the material of experience on which the prediction is built (sources of law)". Where the probability is high because the basis is a statue or an established precedent, the degree of validity of a rule is high; where the probability is low because there is no decisive authority, the degree of validity is low.

The criticism originally levelled at Ross that he ignored the regulative function of norms by saying that they are only addressed to courts was partially met by his later modification that, from a psychological point of view, norms are also addressed to individuals. However, his continued insistence that only the former matter still underplays the regulative function. On the other hand, to admit, as he now does, that norms directed at individuals also exist, thereby implying that they, too, are social facts, dilutes the foundation of his structure. The thesis that there can be degrees of validity follows from an identification of validity with eventuality, what actually happens. Is this legitimate? The closely related point is his adoption of an exclusively descriptive point of view. But, as was pointed out in connection with American Realism, the resulting picture is unsuited to the point of view of a legislator or judge. What does validigy signify to them? A judge, for instance, can hardly be predicting his own feelings or behaviour, but it would be quite unrealistic to suggest that validity has no significance for him.

11

PHILOSOPHICAL AND NATURAL LAW THEORIES

NATURAL law theory has a history reaching back centuries B.C., and the vigour with which it flourishes notwithstanding periodic eclipse, especially in the 19th century, is a tribute to its vitality. There is no one theory; many versions have evolved throughout this enormous span of time. Kelsen exposed some of them as masks for political ideologies. But natural law theory should not be dismissed simply on account of its variety. On the contrary, this very fact is an important clue to its understanding. No other firmament of legal or political theory is so bejewelled with stars as that of natural law, which scintillates with contributions from all ages. A single chapter cannot possibly do justice to this rich and varied material, so all that will be attempted here is to deploy those portions of it that will help to embroider the topics which seem fairly central in contemporary thought. Old ideas have been abandoned or refurbished and new ones put forward, while forgotten lessons have blossomed with new significance.

The term "natural law", like "positivism", has been understood to mean a variety of things to different people at different times. (1) Ideals which guide legal development and administration. (2) A basic moral quality in law which prevents a total separation of the "is" from the "ought". (3) The method of discovering perfect law. (4) The content of perfect law deducible by reason. (5) The conditions sine quibus non for the existence of law. Because of these differences it is not always possible to classify a given writer as naturalist or positivist. For instance, it has been pointed out that Scotus, Ockham and Kant have been treated as positivists by some natural lawyers and as naturalists by some positivists; besides which there are wide differences among those who are normally classed as naturalists or positivists. Also, natural law thinking in one form or another is pervasive and is encountered in various contexts. Values, for instance, as pointed out, play an indispensable part in the development and day-to-day administration of law. In a different sphere natural law theory has tried to meet the paramount needs of successive ages throughout history, and an account has been given of the ways in which it supported power or freedom from power according to the social need of the time. All this is part and parcel of its very nature. Further, natural law thinking figures prominently in offering help with two vital contemporary problems, namely, the validity of the unjust law and the abuse of liberty. Positivism, on the other hand, by seeking to insulate legal theory from such considerations refuses to give battle where battle is most needed, perhaps wisely, perhaps to its own discredit, depending on the point of view. Nevertheless, the constant readiness of natural lawyers to meet challenge is a tribute to the springs of their inspiration, which has a vitality like that of the phoenix.

A distinction should be drawn between two kinds of natural law thought, "natural law of method" and "natural law of content". The former was the older, dating from ancient times and was also prevalent in the early middle ages. It concerned itself with trying to discover the method by which just rules may be devised to meet ever-varying circumstances. "It is a prescription for rule-making, not a catalogue of rules". The "natural law of content" was a feature of the 17th and 18th centuries and was characterised by attempts to deduce entire bodies of rules from some absolute first principle. These were manifestations of the then fashionable assertion of "natural rights" and were accompanied internationally by grandiose schemes for ensuring perpetual peace. It was this "natural law of content" which became the target for damaging criticism. The effect was the eclipse of natural law thinking generally throughout most of the 19th century, when it reached its nadir and was superseded by positivism. As long as social conditions remained stable, positivism could flourish. This in turn failed when those conditions were upset by the convulsions that have beset nations since the second half of the last century. It failed because it could give no guidance amidst the challenge to accepted moral and social beliefs; it failed because it could give no help in avoiding or remedying mostrous abuses of power and liberty that have been, and are still, prevalent. With its decline there arisen a new preoccupation with social justice, which includes, among other manifestations, a revival of natural law doctrine. This is more in line with the older "natural law of method" and endeavours to avoid the criticism of the past and to meet the problems of today.

It is against this background that theories of natural law should be approached. Since their concern has always been with the needs of particular ages, only theories with contemporary relevance will be discussed here. Those that were tailored to suit bygone times, e.g., those of Aristotle and Grotius, will not be dealt with. A start might be made with the doctrine of St. Thomas Aquinas (1224/5-1274), which is not only outstanding in itself, but whose enduring value was endorsed in 1879 by Pope Leo XIII, who enabled it to become part of the teaching of the Catholic Church.

St. Thomas Aquinas

The Thomist scheme has to be set in the context of its time. There was, first, a need for stability in a world emerging from the Dark Ages. Secondly, the struggle between Church and State was beginning and there was the need for the Church to establish its superiority by rational argument rather than by force, since secular authority had the monopoly of force. Thirdly, it was necessary for Christendom to unite in the face of the spreading heathen menace and a need was felt for a unifying Christian philosophy. The available philosophic material consisted largely of the natural law philosophies of Greece and Rome. The Decretum Gratianum (c. 140) had already identified the law of nature with the law of God and this paved the way for resort to classical literature as authority. Aquinas endeavoured to meet all three needs and his doctrine may be presented as follows.

There is a connection between means and ends. This is because there is an unshakable relation in the nature of things between a given operation and its result. Natural phenomena have certain inevitable consequences: thus fire burns, it does not freeze. So, one adopts a particular method because of its properties. Another point is that a tendency to develop in certain ways is naturally inherent in things. Thus, an acorn can only evolve into an oak; it will never evolve into a larch or pine. The appreciation of both these, namely, the relation between means and ends and the process of growth towards fulfilment, is open only to intelligence and the faculty of reason. An acorn does not think, but Man does. He appreciates the relation between means and their ends and the destined development of phenomena around him. He can also, within limits, choose for himself the ends which he wants and devise means of achieving them. For example, a person in authority may decide that the health of society is an end worth achieving. He will then consider how best to accomplish this and prescribe appropriate regulations of social behaviour. Laws thus consist of means of achieving ends. (a) The relation between an end and the method by which its fulfilment is sought is initially conceived in the mind of the legislator, but those who are required to conform to his directions can also appreciate the connection by the exercise of their own reasoning faculties. (b) Where the achievement of the end, which the legislator seeks, depends on adherence by others to the patterns of conduct that are prescribed, it is essential that these should be made known to them. Therefore, law in an all-embracing signification is "nothing else than an ordinance of reason for the common good, made by him who has the care of the community, and promulgated".

Though Man can to a large extent control his own destiny, he too is subject to certain basic impulses, which can be perceived by observing human nature. At the lowest level there is: (a) the impulse towards self-preservation; (b) at the next level there are the impulses, shared with other creatures, to reproduce the species and rear children; (c) at the highest level there is the impulse to improve, to take such decisions as are necessary for the attainment of higher and better things. This last is peculiar to Man by virtue of his reason. These basic impulses point in a definite direction; they are seen to be the means of achieving, not only survival and continuity, but also perfection. They are an inescapable part of human nature and show that Man also, to a lesser extent than an acorn, is limited by nature. If then, the framework of human nature is itself a means to certain ends, the establishment of the ends and these means of achievement could only have originated in the reason of some superhuman legislator. This is the eternal law: "the eternal law is nothing else than the plan of the divine wisdom considered as directing all the acts and motions" to the attainment of the ends. But Man, unlike the rest of creation, is free and rational and capable of acting contrary to eternal law. Therefore, this law has to be promulgated to him through reason. This is natural law. There is no need of promulgation to other created things, for they lack the intelligence of Man." The natural law is nothing else but a participation of the eternal law in a rational creature", i.e., the dictates revealed by reason reflecting on natural tendencies and needs. "The primary precept of the law is that good should be done and pursued and evil avoided: and on this are founded all the other precepts of the law of nature". By reflecting on his own impulses and nature Man can decide what is good. In this way he perceives the three basic drives mentioned above. In addition, reason reflecting on experience yields further, more detailed precepts. The moral law thus contains a variety of them of greater or less generality.

Before proceeding further, certain doubts might be mentioned. The fact that reason is needed to appreciate the orderings in nature does not necessarily imply that reason established them; nor does the fact that Man by his reason can set himself a goal of his own and utilise the existing ordering of nature as means for its achievement necessarily suggest that the order in nature was appointed by reason. It might conceivably be argued that it is only the faculty of appreciating order, implanted in the mind, that should be ascribed to the Deity. On that supposition eternal law would be what Man creates in his own mind, not something external to it and comprehensible by reason. This question, of course, strikes at the root of religious belief and, as such, is too large a matter to be debated here. Another important point concerns the nature of the "ought" behind Aquinas's view of natural law. It amounts to saying: Man's nature is such that he is necessarily impelled to seek good in survival, continuity and perfection; therefore, he ought to do things to achieve these and not do things to frustrate them. Superficially it might seem that this is no more than the functional "ought" behind the adoption of a certain course of action as the effective means to a certain end. This, however, is not the case here. With the functional "ought", the failure, or even refusal, to pursue the end is morally neutral. Thus, while it is true that if a person wishes to make a gratuitous promise, he ought to make it under seal, there is no moral failure on his part for not wishing to make such a promise. Aquinas's moral imperative is something different; to go against the ends is morally wrong. it is not wrong because God has forbidden contravention of natural law; God has forbidden it because it is wrong, i.e., contrary to reason by which He Himself is bound. This being so, Aquinas's argument looks as if he is deriving the "ought" logically (by reason) From as "is" (Man's observable nature). Finally, there is another difficulty in that procreation was treated by him as a basic drive of human nature and hence good, but he himself subscribed to clerical celibacy. His answer was that Mankind "ought not only to be multiplied corporeally, but also to make spiritual progress. And so sufficient provision is made if some only attend to generation, while others give themselves to the contemplation of divine things for the enrichment and salvation of the whole human race". This is tantamount to saying that this natural law is addressed to people generally but nobody in particular. If so, the imperative behind it stands in need of elucidation as well as the connection between sin and contravention of natural law.

In addition to eternal and natural law there is divine law, which is eternal law revealed through the Scriptures; and lastly there is human or man-made law. The latter should conform to reason and thus to the law of God. These four, then, eternal law, natural law, divine law and human law, comprise the Thomist system.

This scheme may justly be regarded as the first of its kind in the history of jurisprudence. Its outstanding features were: (i) that it combined ancient philosophy, the law of the Romans, the teachings of the Christian Fathers and contemporary pragmatism with consummate power and skill. But differing from the teaching of St. Augustine, law was no longer the product of original sin, but part of the Divine scheme. Nor is there any suggestion that body and natural things are synonymous with corruption and a clog on the spirit. What is most striking is its uncompromising appeal to reason. Man was created so that he might strive towards perfection within the limits of mortality. Reason dictates that he has, therefore, to be free. God cannot alter this state of affairs. To do so would contradict His own nature, since God Himself is bound by reason. This is a stupendous claim and to match it one surprising that, consistently with this, the law of God itself was declared to be "nothing else than the reason of divine wisdom"; and Christinity was said to be supreme reason: credo quia ration obilis est. (ii) Natural law, as will have been application. (iii) Another most interesting feature is the empirical approach to eternal and natural law. Inferences are drawn from human nature as can be observed by everybody. (iv) Reason becomes the foundation for all human institutions. Social life, whether in the form of families or the state, are founded on human nature. Reason reflecting on this shows that these natural institutions. An extension of this is the ideal of a single organisation of all Mankind in a world-state. (v) Aquinas sought to strengthen the authority of the Church by asserting that human dignitaries were responsible to the Church in matters relating to eternal law, and buttressed that contention with the proposition that the Church is the authoritative interpreter of divine law in the Scriptures. Nevertheless, the state, which existed before the Church, is itself a natural institution. It serves the common good, and by means of its laws should bring about the conditions conductive to Man's proper development. (vi) The test, then, by which laws are to be judged is the following dictate: "every human law has just so much of the nature of law, as it is derived from the law of nature. But if at any point it departs from natural law, it is no longer a law but a perversion of law". (vii) The need is stressed for the union of prescriptive patterns of behaviour, ideals and inward obedience if law is to achieve its objectives. In so far as human laws are founded on reason there is a duty to obey them; from which it would follow that if a law is unreasonable and unjust no such duty arises. But, interestingly enough, Aquinas qualified this inference by saying that there may be subtle dictates of morality which enjoin obedience even to an unreasonable positive law, for instance to avoid social disruption. Unjust laws, he said, "do not bind conscience unless observance of them is required in order to avoid scandal or disturbance". The qualification might well have been a concession to the need of the time to preserve social stability. Even more significant, perhaps, was the implicit recognition of the growing importance of man-made law. (viii) The corollary of this was that an unjust ruler may be overthrown, unless revolution would create as bad, or worse, state of affairs than before. Sedition is a social evil; and he warned against rebellion in circumstances which do not justify it. As before, the qualification reflects the need of the time. (ix) The identification of natural law with reason was destined in later times to bring about a separation of natural law from theology. For with the advent of the Reformation, the Protestants denied the authority of the Church to be the unchallengeable exponent of the law of God; Man was said to have direct access to God through his own reason.

In the era which followed that of Aquinas, the dream of an united Christendom was finally abandoned, Europe emerged from feudalism and there arose the modern municipal state. These developments had to be justified by theories, which were more power-orientated than in the preceding age. Then, abuse of power by sovereigns over their subjects led to revolutionary strings and assertion of fundamental rights of the individual, which called for immunity-orientated theories. Both these movements manifested themselves in successive variations of the social contract theory. Side by side with this, there was international chaos produced by the exercise of unlimited freedom of action by states in their mutual relations, which led to the birth of international law and schemes for perpetual peace evolved out of reason. These factors fostered the rise of "natural law of content" theories, which supposed that by appealing to reason perfect systems could be deduced in detail. Throughout this period the emphasis was very much on the individual and his rights.

Transcendental Idealism

The close of this epoch was marked by another line of thought, which was equally uncompromising in its insistence on individual freedom, but wholly idealistic in character. Kant (1724-1804), whose doctrines were developed by Fichte, taught that sensory perception is the avenue to knowledge of the objective would, but that all such perception is shaped by preconceptions which are given *a priori*. Thus, preconceptions of space, time and causation are the ideas which filter one's experience of nature. In so far Man is part of the world of reality, he is subject to its laws and is to that extent unfree. But his reason and inner consciousness make him a free moral agent. Man thus participates in two worlds, the "sensible" and the "intelligible". Law and morality belong to the latter. The actions of Man as a free agent are governed by aims, and the ethical basis of action has also to be accepted *a priori*. Justice, according to Kant, originates in pure practical reason. People know *a priori* how to act justly. The ultimate aim of the individual should be a life of free will. But it is when free will is exercised according to reason and uncontaminated by emotion that free-willing individuals can live together. People are morally free when they are able to obey or disobey a moral law. Kant propounded two principles of practical reason: (a) "Act in such a way that the maxim of your action can be made the maxim of an universal law (general action)". This is his famous "categorical imperative". (b) "An action is right only if it can co-exist with each and every man's free will according to universal law." This is his "principle of right".

Two points should be noted. The first is the emphasis on the individual. An important feature of Kant's doctrine is his proclamation of the autonomy of reason and will. Human reason is law-creating and constitutes moral law. Freedom in law means freedom from arbitrary subjection to another, and law is the complex totality of conditions under which maximum freedom is possible for all. To this end a separation of powers is necessary to prevent the emergence of a despotic regime, and the sole function of the state is to ensure the observance of law. Kant proceeded to urge that the individual should not allow himsel to be made the means to an end, since he is an end in himself; and further that he should, if need be, retire from society if his free will would involve him in wrong-doing. For Kant did perceive the necessity for rules in social existence, guided by a just general policy—Society unregulated by right results in violence. Social existence and violence are incompatible;

so reason demands that Man has an obligation to enter into society and to avoid wronging others. Such a society has to be regulated by compulsory laws, and if these laws are derived by pure reason from the whole idea of social union under law, Man will be able to live in peace. What is needed is a rule of law, not of men. The second feature is that the Kantain ideal of laws bears no relation to any actual system of law. It is purely an ideal to serve as a standard of comparison, not as a criterion of the validity of law.

MODERN THEORIES

Until the beginning of the nineteenth century natural law theory was a philosophy of content, i.e., it sought to deduce the contents of just laws from fixed premises. That century witnessed a decline in its popularity of many reasons. The existence of absolute principles was convincingly attacked, notably by Hume (1711-1776), who pointed out that there is no causal connection between facts and ideas. One cannot logically derive an "ought" from an "is". Cause and effect is an empirical correlation to be found in the physical science. Conceptions such as good and evil, for example, are subjective emotional reactions. Values are not inherent in nature, nor in justice. Reason can only work out the means that will lead to specified results; it cannot evaluate the latter. It is of some relevance, perhaps, that Hume was writing at a time of comparative tranquility. Whereas the timorous Hobbes, amidst the alarms of the Civil War, reached out for the shelter of an omnipotent sovereign's wing, Hume was concerned, if anything, with preserving stability. Thus, he argued against a discretion that would allow for justice in individual cases, suspecting a threat to stability in relying on a fluid conception such as justice. He favoured instead the firm and inflexible application of rules, although he conceded that these should be wisely designed in the first place and should be changed when conditions demand. On these lines he attacked the prevailing conceptions of natural law. The conception of a perfect, complete, discoverable system was challenged. If there was such a thing, why are there so many divergent interpretations, and why is positive law needed at all? At the dawn of the nineteenth century a reaction also set in against excessive individualism, fostered by later natural law theories, which had resulted in the French Revolution. Then, there grew up in the course of that century a new preoccupation with society, a collectivist outlook of life, which has been gathering momentum ever since. Natural law theories of the age immediately preceding, adapted as they were to an individualist outlook, fell into disrepute.

Objections also came from another quarter. The teachings of historians and sociologists, as pointed out in earlier chapters, laid stress on environment. Historical investigation helped to explode many assumptions. The social contract, in particular, came in for damaging criticism. Research into the early history of society exposed the mythical nature of the contract. The unit in early society was the family, or clan, not individuals. There was, moreover, the technical difficulty that the social contract theory endeavoured to ascribe the validity of law to contract whereas normally the reverse is the case. Some rule has to be presupposed which prescribes that agreements ought to be kept. But, these objections aside, even as a hypothesis to account for the present state of affairs the theory fell short, since it only heaped fiction upon fiction. Alternative explanations of the origin of society not only fitted the facts of today but were truer in themselves.

The *a priori* methods of the natural law philosophers were likewise unacceptable to those nurtured in the pragmatic spirit of science. Natural law postulates were subjected to critical examination with disastrous results. Their bases were revealed as unsubstantiated hypotheses or else the results of false inferences. Where, for instance, is the foundation for the sweeping assertion that Man must always seek society, or that Man is necessarily selfish? Again, it is a wild inference to assume that because certain institutions in different countries are alike, that must be because they are reflecting some universal law. It has even been suggested more recently that the whole idea of natural law is no more than a psychological reflex. The very diversity that is observable in systems of positive law raise in the mind, it is said, an antithesis of a fixed and changeless law. This coupled with an innate tendency to attribute reality to ideas prepares the way for belief in the existence of natural law. For all these reasons it became evident that the increasingly complex problems of the nineteenth century required a realistic and practical approach, not the easy application of abstract preconceptions.

In the new climate of opinion the prevailing natural law theories could not survive, and in their place arose analytical and historical positivism with increasing stress before long on a sociological approach to problems.

On reason for this was the courageous admission of scientists of the extent of which their own subjects were in fact founded on assumptions. Another was the failure of positivists to find answers to the problems that were coming to the forefront. The indispensability of values was increasingly felt as guides for legal development. This need was associated with the increasing use of broad, flexible concepts which admit latitude in application, and also with the realisation that judicial reasoning is creative and far from being purely syllogistic. The shattering effects of world wars, the decline in standards, a growing insecurity and uncertainty have stimulated anew the quest for a moral order, which was a boon undoubtedly afforded by natural law in the past. The alarming growth of totalitarian regimes, both right wing and left wing, has called for the development of some ideological control which could prevent the clock of legality being cast around every abuse.

In these circumstance it is hardly surprising that there has been a return to natural law in a new form, which strives to take account, not only of the knowledge contributed by the analytical, historical and sociological approaches, but also of the increasingly collectivist outlook on life. An important feature is the returning emphasis on a philosophy of method rather than of content, which leaves the details of actual laws to vary with time and place and also opens up a possibility of establishing evaluative criteria empirically.

Neo-Thomism

One form which the revival of natural law has taken is the adaptation of the doctrines of St. Thomas Aquinas. In the face of present-day divergences and conflicting tendencies there was much attraction in the method offered by Aquinas whereby philosophical reflection might find a way of synthesising prevailing needs and circumstances from a Christain point of view. Therefore, Pope Lew XIII's Encyclical Aeterni Patris, 1879, which drew attention to the value of his synthesis and encouraged the adaptation of his method, gave a powerful stimulus to an intellectual flowering already in bud. Although the philosophy of Thomism has come to be very much associated with Catholicism, it is no in fact officially part of it.

Neo-Thomists, as Aquinas's modern followeres are known, are prepared to accept the descriptions of reality provided by scientists, but they maintain that it is for philosophy, starting, like scientists, from certain hypotheses and utilising scientific insights, to give the full explanation of reality through reason and reflection. They also adopt the humanism of Aquinas to steer a course between, on the one hand, an exclusively individualist view of Man and, on the other, a totalitarian view of society in which the individual counts for nothing. Natural law is both anterior and superior to positive law. Aquinas believed that natural law was the attainment of the eternal law of God through the exercise of reason. Following from that the neo-Thomists formulate certain very broad and abstract generalisations, which are so abstract that they can be regarded as universal. In the concentration of these can be regarded as universal. In the concentration of these principles into rules of positive law variations will be found from place to place and from age to age. It is not clear to what extent a dictate of positive law which flouts natural law is void, but the mere fact that a law is unjust does not render it invalid.

One of the principal representatives of this school is Jean Dabin. Who maintained that the law of nature was "deduced from the nature of man as it reveals itself in the basic inclinations of that nature under the control of reason". Since human nature is identical in people everywhere, the precepts of natural law are universal despite historical, geographical, cultural and other such variations. These prescriptions are, however, only broad generalisations, and their detailed working out is left to the

Catholic Church. One of the precepts of natural law is concerned with the good of society, which is the purpose of state and law. The state provides order and laws are means to that end: "ubi jus ibi societas". By virtue of this paramount function the state is superior to all other groups, while state law "is the sole true law". The jus politicum he defined as:

> "The sum total of the rules of conduct laid down, or at least consecrated, by civil society, under the sanction of public compulsion, with a view to realising in the relations between men a certain order—the order postulated by the end of the civil society and by the maintenance of the civil society as an instrument devoted to that end".

Laws may be expressed variously, e.g., in statutes, precedents, custom; but they are general regulations of conduct, not of conscience. They are in the main obeyed, but when they are not obeyed, compulsion under the authority of the state has to be employed. By saying that laws are directed to conduct and not to conscience, Dabin was able to argue that there is a moral duty to obey those positive laws which conform to the natural law principle of promoting the common weal. If a law fails to conform to this principle it is not morally binding, because "everybody admits that civil laws contrary to natural law are bad laws and even that they do not answer to the concept of a law". This is ambiguous. It they are not "laws", there is no question of moral bindingness. What is not clear is whether they remain legally valid, though not morally binding. The question whether it would be immoral to disobey even such a law, because disobedience might be injurious to social stability, is not faced.

In order to fulfil the common good laws have to be adapted to the needs and ethos of the particular community. This is a matter of legal technique. So the actual making and applying of positive law with a view to giving effect to the dictates of natural law is an area which only jurists are competent to exercise. For the rules of the law do not simply put natural law into effect; in most cases a great many practical factors need to be taken into account.

All this reflects the attempt to harmonise the restoration of natural law with the variability of human societies and at the same time to follow the new emphasis on society.

Stammler

Another development was the mode of thought styled "natural law with a variable content", of which Stammler (1856-1938) was an exponent. He first distinguished between technical legal science, which concerns a given legal system, and theoretical legal science, which concerns rules giving effect to fundamental principles. The former deals with the content of the law, the latter relates them to ultimate principles.

He thus proceeded to distinguish between the "concept of law" and the "idea of law", or justice, and he approached the concepts of law as follows. Order is appreciable through perception or will. Community, or society, is "the formal unity of all conceivable individual purposes", and by this means the individual may realise his ultimate best interests. "Law", says Stammler, "is necessary *a priori,* because it is inevitably implied in the idea of co-operation". A just law aims at harmonising individual purposes with that the society. Accordingly, he sought to provide a forma, universally valid definition of law without reference to its content. He defined it as "a species of will, other—regarding, self-authoritative, and inviolable". Law is a species of will because it is concerned with orderings of conduct, other—regarding because it concerns a man's realations with other men, self-authoritative because is claims general obedience, and inviolable because of its claim to permanence. The idea of law if the application of the concept of law in the realisation of justice. Every rule is a means to an end, so one must seek a universal method of making just laws. A just law is the highest expressions of Man's social activity. Its aim is the preservation of the freedom of the individual with the equal freedom of other individuals. In the realisation of justice the specific content of a rule of positive law will vary from place to place and from age to age and it is this relativity which has earned for the theory the name of "natural law with a variable content". In order to achieve justice, a legislator has to bear in mind for principles. These are, firstly, two Principles or Respect.

(1) "The content of a person's volition must not depend upon the arbitrary will of another."
(2) "Every legal demand can only be maintained in such a way that the person obligated may remain a fellow creature."

Secondly, there are two Principles of Participation:

(1) "A person lawfully obligated must not be arbitrarily excluded from the community."
(2) "Every lawful power of decision may exclude the person affected by it from the community only to the extent that the person may remain a fellow creature."

With the aid of these four principles Stammler set out to solve actual problem which may confront the law courts. His solutions may sometimes be questioned on the ground that they do not necessarily follow from his principles, or that they are not the only possible just solutions. He did not deny validity to laws which fail to conform to the requirements of justice. His scheme is a framework for determining the relative justness of a rule or a law and for providing a means for bringing it nearer to justice. The whole approach is basically Kantain in so far as it is maintained that human beings possess certain *a priori* forms of apprehending the idea of law. The difference lies in the variability that is allowed in its content and in the collectivist, rather than an individualist, slant of the whole theory. Despite its ingenuity it has not found wide acceptance.

It is in America that contemporary natural law theory might be said to have found something like a congenial home.

John Rawls

A through-going attempt to formulate a general theory of justice is that of Professor John Rawls (1921-2005) of Harvard University, who writes mainly from the angle of philosophy and political science rather than of law. Natural law is not dealt with as such; but in so far as his scheme is based on reason, concerns social justice and purports to be comprehensive, it is naturalistic in conception. Since its publication in 1971 it has received wide attention.

Professor Rawls assumes that society is a more or less self-sufficient association of persons, who in their mutual relations recognise as binding certain rules of conduct specifying a system of co-operation. Principles of social justice are necessary for making a rational choice between various available alternative systems. The way in which a concept of justice specifies basic rights and duties will affect problems of efficiency, co-ordination and stability. This is why it is necessary to have a rational conception of justice for the basic structure of society. Practical rationality has three aspects, namely, value, right and moral worth. The "concept of right" relates to social systems and institutions, individuals, international relations and also the questions of priority between principles. With regard to social systems and institutions, the concept of right yields "Principles of Justice" and "Efficiency".

The approach to principles of social justice through utilitarianism and intuitionism respectively is considered critically and rejected. The latter in particular is faced with the difficulty of answering, first, Why should intuitive principles be followed? And, secondly, What guidance it there for choosing between conflicting principles in a given case? Professor Rawls endeavours to meet the first question by grounding his own principles in the exercise of reasons in an imaginary "original position"; and the second by calling in aid certain "principles of priority". He arrives at his theory as follows.

Fairness results from reasoned prudence; and principles of justice, dictated by prudence, are those which hypothetical rational persons would choose in a hypothetical "original position" of equality. The insistence on prudence excludes gamblers from participating in the "original position", but will bring in, on the whole, those who are conservatively inclined. The concept of the "original position" is not quite a modernised version of the "social contract", nor is it offered as being anything other than a pure supposition. On the one hand, people in this "original position" are assumed to know certain things, e.g., general psychology and the social science, but, on the other hand, a "veil of ignorance" drapes them with regard to certain other things, e.g., the stage of development of their society and especially their own personal conditions, place in that society, material fortunes, etc. In short, all this is designed to exclude personal self-interest when choosing the "basic Principles of Justice" so as to ensure their generality and validity. What is needed is a form of justice which will benefit everyone, i.e., the disinterested individual's conception of the common good. Leaving aside the wholly fictitious nature of this "original position", it is necessary to question the underlying assumption that what would be judged prudent in these hypothetical circumstance will eventually coincide with what people in actual societies will regard as just. Moreover, the "veil of ignorance" introduces needless complexities into what is no more than the simple requirement of impartial judgment.

The Basic Principles of Justice are generalised means of securing certain generalised wants, "primary social goods", comprising what is styled the "thin theory of the good", i.e., maximisation of the minimum (as opposed to a "full theory"). These primary social goods include basic liberties, opportunity, power and a minimum of wealth. The First Principle of Justice is: "Each person is to have an equal right to the most extensive total system of equal basic liberties compatible with a similar system of liberty for all". The basic liberties include equal liberty of thought and conscience, equal participation in political decision-making and the rule of law which safeguards the person and his self-respect. The second Principle is: "Social and economic inequalities are to be arranged so that they are both: (a) to the greatest benefit of the least advantaged, consistent with the just savings principle, and (b) attached to offices and positions open to all under conditions of fair equality of opportunity". The "just saving principle" is designed to secure justice between generations and is described as follows. "Each generation must not only preserve the gains of culture and civilisation, and maintain intact those just institutions that have been established, but it must also put aside in each period of time a suitable amount of real capital accumulation". With the aid of these Principles Professor Rawls seeks to establish a just basic structure. There has to be a constitutional convention to settle a constitution and procedures that are most likely to lead to a just and effective order; next comes legislation; and lastly the application of rules to particular cases. In this way it is claimed that the Basic Principles will yield a just arrangement of social and economic institutions.

Many criticisms have been levelled at various aspects of Professor Rawls's philosophic methods and economics into which it is unnecessary to enter. One major attack, launched by more than one critic, has been to question whether his conclusions follow from his "original position". For instance, distribution of goods is said to follow need, not merit. How the "original position" yield this? Again, would people in this position necessarily choose liberty? Professor Rawls does not specify any particular period in history, so that the people may find themselves in a time when there is need for power rather than liberty, or, as one critic suggests, the need may be for food in a time of famine rather than liberty. The answer to the last point might be that, as Professor Rawls says elsewhere, liberty is to have priority only after a certain point; but this raises another difficulty with regard to his priority principle, as will appear. Even so, when looked at from an economic or philosophical point of view, it is not easy to see how the balance between liberty and needs follows from the "original position". Indeed, the "veil of ignorance" is so restricted that one wonders how people in that carefully defined state of nescience could arrive at any of the Rawlsian conclusions. Although they are supposed to know general psychology and social science, they are ignorant of the stage of development of their society: what is not clear is whether people in a primitive state of development are supposed to possess the sophisticated psychological and social scientific knowledge of modern people, or whether they are to possess only primitive knowledge. The insistence on excluding motivations of self-interest as well as knowledge of the state of society is designed to make the choice disinterested, but nonetheless it remains personal. It has been pointed out that the fact that something is good for the individual does not imply that it will, therefore, be good for the individual does not imply that it will, therefore, be good for society. Thus, the benefit to an individual of being able to exercise a liberty may be lost to him if it were enjoyed by all. If then, the Basic Principles do not necessarily follow from the "original position", their ultimate acceptance (if, indeed, they do come to be accepted) must derive from their intrinsic moral appeal rather than reason. Thus, the fact that particular principles may have been thought suitable in an "original position" of limited knowledge and uncertainty is no basis for continuing to impose them later in the face of changed conditions and fuller knowledge. If it is contended that people would have chosen the principles anyway even in the light of later knowledge, this can only happen because they are thought to be just *per se*. The "original position" then becomes irrelevant. All this shows that the whole concept of the "original position" and the "veil of ignorance" and what it covers and does not cover only provide a semblance of justification for reaching certain desired conclusions.

A major objection to the method of intuitionism is, as Professor Rawls points out, that it gives no guidance in choosing between conflicting principles. To meet this difficulty he offers certain "Principles of Priority". Such priority is "lexical", i.e., the first has to be fully satisfied before the second falls to be considered. The First Priority Rule is the Priority of liberty: "liberty can be restricted only for the sake of liberty". He continues: "(a) a less extensive liberty must strengthen the total system of liberty shared by all; (b) a less equal liberty must be acceptable to those with the lesser liberty". The Second Priority Rule is the lexical priority of justice over efficiency and welfare: "(a) an inequality of opportunity must enhance the opportunity of those with the lesser opportunity; (b) an excessive rate the saving must on balance mitigate the burden of those bearing this hardship". These principles, in effect, ensure that as between liberty and need, liberty prevails; as between need and utility, need prevails, and as between liberty and utility, liberty prevails.

An objection to the lexical priority of liberty is that if equal liberty is accorded such priority, then anything involving unequal liberty can never fall to be considered, since the former has to be fully satisfied before one passes to something else. Even more seriously, Professor Rawls concedes that liberty is to be given this kind of priority only after certain basic wants are satisfied. But if liberty is not prior to needs all time, lexical priority becomes meaningless.

With reference to the individual, Professor Rawls contends that reason yields principles of natural just institutions, to help in establishing just arrangements, to render mutual aid and respect, not to injure or harm the innocent. The fairness principle gives rise to obligations, including promises; and in connection with fairness he strikes a topical note when discussing civil disobedience. The principle is that one should play one's part as specified by the rules of the institution as long as one accepts its benefits ("fair-play"), and provided the institution itself is just, or at least nearly just, as judged by the two Basic Principles of justice. Civil disobedience is said to be justified when "substantial injustice" occurs, all other methods of obtaining redress fail and disobedience inflicts no injury on the innocent. In these circumstance disobedience is an appeal to the society's sense of justice, which, it is said, is evidenced by the reluctance of the community to deal with it. This is hardly in accord with observed facts; it is more realistic to say that such reluctance is rooted more often than not in apathy and even fear, no matter how strongly people may condemn the disobedience.

In the result, it would seem that Professor Rawls has not succeeded in showing how his principles, desirable as they may be, derive from reason. Leaving that aside, however, it should be noted that the thrust of his theory is for stability, especially in Part Three of his book where he deals with objectives, and in his emphasis on obedience grounded in fair-play.

Law is only one institution of social justice in Professor Rawls's scheme. Professors Clarence Morris and Jerome Hall make it their exclusive concern, which makes their theories less extensive in scope.

Clarence Morris

Professor Morris (1893-1981) begins with the proposition that "justice is realised only through good law". Laws without just quality are doomed in the long-run; but the implication of his statement that justice cannot exist without good law does not follow. Justice may be realised through many other institutions; indeed, according to Marx and Engels in a communist society laws will wither away and justice for all will remain. Apart from the likelihood or otherwise of this prediction being fulfilled, it needs to be borne in mind that they were using "law" in a narrow sense, as Engels went on to say, though "law" will disappear, there will remain "an administration of things". Professor Morris, however, uses "law" in a much broader sense. "I use the word 'law'", he says, "to mean more than statutes and ordinances; it includes both adjudicated decisions of cases and social recognition of those legal obligations that exist without governmental prompting" (customs and practices).

Justice is on the three principal justifications of law, the other two being rationality and "acculturation". His theory concerns the method of realising justice and is not a theory of just content. "Doing justice" through law means that law-makers serve the public by advancing its "genuine aspirations", which are "deep-seated, reasonable, and non-exploitative". Law-making contrary to them is doomed to failure, for without public support legislators toil in vain. One difficulty lies in knowing who constitutes the "public". Would Jews in Nazi Germany or Africans in South Africa count as the "public"? "Genuine aspirations" is a vague phrase, as Professor Morris admits. To speak of them as "deep-seated, reasonable, and non-exploitative" does not carry the matter much further. Who, for instance, decides what is "reasonable"? In South Africa today it is not unfair to say that a majority of the European minority regard many African aspirations as unreasonable, and may even feel that some exploitation of Africans is reasonable. Such sentiments are deep-seated. Yet, the whole tenour of Professor Morris's book seems to be against regarding that regime as just. Another question is why it should be supposed that justice is achieved only so long as legislators follow public aspirations. May they not, with justice, sometimes seek to lead? The point is not faced.

The second justification of law, rationality, concerns the reasoning processes of the law, both judicial and legislative. Reason is a major ingredient of justice, but is of a special kind. By accepting judicial appointment, a judge is said to incur a duty to implement public aspirations within the leeways of the judicial process. Although legislation, too, must reflect them, this does not imply that an unjust law is not a "law"; a court remains bound to apply it. At this point Professor Morris enters the familiar ground of judicial reasoning and legislative techniques, which need not be rehearsed.

The third justification is "acculturation", which is conformity with culture. The purport of a statute, for example, can be more easily gathered when one is in tune with the legislator's cultural environment, and the point is developed with reference to ancient Chinese legislation. Under the heading of "acculturation" is included a pea for an awareness in law-making of man's responsibility towards his environment, since destruction and pollution of this will redound on himself. What is not clear is whether the idea of justice is here being stretched to cover conservation.

Professor Morris's general thesis is that law has to be justified morally, socially and technically. He does not specifically assert that just quality is a necessary condition of the continuity of laws, but this seems to be implicit. He certainly of the continuity of laws, but this seems to be implicit. He certainly stops short of saying that just quality is a requirement of the validity of a "law", for he does speak of "unjust laws". So, mindful of the point made at the start of this chapter, perhaps Professor Morris is not to be classed as either naturalist or positivist, for his thesis would not be rejected by either side.

Jermoe Hall

Not only does Professor Hall (1901-1990) insist on unifying moral, social and formal considerations, but he also takes the further step of saying that moral value needs to be included in a definition of positive law. It is certainly appropriate to treat him as a naturalist.

Until the time of Hegel, jurisprudence was treated as part of philosophy. Since then it has become fashionable to diversify different aspects of philosophy, including jurisprudence. The positivist belief in the "neutrality" of jurisprudence as an autonomous discipline is said to be associated with belief in logical analysis as a "neutral" method of reasoning. It is obvious, however, that logical analysis will yield neutral results only if the premises are neutral; if values are part of the premises, then the results of logical anlysis are likewise value-laden. The real issue is how one should view the premise, i.e., the subject-matter of jurisprudence, namely, "positive law". The time has come, says Professor Hall, to re-unite disciplines, and to this end he argues that jurisprudence should be "adequate" in the sense that it will combine positivist, naturalist and sociological study, namely, rules, values and social conduct. The result will be what he calls "integrative jurisprudence". The focal point of this is the action of officials, and he calls the concept "law-as-action". The word "action" is preferable to "behaviour"; "behaviour" occurs, whereas "action" brings in the idea of purpose guided by the value of achieving goals. Law-as-action from the point of view of officials relates rules, values and social behaviour in the following way. Rules come in to explain official actions in prescribing, judging and ordering and applying sanctions. Values come into the idea of validity. The way in which validity is understood depends upon whether law is viewed as law-as-rules or law-as-action. The former leads to a Kelsenian-type concept whereas the latter will include moral attitudes, principles and ideals. Thus, it is not sufficient to say of the actions of officials in deciding disputes that their decisions are in conformity with law, one has also to say whether they are correct, fitting or useful. "Correctness" reflects sound values in the rules, which means that from this perspective rules, too, acquire moral validity. In so far as law-as-action concerns the achievement of goals, "correctness" also partakes of the morality of the goals. Social behaviour comes in through the idea of the effectiveness of law, which covers a whole range of phenomena, including sanctions, mere conformity, conscious obedience and compliance (obedience plus approval). Obedience has to be gauged in relation to results, which are aimed at, as distinct from consequences, which simply occur. So, probable consequences have to be considered, which necessitates continuous re-assessment. Even the very enforcement of a law alters the facts in the sense that the situation is different after enforcement from what it was at the time the law was made. Laws, therefore, are effective when actual behaviour in accordance with then maximises the values of their goals.

The conclusion thus becomes irresistible that, when looked at from the point of view of law-as-action, moral value must be included in any definition of positive law. In addition, Professor Hall points to customary law which, he says, represents experience in settling problems in just and rational ways. "It is deliberate blocking out of the history of juridical experience that supports restrictive positivist analysis." He also points to the avowal of a "minimal natural law" by at least one modern positivist as "tantamount to surrender".

The need still remains to distinguish positive law from morality and other norms, and to this end he offers six criteria for law: (i) ethical validity reflected in certain attitudes; (ii) functions; (iii) regular (rather than systematic) character; (iv) range and character of public interest expressed in a state's laws; (v) effectiveness, which, if tied to the moral validity of law, has both a descriptive and prescriptive meaning; (vi) supremacy and inexorability in its sphere of relevance. Only law possesses all six features.

The main difficulty about Professor Hall's thesis is a practical one. For all the persuasiveness of his theoretical demonstration that a moral value has to be included in a definition of positive law, the question remains: how does this help in the day-to-day business of law-as-action? What is the correct, fitting or useful action to be taken by a judge if he is confronted, e.g., with a duly enacted decree requiring the killing of all new-born babies in order to save the state from the effects of the population explosion? Nowhere does he say that an immoral law is not "a law". Validity in the sense of law-quality for the purpose of deciding this or that case is different from validity in the sense of law-as-action. The practical implications of the latter are unclear. An explanation may lie in the fact that his theory presupposes a continuum of time. His thesis that morality must be included in a definition of law has to be understood in that context. Moreover, his stress on the need to integrate rules, morality and sociology, and the need to study law-as-action (functioning) give striking support to many of the contentions previously advanced in the present book.

Side by side with attempts, such as these considered, to work out a natural law of method, there have also been endeavours to base natural law on fact. Of especial interest in this connection is the theory of John Wild (1902-1985). He proceeds on the idea that "there are norms grounded on the inescapable pattern of existence itself", and his method of arriving at these is not that of logical deduction, but a different though equally logical process, namely, "justification". "How", he asks, "is moral justification to be explained? We cannot explain it without recognising that certain moral premises must somehow be based upon facts". The core of his thesis is that "value" and "existence" are closely intertwined. Existence has a tendency towards fulfilment or completion, and if the completion of existence is considered good, then existence itself must be valuable. The same act is good so far as it is realised, but evil so far as it is frustrated or deprived; an influence that enables something to act is good for it, and one that frustrates it is bad. Goodness, then, is some kind or mode of existence, evil is some mode of non-existence or privation.

Tendencies are the facts on which value-statements are founded. All individuals share in a common human nature, which has existential tendencies and which move them to their natural end. Such tendencies are at the root of the feeling of obligation which men possess. From it one can pass back to the values which require the act obliged, from the values to the needs which they satisfy, and factual evidence can be produced to demonstrate that these needs are essential rights. Accordingly, Wild reaches the following conclusions: (1) The world is an order of divergent tendencies which, on the whole, support one another. (2) Each individual entity is marked by an essential structure which is shares in common with other members of the species. (3) This structure determines certain basic existential tendencies that are also common to the species. (4) If these tendencies are to be realised without distortion or frustration they must follow a general dynamic pattern. This pattern is what is meant by natural law. It is grounded on real structure and is enforced by inexorable natural sanctions. (5) Good and evil are existential categories. It is good for an entity to exist in a condition of active realisation; if its basic tendencies are hampered and frustrated, it exists in a evil condition. When all these principles are applied to human nature, two ethical theses may be derived: (a) the existence of norms founded on nature; and (b) the good for Man as the realisation of human nature. Natural law may therefore be defined as "a universal pattern of action applied to all men everywhere, required by human nature itself for its completion.

Wild's opponents, notably Kelsen and Julius Stone, have fastened on the hiatus between fact and norm in his theory. There may be factual grounds for the content of the rules of natural law, but these do not show that natural law ought to be binding. Again, it may be a fact that human beings have certain tendencies and have a sense of obligation; but they do not explain why people ought to obey this sense. Mere existence is not enough, since, in Wild's view, the fact is the tendency of existence towards fulfilment or completion. How are these to be determined? Opinions will vary so enormously that this tendency ceases to be objective fact and becomes purely subjective. Besides, the fulfilment of existence of one entity may thwart or destroy the existence of another, and in such a case one wonders which is the natural law.

A different line of argument is adopted by Professor Lon L. Fuller (1902-1985), who might perhaps be regarded as the leading contemporary natural lawyer. The core of his thesis concerns the conditions 'sine quibus non' for the functioning of laws. For him, law "is the enterprise of subjecting human conduct to the governance of rules". Its morality has two aspects, external and internal. "External morality" is the "morality of aspiration", ideals; and towards the end of his book he submits that it is possible to derive a "substantive natural law" from it. This is more than a recipe for mere survival; it is a recipe for "meaningful contact with other human beings" whereby men can improve and enrich themselves. This substantive natural law concerns itself with those fundamental rules without which such meaningful co-existence could not obtain. There is also the "internal morality" of law, which makes no appeal to external standards, but is, in Professor Fuller's own words, "a procedural version of natural law". It is the morality that makes the governance of human conduct by rules possible. A judge may well stay neutral with regard to external morality, but it would be "an abdication of the responsibilities of his office" for him to stay neutral with regard to the internal morality. The content of it, which has been considered in connection with the functioning of duty, consists of eight desiderata: (i) generality, (ii) promulgation, (iii) prospectivity, (iv) intelligibility, (v) unself-contradictoriness, (vi) possibility of obedience, (vii) constancy through time, and (viii) congruence between official action and declared rules. This "inner morality" is not something superimposed on the power of law, "but is an essential condition of that power itself"; it is, in other words, "a precondition of good law". Immoral policies are bound in the end to impair the "inner morality" and so the very quality of law.

It was argued earlier that these are conditions 'sine quibus non' for the functioning of duties. If they are called "natural law", they are "natural" in that they are founded on the nature of things—human beings and human society are made in such a way that their natural limitations constitute the conditions for the successful functioning of duty-creating laws. It will be noticed that these conditions apply to the governance of any society of human beings so that they do not of themselves help to distinguish the functioning of the rules of a legal system from those of a club; nor does Professor Fuller claim that they do. The question may be raised, however, as to what a judge should do when faced with a decree violating the "internal morality", e.g., that of Caligula, which was promulgated in such a way that no one could read it. Should he refuse to acknowledge it as "a law"? Professor Fuller does not give an answer. In the sort of regime in which the "internal morality" is likely to be violated, a judge who refuses to accept a decree on this ground will receive short shrift indeed. So Professor Fuller's thesis likely to avail least where it would be most needed.

Professor Hart and others have drawn attention to a different point. The former has pointed out that the eight desiderata are "unfortunately compatible with very great iniquity", e.g., Herod's order for the massacre of the innocents satisfied all the conditions. Professor Fuller's reply is do doubt whether an evil rules could pursue iniquitous ends and also continue to respect the "inner morality". He calls for "examples about which some meaningful discussion might turn" and which would show that "history does in fact afford significant examples of regimes that have combined a faithful adherence to the internal morality of law with a brutal indifference to justice and human welfare". This is hardly an answer, but it does reveal an interesting point about the difference of opinion here. His contention is that iniquitous regimes have not continued to exist, nor could they continue to combine evil policies with fidelity to the "internal morality". In other words, he is thinking in a continuum, which is consistent with his whole idea of conditions needed for the continued functioning of laws. Professor Hart's objection concerns the position here and now of an iniquitous decree rather than the question of its continuance. In other words, the two parties are not at issue since they are thinking in two different time-frames.

Professor Hart (1907-2000), who is perhaps the leading contemporary positivist, has himself essayed an incursion into natural law. He admits that there is "a core of indisputable truth in the doctrines of Natural Law", if survival is taken as the minimum aim of human existence. The conditions 'sine quibus non' for achieving this end require that account be taken of five "facts": (i) human vulnerability, (ii) approximate equality of people, (iii) limited altruism, (iv) limited resources, and (v) limited understanding and strength of will. Because of these there is a "natural necessity" to protect persons, property and promises in varying degree. This necessity imposes some limit on the content of laws and this, he says, is the answer to a positivist who thinks that laws may have any content. It is by no means clear what this last statement implies. Professor Hart would hardly maintain that a law contrary to any of his five requirements of void, for he has strenuously upheld the positivist separation of law and morality and has urged that is both intellectually honest and conducive to clarity to say "This is law; but it is too iniquitous to be applied or obeyed." Such being his position, it would seem that the five requirements only furnish a standard of evaluating actual laws and guidelines for what they ought to be. Yet, his assertion that they are the answer to a positivist who thinks that laws may have any content suggests something more than this, something quite an-positivist. Another point is that, even as quidelines, the requirements are too vague to offer meaningful guidance. Thus, human vulnerability has not prevented life in most modern societies being made increasingly hazardous through various technological advances. Does vulnerability require that law should be used to discontinue such activities, or only to provide suitable compensation when injuries are sustained? If it is the latter, it seems odd that the minimal natural law should manifest itself, not in seeking to avoid threats to one of its basic "facts", but only in seeking a remedy in ways which can hardly "remedy"; for no amount of money can mend broken bones. Again, the "approximate equality" of people suffers from the weakness, previously noted, that everything depends on the criterion of equality and who applies it. Finally, it is to be observed that survival even as the minimum aim of human existence, as well as the five "facts" of the human condition, are not supported by any evidence, i.e., they are intuitive, self-evident. Professor Fuller has doubts about survival, even as an assumption: survival may be a means to other ends, but as the core of human striving, he says, it is open to question.

It may seem ironic that this account of natural law should end with a leading positivist expounding on the "core of indisputable truth in the doctrines of Natural Law". But this may at least indicate that the gulf between the two groups is not as wide as it used to be. Positions are less clear-cut now. It further underlines the point that classification into "naturalist" and "positivist" applies to views, not individuals. Certain doctrines may be labelled "naturalist" and others "positivist", but people may subscribe more or less strongly to one type or the other depending on the issue.

Implications of a Temporal Approach

The temporal approach, as outlined in the first chapter, only offers a way of looking at phenomena and not some new revelation. Jurisprudential study has broadened immeasurably in modern times, and the theme of this book has been to emphasise the essential inter-relation between law and other disciplines, principally philosophy, sociology and ethics. No one can be a good lawyer who only knows the law. It does not require a temporal approach to appreciate the connection between law and these other subjects, but such an approach can provide a framework which will unite their study. Whenever phenomena are viewed in a continuum, factors but for which they would not come into being, continue to be, and function become an integral part of one's concept of them. Origins include moral and social factors, reaching back perhaps to the very springs of governmental and other established social institutions. Function, or purpose, brings in the study of policies and values and the multifarious parts these play. They help to relate contemporary problems to the whole sweep of human though from ancient philosophies down to the most modern. Functioning brings in the actual operation of laws in society, including the important parts played by the institutional structure of society, the interplay of social and moral factors, and so on. In this connection the study of legal concepts also comes in, for they are necessary instruments in the task of doing justice in deciding disputes.

In addition to this, a temporal approach might help by assigning inquiries to their appropriate context. It has been suggested, for instance, that statutes should be thought of in a continuum, since they are designed to operate over indefinite periods of time. This will make it easier to see that statutory interpretation is an open-ended process of applying a given set of words to ever-changing situations rather than a linguistic exercise in trying to elucidate the referents of words. There is an *ad hoc* character about the latter, which is quite out of keeping with the nature of the enterprise, which should be statute "application" or even "construction", not "interpretation". It is submitted that the present unsatisfactory position is the result of approaching this task in the wrong temporal context. So, too, the ratio of a judicial precedent is not some "thing", which can be isolated here and now, but an open-ended process of continuous adjustment. Again, the dispute as to whether or not sanction in an essential part of the concept of duty is the product of a failure to see that each view is appropriate in its own context. Sanction is indeed part of the duty concept when duty is viewed in a continuum, where its functioning falls to be considered and with it the machinery of enforcement. But viewed as a tool of legal reasoning for the purpose of doing justice in this or that case. The concept of duty divorced from sanction is frequently used. The controversy arises when an inference from one time-frame is illegitimately transferred to the other. "Validity" (law-quality) is a concept which is appropriate in the present time-frame, where the question, Is this proposition "law"?, is asked with a view to identifying it as "law" for the purpose in hand, usually the deciding of a dispute. It is necessary to keep the means of identification as clear-cut as possible. One does not have to consider the decision of this or that case when thinking in a continuum, so different questions are asked: Why was this criterion of validity adopted? Why does it continue to be adopted? The operation of Savigny's mystical Volksgeist is discernible, if at all, only over a continuum, but his mistake, it is submitted with respect, was to utilise a factor operative in a continuum as a criterion of validity here and now. Professor Hart, whose concept of law and society imports continuity, changes his ground in order to defend positivism and he shifts his argument to the need for clear-cut criteria of validity in the day-to-day business of identifying "laws".

The temporal approach cannot resolve every puzzle, but it might at least shed new light on some. In connection with custom, there is the age-old antinomy between the apparent bindingness of customs and the unlimited discretion which courts appear to have in accepting or rejecting them. At least an explanation of why this problem has arisen, if not a solution, is suggested by a consideration of the requirements of custom in a temporal perpective. Two other famous controversies need separate treatment. They are the question whether international law is "law", and the positivist-naturalist debate.

The Problem of International Law

International law did not fit Austin's definition of "law properly so called", so he excluded it from further consideration; which was unobjectionable in itself. Unfortunately what he said, in effect, was, "This is the definition of 'law' which I propose to adopt. It is the proper meaning, and I exclude international law because it is not properly called 'law'". As might have been expected, international lawyers, incensed at this cavalier denigration of their subject, took issue with him. Had they, for their part, simply replied: "Use the word 'law' how you like, but we shall use it for our subject," no controversy need have arisen. Instead, they took issue with him on the "proper meaning" of the word "law". To this extent the controversy was verbal and sterile.

It is an undoubted fact that the respect which states pay to international law is less than that which individuals pay to municipal law. There has always been a need to enhance the prestige of international law by calling in aid the magic of the word "law", especially in creating a sense of obligation. This is one reason why international lawyers are sensitive about Austin's exclusion of their subject from his imaginary paradise and why they are so anxious to avail themselves of the emotive connotation of the word "law". Professor G.L. Williams pointed it out very clearly:

> "The word 'law' stimulates in us the attitude of obedience to authoritative rules that we have come through our upbringing to associate with the idea of municipal law. Change the word for some other and the magic evaporated. Accordingly these writers felt obliged to embark upon the unprofitable discussion as to the 'proper' meaning of the term 'law'."

Hence the attempts to prove that the subject is "really" law.

Professor Hart thinks that the controversy is more than just a disagreement about words, because the application of the general term "law" to a whole discipline like international law is different from the application of a name to some object. The question, he says, is one of analogies. (a) There are rules prescribing how states ought to behave, which are accepted as guiding standards just as in municipal law. (b) Appeals are made to precedent, writings and treatises as in municipal law; not to rightness or morality. (c) Rules of international law, like those of municipal law, can be morally neutral. (d) Again, like those of municipal law, they can be changed by conscious act, e.g., by treaty. Accordingly, Professor Hart submits that there are sufficient analogies of content, as opposed to form, to bring rules of international law nearer to municipal law than to any other set of social rules.

Despite these resemblances, two important differences should not be overlooked. One is that the subjects of international law are primarily states, and the disparity in strength between them far exceeds that between individuals in society. Besides, there are other institutions which have claims, duties, etc. but which are not states. Examples would be the United Nations Organization, the Holy See between 1871 and 1929, various other specialised agencies and so on. Individuals as such are increasingly becoming subjects of international law, which enhances the disparity between the various subjects.

The other difference is that whereas the courts of a municipal order appeal to the same criterion, or criteria, by which to identify "laws", there is no co-ordination in the ways in which rules of international law are identified. There is no singly criterion of identification, because there are unrelated sets of tribunals, each of which identifies international law differently. There is, first, the International Court of Justice, which identifies its rules with reference to Article 38 of the Statute of the Court. Paragraph (1) specifies treaties, custom, general principles of law, and, subject to Article 59, judicial decisions and writings of jurists. Paragraph (2) empowers the Court to decide 'ex aequo et bono' if the parties agree. There are other international tribunals, such as arbitration tribunals, which are not bound by the Statute of the International Court. They may, and usually do, resort to much the same sources, namely, treaties (especially the treaty setting up the tribunal) custom, general principles of law, judicial decisions and writings of jurists. Municipal courts also are often called upon to apply principles of international law. Their criteria of identification are regulated by their own municipal systems. A British court, for instance, finds rules of international law primarily in statute and precedent. Only in the absence of a rule of statute law or common law applicable to the case in hand will it go outside and, even then, only as a matter of discretion.

When one considers international law in a continuum the differences become still more pronounced. In the first place, it follows from what has just been said that no consistent answer can be given to the question why the criteria of identification were adopted. In most cases the adoption is *ad hoc,* for the purpose of the instant dispute, not once and for all. The predictability of decisions in any international tribunal is less than in municipal tribunals because there are fewer agreed rules and because of the greater intrusion of political considerations and national self-interest. Indeed, "vital interests" and "national honour" prevent every important issue ever going before courts.

Far more interesting is the manner in which rules of international law work, with which is associated the question of obedience to it. The basis of the binding force of international law is commonly ascribed to consent, but this is not a satisfactory explanation. A basis in consent presupposes some rule which makes consent obligatory; and the basis of that rule then requires elucidation. Again, if consent is the basis, it would follow that once consent is withdrawn, the obligation to obey ceases. It has been pointed out with regard to municipal law that consent is quite unrealistic. Individuals are never asked if they consent to be bound by municipal laws, which are treated as binding regardless of consent. The point only arises when some dissident declares that he no longer accepts a law, in which event the question is not whether consent makes a law binding, but whether withdrawal of compliance can deprive it of its obligatory force; which is a different matter. Here, the coercive power of the state, manifested in its sanction machinery, comes into play, and this is so over whelming as to make it quite immaterial what the individual thinks. Accordingly, as has been suggested, there is not point investigating "the binding force" behind laws as if this is some "thing" which can be isolated but it would be more meaningful to ask: Why do people obey? And, What machinery is there for dealing with disobedience?, The so-called "binding force" rests in the psychological reactions inducing people to obey, among which fear the organised force is one factor. In the international sphere, there is no effective machinery for applying overwhelming, organised force. The principal reasons why states choose to obey international law are fear, if at all, of their neighbours and self-interest. Fear operates through war, reprisals, retorsion, pacific blockade and naval and military demonstrations. These have comparatively little effect and, in any case, are calculated to deter weak rather than strong states. Fear of action taken by the United Nations Organisation is very slight, for such action if inhibited by the use of the veto in the Security Council. The greatest shortcoming of international law is the absence of effective machinery to carry out sanctions. In any case, such action as might be taken is more likely to influence weak rather than strong states. The result, therefore, is that whether or not a given strong states. The result, therefore, is that whether or not a given state at any time abides by a given rule of international law depends upon a balance between various considerations, e.g., a desire to secure fair treatment for its own nationals at the hands of other states, nationalism, tradition, morality, diplomacy, economic interests and, possibly, fear. All this makes the working of international law very different from that of municipal law. In brief, international law continues in being mainly because states find in it a useful instrument of policy.

The result of all this is that when one considers the matter in the present time-frame the resemblances between international and municipal law are such as to tilt the balance in fauour of hallowing the former with the sanctity of "law"; when one considers it in a continuum the functioning of international law is so different from municipal law that the balance gets tilted the other way. The temporal approach does not answer the question whether international law is "law" or not, but it could account for the persistence of the question and why it resists all efforts to lay it to rest.

The Positivist-Naturalist Debate

In the course of the discussion of the is ought dichotomy it was pointed out that a total separation of the "is" and the "ought" is not possible. Law is what it ought to be. For instance, in rule-making and rule-shaping, including the constant re-structuring of concepts, it is undeniable that moral, social, political and other such factors make them what they are; and where there is no authority on a point, the judge will declare the rule to be what he feels it ought to be. Again, principles and doctrines, as Professor Dworkin has argued, "are" law now, but they are themselves pointers to what laws ought to be.

When naturalists talk of the moral quality of law they are thinking of law in a continuum i.e., as a purposive social activity extending over an indefinite period of time. They are certainly able to make out a powerful case. A separation of law from morals is not possible when the moral quality of law is one of the factors that brings it into being and determines its continued existence; all such factors are a part of the concept of law as a continuing, functioning phenomenon.

Positivists, on the other hand, think mainly in the present time-frame where the need is to determine whether a given precepts is or is not a "law" for the purpose in hand. Their case for resting identification on a purely formal criterion is over-whelming?

So far naturalists and positivists are not at issue, and the fact that they have been operating in two different frames of thought can be revealed by a few writings. When Austin, for instance, declared that "a law" is the command of a sovereign supported by a sanction, he was only providing a method, inaccurate at that, of identifying what he called a "positive law". Nowhere did the concern himself with the conditions of continuance. Kelsen's hierarchical scheme is a demonstration of how the law-quality of every norm at any given moment is derived from the Grundnorm; and by insisting on "purity" for his theory he excluded all dynamic forces that make for continuity. Professor Hart begins by equating "law" with "legal system", which is an on-going phenomenon; but in arguing the case for positivism he bases it on the need for a clear-cut method of identifying laws at any given moment of time. Elsewhere he has alluded to "the acceptable proposition that some shared morality is essential to the existence of any society". Thus, when he thinks of continuity, morality is seen to be essential; when he thinks of the need here and now for clear-cut, formal means of identifying laws, he shifts over into the present time-frame.

On the other hand, when Professor Fuller, a naturalist, proffers his eight conditions, which comprise the "inner morality" of law, he is stating, as has been pointed out, indispensable requirements for the continued functioning of laws. His positivist critics have not been slow to point out—(a) that all these conditions are compatible with very great iniquity, and (b) that there is no reason why an immoral precept may not be likened to a "sick law", but a "law" nonetheless. Both these objections betray clearly the critics' obsession with the present time-frame of thought in which alone they are meaningful. For they overlook the crucial point that the conditions required to keep a thing going, to cure or kill it are included in any conception involving its endurance. An unjust law may indeed satisfy the eight conditions and even function, but Professor Fuller's point is that it will not continue to function. However, he does not answer the question whether or not an immoral precept is to be treated as "law" at this moment. He side-steps that point by instead whether "history does in fact afford significant examples of regimes that have combined a faithful adherence to the internal morality of law with brutal indifference to justice and human welfare". This is a matter of continuance and shows that he, for his part, is thinking in a continuum. The time-frame approach thus shows that the two sides are not on the same plane.

The inclusion of both a formal and moral element will ensure that there will continue to be some separation between what is law and what ought to be law so that the latter can serve as a standard by which to evaluate the former. What naturalists are anxious to secure is that precepts, which violate minimum morality, will not become "laws".

It is necessary to separate two questions: Is there presently a minimum moral criterion of validity? and Ought there to be such a criterion? With regard to the first, the answer must be in the negative, save where a moral element has been written into a constitution in some form or other. There have been occasional judicial utterances of wider import, but these are not decisive and should not be generalised.

The second question is whether a minimum moral element ought to be incorporated into the criterion of validity. Naturalists, arguing on the basis of the conditions essential to continuity, advance good reasons why it should be. Positivists, while not questioning the desirability, advance equally cogent reasons why a moral test as such would be impracticable in the daily workings of the law. This casts the onus squarely on naturalists to find a practicable way of incorporating a moral test into a formal criterion of validity. It is proper that they should accommodate themselves to a formal test, since the method of identifying laws for the purpose of daily business has to be clear-cut and impersonal for the compelling reason given by positivists. Indeed, if naturalists choose to enter the lists in the present time-frame, as they are doing here, they must submit to the requirements dictated by its circumstances. If such a method could be found, then both positivist and naturalists should be satisfied, the former because their insistence on a formal test will have prevailed, the latter because their demand for a minimum moral criterion will also have been met. Though it is doubtful if any of them can be regarded as providing a wholly satisfactory answer. So, finding such an answer remains an unattained goal in the general pursuit of social justice, but there is no reason why positivists and naturalists should not co-operate in making the quest a joint enterprise.

The Temporal Approach to Natural Law

The "natural law of method" is a way of working out just laws, and the 20th century has seen versions of "natural law with variable content". The temporal approach is in line with this thinking. Factors but for which a thing would not be and continue to be and function are part of the conception of it as a continuing phenomenon. The nature of things being what it is, such factors dictate a "natural law of existence". The "ought" behind it is that behind the conditions 'sine quibus non' of achieving any end in this case, continuity. It is not the "ought" from an "is". Such an approach is politically neutral in that it does not support any particular kind of order. Even if the present one were shattered to pieces and a different one established, the continuance of that, too, will require the same conditions.

The Temporal Approach to Legal System

Bentham and Austin, it will be remembered, regarded legal systems as the sum-total of its laws. Bentham saw truly that any ordinary regulation, e.g., a statutory provision, in made up of several provisions, but by "a law" he meant one which is undividuated" in a jurisprudential sense. For him, the core of every law was an act-situation and an aspect of the sovereign's will in relation to it. Consistently with this, he distinguished between a law prescribing, e.g., "You ought not to do X", and a separate law prescribing the sanction of you do X. Kelsen, on the other hand, rolled these two into one by making the former a condition of the latter: "If you do X, then sanction Y ought to be applied". It was pointed out that of the two Bentham's way of regarding the matter was preferable. Even so, there are certain shortcomings about his conception. The most obvious of these stems from his commitment to an imperative basis for law, which *inter alia,* led him to treat whole branches such as contract and property as being only the "qualificatory" and "expositary" parts of other laws for-bidding, e.g., breaches of contracts or meddling with property.

Accordingly, it is submitted, first, that the idea of sovereign will should be abandoned, and, secondly, that instead of making act-situations the core of every law, the different functions of laws be used instead. In this way a broader treatment might be achieved and also one that will not diverge from the ordinary uses of the term "a law". Laws have different functions: they may (i) impose duties, (ii) create or acknowledge liberties, (iii) create, change or abolish other laws, (iv) specify conditions for the effective exercise of powers, (v) create immunities, (vi) define the use of labels (e.g., "person", "simple contract"), and (vii) regulate the incidence of claims, duties, powers, etc. (e.g., the duty to support an illegitimate child lies primarily on the mother).

Another objection to Bentham is that a legal system is much more than the sum-total of its laws. The very word "system" implies the pattern of their inter-relation and also continuity. With regard to the first, just as a railway system is more than the sum-total of tracks and rolling-stock, so too with a legal system. One of the most important unifying links in the pattern is validity. The validity of laws, i.e., the "legal" quality of every part of the legal system, derives from a common source or sources (e.g., statute, precedent and immemorial customs in Britain), or Grundnorm in Kelsen's terminology. What this implies is that the creation and conferment of duties, powers, etc. is limited to one body, or limited number of bodies. But there are also principles, doctrines and standards, which are "law", but which do not derive their validity in this way. The law-quality of laws emanating from the Grundnorm as well as the law-quality of principles, etc. depend on acceptance by courts. At this point the signal importance of institutions beings to emerge. Not only is the institution of courts and the place they occupy in the organisation of society of crucial significance, but so are other institutions, e.g., that which produces legislation. Thus, it is not just the assent of the Queen, Lords and Common that constitutes a statute, but only such assent after it has been given through the institution of Parliament and its institutionalised procedures. Other unifying factors in the pattern of a legal system are: the interpretation of laws and the ordering of sanctions are entrusted to specified institutions acting according to set procedures; and the sanctions themselves are limited in number and entrusted to certain other institutions to execute. If "legal system" is not simply the sum-total of laws, there is no inconsistency in saying that the provisions of sanctions is a feature of legal system, though not necessarily of every individual law.

Thus far the picture is of the formal structure of a legal system. But the word "system" also implies continuity. Since any concept of inter-relationships and organisation is pointless except in connection with the way in which they hold together while functioning. The inclusion of powers in a concept of law makes a temporal perspective unavoidable, since, as pointed out, the power, e.g., to make an offer and the power to accept and the claim-duty relationship which they create cannot co-exist. If, then, a time dimension has to be introduced, the implications of this have to be faced. The endurance of a legal system is of course on a much larger scale than this limited example suggests. In the context of endurance on important question that has to be asked is: What is the function of a legal system? To which the predominant answer is: To do justice. Not only is justice its purpose, but the quality of justice is a condition of its continuance. It is not possible to maintain a system indefinitely through fear; people must have faith in it as being substantially a just order and as dispensing substantial justice. Doing justice in deciding disputes is the principal concern of lawyers. This is a task which brings into consideration the equipment used in legal reasoning and above all values, which play so decisive a part in the decisional process. Doing justice further involves consideration of what is actually accomplished in social life through the operation of laws and decisions. So the attribute of justice has to be incorporated into any concept of legal system.

The establishment and maintenance of a just order requires for a start a just allocation of benefits and burdens. Two essential pre-requisites for this are moral restraint in the exercise of power by those who have to decide these matters, and moral restraint in the exercise of liberties of action by all those who are in a position to wreck any scheme of allocation. Positivists on their own confession are unable to help with these problems. Their purely formal concepts of law and of legal system are like charts depicting the structure of a machine without its motive power. But the structure of every machine has to be worked out so as to make controlled use of motive power, and all formal depictions of structure are based on the assumption that there is, or will be, such control. Legel machinery is but partly the product of human calculation; it is also the product of ideological and social forces over which human control is limited, since human beings as members of society are themselves in the grip of these forces. There is thus all the more reason to incorporate control of these forces into a concept of legal system, for otherwise uncontrolled forces can shatter the system and society. The recurrent tragedies of history have resulted, not from the support given to power or liberty according to the paramount need of the age, but from failure to control whichever movement was in the ascendant. A contented society is the antithesis of tyranny and anarchy. It has been observed that natural law theory is in a sense always a reaction against abuse: abuse of power, which is tyranny, or abuse of liberty, which is anarchy.

Two conditions 'sine quibus non' for the continuity of any legal system are thus control of power and of liberty. Power is manifested through laws. If this were to come about, it could be accommodated within a formal concept. This, however, is not enough. A formal structure stands until changed and, as pointed out, failure to adapt to change is as much an abuse of power as direct exercises of it. What is needed is a concept of legal system which transcends formality and embodies control of power as an indispensable part of the very idea of law. The same applies with even greater force to the restraint of liberty, since the problem of its abuse cuts even deeper than that of power. One must begin by asking whether one wants society at all; and if one does, the next question is how it would be possible to have a stable society without providing safeguards against the two most potent forces of destruction, namely, abuse of power and abuse of liberty. Some exercise of power there will have to be in order to suppress certain forms of liberty. Outside the area of prohibition, restraint on liberty can only come from self-restraint and self-discipline, for which there is no alternative but the acceptance of a set of shared values, which results from faith in a just way of life, namely religion. The sooner the implications of this are realised the better. The question what sort of concept would be appropriate for this purpose will depend, in the first place, on whether liberty is treated as falling within or outside a concept of law. Clearly, it can form no part of a concept which confines "law" to positive regulation of conduct . It was pointed out in a earlier discussion that there is justification for including all aspects of conduct within "law", whether positively or negatively regulated. Besides, apart from specific regulation, the law can indirectly influence the exercise of law itself depends on a sense of freedom with responsibility. On this view it is necessary to bring liberty within a concept of law. The choice between the two kinds of concepts, that which includes and that which excludes liberty, is not dependent on logic, but is simply a question of which is more suited to the task of law as one sees it. To rule is to educate; that is a lesson which has been preached from ancient times down to the present. Education includes education in values and in moderation, which is inspired by breadth of vies, and dispassionate, of fear and both of them hinder the development of ideas. No matter how difficult the task of curbing these may be at present, the failures of today can be made into stepping-stones towards the success of tomorrow.

John Wild

The theory of John Wild (1995) proceeds on the idea that "there are norms grounded on the inescapable pattern of existence itself." His method of arriving at these is not that of logical deduction, but a different process, namely, "justification". He asks: "How is moral justification to be explained? We explain it without recognizing that certain moral premises must somehow be based upon facts." The core of his thesis is that "value" and "existence" are closely intertwined. Existence has a tendency towards fulfilment or completion. If completion of existence is good, existence itself must be valuable. The same act is good so far as it is realised, but it is evil so far as it is frustrated. Goodness is some kind or mode of existence and evil is some mode of non-existence or privation.

According to Wild, the world is an order of divergent tendencies which, on the whole, support one another. Each individual entity is marked by an essential structure which it shares in common with other members of the species. This structure determines certain basic tendencies that are common to the species. If these tendencies are to be realised without distortion or frustration, they must follow a general dynamic pattern. This pattern is what is meant by natural law. It is grounded on real structure and is enforced by inexorable natural sanctions. Good and evil are existential categories. It is good for an entity to exist in a condition of active realisation. When all these principles are applied to human nature, three ethical theses may be derived viz., the universality of moral or natural law, the existence of norms founded on nature and the good for man as the realisation of human nature. Natural law may be defined as "a universal pattern of action applied, to all men everywhere, required by human nature itself for its completion."

Fuller

Prof. Lon L. Fuller (1902-1995) is regarded as the leading contemporary natural law lawyer. He does not contend that the rules of a legal system must conform to any substantive requirements of morality or any other external standard. He maintains the need for rules of law to comply with "internal morality." Initially, he draws a distinction between morality of duty and morality of aspiration. The former corresponds to an external morality of law. It consists in those fundamental rules without which society cannot exist. He sees law as a "purposive activity." The morality of aspiration exhorts mankind to strive for ideals' and fulfil their potentialities in a Platonic way. He gives eight typical ideals or formal virtues to which a legal system should strive viz., generality, promulgation, absence of retroactive legislation and certainly no abuse of retrospective legislation, no contradictory rules, congruence between rules as announced and their actual administration, clarity, avoidance of frequent changes and the absence of laws requiring the impossible. These principles of legality are not basic conditions which every system necessarily fulfils, but constant pole stars guiding his progress. The greater its success, the more fully legal such a system is.

Fuller is critical of the assertion of Dworkin that while baldness is a matter of degree, a line can be drawn between law and non-law. To quote Fuller: Law does not just fade away, but goes out with a bang.

Fuller does not develop the relationship between the form 'in which legal rules are expressed and their content. The Nazi legal system was faithful, with one possible exception, to the cannons of Fuller and yet it was able to promulgate the Nuremberg racial laws which were utterly offensive to all human values. Fuller must surely believe that form has a direct bearing on content as otherwise his principles would be nothing more than the tools of an efficient craftsman.

The view of the critics of Fuller is that Fuller betrays con-fusion between efficacy and morality. Hart objects "to the designation of these principles of good legal craftsmanship as morality, in spite of the qualification 'inner', as perpetrating a confusion between two notions that it is vital to hold apart the notions of purposive activity and morality".

Hart points out that the eight desiderata of Fuller are "unfortunately compatible with very great iniquity", e.g., Herod's order for the massacre of the innocents satisfied all the conditions. The reply of Fuller is to doubt whether an evil ruler could pursue iniquitous ends and also continue to respect "inner morality". He calls about which some meaningful discussion might turn and which would show that "history does in fact afford significant examples of regimes that have combined a faithful adherence to the internal morality of law with a brutal indifference to justice and human welfare." The contention of Fuller is that iniquitous regimes have not continued to exist, nor could they continue to combine evil policies with fidelity to "internal morality".

Castberg, a Norwegian jurist, refers to natural law in the sense of rules of ideal laws which are adapted to the oft changing conditions of life.

D'Entreves states that natural law contains the elementary principles which man must respect as long as they are what they are and propose to set-up a viable society. He puts certain queries and asks: Are we to conclude that natural law is central and privileged sphere of morality distinguished by its sacred and inviolable character? Does it mean that outside the sphere of the minimum content, laws of any iniquity may stand? And even within it, what is the status of laws which flagrantly violate the minimum protection for which Hart's natural law stands? Are such laws and, if so, what, if any, is the right of resistance? To what extent can evil permeate a system before that becomes no more than a suicide club?

The most significant revival of natural law thinking in our time is to be found in contemporary German legal philosophy. This revival springs directly from the reaction against the excessive and, in the later phases of the Nazi regime, Nihilistic manifestations of legal positivism. German legal philosophers and law courts have sought to rethink and reformulate the relation of "higher law" principle and positive law. Deeply moved by the excesses of absolute State sovereignty perpetrated by the Nazi regime, Gustav Radbruch states that since law is, in its very nature, destined to serve justice, certain types of positive law cannot be defined as law and this applies to the whole portions of National Socialist Law. Radbruch was conscious of the extreme difficulty of separating "non-law" from merely "bad" or "unjust" law and the need to reserve the decision on those matters to institutions like the supreme constitutional court.

H. Krabbe, a Dutch jurist, strongly adheres to the "social conscience" or the "recognition" of law by those whom it applies. He admits no other authority as a true source of law. According to him, law is to the individual or groups of individuals in the same way as the theory of auto-limitation is to the state. This collective conscience becomes the corporate aspect of natural law. As for the individual judge or legislator who has to explore and expound the collective conscience, much stress is laid on his instinct or intuition, that is, his own moral sense and his own intelligence.

The view of Prof. C.K. Allen in *Law in the Making* is that reduced to its simplest language, the revived natural law appears to "mean little more than that the magistrate must judge as justly as he can, and the legislator must make laws as wisely as he can, in accordance with the prevailing ideas of justice and utility with which, it is to be hoped, (and, after all, it cannot be more than a hope), law-makers and law-dispensers of a particular community are imbued by training and experience." Again, "the new natural law does not seem to contain any very novel truth, or to be very felicitously named; and it probably would not have been so much canvassed on the continent had it not been associated with a movement for a moral, liberal and elastic judicial technique, *la libre recherche scientifique,* than has been orthodox in most European countries and also with controversies concerning the nature and limits of the powers of the State. Apart from these special problems, its chief value has been to counteract the tendency to exaggerate the purely historical and fortuitous circumstances of legal growth, at the expense of the moral principles from which law may sometimes be judicially separated, but can never be divorced a *vinculo matrimonii.*"

Hart

Prof. H.L.A. Hart (2000) is in many ways the leader of contemporary positivism. In his book entitled *The Concept of Law,* Hart has attempted to restate the position of natural law from a semi-sociological point of view. He points out that there are certain substantive rules which are essential if human beings are to live continuously together in close proximity. To quote him: "These simple facts constitute a core of indisputable truth in the doctrines of natural law." Hart puts emphasis on an assumption of survival as a principal human goal. According to him, we are concerned with social arrangements for continued existence and not with those of a suicide club. There are certain rules which any social organisation must contain and it is these facts of human nature which afford a reason for postulating a "minimum content" of natural law.

Hart does not state the actual minimum universal rules but certain facts of "human condition" which must lead to the existence of some such rules but not necessarily rules with any specific content. According to Hart, those facts of human condition consist of human vulnerability, approximate equality, limited altruism, limited resources and limited understanding and strength of will. In the light of these inevitable features of human condition, there follows a "natural necessity" for certain minimum forms of protection for persons, property and promises. "It is in this form that we should reply to the positivist thesis 'law may have any content'."

Hart does not suggest that, even if this analysis of human society is accepted, this must inevitably lead to a system of even minimal justice within a given community. He accepts the fact that human societies at different periods of history have displayed a melancholy record of oppression and discrimination in the name of security and legal order as in the case of systems based on slavery, or systems based on positive religious or racial discrimination.

Hart's view of minimum content for natural law has been criticised. It is contended that this approach should not be confused with an attempt to establish some kind of "higher law" in the sense of overriding or eternally just moral or legal principles, but is merely an attempt to establish a kind of sociological foundation for a minimum content for natural law. The justification for the use of the term natural law is that regard is paid to what is suggested to be the fundamental nature of man as indicated in the five facts of human condition by Hart. However, these "facts" are extremely vague and uncertain in most respects. They do not depend upon sociological investigation, but are really an intuitive appraisal of the character of the human condition. Lord Lloyd points out that it is difficult to see how any real minimum content whatever can be based upon such principles. The factor of human vulnerability restricts the use of violence but the need for human survival has not prevented the acceptance in many. societies of the exposure of infants or the killing of slaves or children by those exerting power over them. A society may actually base its survival upon the need for human slaughter. The ancient civilisation of Mexico possessed a religious and a State system which required the perpetual propitiation of the gods, by continuous human sacrifice on a massive scale. In relation to such a society, it seems difficult to talk in terms of individual human vulnerability as it might be conceived in a developed modern State which acknowledges as a fundamental principle the value of individual life and security.

Although Hart refers to the implications of approximate equality between human beings, he himself recognises that no universal system of natural law or justice can be based upon the principle of impartiality, or that of treating like cases alike. The rule of equality cannot be derived from any formal principle of impartiality. The idea of equality or non-discrimination is essentially a value judgment which cannot be derived from any assertions or speculations regarding the nature of man. No insistence on the idea of impartiality or the rules of natural justice, or the "inner morality" of the law in the sense used by Prof. Fuller, can afford a basis of arriving at such a principle as that of non-discrimination. This is fully recognised by Hart himself when he writes that the idea of impartiality is "unfortunately compatible with very great iniquity."

D'Entreves points out another gap in his treatment of natural law by Hart. While Hart accepts the positivist view that the validity of a legal norm "does not depend in any way on its equity or iniquity", he maintains that natural law contains "the elementary principles which man must respect as long as men are what they are and propose to set-up a viable society." D'Entreves asks: "Are we to conclude that natural law is a central and privileged sphere of morality distinguished by its sacred and inviolable character?" Does this mean that outside the area of the minimum content laws of any iniquity may stand? and even within it, what is the status of laws which flagrantly violate the minimum protection for which Hart's natural law stands? Are such laws law and, if so, what, if any, is the right of resistance? To what extent can "evil laws" permeate a system before that set-up becomes no more than a suicide club?

Prof. Dias observes that it may seem ironic that this account of natural law should end with a leading positivist expounding on the "core of indisputable truth in the doctrines of natural law", but this may at least indicate that the gulf between the two groups is not as wide as it used to be. Positions are less clearcut now. It further underlines the point that classification into "naturalist" and "positivist" applies to views and not individuals. Certain doctrines may be labelled "naturalist" and others "positivist", but people may subscribe more or less strongly to one type or the other depending on the issue. (*Jurisprudence*, p. 684).

It is clear from what has been stated above that the concept of natural law has changed from time to time. It has been used to support almost any ideology—theocracy, absolutism and individualism. It has inspired revolutions and bloodshed. It has provided a firm ground for theorizing and expressing the ideas and thoughts of a particular age. It has influenced positive law and modified it. The theories of natural law have helped the development of law. A large number of principles of natural law have been embodied in the legal systems of various countries. Examples can be given from the legal systems of England, the United States and India. So far as England and the United States are concerned, a reference to them has already been made. As regards India, a number of legal principles and concepts have been borrowed from England and many of them are based on the principles of natural law. The examples of some of them are "justice, equity and the good conscience", quasi-contract reasonableness in tort. The Constitution of India also embodies a number of principles of natural law. It guarantees certain fundamental rights to the people of India and gives the Supreme Court of India and the High Courts the power to exercise control over administrative and quasi-judicial tribunals and one of the grounds on which the orders arc set aside, is the violation of the principles of natural justice. The principles of natural justice are incorporated in Article 311 of the Constitution which provides that no civil servant can be dismissed, removed or reduced in rank without giving him reasonable opportunity of showing cause against the action proposed to be taken against him.

In recent years, the ideas of natural justice have become more and more important and have been relied upon by the Supreme Court of India and High Courts in their decisions. In *A.K. Kraipak* v. *Union of India*, the Supreme Court observed that the aim of the rules of natural justice is to secure justice or to put it negatively, to prevent miscarriage of justice. These rules can operate only in areas not covered by any law validly made. They do not supplant the law of the land but supplement it. The concept of natural justice has undergone a great deal of change in recent years. In the past it was thought that it included just two rules, namely, (i) no one shall be a judge in his own cause (*nemo debet esse judex propria causa*) and (ii) no decision shall be given against a party without affording him a reasonable hearing (*audi alteram partem*). Very soon thereafter, a third rule was added which provides that quasi-judicial inquiries must be held in good faith, without bias and not arbitrarily or unreasonably. In the course of years, many more subsidiary rules have been added to the rules of natural justice. Till recently, it was the opinion of the courts that unless the authority concerned was required by the law under which it functioned to act judicially, there was no room for the application of the rules of natural justice. The validity of that limitation is now questioned. If the purpose of the rules of natural justice is to prevent miscarriage of justice, one fails to see why those rules should be made inapplicable to administrative inquiries. It is not easy to draw the line that demarcates administrative inquiries from quasi-judicial inquiries. Inquiries which were considered administrative at one time are now being considered as quasi-judicial in character. Arriving at a just decision is the aim of both quasi-judicial inquiries as well as administrative inquiries. An unjust decision in an administrative inquiry may have more far-reaching effect than a decision in a quasi-judicial inquiry. The rules of natural justice are not embodied rules. What particular rule of natural justice should apply to a given case must depend to a great extent on the facts and circumstances of that case, the framework of the law under which the inquiry is held and the constitution of the tribunal or body of persons appointed for that purpose. Whenever a complaint is made before a court that some principle of natural justice had been contravened, the court has to decide whether the observance of that rule was necessary for a just decision of the facts of that case. In the case pending before the Supreme Court, the selections were set aside on the ground that they violated the principles of natural justice as one of the members of the Selection Board was himself interested in that selection. (AIR 1970 SC 150).

In *Maneka Gandhi* v. *Union of India*, the Supreme Court observed that natural justice is a great humanising principle intended to invest law with fairness and to secure justice. Over the years, it has grown into a widely pervasive rule affecting large areas of administrative action. The soul of natural justice is "fairplay in action" and it has received widest recognition throughout the democratic world. The Supreme Court held that even the procedure laid down by law must be right, just and fair. It is liable to be set aside on the ground that it is not reasonable. (AIR 1978 SC 597).

12

ORIENTAL AND CONTINENTAL APPROACHES

Sir Henry Maine in his Ancient Law observes, 'The Hindu Code, called the Laws of Manu, which is certainly a Brahmin composition, undoubtedly enshrines many genuine observances of the Hindu race, but the opinion of the best contemporary orientalist, is that it does not, as a whole represent a set of rules ever actually administered in Hindosthan. It is, in great part, an ideal picture of that, which in view of the Brahmins ought to be the law.' This statement of Maine presupposes the absence of any systematic procedural law during the time of Manu and other authors of the Smrtis. J.D. Mayne has refuted the view adumbrated in Ancient Law and maintained that the Smrtis were partly based upon contemporary and anterior usages, and, in part on rules framed by the Hindu jurists and rules of the country. Smrtis and Digests were not private law books but were recognized authorities in the courts and tribunals of the country and that the Smrti rules were concerned with the practical administration of justice. The present book aims to show how the administration of justice in the times of the authors under investigation i.e. between 200 and 700 AD as depicted in their codes was based on practical rules and how the law of procedure was developed during the last stage of the compilation of the Smrtis.

Although the germs of the judicial system in ancient India are to be found in the earlier Smrtis and other works the judicial procedure as observed in the king's court is hardly to be traced in them. Even Manu and Yajnavalkya who are looked upon as authorities on early Hindu legal systems, are very brief. As observed by Maine, 'we can see that Brahmanical India has not passed beyond a stage which occurs in the history of all the families of mankind, the stage at which a rule of law is not yet discriminated from a rule of religion.' It is only during the time of Narada, Brhaspati and Katyayana that we find a systematic attempt to lay down the procedural law. In the works of these law-givers we find a much developed and systematic picture of the judicial procedure as followed by the law courts in ancient India and particularly in the code of Narada we trace definite rules about the nature and characteristics of a judicial procedure and it is in his work that one finds a systematic and exhaustive discussion of the various aspects of the administration of justice. While Narada fully describes the various aspects of *vyavahadra* or a judicial procedure, Brthaspati enumerates in detail several other aspects of it such as the function of the members of a court, different titles of law, ordeals and so on.

As already stated the Hindu law of procedure is a later development of the Hindu judicial system and it would not be out. of place to take a brief survey of the legal outlook of the Aryans as depicted in their early literature such as the Vedas, Brahmanas, Dharmasutras and so on that preceded the Smrtis with a view to having some idea of the concept of law of the early settlers of India.

Survey of the nature and concept of law prior to the Smrtis of Narada, Brhaspati and Katyayana

The concept of law in the history of legal philosophy varies from time to time and in the remote period of the Veda law was synonymous with *dharma,* which again, to a certain extent, corresponds with the Vedic concept of Rta, denoting the supreme transcendental law or the cosmic order by which the universe and even gods were governed and which was ultimately connected with yajna-sacrifice. On the relation of Rta and law Beralzeimer in his work on '*The World's Legal Philosophies*' says, 'Closely connected with the religious and the philosophical use of the Aryas are certain fundamental positions in regard to philosophy of law which in turn became the antecedent of later legal and ethical developments among the Greeks and the Romans.' According to him the Rta is the foremost among the philosophical conceptions and is the governing force both of the universe and the divine ordering of earthly life. Dharma as one of the aspects of Rta refers specifically to the moral function of rewarding good and punishing evil. It would therefore be appropriate to have a survey of the development of the conception of Hindu Law as is to be found in the oldest records of the Hindus viz. the Vedas and the literature that follows.

Rgvedic Period

Although in the Rgveda we do not find any reference to positive law, we do find therein some contribution from the Vedic Seers to the Vedic thought that has a direct bearing on the positive law of the later period of the Smrtis. The conception of *rta* in the Rgveda is the foremost among the vedic conceptions of law. The Rgveda says that *rta*, the external law, is firm and immutable (*rtasya drdha dharunani santi*) and not flexible. It is the ordering principle not only of earthly life but it binds even the gods inasmuch as it regulates the movements of sun and the moon. The days and nights are caused because of the influence of *rta*. Mitra and Varuna, the twin gods, who are associated by the Vedic Aryans with the administration of justice and who are the lovers and cherishers of law are said to have obtained their mighty power only through *rta*. Order and harmony, both in earthly life and the divine life, are said to be due to existence of *rta*. As the ordering principle of earthly life it is imbued with human purposes and is for the human benefit. The Rgvedic *rta*, which was conceived as the binding force was generally associated with rituals, which gave it strength and obligatoriness.'Transgression of these rules is not merely a violation of human laws to be enforced by human sanctions but was supposed to be punished in this life and hereafter by supernatural forces.' The association of law and religion continued not only during the post Rgvedic literature such as the Atharveda, the Brahmanas, the Upanisads and the Dharmasutras but also in the latest stages of the evolution and the growth of law.

The Rgvedic philosophy or conception of law thus centred round the idea of *rta*, which was born along with truth even prior to all existence. 'According to the Vedic Rsis before there could be any society, before there could be any social ideality, *rta* evolved: the ordering principle came into existence even before there was any diversity; the whole existed even prior to its parts.' Out of this conception of the Rgvedic *rta* evolved the Hindu ideal of truth and non-injury which were considered as the basis of the Hindu law. The people of the Rgvedic period were religious-minded and abstained from causing injury to others. They were therefore free from litigations which arose in later times as men became greedy and envious.

Post-Rgvedic Period

The post-Rgvedic literature comprises the three Vedas, viz., the Yajurveda, the Samavda and the Atharvaveda; the Brahmanas, Aranyakas and the Upanisads followed by the Dharmasutras. This vedic literature subsequent to the Rgveda, though vast in extent, contains no profitable information as regards the nature and concept of law, nor about its development. Since the Samaveda is a mere echo of the Rgveda, it has the same conception about *rta* as is found in the Rgveda. Following the Rgveda, the Samaveda also declares that Mitra and Varuna, who are the up-holders of law and administrators of justice, have obtained their mighty power through *rta*. The Samaveda conception of law is thus similar to that of the Rgveda and it looks upon *rta* as the declaration of an eternal and immutable code.

In the Aharvaveda we meet with the idea of what law is. Its conception of law is also similar to the one contained in the Rgveda. Like the Rgveda, the Atharvaveda also looks upon *rta* and Satya as the basis of law. It declares that 'Truth is the base that bears the earth; by Surya are heavens upheld. By law the Adityas stand secure and Soma holds his place in heaven.'

As already stated above, during the Rgvedic and the post-Rgvedic period the conception of law centred round the attempts to determine the nature of law. The vedic seers discussed the nature of *rta* as the upholder of law and as an ordering principle; but little thought was given to define the end of law, which as a specific subject gradually gained importance, and one has to turn to the Brahmanas and the Upanisads to find how therein the philosophy of law occupied itself with this end. It is for the first time that we find in the Brahmanas and the Upanisads a conscious thinking about the end of law. They declared that the end of law was the preservation of the social 'status quo.' The general security of the society was for the first time conceived by the philosophers of this period. To them general security could be maintained only through securing preservation of the existing social institutions. They looked upon law as the guiding principle which aimed at setting man in his proper predetermined place, thus avoiding friction with others.

The Upanisads, too, looked upon truth and law as synonymous. To them declaring the truth was equal to declaring the law and vice-versa.

Dharmasutras

It is noteworthy that the king, who was considered to be the head of the administration of justice in the later works on Dharmasastra, had a subordinate position during the vedic period. In the opinion of the Brhadarnyaka-upanisad law exists without the sovereign and is above the sovereign. The theory of the 'Divine Right of Kingship' does not seem to have been favoured by the authors of the Vedic literature prior to the Dharmasutras.

The Sutras represent the last phase of the vedic literature. They were composed to reduce the mass of matter contained in the ritualistic literature of the Hindus. These Sutras are classified into three categories viz., (i) Srautasutras, (ii) Grhyasutras, and (iii) Dharmasutras. The first two being devoted to the treatment of ritual and domestic ceremonies are not of much importance to a student of Hindu law. For a fuller account of law as it existed in the Sutra period we have to turn to the Dharmasutras, which include not only the precepts for the moral duties of all Aryas, but also the special rules regarding the conduct of kings and the administration of justice. These Dharmasutras cover the whole range of topics of law contained in the later metrical Smrtis attributed to Manu, Yajnavalkya and others. Among the topics of law that are to be found in the Dharmasutras the following few might be mentioned: 1. Legal procedure, 2. The Parisad or the legal assembly, 3. Evidence, 4-5. Marriage, 6. Niyoga, 7. Possession and ownership, 8. Stridhana, 9. Partition, 10. The Law of debt, 11. Relations between Master and Servant, 12. Trade laws, 13. Theft, 14. Gambling, 15. Sexual offences and so on.

Although the Dharmasutras describe briefly the various topics of law, their analysis reveals the fact that the laws as propounded in these Sutras were originally concerned with ceremonial and religious conduct with the infliction of penance as the spiritual counter-part of the punitive measures of the royal or Arthasastra administration of criminal law. They took into account the spiritual and moral uplift of the man in society and according to them the offender was not a criminal to be condemned by the society but a sinful person who could atone for his wrongs by submitting himself to penances. Whate'er references to the legal topics we find in the Dharmasutras are, therefore, incidental and are not the main features of their subject-matter. Although one finds in these Dharmasutras several topics of law as enumerated above, they were not the exclusive codes on civil or positive law. As already observed they were treatises written for providing rules of conduct and guidance for the different stages of life and rights and duties of different castes in the early Hindu society. They contain much more of ritual than law, and a great deal more about the impurity caused by touching impure things than about punishment. Nevertheless, from the discussion of law in the Dharmasutras one can infer that they were the earliest works in which some details of the future Hindu law, as propounded by the later law-givers, are available. Although purely legal matters are scanty in these books, they speak of law, in the course of their discussions, as much as it was necessary for the regulation of the society as a whole, with the king as the head of the administration of justice and the Brahmana at the head of the religious and social set-up.

As regards the legal character of the Dharmasutras Sir Henry Maine observes. 'They are intended to guide the faithful Hindu of the three higher castes from birth to death and give him directions for living first as a student of holy books next as a religious ascetic or hermit.'

'This remarkable distinction of life runs through the whole series of sacred legal writings and only disappears when they become mere law-books. When a student returned as a house-holder he became a citizen and attended to his family and civil affairs. It is therefore the second period of life as a house-hold to which we must look for whatever light the sacred laws of the Hindus may throw upon the ancient history of law."

The law, civil or criminal, as enforced by the king first makes its appearance in the Dharmasutras. Although in the Rgveda there is no trace of the king administering justice and there was little scope for the royal authority, the role assigned to the king and his functions is always increasing. During the Sutra period, however, the king is only represented as the auxiliary of the spiritual director. He has to enforce penances. In this connection Apastamba says that if any person transgresses the order of the spiritual teacher he should be taken before the king, who, in consultation with his domestic priest, learned in law and science of governing, would order for the performance by forcible means, excepting corporal punishment and servitude, if he were a Brahmin. In the case of men of other castes, the king after having examined their actions, may punish them even by death. From this point of view the law proper emerges for the first time in the Dharmasutras where the king is entrusted with the duty of administering justice.

Manu and Yajnavalkya

The codes of Manu and Yajnavalkya represent a still further stage in the development of the concept of law and it is in these treatises that we find the king assuming more power as the fountain head of justice. With the increased importance and functions attributed to the king, there is a change in the sacerdotal view of his relation to law. The principal duties of the king according to these law-givers were considered to be to protect the subjects to see that the rules of Varnas and Asramas were carried out, and to punish the wicked and do justice to the persons wronged. The Manusmrti and the Yajnavalkyasmrti lay down elaborate rules regarding the daily duties of the king from morn till night. Among the primary duties of tile king are the administration of justice and the punishment of the offenders. According to Kautilya, the king is to attend to the administration of justice during the second part of the day. Manu states that the king desirous of looking into the disputes of people should enter the hail of justice and there decide every day the causes of litigants. The Smrtis looked upon the administration of justice as a personal concern of the king and that an impartial attitude towards law yielded the same reward to the king as the performance of a Vedic sacrifice. All these references in the two Smrtis to the administration of justice by the king tend to show how the king gradually came to have a prominent place in the administration of justice during the post-Vedic period.

Narada, Brhaspati and Katyayana

The law-books of Manu and Yajnavalkya, in spite of their being the codes of civil law, contain much of sacerdotal matter such as acara or the rules of conduct for persons of all castes and in the different stages of life. They also dealt with the expiation for the commission of sin. We have therefore to look to later treatises such as those of Narada, Brhaspati and Katyayana in whose law-books we find what is known as pure positive law. All these three jurists exhibit an excellent analytical insight and the most perfect legal acumen in elaborating and explaining the juristic principles and philosophy. They represent the last phase of the development of Hindu law and it is in them that we find the most perfect specimens of juristic speculation and the most systematic and methodical treatment of legal topics like evidence, law of debt, ownership, contracts and partnership, inheritance and so on.

The treatises of these three law-givers are simple law-books in which the ancient Brahmanical system is conspicuously absent and is tempered in its phases by the good sense and equity of the Schoolmen. Portions of these books which deal with several local topics are particularly remarkable because of their legal doctrines which could be favourably compared with some of the modern theories. Some of the sections of the Indian Civil Procedure Code, Indian Evidence Act, Contract Act and a few others resemble the rules propounded by Narada, Brhaspati and Katyayana. Because of the purely juristic character of the three Smrtis under study and their advanced views on legal matters, Mm. Dr. Kane has aptly described them as the triumvirate in the realm of the Ancient Hindu Law and composition of the Hindu legal literature. The law-codes of these authors belong to the latest productions of the Smrti epoch of Hindu law, and their legal character as also their juridical content are decidedly more advanced than those of either Manu-or-Yajnavalkya Smrti.

The foregoing remarks show how the concept of law emerged from its earliest stages in the Rgveda and developed through the following centuries in the post-vedic and Smrti period. The origin of the Hindu Law is to be found among the early settlers, who came to the Indian soil three or four thousand years ago. We have vague traces of the concept of law in the earlier records of the race known as the Aryan, but the law proper is only found for the first time in the Dharmasutras as administered by the king.

There is a long history before the pre-Vedic stage of law as found either in the Dharmasutras or in the later law-books known as the Smrtis. While these treatises proclaimed the king as the upholder of justice and the punisher of the wicked, in the Rgveda there is no trace of the king administering justice. There we find a conception of a binding force called *rta*, which is generally associated with ritual which gave it strength and binding force. Violation of it was an offence against human law, not only to be met by human sanctions but was also supposed to be punished by supernatural powers. The recognition of ordeals in the future legal system is probably a relic of this belief. Further, wrongs could be set right by expiation or penance. This association of law with religion continued even to the latest stages of the growth of law and even the law-givers like Narada, Brhaspati and Katyayana, in spite of their secular, advanced and radical views, could not dissociate themselves from the time-honoured association of law and religion characteristically embodied in the word Dharma.

Sources for the Study of the Smrtis of Narada, Brhaspati and Katyayana

The Vedas, and the Dharmasutras followed by the Smrtis are the well-known sources for the study of Hindu law. For our purpose, however, it is the commentaries and the digests that are more important and could be studied from two points of view viz. (1) their character, and (2) their importance for the studsy of Hindu law, especially as laid down in the three Smrtis under study. Some of the commentaries and digests like the Smrticandrika and the Smrtimuktaphala are particularly significant for our study as they contain numerous citations from the Smrtis of Narada, Brhaspati and Katayayana. It is from the numerous citations in the commentatorial literature and the digests that the Smrtis of Brhaspati and Katyayana have been made available to us in reconstructed form.

Character of the Commentaries and the Digests

The commentaries and the digests mark the most important and the final stage in the development of Hindu law. When the commentaries on the Dharmasastra works, particularly the Smrtis, came to be written, all the reputed Smrtis had acquired some authority. In many cases there were apparent discrepancies among the several Smrtis and the task before the commentators and the compilers of digests was to reconcile them and to adapt them to the existing conditions of the society of their times. A study of a few important commentaries and the digests shows that these works were not merely in the explanatory form or mere collections of different Smrti texts on several topics. They contained matter and expositions of different topics which prove that their authors were themselves practical lawyers, who were conversant with the law as administered in the king's court as well as with the rules of conduct. These men developed law not only with reference to the sacred traditions but also with equal regard to the practical requirements of the society. This is evident from the commentaries of Asahaya on the Naradasmrti, the Mitaksara on the Yajnavalkyasmrti, commentaries of Medhatithi and Kulluka on Manusmrti and also from the digests like the Smrti-candrika, Caturvargacintamani of Hemadri, Smrtimuktaphala of Vaidyanatha, Vyavaharamnayukta of Nilakantha and many others. As already stated these works were not merely glossaries of the previous works nor did they merely contain citations from the Smrtis. They depicted the every-day life in their period which helped to throw some light on the practical working of the Indian law in their times. Dr. Jolly, in order to illustrate this point, quotes in his translation of the Nadradasmrti (SBE, XXXIII, p. 43n) a full passage from Asahaya's commentary pertaining to a suit between Mahidhara and Sridhara, which gives a vivid picture of the way in which judicial proceedings used to be transacted in ancient India. The story given by Asahaya illustrates the doctrine that the liability to pay the debts contracted by an ancestor extends to the great-grandson. This view is, of course, opposed to the opinion of Vijnanesvara, who maintains in the Mitaksara that the liability ends with the third generation, i.e. with the grand-son. As regards the true role of the commentaries (and also probably of the digests) the Judicial Committee observed that 'the commentators, while professing to interpret the law as laid down in the Smrtis, introduced changes in order to bring it into harmony with the usages followed by the people governed by the law; and that it is the opinion of the commentators which prevails in the provinces where their authority is recognized.' (*Atmaram* v. *Bajirao*, 1935) (62. I.A. 139). The Committee further observed that 'in the event of conflict between the ancient text writer and the commentators, the opinion of the latter must be accepted'.

Their Importance for the Study of Hindu Law

The commentaries of the Smrtis and the digests assumed that the Smrtis constituted a single body of law. They therefore tried to reconcile the discrepancies, if any, between any two or more Smrtis by their own reasoning and also in the light of usages and customs that prevailed from time to time. As a result of this, the commentaries and the digests assumed greater importance and were recognized as authoritative in different parts of the country. Different Schools of Hindu Law owe more to this literature than to the original Smrtis. In a large part of India the Mitaksara School prevails with its sub-Schools, while in Bengal the Dayabhaga School has attained greater prominence.

The real importance of these commentaries and the digests lies, however, in the fact that they served a very useful purpose in pre-serving and in giving account of the different Smrti texts as they were available to them. As a matter of fact many important Dharmasastra texts would have been completely lost to us had they not been referred to or quoted in the commentatorial or digest material. Numerous citations are available to us from the codes of Brhaspati and Katyayana, which have now been lost to us and could be reconstructed to a reasonable extent with the help of the citations thereof in various commentaries and digests. The Smrticandrika, for example, which is very early digest work composed in South India, contains as many as 600 verses from the Katyayanasmrti and an equal number from the code of Brhaspati.

Date and Character of the Three Smrtis

As already observed the codes of Narada, Brhaspati and Katyayana from the latest stage in the development of Hindu Law covering a period of about 500 years from 200 to 700 AD. Hitherto only the code of Narada was available for study. It is in two recensions arid complete. A third recension of the same has been discovered and is published in the Trivendrwn Sanskrit Series under the title 'Naradiya Manusamhita'. It does not, however, differ much from the edition of the Naradasmrti edited by Dr. Jolly in the Bibliotheca Indica Series. Jolly subsequently discovered an old manuscript (dated 1407) of the Naradasmrti from Nepal. It contains two additional chapters, one on theft and the other on ordeals. Dr. Jolly rejects the chapter on ordeals as unauthentic and includes the section on theft as an appendix in his edition and the English translation of the work published in the Sacred Books of the East Series.

The other Smrtis viz., (i) Brhaspatismrti, and (ii) Katyayanasmrti were known for a long time only through citations in various commentaries of the different Smrtis and in the nibandhas. Because of their importance they were profusely quoted by later compilers of works on Dharmasastra and although the two Smrtis were completely lost to us their numerous citations enabled Prof. Rangaswamy Aiyangar and Mm. Dr. P.V. Kane to reconstruct them. Dr. Kane reconstructed the Katyanasmrti on the basis of citations and could collect 976 verses. This collection was supplemented by Prof. Aiyangar, who collected as many as 121 additional verses of Katyayana from a single digest viz., Varadaraja's Vyavaharanirnaya. He published these stanzas in the P.V. Kane Festschrift published in 1941.

The Brhaspatismrti has been similarly reconstructed by Prof. Rangaswamy Aiyangar. For this purpose he utilized nearly two hundred texts, including those still in manuscript from. The number of stanzas (including under them a few prose passages) dealing with the vyavahara portion is 1271, which is nearly double the number collected by Dr. Jolly for his English translation of the work. In his edition Prof. Iyangar has also included the non-vyavahara portion of the Brhaspatismrti, the aggregate number in the edition amounting to 2300 stanzas, exclusive of the prose passages.

The two Smrtis, available to us as they are in a reconstructed form, are far from being exhaustive and complete. Being reconstructed from scattered quotations in the commentaries and the nibandhas, gaps appear in their arrangement and sequence of topic and in spite of the strenuous efforts made by the two scholars at their systematic arrangement they look like (patch-work) pieces sewn together.

The three Smrtis, which are now available deal mainly with law properly so-called as would appear from their contents. They treat law by itself without any reference to the rules of penance, diet and any other religious topic. They throw a new and important light on the political and social institutions of ancient India at the time of their composition. We shall now proceed to discuss the date and character of the three individual Smrtis under study.

Naradasmrti

Narada, the oldest of the three law-givers lived probably immediately after Yajnavalkya and long after Manu. As Narada does not mention Yajnavalkya by name it is possible that by his time Yajnavalkya's code had not reached the status of an authoritative work in legal literature. Dr. Jolly observes that there was considerable interval of time between Manu and Narada and since Manu flourished, according to Dr. Buhler, between 2nd century BC and 2nd century AD, it would seem to follow that the Naradasmrti could hardly belong to an earlier period than the fourth or fifth century AD. Dr. Kane has criticized Jolly's views for assigning a date later than 300 AD to Narada and has held that Narada flourished in the first centuries of the Christian era i.e. between 100 and 300 AD.

As already observed the Naradasmrti is now available in two recensions. These recensions of the Naradasmrti which are now available in print deal exclusively with the *vyavahara* topics of Dharmasastra. Herein he differs from his two predecessors, Manu and Yajnavalkya who deal with what may be styled as Dharma—the *vyavahara* portion containing mixed matter of law and religion, the acaradharma, prayascitta, etc. Narada's code covers the whole area of law secular, the law civil and criminal. This may be said to be true of the two codes of Brhaspati and Katyayana. By the time these three codes came to be compiled there appeared a stage in the history of Hindu a law when this unaccountable amalgamation was rejected and the law proper restored to its original entity.

Narada merely professes to be a compiler of the traditional law that handed down from what was known as the Manavadharmasastra. In the Introduction to the Naradasmrti he states that it is an abridgment of a larger work of Manu and refers to the four successive versions of Manu's work. According to him the original code of Manu consisted of one hundred thousand slokas or 1080 chapters. This was reduced to 12,000, 8,000 and 4,000 slokas respectively in subsequent versions. The extant Naradasmrti constituted the ninth chapter of the original code which was headed 'judicial procedure.' There, Narada, the divine sage, composed an introduction in Sutra style. This part of Narada's abridgment of the ninth chapter of Manu's code is designated as 'Matrka' or Vyavaharamatrka, containing a summary of proceedings-at-law or general rules of procedure. After the introduction he proceeds, like a true jurist, to discuss the object and necessity of the administration of justice, which according to him consists of (1) Legal procedure, (2) The plaint, (3) The description of the different courts of justice, and (4) The judgment. He then proceeds with the discussion of the eighteen titles of law or causes of dispute among men in the most scientific, systematic and precise way, indulging in more and sub-divisions of the topics and of law. Thus, for example, judicial procedure, according to him, has four feet, four bases, four means, it benefits four and produces four results. He further sub-divides the eighteen titles of law into one hundred and thirty-two branches, and states that on account of the multifariousness of human concerns a judicial procedure is said to have a hundred branches. The plaint and the answer necessarily play an important part. Narada states a rule as to when the claimant should proffer his claim and the defendant should submit his reply to the plaintiff's claim. As regards the answer to a plaint Narada discusses at length its four-fold nature such as denial, confession, special plea and a reply based on a plea of former judgment or res judicata. Under this topic Narada also enumerates the defects of a plaint which according to him are of seven types viz., (1) Relating to a different object; (2) Meaningless; (3) Improper statement of the amount claimed; (4) Wanting in propriety; (5) Deficient writing; (6) Redundancy and (7) A plaint which is damaged. Narada mentions different grades of courts which are kula (gatherings), sreni (corporations or guilds), ganas (assemblies), one appointed by the king and the king himself; of these each succeeding one is superior to the one preceding in order.

The code of Narada consists of two main divisions. The first part deals with the procedural law viz., the necessity of the administration of justice, the nature of the plaint, the constitution of the court, nature of evidence, witnesses and so on. The second part enumerates and discusses the eighteen titles of law with remarkable clarity. But in spite of his scientific treatment of the subject-matter of law, Narada many a times mixes up different topics which appear, at times, irrelevant to the subject-matter of discussion. For example, in his discourse on the 'Recovery of debt,' which is the first among the eighteen titles of law, Narada includes topics like modes of proof, kinds of witnesses, valid and invalid evidence, etc. which should form part of the procedural law dealt with in the first part of his treatise. Similarly, under the topic of 'Mutual duties of husband and wife,' which is the twelfth topic of law, Narada mentions and describes fourteen kinds of impotent persons.

Narada is generally looked upon as a law-giver of advanced views and theories. He is also more exhaustive than either Manu or Yajnavalkya, especially on the topic of ordeals. But at the same time he is more conservative than his predecessors. For instance, where Yajnavalkya recognizes the right of a widow to succeed to her deceased husband, Narada does not.

Narada, like Brhaspati and Katyayana, was well-known as a legal writer as will be evident from numerous quotations from his code to be found in the later commentaries and digests. In this connection Prof. Jolly observes, 'The repute of Narada as a legal writer appears to have been so great that upwards of half his work has been embodied in the authoritative compositions of the medieval and modern writers in the province of Sanskrit law.'

The Naradasmrti is generally considered to be a leading code in the history of Hindu law. In point of time it was the last of the three leading codes viz., Manusmrti, Yajnavalkyasmrti and the Naradasmrti. Regarding its importance and legal character Mr. Mulla observes, 'It affords a great help in deriving a reliable knowledge of the line of evolution which Hindu Law and Jurisprudence had pursued during the remarkable era of the Dharmashastra. . . . There is intrinsic as well as other evidence to show that the work has been compiled after there has been remarkable political, economic and social progress in the country, when the highest intellectual capacity of the people had already produced the philosophy of the Upanisads out of which had been developed the doctrine of karmayoga, and when considerable advancement had been made in Hindu Jurisprudence.'

Brhaspatismrti

Brhaspati is later than Narada. Jolly assigns Brhaspati the 6th century AD. But Kane after thorough examination of the internal and external evidence, especially taking into account the fact that Katyayana looked upon Brhaspati as an authority, remarks that 'Brhaspati must have flourished several centuries before and therefore cannot be placed later than the 4th century A.D.' A comparison of Brhaspati's work with Naradasmrti suggests that it must have been compiled one or two centuries after Narada and at a time when in many branches of it the law had made further strides in its line of development. As Brhaspati is thoroughly acquainted with the extant Manusmrti and with the code of Yajnavalkya and also probably with the code of Narada, he must have flourished between 200 and 400 AD.

The code of Brhaspati is available to us in a reconstructed form. The original code has been lost to us and it is doubtful if it could be recovered. Buhler, however, believed that the Smrtis of Brhaspati and Katyayana were available till recently; but there is nothing to justify his belief. If it were so, manuscripts of these works could have been available so far. We have therefore to rely for our study of Brhaspati on the reconstructed text, which has been edited by Prof. K.V. Rangaswamy Aiyangar based on citations from the Brhaspatismrti in medieval and later works on Hindu Law. The edition referred to is divided into the following seven sections viz., 1. vyavaharakanda, pp. 1-230; 2. samskarakanda, pp. 231-308; 3. acarakanda, pp. 309-325, 4. sraddhakanda, pp. 326-352; 5. asaucakanda, pp. 352-364; 6. appaddharmakanda, pp. 365-372; and 7. prayascittakanda, pp. 373-386. It will be seen from this division that a major portion of the Smrti deals with *vyavahara* topic, with which we are mainly concerned.

From the classification of the Brhaspatismrti as it is now available to us it would be seen that it contains also the non-*vyavahara* portion, though very meagre as compared with its *vyavahara* counterpart. Citations of such topics from the Smrtis of Brhaspati and Katyayana occur in the Dharmasastra commentaries and the digests. An exhaustive survey of these might reveal the existence of larger non-*vyavahara* portion in these two Smrtis. Out of the total number of 2300 slokas collected by Prof. Aiyangar from numerous works, 1271 verses deal with the subject-matter of law proper. The distribution of the slokas under different topics in the printed edition is as under:

1. Vyavahara	*verses*	1271
2. Samhskara	*verses*	557
3. Acara	*verses*	101
4. Sraddha	*verses*	155
5. Asauca	*verses*	76
6. Apaddharma	*verses*	51
7. Prayascitta	*verses*	89
Total		2300

The *vyavahara* section of the Brhaspatismrti reveals the fact that Brhaspati was the first law-giver to make a specific distinction between civil and criminal suits. According to him the law-suits are of two kinds, viz., 1. Arthasamudbhava or civil, and 2. Himsasmudbhava or criminal. The former originate in demands regarding wealth, while the latter in injuries. Those originating in money are of fourteen sorts; and those arising from injury are of four kinds.

Brhaspati not only follows Manu in many respects but he also looks upon Manu as supreme authority. Whatever is opposed to the dictates of Manu is according to Brhaspati unacceptable and fit to be discarded. In several places he refers to Manu's text, explaining and defining the laconic terms of Manu. For example, Manu refers to only two kinds of ordeals, while Brhaspati speaks of nine. Similarly, Manu mentions four varieties of interest but does not explain them. Brhaspati explains the terms more elaborately. Because of his explanatory role on certain matters occurring in the Manusmrti, Kane styles him as a varttikakara of Manu. Jolly makes a similar remark and observes, Brhaspati even when not referring to Manu presupposes throughout an acquaintance with his code and a very large portion of his Smrti is devoted to the interpretation of technical terms or to the elucidation or amplifications of the somewhat laconic enumeration of Manu.'

The Brhaspatismrti has been considered to be the most precious relic of the Hindu law containing a very full exposition of the principles of law. The very fact that the editor of the Brhaspatismrti could collect nearly 2300 verses ascribed to Brhaspati from various commentaries and digests is in itself a glowing tribute to Brhaspati's lucid and full treatment of the subject and the authoritative character of his code. It also shows how favourite he was among the digest writers. Brhaspati does not mix up the subject-matter of law with other topics like Narada but in many essential points he agrees with his predecessor. Like Yajnavalkya and Narada he mentions different grades of courts such as kula, sreni, gana, etc. ending with the king and each succeeding one being superior to the one preceding and the king as the highest court of appeal.' This is evident from the trial scene in the Mrcchakatika, where Carudatta being declared guilty of committing the murder of Vasantasena, the judge says 'our authority is (only) with regard to the decision; in other matters it rests with the king.'

Like the different grades of courts Brhaspati also mentions four kinds of courts viz., one established (pratisthita), not established (apratisthita), a court established by royal order with authority to use the royal seal (mudrita) and a court in which the king himself attended to the administration of justice (sasita or sasitrita). Following Narada, Brhaspati lays down a rule that a legal decision should not be arrived at merely on the basis of sastra and that where a decision is not based on proper reasoning there is loss of dharma and in such cases there is every likelihood of an innocent person being held guilty or *vice versa*.

Brhaspati gives such elaborate rules and definitions regarding the judicial procedure from the filing of the complaint to the passing of the final decree that he can stand comparison with the modern jurists.

Katyayanasmrti

The third Smrti analogous to the codes of Narada and Brhaspati is the code of Katyayana. For a long time this code was not available and was known only through citations. Like Brhaspati, Katyayana also was a reputed author and a large number of citations from his code has helped us a good deal in having an exhaustive, though not complete, code in reconstructed form. Katyayana's code as it is now available to us deals with civil law only, devoting a very small portion to the treatment of crimes.

The contents of the Katyayanasmrti are practically the same as those of its two predecessors viz. Naradasmrti and Brhaspatismrti. In the Katyayanasmrti as it is reconstructed we find the following topics discussed by its author: Katyayana starts with the characteristics of a king and his duties, the chief of these being the protection of the subjects, eradication of the thorns of the society (i.e. offenders), reverence to Brahmins and so on. The characteristics of *vyavahara* or judicial procedure are enumerated next. Katyayana agrees with Narada and Brhaspati in regarding the judicial procedure to have four stages viz., the plaint, defence, deliberation as to the burden of proof and adducing of proof. According to Katyayana the two main branches of *vyavahara* are Dharmasastra, i.e. sacred law and Arthasastra, i.e. science of politics and government. Its result is also two-fold viz., success or defeat in a law-suit.

In the first part of his code Katyayana describes in detail topics like the four divisions of *vyavahara* such as dharma, *vyavahara*, caritra and rajasasana and their relative merits; the hail of justice; members of the court;

method of examining the plaintiff, the defendant and the witnesses; sureties; characteristics of a plaint and its defects; different kinds of reply; ordeals; different kinds of documents and so on; the eighteen titles of law are also discussed briefly. Under the first title of law viz., the recovery of debt are included topics like rates of interest; rules as to the recovery of debt; deposits; sureties; their liability; liability of payment of debt when there are several debts; son's liability for the debts contracted by the father and so on. Katyayana also deals with the law of crimes which include abuse and defamation; injury; violence; theft and adultery.

Katyayana's date can be fixed only approximately from external evidence as no personal information about him has come down to us. According to Dr. Kane, Katyayana must have lived between the 4th and the 6th cent. AD or roughly between 300 and 600 AD.

Since Katyayana flourished after Narada and Brhaspati he refers to them frequently. It also appears that he has followed his two predecessors in his treatment of the subject-matter of law. He closely follows both the writers in legal phraseology and in technique. But he is not a blind follower of the previous writers. Thus while mentioning the four stages of a trial he does not merely copy Narada's statement but devotes a number of verses to illustrate and expound Narada's views. His views on a woman's property and on gains of learning are far more illustrative than those of any other law-giver. As regards Katyayana's lucid exposition of the topic of Stridhana Mm. Dr. Kane observes, 'Katyayana's treatment of *stridhana* has attained classical rank. It appears that he was probably the first to define carefully the several kinds of *stridhana* (such as *adhyagni, adhyavahanika, pritidatta, sulka, anvadheya* and *saudayika*), to lay down woman's power of disposal over the several varieties of *stridhana* and to prescribe lines of devolution to *stridhana*.'

Special Features of the Three Smrtis and their Contribution to Hindu Law

We shall have occasion to discuss fully the salient features of the three codes in the chapters to follow; nevertheless they are briefly described here.

The most striking feature of the three codes of Narada, Brhaspati and Katyayana is that all of them deal exclusively with the topic of *vyavahara* or the administration of justice as contrasted with the earlier codes, most of which include other religious matter as well. Though in some later works the non-*vyavahara* portion ascribed to Narada and Brhaspati is to be found, the extent of such references is so meagre that it can safely be ignored for our purpose. The code of Katyayana, as is now available, contains solely *vyavahara* portion.

Another striking feature that appeals to the student of the three codes is their elaborate, systematic and scientific exposition of the different topics of law. Although in many respects the three jurists seem to follow their predecessors like, Kautilya, Manu and Yajnavalkya, they also differ from them in many essential matters. There is difference among the three jurists and their predecessors as regards the nomenclature of the topics of law. It is in the codes of Narada and Brhaspati that we find for the first time a marked distinction of the disputes as civil and criminal. Further, in the treatment of ordeals all the three law-givers are more exhaustive than any of the other Smrti-writers. Similarly, in topics like the recovery of debt and others the rules given either in Manusmrti or in the Yajnavalkyasmrti are sketchy as compared with those of the three Smrtis under study. Manu mentions only four kinds of interest; but Brhaspati defines clearly every kind of interest. Many new and technical expressions are to be found in the three codes. For example, Narada explains the word *hodha* which cannot be found in any other Smrti. *Hodha,* according to Narada means 'one's property when lost or stolen.' Similarly, in the Katyayanasmrti we find two peculiar terms viz., stobhaka and *sucaka*. These are the two persons who bring to the notice of the king certain offences; but there is a slight distinction between the two. A *sucaka* is a person who is appointed by the king to detect wrong-doings of people and who on coming to know of such incidents brings them to the notice of the king; while a *stobhaka* is one, who solely with a view to obtaining money and without being urged by the king acts as an informant of the crime.1 Katyayana, as compared with Narada and Brhaspati, seems to be very fond of using new terms and definitions such as those of *vyavahara, pradvivaka, dharmadhikarna* and so on; but his definition of two kinds of decrees is peculiar. Ordinarily a decree either in favour of the plaintiff or the defendant is known as the *jayapatra* or a document of success in a law-suit. But Katyayana uses two separate terms for a decree viz., 1. Pascatkara and 2. Jayapatra. The former according to him is a judgment given in favour of the plaintiff after a hot discussion and contest between the plaintiff and the defendant, while the latter constitutes a judgment given on admission by the defendant or a judgment dismissing the suit on various grounds. Such instances of new and technical terms to be found in the three codes could be multiplied.

Scope of the Present Book

The present book aims to establish the view by a comparative study of the Smrtis of Narada, Brhaspati and Katyayana, who deal primarily with the procedural law, that at least in the days of the three authors the law of procedure had developed to a considerable extent and that the mixture of law and religion as we find in the earlier Smrtis including those of Manu and Yajnavalkya was done away with. A brief survey of the provisions of the three codes on the administration of justice and of the different topics of law as profusely described in the book will, therefore, be of great advantage as it will enable us to get a correct picture of the entire subject-matter as presented in the book.

Both Narada and Brhaspati state that in good old days people were religious-minded and unharmful. There was therefore no scope for litigation. But when they became overpowered with greed and hatred naturally dharma vanished from among them giving scope for litigation. The king was therefore appointed to decide law-suits, because he is the up-holder of justice and has authority to punish. This is the beginning of the administration of justice as followed in the king's court and as described in the Smrtis, particularly in the later law-books. The picture we find in these law-books is that of the administration of justice as observed by the king in his capacity as the up-holder and fountain-head of justice. The law-books therefore provide that it is the duty of the king to look after the administration of justice personally. The king should take his judgment seat, being equitable to all beings, discarding selfish interests and being just in the reward or punishment according to the good or bad actions of human beings. When owing to the pressure of other duties he is unable to attend the court personally he should appoint another person, preferably a Brahmin learned in the science of law to look after the affairs of the court. The king or the judge does not, however, administer the law singly. We find in the Smrtis references to a body called the *sabha* and its members, the *sabhasadas,* whose duty it was to express their opinion in a law-suit and this opinion was generally binding on the king or the judge. As the law developed the scope of the members of the judicial assembly widened. Several provisions regarding the constitution of the *sabha,* qualifications of its members and such other matters received the attention of the law-givers. While in early days the members of the judicial assembly consisted mostly of the Brahmin class, in the days of Katyayana even ordinary people; such: as men from merchant class of good birth and conduct, aged, wealthy and free from greed became its members. It will thus be seen that the judicial assembly or the *sabha* formed an important feature of the ancient Hindu judicial procedure. It consisted of members whose duty was to help the king or the Chief Judge in the proper administration of justice. They were expected to be proficient in the science of law, truthful and impartial. The function of the judicial assembly has been mentioned in detail by all the three law-givers, which shows the important role played by the *sabha* in the administration of justice in old days. An important change, is, however, to be noticed in the days of Katyayana in the constitution of its members. For a long time, even up to the time of Narada and Brhaspati the members of the assembly were recruited mostly from the Brahmin class, proficient in the science of law. But in the days of Katyayana even people from the merchant class could act as assessors provided that they were of good birth and conduct, wealthy and free from greed, showing thereby the importance gained by the merchant class in society in course of time. The history of the judicial assembly shows how gradually this body came to occupy an authoritative position and how its opinion was more or less binding on the king.

Judicial Procedure

The sanskrit word for judicial procedure is'*vyavahara*. According to Narada a judicial procedure is of two kinds viz., one with a wager (*sapana*) and the other without a wager. In the former case a litigant has to lay a wager on the truth of his claim. This distinction is peculiar to Narada, who describes at great length the characteristics of *vyavahara* or judicial procedure. Brhaspati also mentions a few peculiarities and throws more light on the function of each of the ten kinds of members of a judicial assembly which are merely enumerated by Narada. The classification of the eighteen topics of law has been accepted by almost all the Smrtis though they differ in their nomenclature and order.

The Trial

The trial in the period of Smrtis seems to have been mostly attended by the king personally and when he could not do so some person who was called a *pradvivaka* or a chief judge supervised the proceedings of the court. The trial begins with the narration of the plaintiff about the grievance caused to him by the defendant, who is then summoned and if the king (or judge) is satisfied that there is sufficient for the conduct of the case before him. It is to be noted that before ground for investigation and for proceeding with the suit he orders the commencement of the trial each party to the suit has to furnish surety and if any of the litigants failed to do so he becomes liable to be kept in charge of a guard or the court's officer called the *sadhyapala*. After the filing of the complaint and the reply of the defendant the judge deliberates with the assessors as to the responsibility of the burden of proof and the mode of adducing evidence. The complainant or the plaintiff has to establish his case with adequate proof; otherwise he is liable to lose his case. This is almost similar to the provisions of Orders XLV and XVIII of the Civil Procedure Code and sec. 102 of the Indian Evidence Act. The part of the judicial procedure relating to the adducing of evidence is known as the *kriyapada*. The chief judge has to decide as to which of the two contending parties should have the right to begin his case. The common rule is that a person who files the complaint should have a right to begin. But according to Narada and Katyayana the right belongs to the person who has suffered greater injury rather than the party who first filed the complaint. Brhaspati lays down that even the caste of the parties should be taken into account.

Some Aspects of the Judicial Procedure Summons

The topic of summons has been described by the three Smrtis in detail. In the early law there does not seem to be any provision for bringing the defendant before the court by a process of the court and it was primarily the business of the plaintiff to produce the defendant before the court. But Brhaspati and Katyayana state that the king should summon, either through a letter under his seal or through an attendant, the defendant, the latter adding that before a summons is issued to the defendant the king must satisfy himself that the cause of action is judicially entertainable. Detailed rules are to be found in the codes of Narada and Katyayana regarding persons who should not be summoned. These provisions may be compared with those of sec. 132 of the Indian Civil Procedure Code which exempt certain classes of women from personal appearance in the court. Although in exceptional circumstances some person other than the defendant is allowed to represent him, in matters of grave crimes a representative is not allowed either for the plaintiff or the defendant and therefore it is the duty of the person summoned to attend the court and if any person fails to attend even when called by the court he is liable for punishment.

Restraint

The provisions regarding restraint show that the plaintiff can proceed to arrest the defendant if he apprehends that the defendant is likely to abscond. During the days of Narada, however, it appears that the defendant could be arrested only under an express order of the king or the court. This arrest is of four kinds. Provisions are also to be found in the three Smrtis which lay down that certain types of persons, i.e. defendants are exempted from being arrested and if the plaintiff tries to restrain them he is punishable under law. Rules as to when a defendant should not be arrested are also recorded and in such cases if the defendant breaks restraint he is not held guilty. The term for restraint is *asedha* and appears to be a sort of injunction placed on the movements of the defendant either by the plaintiff or by the court pending the issue of summons.

Surety

Surety in a judicial trial appears to be a special feature of the ancient Indian judicial system. This surety is generally a surety for the appearance of the litigant parties and should be distinguished from a surety for the debtor in monetary transactions. Since a surety has to be furnished by both the plaintiff and the defendant both the contending parties are liable for the default committed by them in respect of furnishing a surety. Every person, however, cannot act as a surety and the Smrtis enumerate a category of persons who cannot act as sureties. According to Katyayana if any of the parties fails to give a surety as required by law he should be kept in charge of a person of the court called *sadhyapala*, who represents a modern bailiff.

The Judgment

The judgment is the last and important part of a judicial trial. The judge issues to the successful party a document known as the *jayapatra* or a deed of success in the litigation. This *jayapatra* corresponds to a modern decree in a judgment suit. In this respect we find important but divergent views of the three law-givers. Narada and Brhaspati state that if a person against whom several claims have been made having first denied the entire claim afterwards admits only a portion of it, he should be compelled to pay the entire amount claimed; whereas according to Katyayana where the witnesses depose only with a portion of it, the entire claim is dismissed. The contents of a judgment are given by the three authors but Katyayana is more systematic and exhaustive.

The three authors mention a four-fold characteristics of a judgment which are described fully under the section on rules regarding decision. The four aspects of a decision are: (1) Dharma or moral law, (2) Vyvavahara or judicial trial, (3) Custom, and (4) Royal edict. With reference to the last Brhaspati and Katyayana differ from each other as regards the king's authority pertaining to custom. Brhaspati maintains that a king can give a verdict according to his own inclination disregarding the established custom or usage, while Katyayana holds that the decision based on royal command should not be in conflict with the rules laid down by the Smrtis or the usages of the country. With regard to the contents of a judgment both Narada and Brhaspati are very brief and less systematic than Katyayana, who states that a decree should contain a record of the following particulars:

1. Statements of the plaintiff and the defendant.
2. Reply filed by the defendant.
3. Testimony of witnesses.
4. Decision of the dispute.
5. The manner in which the subject-matter of dispute has been considered by the king or the judge.

A few provisions regarding an *ex-parte* decree are found only in the code of Katyayana where he mentions that an *ex-parte* decree may be ordinarily passed in favour of the plaintiff when the defendant remains absent except when the absence is caused by factors beyond his control.

Adjournments

The ancient Hindu law dealt with this aspect of a judicial trial and the tendency of the earlier writers seems to be against allowing adjournments to the contending parties. During the last period of the Smrtis, however, this tendency seems to have been softened and during the time of our authors we find many rules which permitted adjournments under certain circumstances. The practical aspect of the question is not lost sight of and in a few cases of importance adjournments are refused. In criminal matters no adjournment is allowed while in civil disputes adjournments are allowed at the discretion of the court. For deposition of witnesses no time is granted because it is believed that a serious fault of turning away from justice would arise by allowing adjournments in matters of deposition.

Recognized Agents or Pleaders

Scanty provisions are found in the three Smrtis on this topic. It is a matter of controversy whether jurists who functioned like the advocates of today existed in old times. From a few instances it appears that representatives were allowed to appear for the litigant parties and when they appeared on behalf of any party, the victory or the defeat is supposed to be of the contending parties and not of the persons who represent them. One important rule in this respect seems to be that in criminal suits, especially in offences of grave nature, no representative is allowed and the parties to the suit have to be present in the court.

Retrial

The word for retrial is *'punar-nyaya'* and the rules provided by the Smrtis are generally analogous to those of the Civil Procedure Code. It is allowed where one of the litigants believes that the decision arrived at was contrary to justice. It is, however, refused in suits where the party has been defeated because of his own wrong statements. Appeals were preferred from the lower courts to the higher tribunals and finally to the king.

Jury System

The only reference which enables us to believe about the existence of the Jury system in ancient India is the mention of the assessors who happened to be the members of a judicial assembly, called the *sabha*. They expressed their opinion in law-suits and helped the king in the administration of justice. Dr. Kane, however, believes that in ancient India the jury system was resorted to for settling complicated questions of law.

The section on the constitution of the court shows that it was the duty of the king to attend to the administration of justice personally. It also discusses the role of assessors in a trial, different kinds of tribunals such as *kula, sreni, gana* and so on, which are invested with power to dispose of cases that are brought before them. These subsidiary courts resemble the modern *panchayats*. Appeals are preferred to the king on the decisions of these subordinate courts. The important development in the constitution of the assessors of the court from previous times to the time of Katyayana seems to be that in his days even ordinary people were included among the *sabhas* of the court which was previously the privilege of only the Brahmin caste. Brhaspati has a peculiar category of courts known as 1. Stationary, 2. Not stationary, 3. A court directed by the king and 4. A court furnished with a signet ring. Characteristics of each of these have also been stated by him.

Court House

Of the three Smrtis only the code of Brhaspati gives us a picture of the court house. It mentions how a court house should be situated and the respective places that should be occupied by the king, the chief judge, the assessors, the scribe and the accountant. The equipment of the court viz., gold, fire, the law-books, water, etc. are also mentioned by Brhaspati along with the purpose for which these articles should be used.

Plaint and Reply

The plaint and the reply of the defendant which form the first two stages of a judicial trial are systematically discussed in the three Smrtis of our study. A survey of the provisions regarding plaint shows its different aspects such as: 1. Its nature and contents, 2. Its classification, 3. Essentials of a valid plaint, 4. Defects of a plaint, 5. Amendments to a plaint, and 6. Characteristics of a good plaint. The provisions of the three Smrtis in respect of the above classification can very well be compared with modern law.

The law of evidence which is known as the *kriyapada* forms the third stage of the ancient Indian judicial procedure. The parties to the litigation have to put forth evidence in support of their claims. This evidence is of three types viz., (1) Documentary, (2) Testimony of witnesses, and (3) Ordeals. The last is known as the divine proof and should be resorted to only when human proof is not available. In the cases of disputes pertaining to immovable property possession is also considered as an additional means of proof. In the opinion of Narada and Brhaspati documentary proof is the most superior and acceptable of all the three modes of proof. A document should be free from all ambiguities and perfect in all respects. Its contents should not be opposed to the usages of the country. The eleven kinds of documents dealt with exhaustively by Brhaspati show the importance of documentary evidence in ancient judicial procedure of India. Of the two kinds of documents viz., *sasana* or a royal grant and *laukika* or public document, the latter required certain formalities to be observed. A deed of debt should contain apart from the name of the royal family, etc. the name and caste of the creditor and the debtor, the nature of the property, rate of interest and the signature of the witnesses. If a document is torn or stolen or burnt, a fresh document could be executed. But before producing such secondary evidence the parties must satisfy the court that they have made a thorough search for the original document. The party should also satisfy the court with genuine reasons for the loss of the original document. Before admitting a subsequent document the testimony of the sub-scribing witnesses to the original documents should also be taken. But Brhaspati seems to be against admitting secondary evidence and maintains that a document which is reported to have been lost or destroyed or has its contents defaced, should be considered as a false document and hence invalid. From the opinion of the jurists in old days it appears that as in modern times primary evidence should be insisted upon and that secondary evidence should be accepted by the courts only in special circumstances.

The entire topic of documents as discussed in the three codes shows that in the later period of the Smrtis there was a tendency to make fabricated and false documents. In Brhaspati's time this tendency seems to have been on a larger scale as will be seen from his warning against clever forgers who fabricate false documents. In Katyayana's time we find more provisions for testing the validity of documents supported by the testimony of subscribing witnesses and even by ordeals if necessary.

From the documents we pass on to witnesses, the essential requisite of which is that there must be direct witnesses to a transaction that has taken place. The law of the Smrtis shows that ordinarily witnesses of the plaintiff should be examined first except in special circumstances when the witnesses of the defendant should get priority. As regards the evidence of the persons who are away we find provisions which are similar to those of the Indian Civil Procedure Code regarding evidence by commission. Katyayana, however, expressly says that the witnesses should be examined only in the hail of justice and not elsewhere except in the cases of disputes concerning immovable property. As regards the manner of deposition the general rule is that the witnesses should be asked to state the truth. The exhortation of the presiding judge, however, differs according to the castes of the witnesses. Elaborate rules have been framed by Narada on the exhortation by the judge. The provisions of the Smrtis insist that the witnesses should possess certain essential qualifications. They should be of good families and of unimpeachable character. According to Katyayana they should be preferably of the same caste as of the litigants and that the litigants of lower castes should not engage people of higher castes as witnesses. Further, in the case of women, the witnesses should preferably be women. Narada records a long category of persons whom he considers as incompetent witnesses. Persons who have no veracity or integrity cannot act as witnesses. So also persons of unworthy character such as a public dancer, seller of spirituous liquor, snake-catcher and so on. A few relatives are also excluded from being witnesses. According to Katyayana a person who is dependent upon another person should not depose on behalf of his master. With regard to incompetent witnesses Narada and Katyayana lay down an important rule that a person considered incompetent to act as a witness in a civil suit can depose in a criminal case because, they say that in criminal matters men with requisite qualifications are not always likely to be available. But even in such cases, Narada says, that a minor, a woman, a single person, forger of deeds and such other persons should be scrupulously avoided for deposition as each one of them is likely to make false statements for one reason or other. Narada and Katyayana have only two kinds of witnesses viz., 1. *Krta* or appointed by the parties and 2. *Akrta* or not so appointed. Brhaspati on the other hand mentions twelve kinds of witnesses and explains their functions as well. In a few cases witnesses are dispensed with. These are called *asaksipratyah* i.e. capable of being proved without witnesses. According to Narada certain acts of persons are indicative of their motive to commit crime and if as a result of such signs or acts any wrongful act is committed the logical inference would be that the author of the crime must be the person possessing the visible signs and in such cases no witness is necessary. These provisions are fully in agreement with the provisions of sec. 114 of the Indian Evidence Act which lays down that the court can infer from certain circumstances whether an offence has been committed or not.

As regards the number of witnesses there does not seem to be any agreement among the three law-givers. Their number varies from three to nine but testimony of even a single witness is admissible according to Narada and Katyayana depending on circumstances. The general rule, however, seems to be that the witnesses should not be less than three and in even numbers. Where the number of witnesses is equal Brhaspati maintains that the testimony of more virtuous and religious-minded people should be relied upon. Impeachment of the credibility of witnesses was a feature of the old Hindu law as it is today as laid down in the Indian Evidence Act. Two noteworthy provisions of the three Smrtis in this respect are that (1) If a party tries to cast aspersions on the character of a witness, whose veracity cannot be questioned, he is liable to be fined, and (2) The draw-backs of the witnesses, if any, should be shown before they depose and not afterwards.

Possession of any property—whether movable or immovable—has always been considered as one of the most important modes of evidence leading to the inference of its ownership. The law as laid down by Narada and Brhaspati in this respect shows that possession ripens into ownership provided that it is either accompanied by a title or has been for a very long time. It is a debatable point whether mere title without possession creates ownership in a property. But Narada expressly states that in such cases mere title has no validity. The provisions of the three Smrtis in matters of long possession indicate that according to Katyayana an unbroken and continuous possession of a property for three generations and enjoyment of any property beyond living memory (*asmartakala*) according to Narada and Brhaspati creates ownership in a property even though such possession has been obtained unlawfully by the ancestors of the persons who occupy it. In the case of adverse possession Narada has a significant rule which provides that a pledge, boundary, the property of a minor, open deposit, an *upanidhi* deposit, women and what belongs to a king or a learned Brahmin cannot be owned even by adverse possession. It should be noted that a property held by a relative or friend in a fiduciary character is exempted from the application of the rules for adverse possession and to a certain extent the provisions of section 10 of the Indian Limitation Act are analogous to these rules.

As already stated ordeals are considered to be beyond the scope of human proofs and are resorted to only under special conditions. An important rule as laid down by all the three law-givers is that when human proofs such as documents, witnesses or possession are available, there is no scope for divine proofs or ordeals. Similarly, ordeals are not administered in disputes of immovable property or in petty cases. The different ordeals mentioned are to be used in particular cases and in particular seasons.

The division of the several topics of Jaw into eighteen is a special feature of the Hindu law and is accepted by almost all the Smrtis, though they differ in their order and nomenclature. There is no ear-marked distinction between criminal and civil suits. But Narada and Brhaspati seem to be aware of such distinction. Brhaspati states that fourteen of the titles pertain to civil wrongs, while the remaining four deal with criminal wrongs. Although this distinction is mentioned we do not find any reference to the two kinds of courts, one for civil suits and the other for criminal, as in modern days. Probably both kinds of suits were tried by the same courts. An important distinction is made as to what are known as miscellaneous suits (*prakirnaka*) and the remaining seventeen classes of disputes. In the case of the former it. is the king and his officers that take an initiative action in filing a suit; whereas in the latter case it is the plaintiff or the complainant that sets up a claim against the defendant in a court of law.

An analysis of the different topics of law as laid down in the ancient Indian Smrtis as also in the three Smrtis under study enables us to classify them into five main divisions viz., 1. Monetary laws, 2. Service laws, 3. Group laws, 4. Land disputes, and 5. Criminal laws. Monetary laws deal with the topics of law of debt and deposits of various kinds. The law of debt lays down rules for interest, sureties, repayment of loan, liability of different persons for the payment of debt and so on. The three authors mention different kinds of deposits with respective characteristics of each. In the service laws the three law-givers thoroughly explain the mutual relations between master and servant, teacher and the apprentice and between the employer and the employee together with their rights and responsibilities as well as duties towards each other. The group laws speak of partnership business and joint undertakings by groups or associations of people. In the cases of partnership the duties, rights and liabilities of every partner are specifically mentioned. Provisions regarding sale and recession of sale or purchase which deal with the rights and responsibilities of the seller and the purchaser may also be included under contracts. Some of the provisions of the law of sale and purchase are similar to those laid down in the Indian Contract Act. The land disputes as we find them in the three Smrtis mainly discuss about the boundary marks of fields, etc. and easements. Lastly, the criminal laws as found in the three codes can be classified under the following six heads:

1. Offence by words (*vakparusya*).
2. Assault or *dandaparusya* dealing with different kinds of assaults.
3. *Steya* or theft.
4. *Sahasa* or violence resulting in injury.
5. *Strisamgrahana* or adultery.
6. Miscellaneous offences known as *prakirnakas* which deal with litigations instituted by the king or his officers.

From the survey of the contents of the three codes as adumbrated above it will be seen that the three jurists are of advanced views so far as several matters of Hindu jurisprudence are concerned. They lay down a number of principles on a variety of subjects. Although they faithfully follow the previous codes of Manu, Yajnavalkya and others, in certain matters they differ from them in many important particulars. They all uniformly recognize the superiority of custom and state that the custom is powerful in overriding any text of Hindu law. Narada, Brhaspati and Katyayana give exhaustive rules pertaining to civil and criminal law and in spite of their adherence to the views of their predecessors they are not servile nor do they hesitate to proclaim boldly whenever they differ from traditional views. They made such changes as were in conformity with the changes that took place in social, religious, economic and political conditions of their times. A reference from Katyayana's code will illustrate this remark. All the Smrti writers prior to the three law-givers of our study state that the king's legal assembly or the *sabha* should include only Brahmins and persons versed in the three Vedas, as assessors. But as already stated Katyayana says that the *sabha* should also consist of a few merchants of good birth and conduct, aged, wealthy and free from greed. This development shows the importance gradually gained by the merchant class during the days of Katyayana. In older Smrtis merchants were not included in the king's assembly because that community was probably held in low esteem. Another instance of the hold of social conditions could be seen in the laws about gambling. Manu emphatically condemns gambling and says 'gambling and prize-betting should be driven out of the state by the king. These two faults of the kings are the means for destruction of the kingdom.' This strict condemnation of gambling gave way to regulated gambling during the time of Narada, Brhaspati and Katyayana. The rules regarding the play of dice as stated by Narada indicate a larger prevalence of the game leading to relaxations of restrictions and although Brhaspati refers to the condemnation of gambling by Manu, he says that the law-givers have permitted it because it brings revenue to the king. Lastly, Katyayana, in spite of his resentful attitude towards gambling as promoting anger and creating ill-will and wickedness among the people, submits to the popularity of the game among the society and says that if gambling is to be allowed by the king it should be an open gambling and not a secret one and further that it should be made use of for yielding revenue to the king's treasury.As in certain other branches of knowledge, whether it be science, art or sculpture in which India has had the proud privilege of being a pioneer, so it has been in the matter of knowledge of law. The present legal system may not have been the one obtaining in the early ages, but references that occur in Vedas, Smritis and Sadachar clearly show that India had once been very rich in Jurisprudence. Indian or Hindu Jurisprudence showed its visible roots at least 3000 to 4000 years ago, if not earlier.

Law and its rules were conceived as the orders of Dharma. Dharma has been the origin of Hindu Law or Hindu Jurisprudence. The word Dharma has been used in several senses but its most dominant association has been with MAT or religion as Hindu Dharma, Isai Dharma, Muslim Dharma, Jain Dharma, Parsi Dharma., etc. But, it has also been used with equal prominence in reference to a particular code of conduct, which descended up to Sutrakal, the age of scripture. Chief Sutra-Karas (religious script writers) viz., Gautam, Bodhayan, Apastamva and Vashishtha have written about marriage, son, property, crime, punishment, etc. in the shape of Sutra. In Vashishtha Dharma-Sutra, widow-remarriage and divorce are found.

After *Sutra-Kal,* Smritis have been accepted as the main source of Hindu Jurisprudence. Smriti means memory of those who knew Vedas. They are considered to be the links between Vedas and the traditions of the Vedic period. The outstanding Smritis are Manu-Smriti, Yajnvalkya-Smriti, Narad-Smriti, Brihaspati-Smriti and Katyayan-Smriti. Manu has divided his Smriti into three parts, viz., Achar, Vyavvahar and Prayashchit, and framed rules in respect of each of them. Narad-Smriti has been considered to be more progressive in comparison to Manu-Smriti or Yajnavalkya-Smriti. According to this Smriti, the king had the power to make rules different from those mentioned in Smrities. Brihaspati and Katyayan Smrities mainly dwelt upon Vyavahara (civil law) and Stridhan.

Besides four sources of law (Surti, Veda, Smriti and Sadachar) mentioned above, there is yet another source called 'self-satisfaction' though it is accepted as a source of law in a very limited sense. Manu's citation of Shila is stated to be interrelated with Smriti.

The theory of Hindu Jurisprudence, acclaims the king and the judge as of divine origin. Similarly, law and justice are also said to be of divine origin. King was created by God primarily with the object of protecting his subjects on his behalf. The King has to take the responsibility of administering justice even if he would have done so with assistance of judge appointed by him. It is the King who was, it is believed, answerable to God who would take an account from him.

From the time immemorial, Hindu Jurisprudence is rooted in Hindu religion. A custom that is good for the society was necessarily to be unavoidable for pleasing a deity. In the words of P.N. Sen "Hindu Jurisprudence may be regarded as Hindu law viewed from the standpoint of jurisprudence, or as jurisprudence effected through the medium of Hindu Law."

The whole conduct of a man through his life, being born in a Hindu family is the concern of Hindu Jurisprudence. In fact, the Hindu Jurisprudence comes in play even before the man is born, i.e. as soon as he is conceived in the womb of his mother. When he is conceived, a conception ceremony called the Garbhadhan ceremony or Samskar is held. Similarly, Janm Samskar as birth, Upanyan Samskar as sacred thread ceremony are held. The sacred thread ceremony was considered to be one of the most important ceremonies of man's life because this was an occasion when his real birth is recognised and with it he was given to the world of "God Knowledge" wherefrom the beginning of Brahmcharya takes place. Vidyarambh Samskar or the beginning of education ceremony was done with markable festivities. After completion of education, man had to begin his Grahasth Ashram after getting married. This again was one of the most important samskars of man's life. This was followed by the 'ritu santi' samskar or consummation ceremony. At the death, Dah Samskar and for Moksh the salvation samskar was performed. Similarly, Ashram Vyavashta of four ashramas demarcating four stages of man's life was also a part of Hindu Jurisprudence. It is, thus, clear that"Hindu Jurisprudence bears a distinct imprint of its own."

In the eternal words of Mayne "Hindu law has the oldest pedigree of any known system of jurisprudence. and even now it shows no signs of dcscriptitude," One of the characteristics of Hindu Jurisprudence, as emphasised in *Sri Balusu Gurubinga Swami* v. *Sri Balusu Ram Lakshamana,* where their lordships of Privy Council observed: "Hindu Jurisprudence does not draw any line of demarcation between ceremonial rites and rules, between moral and religious information and strict legal precepts."

There are two main difficulties in the study of Hindu Jurisprudence. In the first place, Hindu Jurisprudence is an inextricably mixed version of law and morals, and secondly modern jurisprudence being founded upon Roman Law, the concepts of Hindu Jurisprudence are not adaptable to such juristic studies. Both these aspects are ably explained by P.N. Sen in the following words:

> "The Hindu Bharma-Shastras, which are the principal sources of Hindu Law, do not confine themselves to the enunciation of juristic

rules for the guidance of human conduct; ceremonial rules, moral and religious injunctions and strict legal precepts, are found mingled up and no clear line of demarcation is uniformly maintained, so as to keep them separate, and prevent confusion of ideas in the minds not sufficiently familiar with the rules of logic and Canon of construction by which they have to be discriminated from one another. In the second place, difficulty is due to the peculiar character of the science of jurisprudence itself. Jurisprudence, as we have, pre-eminently as Western Science; it had its foundation in the Roman Law, the result is that in the study of Jurisprudence, whatever may be the system of law which furnishes us with materials for the same, we start with certain pre-conceived ideas about and a prearranged scheme of classification for juristic conceptions borrowed from the Roman Law. This works well enough so long as we confine our attention to the western systems of law, for they have all, more or less been based upon and influenced by the Roman Law, but to approach the study of Hindu Law with an exception to find the exact counterparts of the ideas, classifications referred to above may not always prove equally convenient or successful. In order to be properly appreciated and understood, Hindu Law must, therefore, be studied from within, with such light as it itself affords under such guidance as we may receive from a study of analytical and comparative jurisprudence as regards the points on which we should bestow our special attention; and when this way we succeed in grasping the fundamental conceptions and principles contained therein we may proceed to arrange and systematise them with reference to similar topics in other systems of law and compare and note striking points of similarity or contrast wherever such comparison may be instructive or interesting."

So far as legal system prevailing in ancient Indian society is concerned, it was closely knit into three pillars, on which all the legal concepts rested. They were Rta or Rita (Vrat), Dharma and Achara; Rta was a sort of moral principle. The Dharma stood for a code of conduct sanctioned in the Dharmashastras. A council or Parishad which was then called Parshat, was constituted comprising four learned people having deep knowledge of Vedas. These persons used to pronounce Dharma which was binding on all. It carried a sanction. Achar (actual conduct) was treated as a sort of precedent because it reflected the practices and behaviour through life of the learned and wise men of the time. In due course of time, such Achar or practices became precedent and acquired the force of social traditions in the shape of customs and usages. It corresponded with customary law of to-day.

The Vedas, Smritis and Sadachar were the sources of law. However, the Vedas were considered to be the main source of law. The orders of the King were also considered to be the source of law. In the event of any confusion or conflict between Vedas and Smritis, the Vedas were given precedence. The judges assured equality before law at all costs. The King was bound to punish all offenders equally and he did not have any margin for discrimination. Supremacy of law was, thus maintained. Even a King could not be spared for his wrong doings. In fact, the King had to pay fine one thousand times more than an ordinary citizen. The judges were also under law and it was enjoined upon them to follow it like other ordinary citizens. They had to be quite conscious of their duty and had to pay a heavy fine for miscarriage of justice.

Nothing could become a part of law which was against public conscience, the king had to follow the established customs and usages and also the practices of holy and wise men in laying down law on any point, Dharmashastra emphasised that only those were to get the protection of law, who abided by it.

There were clear laws on many social and economic aspects of life. Laws were available on breach of contract, repayment of loans, taking away things without the consent of the owner even in his presence or in his absence, stealing a thing and afterwards disposing it of in consideration of something, partnership, wages for the work done, exchange of things if not subsequently liked by the purchaser, relations between master and servant, defamation, assault, thieving, robbery, disputes as to ownership of land, misbehaviour or misconduct towards women, gambling, etc.

According to Manu, the Hindu law-giver, the God, provided for Danda i.e. punishment and gave to the King for getting it implemented. Due to provision of Danda, people feared to infringe the rights and other things. Administration of Justice and punishing the criminals were the most important duties of the King. According to the provisions of Vajasanyasi Smriti, the King had to see that the stronger one does not harass the weaker and that the King's goodness is shared by all. The principles of deterrent punishment, reformative and of probation were followed as provided for in Dharmashastras. According to Dharmashastra, four theories of punishment existed, viz., Vak-danda, Dhig-danda, Vadha-danda and Dhan-danda. The modern concepts of all the four punishments are reprimand, censure, capital and corporal punishment and fine respectively. It would be seen that reprimand and censure punishments were there with a view to giving the criminal a chance to reform himself. According to Manu-Smriti, for repetition of crime all the four punishments were sanctioned. Compensation to the victim was also allowed and if the King's men failed to recover property, the King had to compensate it from his own resources. It is also provided for in Manu-Smriti that the King who has his realm free from theft, adultery, insult or intimidation and the like, gets heaven after death.

Yajnavalkya mentioned four types of courts as follows:

THE KING'S COURT

|

THE PUGA COURT

|

THE SHRERIN COURT

|

THE FAMILY COURT

The King's court was always presided over by the King himself while other courts were presided over by the judges appointed by the King. The courts below the King's court were subordinate to each other in the hierarchy depicted above and, therefore, their appeals lay in the same order. The King's court was the highest court like our Supreme Court, whose judgments were final for ever. The judges were assisted by the so called assessors. Detailed rules of evidence both oral and documentary existed. No money was charged as court fee but the loser had to pay some percentage of the claim which he lost.

The rule of Dharma, which may be called the rule of law, prevailed as recognised by the society. Recognition of eight types of marriages, i.e., *Brahma vivah, Daiva vivah, Arsha vivah, Prajaptya vivah, Asura vivah, Rakshash vivah, and Paishach vivah* was in vogue. Following were the characteristics of marriages:

(1) Marriage was considered to be one of the most important religious sacraments.

(2) Endogamous marriages were recognised according to which marriages only within castes were considered to be ideal.

(3) Religious aims of marriages were recognised. The performance of five Yajnas, i.e. *Brahma yajna, Deva yajna, Pitra yajna, Bhut yajna and Atithi yajna were considered essential and Pitra yajna* was not possible without marriage. Sex satisfaction was the remotest aim of marriage.

(4) Restrictions were imposed on Sagotra, Sapinda and Sapravara marriages. In no society of the world this characteristic is found except in Hindu society.

(5) Widow marriage was prohibited. The provisions to this effect in Shastras prohibit remarriage under any circumstances. However, Vashishtha Dharma-Sutra allowed it.

(6) In no circumstances the divorce was allowed. The union of husband and wife is said to be the act of God and hence it is only He who could allow divorce and nobody else. Thus, in practice, divorce was not allowed. But, Vashishtha was in favour of it.

The aim of Hindu marriage, as is apparent from the above, was performance of religious duties, progeny, sex, discharge of family obligations, discharge of social obligations, development of personality, etc. According to religious necessity, begetting a son is absolutely essential in order to attain salvation for a Hindu father. Salvation is the supreme object of every Hindu individual in order to get rid of re-birth. According to social obligation, repayment of legal (Vyavaharik) debt is the pious obligation of a son. If the son fails to clear off the debts of his father, the soul of the deceased will never get peace. However, he is not under any obligation to pay off illegal or *avyavaharik* debts. If the debt of the father was contracted for an immoral purpose, the son is not under any pious obligation to pay it.

In addition to the Auras, the legitimate son, there were twelve other kinds of secondary sons, viz., Dattak, putrika, putra, Kshetraj, Kania, Gudhaja. Kritrima, Paunarbhav, Krita, Apvidha, Svayam datta and Nishadha were recognised by the Dharmashastra. The bride was considered holding legal titles or status of wife and sons got the right of inheritance.

The Hindu Marrage Act, 1955 and Special Marriage Act, 1954 are main sources of law in regard to the modern concept of marriage and divorce. Hindu Marriage Act, 1955 provides for marriage and divorce. It prescribes only monogamy and prohibits polyandry or polygamy. Sections 494 and 495 of the Indian Penal Code provide for penalties against polygamous marriages. Marriages are to be solemnised according to customary rites. Civil marriages (i.e. Marriages under the Special Marriage Act, 1954) are, however, to be performed according to its provisions. According to the provisions in the acts, a Hindu spouse can solemnise his marriage under either of the two enactments. A Hindu can marry a non-Hindu also.

Under the Hindu Marriage Act, the marriage may be solemnised in accordance with the customary rites and ceremonies of the either party and if such rite and ceremony includes *saptapadi* then the marriage is complete and binding as soon as the seventh step has been taken. But, under the Special Marriage Act, the ceremony or rite is not essential. The marriage is complete as soon as it is registered before the Marriage Registrar. The two Hindus can, however, marry only when neither of them has any spouse living.

The institution of Hindu marriage is the most important of all the sixteen sacraments. According to Hindu belief, couples are settled in heaven and their union lasts from eternity to eternity. Since marriage is considered to be sacred union of the souls rather than of two bodies, the idea of divorce or remarriage had been eclipsed after *Sutra-period* in the Hindu society.

However, the Hindu Marriage Act provides for the judicial separation and divorce. Both the Acts make a provision for divorce on mutual consent of the spouses. They are, however, not free to apply for the dissolution of marriage within one year of the solemnisation of marriage. This provision has been made with a view to allowing sufficient period for trial of matrimonial alliance and also that the new spouses do not take impulsive, rash, hasty, irresponsible and frivolous action. The court may, however, in any exceptional case, allow petitioner to prefer suit with a view to avoiding hardship meted out to them. The limitation for petition of divorce under Special Marriage Act, 1954, has also been reduced from three years to one year.

The concept of adoption is another characteristic of Hindu Jurisprudence. The provision for adoption is for the fulfilment of religious duties and to continue the ancestral line of the man. This contention has been supported from the text of Baudhayan when it speaks that religious motive in respect of adoption cannot be denied.

In old Hindu Jurisprudence, daughters were not given any share in the presence of son in the property of their father. But, by virtue of new provisions contained in the Hindu Succession Act, 1956, they are now entitled to get the share in the property of their father. This provision has put women at par with men in respect of inheritance in the modern times. Women are, thus not being discriminated in matters of succession on the ground of sex.

An important characteristic of Hindu undivided family has been the coparcenary for the joint family system. According to this concept, every coparcener has equal right of possession and its utilisation. No member of the family has any special interest or right in the joint property. Neither of the coparcener has any definite or fixed part of right. Every coparcener has equal and joint right of use of property and for this purpose he can sue other member of the joint family. He has a right to claim for partition of property. One coparcener has the right to check another coparcener from misutilization of coparcenary property.

In Hindu coparcenary the son, grandson and great grandson acquire an interest by birth in the coparcenary property. As soon as a son is born, he becomes coparcener and gets equal right in the coparcenary property. Thus, the coparcenary starts with the birth of a son. The superior status of a son is a unique feature of Hindu coparcenary where he is born with the property.

The Hindu coparcenary property is distinct from the joint property of English law where the male issue does not acquire any interest in it by birth.

ISLAMIC JURISPRUDENCE

The first and foremost principle of Islamic Jurisprudence is Iman or Faith in God and acknowledgement of His authority over our actions. The second principle is the belief in the prophethood of Mahomed. God alone is the legislator in Islam. Mahomed is a Legislature and the Quran is the law-book.

There is no sharp distinction between law and religion in regard to Muslim Jurisprudence. In this context, Mr. Justice Mahmood observed, "It is to be remembered that Hindu and Mohammadan laws are so intimately connected with religion and they cannot readily be deserved from it." Thus, it is admitted that there is intimate fusion of law and religion in the Islamic system of jurisprudence.

On account of this fusion, there is no clear distinction between the substantive and the procedural laws. The religious doctrines and principles are of great significance. Therefore, procedural law or adjective law has not been distinctly treated in the Islamic Jurisprudence.

The expositions of the Islamic Jurisprudence in general are of three descriptions; the first termed Osool, which treats the fundamental principles of the law in matters both spiritual and temporal, as derived from the Quran, the second Sonnan, which treats the traditions; the rules and precepts of jurisprudence with respect to points not touched upon in the Quran and the third Fatavee, which consists of the recital of decisions upon cases.

The Islamic Jurisprudence begins after the advent of Islam which was actually associated with the prophet Muhammed Sahib. Islamic Jurisprudence did not get the impetus from the Arabic Society nor with any government but it was developed with the concerted efforts of prophet Muhammed Sahib and his other successors. In fact, he has impressed the Arabians by posing himself as a prophet or the messenger of God. People accepted him as prophet and relied on him for every walk of life. Muhammed Sahib preached a religion with the name of Islam, and every utterance of the Islam gave the idea of various principles of social sciences such as politics, economics, law, etc. Islam was codified in the form of Quran verses, which give the idea of personal behaviour and family life of the human beings. This is called the personal law of Muslims. Since these laws were accepted by the Mohammedans, it was called Mohemmedan law. The term Mohammedan law is also very controversial. Some authors like Fyzee employed the nomenclature Muhammedan law. Others like Mulla used the term Mahommedan law for it. Some other jurists called it as Muslim law or Islamic law. During the British period Islamic law was considered as Anglo-Muhammedan law. It is immaterial what terminology is used, it implies the family law of the Muslim community, which is unscientifically divided into Shia and Sunni sects. Sunni sect is again divided into various sub-sects like Honafeie, Shafei, Malika and hanbali, Asharia, Ishmalia, Zaideya sub-sects. These sects and sub-sects are commonly found throughout the whole world. India is thickly populated with Hanafei Sunni community but in South India Ithna Asharia of Shia sect are in dominant position. In Lucknow, the Shia Muslims are in majority.

In fact, Islamic Jurisprudence enriched the various branches of law such as International law, family law, civil law and criminal law of the various legal systems of the world. Under Muslim personal law, the concept of marriage, dowry, divorce, guardianship, maintenance, will, succession and inheritance which are derived from the various sources such as Quran, Sunna, Hadish, Ijma, Qiyas, etc. have been very scientifically observed since classical period of Islamic Jurisprudence.

The Muslim law of marriage is like a contract and not a sacrament and as such it can be dissolved like a civil contract by judicial and extra-judicial methods under law of marriage. some peculiar observations are noteworthy:

(1) Indian Majority Act is inapplicable in regard to the determination of the age in case of the Muslim marriage. In Muslim law a person is treated major at the age of 15 years irrespective of sex. This age is called the age of puberty. However, this age may differ from 9 years to 12 years as reported by Hidaya and Privy Council in case of Shia community, when a female may be treated as a major at the age of 9 or 12 years with the early start of menstruation.

(2) Islamic Jurisprudence made provision for the minors' marriage with the consent of guardian but, however, this marriage can be repudiated at the age of 15 years both by male or female. This is called option of puberty, i.e., Khiyapralbulugh which is one of the notable provisions of the family-law of Muslim community.

(3) The provision of polygamy under Muslim law is one of the salient features of the Islamic Jurisprudence. On the other hand, polyandry has not been recognised there.

(4) The Islamic Jurisprudence incorporates the principle of prohibited degree relationship in whom marriage should not be celebrated- these relations are of consanguinity, affinity and fosterage. Marriages in these relationships are null and void. The marriages in such relations are illegal and children procreated by such parents are not entitled to inheritance of their property. One cannot marry two real sisters at a time. Such kind of marriage is not void but irregular and can be regularised by divorcing one of the two sisters.

(5) Under Muslim Jurisprudence, a woman cannot marry another Muslim during the period of iddat. The iddat period during which a marriage is prohibited is four months ten days in case of death of husband and three lunar months in case of divorce. The provision of iddat has been incorporated with a view to ascertaining paternity of the child with previous husband. Hence, to determine the paternity of child, a woman cannot marry immediately after the dissolution of marriage. She should wait for remarriage till the delivery of child or for four months ten days or for three lunar months. The marriage contracted during these days is not void but irregular. It can be regularised by observing the iddat period even after the marriage.

(6) Under Islamic Jurisprudence there is a provision of restitution of conjugal rights.

(7) Muta marriage under Islamic Jurisprudence is a peculiar system of marriage which grants temporary right of co-habitation to the contracting parties. This system of marriage is not recognised by any other legal system of family law of the world. It is a temporary marriage which may last even for an hour. The Muta marriage is only recognised by Ithna, Asharia Muslims of Shia sects. It is a kind of prostitution which is contracted in the lower strata of Shia community.

The another remarkable Muslim family law is the concept of dower which was originated with a view to ameliorating the status of women in Arabia, who were treated like cattle and divorce was granted to them arbitrarily. The institution of dower is unparallel in Islamic Jurisprudence. The dower is given by husband to his wife at the time of marriage or after marriage. Wife can realise it from her husband even if it has not been mentioned in the marriage register at the nuptial ceremony. She can realise it from the property of the husband even after his death. She can retain the property of her husband in her possession till the payment of dower by the heir is made to her. This right is not known as widow's right of retention. Even in case of death of the wife, the husband or her heirs are entitled to get the share of dower which was not paid to the wife in her life-time.

The concept of divorce is a worth-noting feature of Islamic jurisprudence. Mohammedan law has made provision for the dissolution of marriage. Certain restrictions were placed on the unlimited licence of the pre-Islamic days to dissolve marriage at any time. The Muslim Jurisprudence has conceded to the wife the right to secure a divorce in certain cases, but her power is not arbitrary and is very limited. The rights of the wife have now been extended very considerably.

The term 'divorce' and Talaq are often treated as synonymous. The term 'Talaq' is also used, sometimes in the more comprehensive sense comprising all separations of the wife from husband, for causes originating in the husband but it is also used in the restricted sense of Talaq. The term divorce is generally used for dissolution of marriage in any of its forms. Talaq is one of those forms. With the march of time, the unilateral divorce and triple divorce were introduced with a view to creating fear amongst the marriage partners. The marriage was treated as dissolved as soon as divorce was granted by the husband to his wife. Really, the concept of divorce under Muslim law is also based on some concrete principle of society, which has been acknowledged by the Islamic Jurisprudence. Prophet Muhammed Sahib recognised various forms of Talaq, which are still prevalent in the Muslim community.

The institution of arbitrary Talaq at the sweet will of the husband exists since the pre-Islamic days. In those days, there were no restraints whatsoever. The husband was at liberty to pronounce Talaq any number of times and to revoke it by taking the women back and resuming marital connection. This power of divorce was recognised by the prophet but he imposed certain moral and legal restrictions which constitute some checks on the husband's powers.

Subsequently, the different forms of Talaq were not considered satisfactory because they, in fact, strengthened the hands of husband for divorcing his wife. As a result of this, Indian Parliament passed "Dissolution of Marriage Act, 1939" in order to get rid of the existing anomaly in the field of divorce. By virtue of the provisions of this Act, women have been given certain rights for divorcing their husbands.

One of the peculiar and most important concepts which had been recognised by the prophet Mohammed Sahib was the concept of re-marriage under Islamic Jurisprudence. If husband has divorced his wife, he can re-marry her immediately but the following points must be observed with respect to such re-marriage:

(i) After divorce wife should observe iddat period.

(ii) After iddat she should be married with other Muslim.

(iii) He should intercourse with her.

(iv) He should divorce her.

(v) She should observe iddat period.

(vi) After iddat, the previous husband can marry that woman.

If these steps are not followed, marriage would be irregular but not void. It can be regularised even after the marriage by observing the aforesaid steps.

Similarly, the law of will has also been very scientifically based under Muslim Jurisprudence. A testator may execute will in favour of legatee to the extent of only one-third of his property and not the whole property. A will cannot be executed in favour of testator's heir except with the consent of the heir.

Under Islamic Jurisprudence there is a provision for gift i.e., Hiba, where a Muslim having the ownership of property may dispose of this property to another Muslim without any condition or consideration. Under modern Muslim law, life interest by way of gift of usufruct can also be given to another Muslim.

Under Islamic Jurisprudence, the law of Waqf is also well developed. Any Muslim who is of sound mind, having the ownership of property may dispose of his property in the name of almighty God for religious, pious and charitable purposes. Hence, as soon as *wakf* i.e., creator of *wakf* has vested his property in the *wakf* his right of ownership is extinguished except in Hanafi law. In Hanafi law the right of wakif's ownership is not extinguished even after creation of *wakf*. This view is only prevalent in Hanafi community. Prior to the Wakf Act, 1913, a family *wakf* could not be created but after introduction of this Act, a family *wakf* can be created. The *wakf* property is managed and supervised by a person who is called Mutwalli.

Another principle of Islamic Jurisprudence is law of pre-emption. Although the notion of pre-emption was not originally found in the Quran or Sunna, yet it has been adopted in the Muslim community through equity, justice and good conscience. The law of pre-emption is the right of substitution in the shoes of vendee and it is an incident to the property and not to the sale of property. But, Mitter J. in *Sheikh Kudrutulla* v. *Mahim Mohan Shalt*, observed that law of pre-emption is a right of re-purchase and it is an incident to sale and could not exist prior to sale. Under Hanafi law, co-sharer and participator in the property and neighbour can claim right of pre-emption and they are called as pre-emptors. In Shia law and Shafei law only co-sharer can claim right of pre-emption.

The right of pre-emption cannot be claimed in arbitrary manner. There is a specific procedure under Muslim law for claiming such right. If that procedure has not been followed, the right of pre-emption would fail. The right of pre-emption was also prevalent in the Hindu-community in ancient times.

The right of pre-emption can only be claimed after the sale and under no circumstances prior to sale. It can also not be claimed when the property has been transferred by way of gift, exchange. lease, licence, *wakf* or any kind of transfer other than sale.

The right of pre-emption may be lost when the pre-emptor waived his right and not claimed the pre-emption. The death of pre-emptor and release by accepting some consideration by pre-emptor are also the means through which he can extinguish his right of pre-emption.

The Indian Succession Act, 1925 acknowledged and adopted various aspects of Muslim personal law in regard to succession of Muslim community. Under Muslim law, after the death of a Muslim, property should be distributed amongst the heirs only after the payment of deceased's debts, death-bed charges, funeral expenses, and other medical expenses. This aspect has been accepted by the Indian Succession Act.

The Muslim law of inheritance is very scientifically established by the Prophet, where each member of the deceased's family has been given due share. The distribution of shares of the deceased's property is already fixed both in Shia and Sunni community. The significant point in both the communities is that women are given the right of inheritance in the property as it was not prevalent in the pre-Islamic Arabia, i.e., prior to the Prophet.

After discussing the fundamental tenets in regard to the personal laws of the muslim community, it is necessary to give some idea about Muslim criminal jurisprudence. Hindu criminal jurisprudence obtaining in various ancient codes was prevalent in ancient India. However, in medieval period, it disappeared when Muslim rulers came in power. Henceforward, the people were made necessarily subject to the criminal jurisprudence of the new conquerors. The origin and fountain of Muslim criminal jurisprudence is the Quran. In all ages since the advent of the Prophet, it has been the sole code both of criminal jurisprudence and of civil duties. Subsequently, during the British period, when the Indian Penal Code, 1860 came into operation, the Muslim criminal jurisprudence died its natural death and every Indian irrespective of caste, creed and colour became subject to the provisions of the said code in respect of criminal liability.

The religious Shariat law discriminated against women in matters pertaining to property and marriage. The Prophet recreeded in the pre-Islamic Arab days that the Muslims take up to four wives. He was, by this decree, in fact, putting a restriction on exploitation of Arab women which was rampant in his days. Now the time has come to change this Shariat law to suit the needs of the country. A drastic change is necessary in the personal laws of Muslims including the Muslim Shariat law which did not give equal status to women. However, the Muslim community may resist any move to form a common civil code which is evident from the public utterings of the Muslim leaders in India.

COMPARATIVE JURISPRUDENCE

Jurisprudence is generally differentiated from comparative law but it seems difficult as to how jurisprudence can survive without the comparative law. There have been many debates on the nature of comparative law and comparative jurisprudence. It would be seen that on the basis of certain definitions of comparative law no difference between the two is pointed out and both are inseparable.

The phrase 'comparative jurisprudence' is employed by many a jurists in different senses but it is generally used for comparative method in the study of law. This method is very useful in the study of analytical jurisprudence. The basic principles which are common in various legal systems of the world are ascertained by the use of this technique. By virtue of this mode of learning, certain universal principles are traced out but they are not good in number because the legal institutions have to discharge their functions in different environments and conditions.

Pollock and Maine have made the use of the phrase 'Comparative Jurisprudence' in their works. Sometimes this phrase is referred to as 'Comparative Legislation'. But, today the word 'Law' is commonly used in place of 'Jurisprudence' and 'Legislation'—which creates confusion in the minds of legal thinkers. However, the phrase 'Comparative Law' denotes the term 'Comparative Jurisprudence' and nothing else. The comparative method is adequately flexible and as such it embraces all kinds of activities which are related to the study of different legal systems. According to Paton, there have been many debates on the nature of comparative law and comparative jurisprudence and in some of the definitions, comparative law is indistinguishable from comparative jurisprudence.

Many comparative jurists identified comparative law with comparative legal history or treated it as ancillary to analytical jurisprudence. As said earlier, the terms 'comparative jurisprudence' and'comparative law' are interchangeably used for the same connotation. In this context, Pollock observes:

> "It makes no great difference whether we speak of historical jurisprudence or a comparative jurisprudence, or as the Germans seem inclined to say, of the general history of law."

While throwing light on the functions of comparative jurisprudence, Holland stated, "comparative law collects and tabulates the legal institutions of various countries, and from the results prepared the abstract science of jurisprudence is enabled to set forth an orderly view of the ideas and methods which have been variously realised in actual system." Maine does not agree with Holland in this respect. He advanced his different view. He laid stress upon the practical aspect of comparative jurisprudence. He ascertained that the main function of comparative law is more or less practical. He said: "The chief function of comparative jurisprudence is to facilitate legislation and the practical improvement of law."

The observations of Maine may be useful to the Indian as the present Indian law needs overhauling and reforms which could be obtained through legislation. Undoubtedly, the comparative method may furnish useful material to Legislatures and law reforms. A distinguished comparative lawyer has said that the phrase 'comparative law' is a strange work. How strange it is, becomes manifest when attempts are made to define it or to ascertain its relation to other forms of learning. The phrase 'comparative law' denotes a method of study and research and not a distinct branch or department of law. If by 'law' we mean a body of rules, it is obvious that there can be no such thing as 'comparative' law. The process of comparing rules of law taken from different systems does not result in the formulation of any independent rules for the regulation of human relationships or transactions. There is no comparative branch or department of law. The emptiness of the phrase has been realised by German lawyers. It connotes a process of comparison only. But in England and most other countries, the term 'comparative law' has become so firmly established that it must be accepted even if it is misleading. The word 'law' in the phrase is sometimes, referred to as comparative jurisprudence and sometimes as comparative legislation.

The use of the phrase 'comparative jurisprudence' is an expression of the belief that the comparative method of study has as its principal objective to aid the historian or the analytical jurist in tracing the origin and development of concepts to all systems of law. However, 'comparative law' is defined as a branch of legal science whose object is to bring about systematically, the establishment of closer relations between the legal institutions of the different countries.

Some jurists are of the view that the comparative method is concerned with space, as the historical method is with time. It collects, examines, collates the notions, doctrines, rules and institutions which are found in ever developed legal system or at least in most systems. This is considered natural, philosophical and serviceable. Bryce indulges in a brilliant fancy when he cites the Praetor as one who might have followed this method in constructing the general or theoretical part of his jus gentium. Salmond defines comparative jurisprudence as 'the study of the resemblances and differences between different legal systems and he says that it is not a separate branch of jurisprudence', but merely a particular method of that science—we compare English law with Roman law—for the purpose of historical jurisprudence in order that we may better understand the course of development of each system.

The main function of comparative jurisprudence is comparison, which is said to be inherent in human mind. Indeed, human psychology and the behaviour of man shows that comparison is one of the most important ways taken by the human mind towards general understanding. Comparison is a natural process of human thought and one cannot escape from it. It is only comparative process that tells us what is good and what is bad. What is heavy and what is light, can only be known by comparison.

We always select our articles, our friends, our life partners by a process of preference which is not always completely conscious. Consciously or unconsciously, knowingly or unknowingly we employ the method of comparison when we finally select or adopt a thing. Selection or adoption presupposes comparison. The importance and well known qualities of a mature legal system can only shine more brightly when compared with other global legal systems. The most valuable function of comparative jurisprudence can be seen in the solution of modern social problems in the international field. The method brings peoples together. In the field of unification of law, the operation of comparative jurisprudence plays a significant role in legislative, academic, practical, sociological and scientific functioning in every society in the modern time.

In the civil law countries, there are two schools of thought with respect to the comparative jurisprudence. The thinkers of one school believe that comparative law is merely a form of legal technique while the philosophers of the other school insist on its scientific nature and classify it as a distinct branch of legal learning. According to the latter, comparative law is of two kinds: (1) Descriptive comparative law; and (2) Applied comparative law.

Descriptive Comparative Law

This is a term which is somewhat loosely employed and embraces many types of comparative work of varying degrees of merit. There is a noticeable tendency to treat any investigation into foreign law as coming under this heading. Descriptive comparative law differs from applied comparative law because it is confined to an analysis of variations between the laws of two or more countries and is not directed to the solution of any problem either of an abstract or a practical nature. A typical instance of research of this character is to be found in the enquiry instituted in 1937 by the League of Nations into the laws which regulate the civil status of women.

Applied Comparative Law

The use of the comparative method with a definite aim in view, other than that of obtaining information as to foreign law, may conveniently be called applied comparative law. The aim in question need not be of a practical nature, it may, for instance, take the form of a comparison carried out either with the object of enabling the legal philosopher to construct abstract theories of law or to assist the historian in tracing the origins and evolution of legal concepts and institutions. The distinguishing feature of this form of comparison is that it does not consist of a mere description of the differences which exist between the concepts, rules or institutions of the laws under examination, but probes more deeply into the matter with a definite purpose in view. Applied comparative law has a practical aim in view such as law reform or the unification of divergent laws. This form of comparative research is the most vigorous and fertile in output.

Abstract or Speculative Comparative Law

There is a third form of comparative law which Rabel has termed 'pure comparative law'. This is also known as abstract or speculative comparative law. It consists of comparison carried out with no other object than to increase the sum total of our knowledge of the law. It is no doubt theoretically possible to conceive of a comparison carried out in vacua which is not descriptive, because it is not solely informative in character, and is not 'applied' because it has no particular aim other than that of scientific curiosity. In any event, research of this kind must be so rare as to be virtually non-existent. If it is confined to an analysis of the differences between systems of law, it would seem to fall under the category of descriptive comparison. On the other hand, if the differences are regarded in the light of the historical development of the law or of the social purposes for which the law exists, then the comparison is likely to lose its abstract character and to assume the guise of 'applied' comparative law.

Purpose

The study of comparative law can serve many purposes. Two of these are of paramount importance. The first is that by comparing it with other systems, it is possible to evaluate the principles of one's own country's legal system and thereby to understand it more clearly. The second aim is that it leads to an appreciation of the influence and indebtedness of the one system to the other or others compared.

Comparative jurisprudence proposes to further our insight into the nature of legal institutions and the spirit of their laws. It is vain to expect comparative law to solve all the problems of legal philosophy. There is a tendency to over-rate the value of the former for the latter, until vitalised by the force of philosophical principles, the most valuable materials are merely building-stores awaiting the design of the architect.

Austin is of the view that by studying different systems of law we shall be better able to detect the faults of our own system. This is the purpose of comparative jurisprudence.

Value

Lord Macmillan has rightly emphasised the importance of studying other systems of law by saying that to him learning another system of law is like learning another language. According to him, study of new system of law not only increases the knowledge of the reader but also renders the system more intelligible and vivid. He is of the opinion that a person. who is bilingual is much better able to appreciate the merits of all the languages he speaks.

Lord Macmillan further says that "I have found this notably in the performance of my duty of administering both the law of England and the law of Scotland in the House of Lords and I do not hesitate to say that the contrasts which emerge in daily debate between the two systems, so very different in their genesis, enable one better to understand and appreciate the futures and merits of each."

Roscoe Pound says that all interpretations go on analogies since we seek to understand one thing by comparing it with another and we construct a theory of one process by comparing it with another. He adds that many varied analogies have been used to interpret law and its history.

Prof. F.F. Stone has rightly remarked that the practice of comparing is one of the human traits. Man compares one event with another, one object with another, one person with another. He says that it applies more directly to law since one sees that the judge must constantly compare one course of action with another, the acts or omissions of one man with those of another and the interpretations placed upon those acts or omissions in order to arrive at his judgments.

The fundamental characteristic of comparative law, viewed as a method, lies in the fact that it may be made applicable to any form of legal research. This method is evenly at the service for the legal historian, the analytical jurist, the judge, the legal practitioner and the law teacher. It covers the spheres both of public and private law; its resources lie open to the economist and to the sociologist, as well as to the lawyer. It may provide important service to the statesman, to the administrator and to the businessman. It can throw light on the obscurities of rules or institutions which do not appear to rest upon traditional or logical foundations. However, on all the events, the comparative method is on trial. Still it is in the experimental stage. In view of this, its classification as to its functions cannot be taken as final.

Criticism

Maine believes that the attempt to build up a system of jurisprudence on observation, comparison and analysis of ideas is due to Bentham and even more to Austin. Austin and Maine are of the view that the aim of jurisprudence is positive law and that jurisprudence can either be particular and national or general and comparative. This is the result of abstraction, because the identical principles of the various legislative systems are the same. General jurisprudence is called by these two writers the philosophy of positive law. The philosophy of positive law differs from the science of legislation, because the former studies the laws as they are, and the second, a branch of ethics or deontology, shows how the laws should be made so that they will conform to a tie, that is, the divine law identified with the principle of general utility.

(i) Hindu Jurisprudence and Islamic Jurisprudence Compared

Manu declared "The Veda, the Smriti (Dharamsashtra), the usage (Sadachar) of good men and what is agreeable to one's soul or self-satisfaction (Atma-tushti), the wise people have declared these to be the four-fold indices of 'dharma' or approved conduct."

These four indices are regarded as the sources of positive law, as understood and obeyed by the Hindus.

We find that the smritis and the established usages may, for all purposes, be regarded as the two principal sources of positive law. Besides, we should also mention the Puranas which are often quoted by commentators and writers of Nimbandhas as authorities on the questions of Hindu law. Jurisprudence is not such a subject with which Puranas may be directly concerned but incidentally sometimes they deal with the questions of law. The Puranas are cited by later commentators and writers on Hindu law as authorities on such questions. It is recognised that the Puranas can never override the Smritis but must yield to the superior authority of the Smritis if any conflict arises between them.

The importance of commentaries and Nibandhas of recognised authority stands on a double basis. In the first place, they collect and harmonise the diverse texts of Dharmashastras bearing on various topics of law, and in the second place, the interpretations which they put, acquire an independent authority in the particular provinces especially governed by them.

Sanction

According to the Hindu ideas, 'Dharma' or sacred law contains its authority within itself; the King is not superior to it, but, like other human beings, is subject to it. The Dharma is an authoritative element because its observance is conducive to welfare and salvation. Its violation is reprehensible because it is sure to lead to misery. The law is supreme. The will of the King is not its originator and its sanction is not derived from an extrinsic or accidental agency, for it contains its sanction within itself in the certainty that obedience to law will lead to welfare and its violation to misery.

Theory of Apurva or Invisible Force

The distinctions between positive law and the ceremonial rule and religious injunctions are found in the special function of the King in the Hindu polity. The law directs an individual to do certain things and avoid certain others, it directs the King, in addition to his other duties, to take steps that the law is respected and obeyed, and to mete out punishment to those who in violation of the law inflict injury upon others, while the positive law is said to comprise of that portion of the law the violation of which calls for the interposition of the King in order to provide an adequate remedy to the injured party, or chastise the delinquent for his transgression, or, if expressed differently, it is that portion of the law which is enforced by the King. So, Yajnavalkya declares, "If a person molested by others in a way which contravenes the Smriti or established usage, complains to the King, that gives rise to a topic for a judicial proceeding,"' and this implies three characteristic elements, namely, (1) transgression of law as laid down in the Smriti or established by usage, (2) injury to some one other than the transgression, and (3) intervention of the King in his judicial capacity.

Dr. P.N. Sen is of the view that if these elements are duly considered, the Hindu conception of positive law would not seem to be very different from the modern or Austinian conception thereof, commands issuing from the King, and the duty of enforcing the same is a self-imposed duty, while according to the former view, the law is issued from a source superior to the King, and the duty of enforcing the same is cast upon him from above, so that the infliction of punishment is itself regarded as a Dharma as indicated in the well-known text of Manu "penalty keeps the people under control, penalty protects them, penalty remains awake when people are asleep, so the wise have recognised punishment itself as a form of Dharma."

It is repeatedly said that the main function of Oriental Empires was the collection of taxes. In the first place, it stresses "law was added because of transgression in the second place it shows that the intervention of the King is called for because, these transgressions cause injury to people other than the transgressors; and in the third place, it indicates that whether the transgression be of some rule of action laid down in the Smritis or of some established usage, in either case it is the intervention of the King, who is the protector of the people and dispenser of justice, that converts religion or customary law into positive law.

The only aspects of difference between the Hindu stand-point and modern or Austinian view are that according to the latter view, law, in its normal form, consists of taxes and the levying of armies, and that they seldom concerned themselves with the enforcing of legal rules, but so far as India was concerned, such an idea reverses the true order of things. According to the Hindu conception, it was the protection of the people, and not the collection of taxes that was regarded as the principal duty of the King, and the administration of justice was one of the chief means to keep the people in order and to protect them in the proper enjoyment of their rights; of course the King had a right; to collect taxes, but the right involved a corresponding obligation to afford protection to those who paid them, and whoever failed to discharge the obligation while enjoying the advantages of the right was condemned. Thus, Manu declared "a king who without protecting his subjects collects revenue from them may be said to be the collector of all impurities, to which they are subject."

To the same effect is the following text of Yajnavalkya which laid down that"whatever sin the people commit being unprotected by the king, half of that goes to the king since he takes revenue from them."

It was, thus, one of the principal duties of the King to administer justice among his people, for administration of justice and maintenance of order go hand in hand and one cannot conceive the one without the other.

Hindu Law and the Muslim Law are the two most important personal laws in India. They have between them many points of similarities and dissimilarities. The important ones are mentioned below:

Origin

Originally, Hindu law was of divine origin. This law covered almost all important aspects of Hindu society such as marriage, divorce, adoption, maintenance, etc. At present, all these aspects are regulated through legislation.

Similarly, Muslim law is also said to be of divine origin. However, legislations such as Wakf Act, 1913; Shariat Act, 1937; and Dissolution of Muslim Marriages Act, 1939 have restored the Shariat law.

Custom

Hindu law recognises custom as source of law. Under the Hindu system of law, clear proof of usage will outweigh the written text of the law. The Hindu Marriage Act, 1955, and the Hindu Adoption and Maintenance Act, 1956 have clearly recognised the validity of customs in certain cases as is provided for in sections 5 and 7 of the Hindu Marriage Act and section 10 of the Hindu Adoption and Maintenance Act.

On the other hand, Muslim law does not recognise custom as a source of law. However, to some extent custom was recognised before 1937 but it has been displaced by the Muslim Personal Law (Shariat Application) Act, 1937.

MARRIAGE

(1) Nature

According to old or original Hindu law, marriage was strictly a sacrament till recently. However, it is showing some gradual change and its character has brought transformation in the nature of marriage.

However, nature of marriage under the Muslim law has been that of a contract which is also known as Ibadat and Muamala. Its character has not changed even in such progressive times.

(2) Conditions of marriage

Under Hindu Law, sections 5, 9, 11 and 12 of the Hindu Marriage

Act provide for the conditions of valid, void and voidable marriages respectively. Sections 5, 6 and 7 provide for the monogamy, free consent, majority in age, parties not to be within prohibited degrees or Sapindas of each other and customary ceremonies are the conditions of a valid marriage.

In Muslim law, distinction of Sahih, Fasid and Batil (in Hanifi law) or Sahih and Batil (in Shia law) marriages are clearly laid down. Effects of these marriages are different from each other. Illegitimate children have no right of inheritance and, therefore, contracting void marriages is discouraged.

(3) Number of wives

According to old Hindu law, generally only one wife could be had. But, in special circumstances, more than one wife was allowable. Under the Hindu Marriage Act, 1955, only monogamy has been provided for. In effect, legally, only one wife can be had at a time.

On the other hand, in Muslim law or Shariat law a Mohammedan may have four wives living at a time.

(4) Divorce

Under the original Hindu law, the marriage was eternal and permanent. Very rare circumstances allowed separation or divorce. The Hindu Marriage Act, 1955 provides for a judicial divorce on certain specific grounds. The law has, thus, made a provision for distressed or deserted spouse. However, since very idea of Hindu marriage is to make it a permanent tie, examining pragmatically, it is not easy to divorce either spouse so quickly.

So far as Muslim law is concerned, a unilateral power was given to the husband to give Talaq to his wife. This right is still in vogue. The wife was allowed to get herself released from the tie of marriage only with the consent of her husband. After 1939, a Muslim wife has been granted right by means of an enactment, to get the marriage dissolved. The law of Talaq provides for this facility. This enactment enables Muslim wives to get rid of their cruel husbands and the provision of Mehr keeps them maintained honourably.

(5) Maintenance of husband

According to Hindu Marriage Act, 1955, husband has also right to claim maintenance from his wife. By this provision, males and females have been kept on equal footing. A pragmatic approach needed such provision.

Under Muslim law, in no circumstances can a husband claim maintenance from his wife. It is only wife who can claim maintenance from her husband irrespective of the fact whether she has means of livelihood or not.

(6) Right to dower (Mehr)

Under original and enacted Hindu law, a wife is not entitled to receive dower or Mehr. Instead, the wife itself is a gift or Kanyadan from the hands of her parents to the hands of the husband.

Under Muslim law, Mehr or dower to the wife from the husband is a part of marriage or marriage contract. Even if, it has been agreed that no Mehr would be paid to the wife, still she is entitled to it and can claim through the court.

(7) Waiting for re-marriage

The original Hindu law did not provide for divorce or re-marriage and as such there was no need of a provision for waiting. Section 15 of the Hindu Marriage Act, 1955, as it provided, no re-marriage could take place unless a period of one year had elapsed from the date of the decree in the court of first instance. Since this provision proved a hardship to the spouse, it was amended in 1976 and now either spouse could marry at any time soon after the decree of divorce.

Under Muslim law, the period of waiting, which is known as Iddat is incumbent and that too on the wife only. This period of waiting has been fixed at three months, or three courses or till delivery, or the longer period of three courses or delivery. However, observance of Iddat is not necessary if the marriage remained unconsummated.

(8) Individuality of wife

The individuality of a Hindu wife is treated on the basis of old, patriarchal society. The status, school, caste or property of a Hindu wife merges into that of her husband. A Shukla girl married to a Misra husband becomes Mrs. Misra after marriage.

It is said that the Muslim wife retains her pre-marriage status, school and caste or property. Her personality does not merge with that of her husband.

(9) Custody of children

Section 6 of the Hindu Marriage and Guardianship Act, 1956 provides for as to who are the natural guardians. They are

(a) In the case of a boy or an unmarried girl, the guardian is father and after him, the mother excepting that the custody of a minor, below the age of five years, shall ordinarily be with the mother.

According to Muslim law, an infant child remains under the custody of the mother. Mother's this right of custody is known as Hizanat. In Hanafi law, the male child until the age of 7 years and female child until puberty remains under her mother's custody. In Isna Ashari law, the mother has a right to custody for up to the age of two years in the case of male and up to the age of seven years in the case of female. It has repeatedly been stated that the mother of the child is the best custodian of all during marriage as well as after separation. It is the mother who is best custodian of her child unless the mother be wicked or unworthy of trust.

(b) In the case of an illegitimate boy or illegitimate unmarried girl, the mother and after her, the father is the custodian according to Hindu law. In the case of a married girl, of course, the custodian is her husband.

The Muslim law on these points is almost the same as Hindu law.

(10) Adoption

Under the original Hindu law, a Hindu husband and in certain circumstances, his widow could adopt a son who has all the rights of a natural son. Under the Hindu Adoption and Maintenance Act, a male as also a woman, whether married, widower, divorcee or unmarried can now adopt not only a boy but also a girl.

So far as Mohammedan law is concerned, Quran specifically prohibits it. According to Quran, child means only a child by birth. Although the prophet himself had an adopted son by the name of Zeyd, the Ulemas have interpreted the Holy Quran to have prohibited the practice of adoption. But, in general no other form of son-ship is recognised and valid. Instead, Islam recognises the rule of paternity. In the following circumstances, paternity of a child may be acknowledged by the father—

(1) where the paternity of a child is not known;

(2) where it is not proved that the claimant is the offspring of Zina; and

(3) where the circumstances are such as do not rebut the presumption of paternity.

However, since the legal status of adopted child is not recognised in Muslim law, he faces an uncertain future. Such an interpretation combined with the practice of polygamy and unilateral divorce by the husband puts the childless wife in a disadvantageous position. Although the Union Government is duty bound to frame a uniform personal law as laid down in the Directive Principles of State Policy, yet it has been discriminating and only Hindu Personal laws are being cared for and not Muslim Law at all.

(11) Pre-emption

Hindu law does not specifically recognize the rules of pre-emption excepting for the dwelling house under the Hindu Succession act. Section

23 of this Act provides that the right of a female heir for the partition of her share does not arise unless male heirs choose to divide their respective shares; but they shall have only the right to reside therein.

Muslim law recognises right to prior purchase of immovable property in substitution of the buyer available to co-sharers or neighbours on such terms as those on which immovable property has been sold to the buyer, its aim being to prevent the induction of a stranger, likely to cause both inconvenience and vexation.

(12) Succession

(a) Under the original Hindu law, two kinds of rules of inheritance, recognised in each of the Mitakshara and of Dayabhaga Schools were in vogue. The rule, in the Mitakshara school is that law of survivorship, up to 3 generations in the male line, in respect of ancestral property and another rule of inheritance, that on the death of an owner; his self-acquired property passes on to his heirs, are recognised. One rule of inheritance, that only on the death of an owner his property passes on to his heirs, is known in Dayabhaga law. The Hindu Succession Act has not improved the position and it has tried to include rules of inheritance of both Mitakshara and Dayabhaga Schools.

In Muslim law, Law of Survivorship is not recognised. The only rule of inheritance is that so long as the owner survives, no one else can have any interest in his property. The property passes on to his heirs only on the death. The rules of inheritance for ancestral and self-acquired properties are one and the same. Thus, there is no difference between movable and immovable property.

(b) In Hindu law, there is a difference between ancestral and self-acquired property on the one hand and between immovable and movable property on the other for the purposes of inheritance in Muslim law, however, there is no such distinction.

(c) Hindu law did not grant to the females full right to inherit immovable property. She could have a woman's estate which is a right to enjoy and maintain but does not give right to transfer. The Hindu Succession Act has given females full ownership of the property which she had in possession at the time of enforcement of the Act.

Muslim treats males and females equal in this respect. Wife, daughter, sister, etc. have been placed in the first category of heirs, i.e. Quranic heirs. Females get full ownership of what they inherit.

(d) Hindu law recognises right of males up to three generations known as birth right or right of survivorship in ancestral property. Thus, a son or son's son can claim partition even during father's or grand-father's lifetime.

On the other hand, Muslim law does not recognise any birth right. There is a peculiar type of right wherein the right of inheritance arises only on the death of a certain person.

(e) The principle of representation is recognised in Hindu law. According to this, the son's children would get the same share, as a branch which their father would have obtained.

Muslim Hanafi law does not recognise any rule of representation. But Shia law, recognises it in a limited extent. By representation is meant the procedure by which one person is said to represent the share recoverable by him, through another person who himself was an owner. If a person dies, a son A and the son of a predeceased son B, A entirely excludes B. The Sunni and Shia schools are unanimous on this point. But when P dies leading three grand sons A by a predeceased son, and B and C by another predeceased son, all these A, B and C are heirs by representation as shown below :

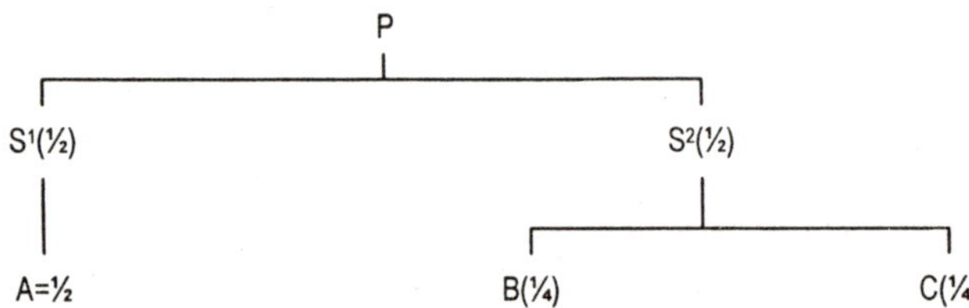

Shia law allows one-half to A and one quarter each to B and C. Shia law allows one-third to each grandson.

(f) Hindu law recognises Stridhan. Stridhan is a property movable or immovable that is given to a Hindu wife during, before or after marriage as gift by parents, husband's parents, relations or friends. A Hindu wife has full ownership over her Stridhan. The rules of inheritance of Stridhan differs according to the source from which it was received.

The concept of Stridhan is not recognised in Muslim law. Every property whether received in inheritance or as marriage gift is the property of a Muslim wife. There is no separate law or rule for the property and rule of inheritance is one.

COMPARISON AND CONTRAST BETWEEN EAST AND THE WEST

The salient features of Eastern concept of law in nutshell have been described in the Rig-Veda as under:

The ancient Indian jurisprudence was permeated by the central conception of Dharma, which bound subject as well as a sovereign. Manu, the great law-giver, lays down that only a being who is honest and true to his coronation-oath and follows the Sastras and rules with colleagues could wield the "dand", not one who is despotic, greedy, stupid and who rules personally.

In eastern jurisprudence, King was considered within the law. It means, he was also bound by the rules of law as it was supreme. Religion, i.e., the Dharma was the prime source of law. In Western jurisprudence, King was thought to be above the law. Law was what King commanded. He was not bound by any norm of law. He was main source of law. In this context, it may be observed that the maxims, 'Kini is the fountain of justice' and 'King can do no wrong' attribute to the divine origin of the King. This ultimately establishes that the dictates of King were tinged with divinity.

Western jurisprudence is based on the concept of rights and hence it enforces them. On the other hand, Eastern jurisprudence is duty-oriented and as such it talks of enforcing the duties. In other words, it is based on Dharma which denotes the Kartavya or duty. Hindu ideas, which are representatives of Eastern philosophy in this regard lay down that "Dharma or sacred law contains its authority within itself, the King is not superior to it but like other human beings he is subject to it." Dr. Priya Nath Sen, after a deep study of the sources of Hindu law has laid down that "the law is supreme, the will of the King is not its originator and its sanction is not derived from any extrinsic or accidental agency for it contains its sanction within itself in the certainty that obedience to law will lead to welfare and its violation to misery. A facile conclusion may be drawn that these laws represent commands issued from God but the Mimansakars maintained that every action had an invisible force designated as Apurva was a relation, super induced not before possessed."

Unlike other laws and particularly eastern laws, Hindu law consists of positive law intermixed with ceremonial rules, moral and religious injunctions. The position of the law that is enforced by the King may be called positive law. As Yajnavalkya declares, "if a person molested by others in a way which contravenes the Smriti or established usage complains to the king, that gives rise to a topic for judicial proceedings."

The part of Hindu law which was positive, had thus, three characteristic elements, i.e., (1) transgression of law as laid down in the Smritis or established usage, (2) injury to some one other than the transgression, and (3) intervention of the King in its judicial capacity, as the King was protector of the people and dispenser of justice and his intervention converted religious or customary law into positive law. The duty of enforcing law is cast upon the King from above so that the implication of punishment is regarded as Dharma as indicated in the well known text of Manu, "Penalty keeps the people under control, penalty protects them, penalty remains awake when people are asleep, so the wise have recognised punishment itself as a form of Dharma."

Hindu law was not the command of any earthly sovereign nor it was established by any political authority. At one time, it was considered to be of divine origin. The divine theory attributed everything to God or religion. In ancient time, the Hindu law was made by sages and philosophers as is made today by legislators. The sages were regarded as semi-divine beings due to their philosophical thoughts and farsightedness. They gave Hindu law which is enshrined in the Dharmasutras, the Dharmshastras, the Arthshastra of Kautilya, etc. Every one including the King was not empowered to make any law but he was responsible to execute it and decide disputes according to it norms. The King's verdict was considered to be a judicial decision of the highest tribunal.

The real difference between Hindu law and the Western conception of positive law is found in the composition of Hindu society, which was governed by the Hindu religion. Hindu law was the result of social organisation while positive law is the outcome of political organisation. The sages not only made the laws but also amended and repealed them according to exigencies of the situations. Such laws were comprehensive and rational. In ancient Hindu society, every person lived for the welfare and improvement of society. This idea is revealed in the scriptures of Hindus. The welfare conception of society was appreciated in the western world only in the beginning of the twentieth century.

This teaching of Hindu society was self-sacrifice for others. This is called as the spiritual achievement of Hindu culture and Hindu Society. The Lord Buddha, King Asoka and Mahatma Gandhi were the embodiment of this culture. The King Asoka conceived and administered a welfare State even several centuries before the birth of Christ. The doctrine of rule of law was recognised in ancient India from the very beginning. It was not a gift of the British rule in India. The Kings and the judges were treated alike. Every one was equal in the eye of law and all were subject to the 'rule of law', even in ancient and medieval India. If a theft was not detected or the stolen property was not recovered, the King had to compensate the aggrieved party out of his own treasury.

It would be seen from the foregoing facts that the Hindu law happens to be the most ancient, comprehensive and highly developed system of law. A close perusal of various legal provisions and the way in which they were put in various Dharmsutras and Dharmshastras, it can be categorically said that the Hindu jurists of the earliest epoch also developed a quite rich legal system to be comparable with any other known system of law as of Rome, Babylonia, Egypt or Greece. According to the provisions included in XII Tables (III-6), of Rome, there were retaliation and extreme form of Patria potestas even to kill sons. There was the most cruel form of law also according to which a debtor could be killed and his flesh distributed amongst creditors without any regard of ratio or pro rata distribution.

The code of Hammurabi illustrates that the capital punishment could be given for trifling offences like theft. Extreme form of Lex Talionis was in existence in Babylonian. "Thus if a builder builds a house for any one and does not build it solid and the house which falls down and kills the owner, one should put that builder to death. If it kills the son of the owner of the house, one shall put the son of the builder to death." Similar other such illustrations are also available there.

The Hebrew law also provided the death penalty not on the innocent boy of the perpetration but direct on guilty person. According to this system "the father shall not be put to death for the children neither shall the children be put to death for the father. Every man shall be put to death for his own sin." The laws of Grotyu (Translated by H.J. Roby) discovered in Greece, provide formulae primarily for slavery, though there are references which pertain to partition, adoption and suretyship also.

According to Hindu law, the creditor, instead of indulging in killing the debtor and taking his flesh, would remain contended in taking recourse to the process of "Dharma", which was a moral pressure put on the debtor to compel him to repay the debt lest some serious calamity might befall him. This was in accordance with the ethical and philosophical background as supplied for Hindu law.

Reference may be made to so many points of law wherein the ancient Hindu Jurists clearly surpassed others. Only one example would illustrate the point. The Hindu jurists clearly set certain rules for practical guidance for discriminating truthful and false witnesses, "An untruthful witness constantly shifts his position, licks the corner of his lips, his forehead sweats, his countenance changes colour, his mouth dries up, he flatters in his speech and very often contradicts himself, he does not look up and is slow in returning answers and contorts his lip, such a person, who exhibits an unnatural aspect either in mind, body or action is esteemed false, whether putting forward a claim on his own account or giving evidence in another's cause. Reliable witnesses generally possess the following qualities:

> "They are religious, generous, of respectable family addicted to veracity, lovers of virtue, candid, having off-spring, wealthy, conformers to traditional and written law."

It is, sometimes, alleged that in Hindu law, the practice of ordeals was there for deciding cases. But, with the practice, several healthy checks, were also there for the application of ordeals, e.g. (1) ordeals were to be avoided if human witnesses were available. "In litigation, documents should be sought first, in absence of documents, witnesses; in absence of witnesses, recourse may be taken to ordeals—this is the injunction of the wise-men." (2) Ordeals could be applied when both the parties were agreeable and when the plaintiff declared himself ready to accept to punishment in case of his defeat. (3) In practice, it was a sort of religious appeal hence it could not be applicable to those parties which were unbelievers, irreligious, Vratyas and great criminals.

If the salient features of the ordeals are closely examined, it would be clear that in many cases, the doctrine of presumption of innocence in favour of the accused will be evident. However, in many cases, there would not be any certainty about the result and the element of chance or probability is always there. There is no mention of ordeals in the Dharmsutras. Manu is said to have mentioned only two ordeals. Ordeals were not peculiar to the Hindu law alone. Trials by ordeals were found in England also and they remained in practice there as late as 1819. In England, ordeals were abolished by an Act of Parliament. As to nature and occasion for the application of ordeals in the trial of cases, Maitland is of the law:

> "If two of litigants, the one contradicts the other flatly of the plain 'you did' of the one is met by the straight-forward 'you lie' of the other; here is a problem which man cannot solve."

A remarkable point of difference between east and west is to be noted with respect to sets of courts. In Rome and England the sets of parallel courts of law and equity had to be resorted to while no such difference was necessary for the genius of the Hindu jurists. It is also notable that like Rome, where there were two classes of people, i.e., Patricino and the Plebians, India also had two categories of people, i.e., Aryans and non-Aryans. In Hindu law, courts as well as administrators applied both, i.e., what was strict law along with what was regarded as equity. It would be seen that the ancient Hindu law was quite progressive in as much as it could suitably accommodate the needs of the hour, keeping in view the growth and progress of the society. Thus, Hindu jurisprudence was flexible and inflexible both and that way it was superior to western jurisprudence.

Ownership and Property in Eastern and Western Jurisprudence

The views of Hindu jurists and western jurists on the conceptions of 'ownership and property' are almost similar. Austin pointed out that "in the Institutes of Gains and Justinian, the right of property of dominion is not defined at all. Things are described, the modes of acquiring property in them are described; servitudes are described; but of the right of property or dominion no direct description is given", and he himself defines the. term property or dominion as being "applicable to any right which gives to the entitled party an indefinite power or liberty of using or dealing with the subject." Similarly, Dr. Holland defines ownership as "a plenary control over an object" but at the same time he points out that according to the maxim "Sic utere tuo ut alienum non loedas" it must be enjoyed in such a way as not to interfere with the rights of others. These definitions clearly point out the approach of the view of Hindu jurists. It would be seen that the resemblance is not confined only to the definitions, but also covers the limitation indicated above. This limitation can also be reduced to the control exercised by the King and by the Sastric injunctions, which are recognised by the Hindu jurists.

The general notion is that a particular thing is the property of a particular man. What does it mean, it has to be made clear. In his commentary on Dayabhaga, Srikrishna Tarkalaukara described that according to the old and established meaning, it signifies fitness for the free disposal and provided for by the Sastra. If an analysis is made to the above saying it would be found that it contains two elements, i.e., (1) the idea of property is solely indicated by the Sastra; and (2) it signifies fitness for the disposal by the person who owns it. However, according to some Hindu jurists, the idea of property is indicated by Sastras and ownership may only be acquired in one of the different modes as recognised by them.

It is also essential to discuss the position of hidden treasure or property the owner of which is not known. The law relating to this, i.e., of treasure-trove has been stated thus, "If the king discovers the treasure-trove, then he will take half and distribute the other half among Brahmans. If a learned Brahman finds it, then he may keep the whole himself; in other cases the king will give one-sixth to the finder, and take the rest himself, but if the finder does not bring the fact to the notice of the king, then he will, on coming to know of it, extract the whole and also punish the finder." However, on the authority of Manu, Mitakshara added that even in such a case if the real owner comes forward and establishes his title, the King will restore the treasure to him after retaining one-sixth or one-twelfth for himself, or, according to Nilkantha one-fourth for himself and one-twelfth for the finder.

It is interesting to compare these rules with Roman and English law on the subject. According to Roman law, if the owner of the land finds any treasure hidden in his land, he could keep the whole of it himself, but if another person found it, the finder and the owner of the land divided it equally. According to English law, neither the finder nor the owner of the land had any interest in it, but it belonged entirely to the crown, and it was an offence not to give notice of its discovery.

Criticism

There is a distinction between treasure-trove and articles lost by the owner and found by stranger. In the former case, all hope of tracing the owner is lost, while in the latter case, the position is different. Therefore, in the case of lost articles found by a stranger, the Hindu law directs that the King must detain them in safe custody for sometime waiting for the owner to claim them. If, however, nobody turns up within that time for claiming these articles, the King may appropriate them for himself after making over one-fourth to the finder. It would be seen that the rules of the Hindu law as stated above are more equitable and just as compared to any such rules available in Western legal system.

Sales

According to the provisions in the Roman law, a sale is not complete and the property does not pass from the seller to the buyer until the buyer has paid the price to the seller or in some way, has satisfied him. However, if the seller accepts the credit of the buyer, the property becomes immediately the property of the buyer. In this way, the Roman law recognises a contract of sale also which is distinguished from a completed sale. The Roman law lays down that a contract comes into existence as soon as the price of sale is agreed upon. But, the title is not transferred until the payment of the price. As a corollary to this agreement, all the risks in respect of the thing contracted to be disposed of all sale, falls upon the purchaser. Thus, the purchaser becomes entitled to all the advantages which may accrue and are attached to the thing though the thing has not been delivered to him.

Prescription

The rules of prescription under the Roman law are similar to those under the Hindu law. However, a few points of difference between them are also there. In the first place, the period laid down for the operation of prescription in the case of movables was shorter under the Roman Law than the Hindu Law. In the second place, the Hindu law does not seem to have allowed the rule of prescription to be operated against any absent owner who had no knowledge of the adverse possession. In the third place, when the possession had no *bona-fide* beginning, a still longer period, viz., thirty years, seems to have been required under the Roman law, to ripen the prescription which went under the name of prescript longisi imi temporis, a provision with which the rule of the Hindu law may be compared and when the adverse possession was not free from verbal protest, a period of three years was essential to put a stop to future disturbance of that possession. To sum up, both the systems reflected accidental resemblances of a striking nature, and where they differ, it cannot be said that the Hindu law suffers from the comparison.

PERSONAL LAWS

Family Relations—Marriage

In ancient Hindu law, no divorce was allowed because marriage was considered to be one of the essential sacraments of the whole span of life. Similarly, it was also enjoined upon the wife to remain faithful to her husband so that there would not arise any cause or excuse for the husband to divorce his wife. At the same time, abandonment of guiltless wife was punishable. In the event of any woman becoming widow, several sacred duties were cast upon her which she was bound to do towards her neighbours, society and especially towards her other family members. Widows were not at all allowed to re-marry irrespective of their age and economic condition of the family.

Manu laid down that one may take a second wife at once if the first wife be guilty of using towards him unpleasant words. However, the husband has certain essential duties to perform, if he marries second wife during the life time of the first one. First and foremost of such duties is that the husband had to pay to the first wife as much as he spends on the second marriage. Thus, the Hindu law did sanction polygamy, it took care to see that it is attended with as little violence to the feelings of first wife as possible. The first wife had to be given some pecuniary benefits on such an occasion.

It was a little anomalous that a man should be permitted to have more than one wife while a woman should be made to remain stick to her husband even after his death. It only shows that the persons who ruled over the Hindu law turned it to their advantages.

Under the Hindu law, a wife is considered to be capable of and allowed to hold property. This property was characterised as Stridhan or women's property.

PUNISHMENT

Sir Henry Maine observed The penal law of ancient communities is not the law of crimes, it is the law of wrongs, or to use the English technical word, of torts. The person injured proceeds against the wrong-doer by an ordinary civil action, and recovers compensation of the shape of money-damages if he succeeds.

In the Hindu law, punishment of crimes occupied a more prominent place, their compensation for wrongs, and the mere payment of compensation to the individual injured, when the injury inflicted was at all serious in its character, was seldom regarded as sufficient to meet the ends of justice.

According to Manu, "A king who punishes those who do not deserve to be condemned and fails to punish those who deserve punishment becomes infamous and is ultimately doomed to hell.

DIFFERENCE OF CASTE AS A DETERMINING FACTOR IN INFLICTING PUNISHMENT

It may be observed that:

(1) In the point of comprehensiveness, the Hindu law in its various branches occupies a fairly high place among the systems of ancient jurisprudence, its conception of legal liability is broad and clearly expressed, though, it has retained the eighteen divisions of the topics of litigation as described by Manu, that has not, in any way, stinted its growth or prevented it from embracing within its bounds the various aspects of judicial relations which the complexity of human affairs may usually bring about.

(2) The administration of justice, according to the Hindu law was actuated by a high sense of duty. and it is impossible to deny

that our law-givers have not taken care to see that the rules laid down by them may not be unreasonable as well as detrimental to the interests of the community. Law stands for the benefit of the people and is a manifestation of the eternal reason which rules the universe. The king cannot afford to over-ride it, the judges cannot dispute its authority and the people have to obey it. It is so not merely because it has the support of temporal authority but because it draws its inspiration from the formation of supreme wisdom.

WILLS

Originally, wills had only very limited scope. The reason for the introduction of wills has varied in different countries. The Athenians, when first allowed to make a will, had to inherit their direct male descendent. The will in Bengal was only operative and allowed to be governed if it was consistent with certain overriding family claims. The Jews were allowed to make will if all the kindered under the Mosaic law were undiscoverable.

In Rome, the will had originally to be made in a popular assembly and it was allowed only when no kindered were discoverable. By and by a dislike of intestacy grew up owing to the unfairness of the Roman law of intestate succession, wherein a child emancipated as a token of favour would be debarred from participation in the property of his father as the even of father's death intestate since the oldest Roman rules of succession were based on the relationship resulting from potestas, not on blood relationship.

However, in English law testamentary succession which was first allowed in respect of movables only was introduced and encouraged by the church on the principle that a party should provide for the poor, through the medium of the church, after his death.

DISTINCTION BETWEEN ROMAN JURISPRUDENCE AND ISLAMIC JURISPRUDENCE

Islamic law is divinely ordained system, the will of God to be established on earth. As God is the perfect being, so is his law perfect and for all time. As the command of God, who is the sovereign of all-Islamic law if positive, i.e., stable, and with justice as its supreme and it is ideal, hence it may be aptly described, in modern terms as 'Positive law in ideal form'. Thus, it is the only law, perfect and pure, universal for all time.

The Islamic Jurisprudence is primarily concerned with the knowledge of the roots of law as distinct from substantive law (knowledge of the branches of law). Islamic Jurisprudence has a special value, because it attaches an ethical value to acts and thoughts. It is the theological foundation of Islamic belief in God, one and indivisible and in the prophethood of Muhammad.

Islam is a perfectly simple religion. The most important feature of this religion is belief in one God and belief in Muhammad as his apostle. The Quran is a sort of spiritual guide which contains counsels and puts forward ideals to be followed by the faithful rather than a corpus juris civilis to be occupied for all times. It was not the intention of prophet and he enlightened Muslim, believes that it was to lay down immutable rules or to set-up a system which was to be binding upon humanity apart from considerations of time and place and the growing necessities arising out of changed conditions. The prophet always asserted that he was a man of like passions with others excepting that he was entrusted with a revelation of truth for the purposes of order, of security and preservation and the maintenance of the new society created by Islam. He laid down rules regulating marriage, inheritance and so forth, but these rules were mostly of a very elementary character and were intended to meet the existing condition of things. The position of Muhammad, indeed, was that of a spiritual teacher, a prophet and not that of a legislature."

The basic differences between Roman law and Islamic law are:

(1) Women under Roman law were under perpetual tutelage. They were not empowered throughout their life to deal with their property without permission of their guardians. The Shari'at, on the other hand, recognizes in principle the complete capacity of women to perform all kinds of lawful transactions.

(2) In Roman law the dowry was a payment to the husband by his wife or one of her family members while in Muslim law the payment is to the wife by the husband.

(3) Adoption was an accepted institution in Roman law while it was not recognised in the Shari'at.

(4) Complication and formalities were quite visible and apparent in Roman contracts and in the Roman rules of procedure, whole the contrary is the case in the Shari'at. In the later, it is a maxim that effect is given to intention and meaning and not to words and forms.

(5) In Roman law, the transfer of debt was illegal whereas in Islamic law it is sanctioned by all schools of jurisprudence without exception.

(6) There are clear differences between the two systems in questions of inheritance and will. In the Shari'at, according to Sunni view, for example, a bequest in a will to an heir is unlawful, while in Roman law, wills were originally instituted for the purpose of appointing the heirs.

(7) The rules of pre-emption and family waqf (endowment) have no similarity in Roman law.

A legal system is described as an integrated body of rules determined by an inner coherence of meaning. Every legal system is of a purposeful enterprise. At the same time, law without justice and morality is no law and cannot survive for a long time. A legal system that does not have a substantial anchorage injustice and morality will be ultimately thrown off. Keeping in view these principles, Islamic law is a code of moral conduct quite different from the case law system where precedent is given full respect and followed by the courts.

RELATIVE POSITION OF CONTINENTAL JURISPRUDENCE AND ANGLO-AMERICAN JURISPRUDENCE

Maine once predicted that Roman law would become the *Lingua Franca* of Universal Jurisprudence and that has proved true.

In 1815, Jefferson denounced the common law doctrine of supremacy of law; when applied by courts in holding legislative acts unconstitutional as a theft of jurisdiction, the era of the uncontested supremacy of the common law appears to be now passing away.

Three characteristic doctrines set off the common law system from all other laws namely, (1) the supremacy of law (2) case law and precedent, and (3) contentious procedure. No person and no act is beyond the law. The supremacy of law is the Germanic doctrine that the State is bound to act by law. Bracton said that the King is "under God and the law" and is as old as our legal system. Our doctrine of precedent is as old as legal system itself. The first precedents were writs and Glanvill's book is a collection of such writs. Bracton relied upon the judgment rolls and his Note Book is quite like a Report contentious procedure is Germanic and characterises English law from before the conquest. But all these three doctrines resolve themselves to a fundamental proposition that law exists for individuals. Its cardinal principle is that law is reason and reason is law. The residuary power of the crown for doing justice among his subjects had been able to serve two crises in legal history when the old polity of local courts become impossible, it gave us the King's courts and the common law when the common law was in danger of fossilizing, the equity was substituted in its place.

Continental jurisprudence is primarily based on codified law as the doctrine of stare decisis is not in operation there. On the other hand, the Anglo-American Jurisprudence is built upon judicial decisions. As a result of this, the major portion of the later system owes its origin to the judicial precedent. For the sake of more clarity we give here the principal aspects of difference between codified and case law systems. In other words, both the systems may be viewed in comparative perspective as follows:

(1) Continental jurisprudence has been decisively influenced by the reception of Roman law; but the Anglo-American law is not so.

Instead, it is the product of gradual historical growth and, therefore, still shows considerable elements of feudalism.

(2) All continental systems are essentially codified; whereas the Anglo-American law is still based on the common law.

(3) From this follows altogether a different approach problems of legal interpretation. Judicial decisions in continental systems are not primary sources of law, but only a gloss on the law. On the other hand in Anglo-American Law, precedent is one of the principal sources of law.

(4) It is an aspect of the contrast of inductive and deductive approach that continental systems, proceeding from general rules to individual decisions, establish general legal principles, whereas Anglo-American system centres round a decision of individual problem and builds up principle from case to case. Such principles as these are, have been developed from a gradual adjustment to practical requirements.

(5) As a corollary to this difference in legal development, Anglo-American legal thinking gives a predominant place to the law courts, while continental jurisprudence thinks of law not only in terms of litigation but also in terms of its general function.

(6) The duality of common law and equity in Anglo-American law is not known in continental systems wherein equity is a principle of interpretation applied to any legal question, but not a special body of law.

(7) All continental systems make difference between private law and administrative law. The former deals with the legal relations between subjects as equals and the latter deals with legal relations between authority of all types and the subject. Anglo-American law has rejected this division and has adhered to the principle of equality of all before the law.

(8) The more abstract and general approach to law of continental jurisprudence has been conducive to the development of legal philosophy, while the pragmatic and empiricist feature of Anglo-American law has had the opposite effect. Therefore, the pre-eminence in Anglo-American law of the analytical school of jurisprudence compared with the infinite variety of continental legal theories.

Decided cases may have some authority but not the sole authority as that of a precedent in the common law system. In contrast to both these systems, decided cases have no authority in Islamic legal system, because the judge in either case is bound to exercise his power of ijtihad or interpretation. In Islamic law, there is no judge-made law.

13

CRITICAL LEGAL STUDIES

A The Critical Legal Studies (CLS) Movement began with a conference held in the US in 1977 as a result of a circular to faculties in US law schools. The initiative came from a group of jurists including Avel, Horwitz, Kennedy, Trubek, Tushnet and Unger, who dissatisfied with the law and Society Association which they thought had become identified with empiricism and behaviourism. The invitation to attend the Conference mentioned only a very vague idea; a gathering a people pursuing critical approaches to the study of law and society. The circular indicated that several of the writers of the circular were trying to develop approaches emphasising the ideological character of legal doctrine and its internal structures. Thus, the critical legal studies movement burst on the scene in the United States in the late 1970s with a series of conferences whereas in Britain the Critical Legal Conference was formed in 1984. The CLS Movement is more a ferment than a movement with those who identify as 'crits' a diverse group perhaps united only by their commitment to a more egalitarian society.

WHAT IS CLS?

"Critical Legal Studies is a broad label encompassing a variety of subversive enterprises to what its members view as the mainstream traditions of scholarship in jurisprudence. CLS is a post-positivist enterprise involving: (i) a critique of the 'objective' scientific method which is seen to underlie traditional scholarship with the claim that 'interpretative understanding must replace positivism', (ii) a change in the way law is viewed. Traditional legal scholarship is viewed as desperately making sense of the world, of holding out law as a coherent and rational body of rules and principles, and the aim of mainstream legal scholarship is to reconstruct rationally particular legal decisions to show how they fit, or do not fit, the proper and rational development of 'law'. Conversely, CLS uses a range of techniques to bring out underlying fissures, contradictions and tensions. Where traditional scholarship divorces the study of law from the study of society and finds the engine for legal development in the guidance of rules, principles and discretions, CLS tells us of the inescapably political nature of life. Deeply embedded in the CLS movement are the motifs of suspicion and scepticism towards any claim for the purity of law; instead we must investigate how law as a field of action maintains its hold over us and contributes to sustaining the legitimacy of the system."

Difference Between 'Realism' and the CLS Movement

The CLS Movement is often compared with the realism. Some classify CLS as radical scepticism and portray it as a development out of American legal realism. But there are many differences between these two schools—

(1) The American legal realists were sceptical of the traditional (positivist) image of law in modern western societies, of legal scholarship's formalism and supposed conservatism. Realists were not sceptical of the outside or external knowledges they thought ought to complement traditional legal scholarship and influence legal department. The CLS Movement is sceptical of orthodoxy. It builds upon insights from social and critical philosophy, literary theory and elsewhere. It draws on the radical political culture of the 1960s generation. It asserts the inescapability of commitment and rejects the aspirations of the preceding intellectual climate's search for value neutrality.

(2) In one sense CLS Movement is a continuation of the Realists' Project, but its objectives are very much wider. The Realists were firmly within the camp of liberalism. The CLS Movement is more radical an attempt to escape the 'crippling choice' between liberalism and Marxism.

(3) Like the Realists CLS rejects formatism, but the Realists saw legal reasoning as autonomous or distinct and CLS Scholars certainly reject the enterprise of presenting a value-free model of law.

(4) A major difference between critical and orthodox (including Realist) legal thought is then that, though the latter rejects formalism, it maintains the existence of a viable distinction between legal reasoning and political debate. Critical legal thought does not countenance the distinction. Critical legal thinkers believe there is no distinctive mode of legal reasoning. Law is politics. Law does not have an existence outside of ideological battles within society.

GROUND FOR CLS MOVEMENT

Robert Gordon in his 'Mood of Disillusionment' (1982) described the legal studies that many academic and students felt in the late 60s, the 70s and the 80s and which provided ground for the CLS movement to flourish. Gordon notes the dissatisfaction with approaches to teaching and studying law and legal practice which emphasised:

(i) The traditional or formalist picture of legal development which the American legal realists had argued against since, the 1920s. American legal realists argued that the notion of legally-led development ought to be replaced with a model of development led by understanding socially desirable consequences.

(ii) The view of lawyers playing their part in a policy science, i.e. law and operating with a social reform attitude to social change presupposed a disinterested, intelligent, governing elite that the lawyer could advise on legislation and policy. As a result, socially interested lecturers and students experienced.

(iii) The absence of real human concerns from the discussions in law schools. Duncan Kennedy in his 'Legal Education as Training in Hierarchy' says that students who join thinking the study of cutting issues of their times were provided with the material of tedious abstract legal concepts. The real life is filled with blood and guts, sex and vomit, hope and depression, oppression and profit—all outside the materials discussed in law schools.

(iv) When progressive students went out to practice they hoped to achieve real change but they soon realised that what looked like victories were often very ambiguous in their outcomes. Therefore, theoretical attention shifted to trying to understand how law served to legitimate the existing social order. One obvious target was legal theory.

(v) The professional concern of prospective lawyers demanded a jurisprudence which fitted them for the demands of professional legal practice. Traditional legal scholarship appeared to create an image of the present state of affairs and the legal system which buttressed and constituted the society as a functionally effective and progressive whole. CLS adherents cannot share this view.

ESSENTIAL TARGETS FOR CLS MOVEMENT

For CLS Movement, Liberalism is one target, so too is Marxism. All systems of thought that make the world seem unproblematic, that render some necessary connection between law and social formations are attacked. Most CLS writers assaulted on legal legislation which are based on the following assumptions—

(i) The assumption of law's neutrality. But for CLS the separation of law from politics is theoretically untrue and mystifies the populace.

(ii) The assumption that legal reasoning is somehow an unproblematic matter. However, CLS substitutes a criticism of the whole idea of a politically neutral 'legal logic'.

(iii) The assumption that laws are positive data of social life, i.e. that they have fixed objective meanings which can't really be challenged; that their validity and significance are settled by objective unchallengeable methods. By contrast CLS writers use a more post-modern form of writing which attempts to free legal analysis from the idea of neutral technicality and show that it is a political instrument.

(iv) The radical contingency and openness of modernity and hence the meaning of social progress.

Legal liberalism serves to preserve a *status quo* of social and economic inequalities. Liberal legal writings and decisions mask this inequality. Liberal legal philosophy talks of law in terms of underlining equality; especially equality before the law as in the notion of the rule of law. CLS movement demands the substitution of legal liberalism with a 'politics of transformation'. This outlook is dedicated to revealing the possibility of change in all forms of social relationships and institutional structures. CLS adopted the following theoretical outlook:

(i) An attack on all claims that there are some kinds of natural laws of history, uncontrollable by human beings. This is a rejection of the Marxist theory of historical materialism.

(ii) The idea that there are social forces or economic forces that control life in some irresistible or objective way is resisted. Rather social life is viewed as being continually created by peoples individual choices and decisions as they coexist.

(iii) A distrust of all theories, and ideas that make the social world seems natural and inevitable.

(iv) The rejection of the idea of moral absolutes.

The approach to law reflects the overall approach to the social. Gordon speaks of CLS generally placing an interpretative or antipositivist view of law in society. The law is one that people construct in order to deal with necessary relationships with other people. Thus, law is hegemonic. CLS adherents are very much concerned with law hegemony is constructed and maintained and in particular with the role that legal ideas have in doing this. CLS strive to deconstruct the abstract stability of legal concepts; legal concepts can only be seen in view of the relations of conflict and choice which underlay them. Law contributes massively to the hegemony of ideas. CLS claims that law is important ideologically.

To combat hegemony and rectification, the CLS movement aims;

(i) To displace the idea that the social world is an objectively knowable scene of natural foundations by the political reality of interpretation. The interpretative approach is intrinsically political. From this it follows that the social world is largely created by humans and therefore, can be changed by humans if they change their ways of perceiving of it. However, the process of political interpretation is often decidedly critical or undercutting, openly deconstructive and playfully trashing towards legal texts and mainstream jurisprudential writings.

(ii) To attack the hegemony of legal ideas. The legal world is not a neutral, inevitable framework of regulation, but a political arena.

(iii) To attack the hegemony of legal liberalism, particularly by showing the internal contradictions in legal ideas.

For CLS the law is a field of action, and how we reach decisions is a product of our 'legal consciousness' rather than our being determined by the material.

LIBERALISM'S CONTRADICTIONS AND CRITICAL LEGAL STUDIES

According to Mark Kelman, liberalism in the eyes of 'Crits' is "a system of thought that is simultaneously beset by internal contradiction and by systematic repression of the presence of these contradictions". In his 'A Guide to Critical Legal Studies', (1987) he says that there are three central contradictions in liberalism. (i) That between "a commitment to mechanically applicable rules as the appropriate form for resolving disputes and a commitment to situation-sensitive, *ad hoc* standards", (ii) "the contradiction between a commitment to the traditional liberal notion that values or desires are arbitrary, subjective, individual and individuating while facts or reason are objective and universal and a commitment to the ideal that we can know social and ethical truths objectively or to the hope that one can transcend to usual distinction between subjective and objective in seeking moral truth"; and (iii) "the contradiction between a commitment to an intentionalistic discourse, in which all human action is seen as the product of a self-determining individual will, and determinist discourse, in which the activity of nominal subjects merits neither respect nor condemnation because it is simply deemed the expected outcome of existing structures.

I. The Fundamental Contradiction Regarding Rules and Standards

Duncan Kennedy, in his article entitled "Form and Substance in Private Law Adjudication" (1976) presented a set of contradictions at the heart of liberalism. He says about rules and standards thus:

The extreme of formal realizability is a directive to an official that requires him to the presence together of each of a list of easily distinguishable factual aspects of a situation by intervening in a determinate way. . . . At the opposite pole from a formally realizable rule is a standard A standard refers directly to one of the substantive objectives of the legal order. Some examples are good faith, due care, unconscionability, unjust enrichment and reasonableness".

The rule is there to implement a substantive purpose, but it does not always succeed. The virtues and vices of standards are a mirror image of those of rules. The choice could therefore be said to come down to a question of which form most effectively carries out the substantive purpose. The liberal effort in law is to produce clear rules in all cases despite the contradiction of form and substance and between rule and principle.

For Kennedy the positions-pro-rules and pro-standards are "an invitation to choose between sets of values and visions of the universe". The formal arguments about the use of rules or standards is thus related to substantive ideals about the proper ordering of society. The jurisprudential position that favours rules is linked with one substantive ethical view (individualism); the jurisprudential view that favours standards with another (altruism). Individualism is considered as liberalism and the belief that all values are subjective; altruism with collectivism and the belief that justice consists of order directed to the achievement of shared ends. The modern era is an age of contradiction: though it is dominated by considerations of morality and policy, the conflict between individualism and altruism remains. The basic tension is that between community and autonomy. Certainly Kennedy's theme is that we need to re-emphasise the communal basis of freedom-liberty is a social rather than an individual matter. Rights discourse disguises the social conditions that need to be considered in defining areas of freedom and constraints in relations between people. For CLS rights divide people into individuals-rights downplay communitarian aspirations. They are the instruments of legal liberalism's mystification.

II. Liberalism's Contradictions—The Facts-Values Distinction, the Reason-Desire Separation

Kelman illustrates by reference to Roberto Unger's 'Knowledge and Politics' (1975). In a nutshell the problem is identified as liberalism's positivist method failing to meet its normative needs, the difficulties it confronts when applying empirical methodology to human desire." Since there is no objective good, only preference satisfaction has any claim; thus good social systems simply accurately aggregate private preferences. Utilitarians by claiming that we are morally bound to seek the maximisation of utility—we don't simply desire to do so. Exponents of CLS would contend, values are not merely matters of taste. Rather they can be considered as universal maxims to govern human relationships, practices and laws.

III. The Contradiction Between Free Will and Determination

Liberal discourse is said to privilege intentionalist discourse, just as it privileges a commitment to the Rule of Law, individualism and value subjectivity. Determinist discourse, by contrast, pictures conduct in backward-looking amoral terms, with conduct simply a last event in a chain of connected events so pre-determined as to merit neither respect nor-condemnation. Kelman shows the ways in which orthodox criminal law, premised on liberalism and therefore on free will, often uses determinist discourse.

RULES AND REASONING

One characteristic of CLS is its rejection of formalism. Formalism has tended to be the fall back position of liberal legal thinking when forced to confront the question: how can a legal system give the kinds of neutral decisions expected of it. Formalists circumvent this problem by insisting that the judge is imposing his values but merely interpreting the words of the law.

In the CLS view, formalism relies on a new kind of essentialism—the belief that there are essential meanings to words. But one theme in CLS writing is to connect adjudication to legislation and to ask the same question about the legitimacy of the exercise of state power in relation of judicial activity as has been asked for millennia about the operation of power by other state institutions. Legal decisions, on this view, are no more neutral than the decisions of a legislature or an executive. Political choices are equally involved.

For Peter Gabel, legal thought is part of a large practice of turning concepts or social roles into things, the practice of 'reifying'. Each person experiences himself as a thing-like function of 'the system'. In Gabel's view, legal reasoning is a system in which "one manipulates concepts that share exactly this rectified and apparently thing-like quality". So long as we know and remember this, it may not matter over-much. But once this knowledge is forgotten or glossed over the abstractions are taken on as beliefs about an objective reality. And at this point we can believe ourselves actually to be living in a world of rights-holders, legal subjects and formal equality. The reification of legal concepts becomes a way of legitimating the *status quo*. But Gabel's views are not subscribed to by many within the CLS movement. Gabel presents legal doctrine "as though it is both infinitely manipulable and firmly constrained by the reified metaphors of common sense and legal consciousness." The chief merit in Gabel's writing is in showing the power of reification in legal thought.

CRITICAL LEGAL STUDIES AND LEGAL PRACTICE

The protagonists of CLS have concerned themselves with the problems of legal practice. They believe that the lessons of critique can radicalise law practice. Thus Gabel and Harris argue that "the very public and political character of the legal arena gives lawyers, acting together with clients and fellow legal workers an important opportunity to reshape the way that people understand the existing social order and their place within it." Their objectives is "to show the way that the legal system works at many different levels to shape popular consciousness towards accepting the legitimacy of the *status quo*, and to outline the way that lawyers can effectively resist these efforts in building a movement for fundamental social change'.

Critical legal scholars are agreed about is that social change is not a matter of clever legal argument deployed by elite lawyers, but it is a process of democratic organisation and mobilisation in which law will play a necessary part. But the CLS subscribes neither to the liberal view that law can be a principal instrument of social change nor to the Marxist view. The CLS position is more complex, reflecting a recognition of the complexity of law itself.

LEGAL THEORY AND SOCIAL THEORY

One of the principal advances of CLS is to demonstrate the need to integrate legal theory within social theory. Critical legal theorists have attempted to introduce into discourse about law the insights and models of analysis of social theory. Roberto Unger, in his article entitled 'The Critical Legal Study Movement', offers what he calls, 'a structure of no-structure'. He describes his programme as 'super-liberalism', "the building of a social world less alien to a self that can always violate the generative rules of its own mental or social constructs and put other rules and other constructs in their place". This represents an effort to make 'social life' resemble what 'politics' is like in liberal democracies, 'a series of conflicts and deals among more or less transitory and fragmentary groups'. He is concerned to protect freedom better and, he sees a crucial role for law and legal thought. This has specific proposals a 'rotating capital fund' to finance projects and effect a 'decentralisation of production and exchange'. The legal counterpart to this is "the disaggregation of the consolidated property right". Unger accepts that some regime of rights is necessary. He, therefore, suggests the creation of four types of rights: (i) immunity rights which establish the 'nearly absolute claim of the individual to security against the state, other organisations and other individuals'; (ii) 'destabilization rights which entitle individuals to demand the disruption of established institutions and forms of social practice that have achieved the 'very sort of insulation and have contributed to the very kind of crystalized plan of social hierarchy and division that the entire constitution wants to avoid'; (iii) market rights which give a conditional and provisional claim to divisible portions of social capital; and (iv) solidarity rights which foster mutual reliance, loyalty and communal responsibility. Unger believes that a society so organised would be better than existing structures. His vision of the future is inevitably based on his understanding of present society.

CONCLUSION

To sum up, CLS contributed the following standard of theoretical achievements:

(i) CLS appears successful in pointing out of inefficiency of a crude positivist position.

(ii) Legal liberalism is depicted not in terms of a moral position, but as mystification.

(iii) While correctly pointing to the complexity of life and the social situations that law must intervene in and partly constitute, CLS overstates the indeterminacy of law and fails to understand that law's closure may be a legitimate pragmatic stance in the face of the complexity of life.

(iv) CLS is a loose label. There are so many projects going on that it is hard to specify core positions.

(v) CLS turns our attention to the hard side of late modernity. If liberalism sees law as a framework of regulations and rules embracing all citizens, CLS is concerned with how equal or unequal law actually is in its effects on different sections of society.

(vi) CLS argues against all forms of closure of the legal, political and social universes—it argues for a radical openness of law, politics, and social formations.

(vii) CLS is a commentary on the fate of 'reason' of thinking itself in modern society.

(viii) CLS offers an account of legal reasoning connected in political theory justifying the power of the state.

(ix) CLS throws light on legal consciousness and the relationship between this and political discourse and social life.

(x) CLS problematises legal education, offers new approaches to legal practice and questions the orthodoxies of legal history.

(xi) CLS situates legal theory within social theory and offers a vision of a different social life, of new forms of human association.

(xii) CLS broadens the scope of jurisprudence beyond the perennial debates, thought now by many to be sterile, between positivism and natural law.

Thus CLS movement has thus, shifted the goal-posts of jurisprudence and broaden the path way of law.

14

FEMINIST JURISPRUDENCE

MEANING OF FEMINISM

The concept 'Feminism' came to public attention in the eighteenth century, most notably in Mary Wollstone Craft's 'A Vindication of the Rights of Women' (1792), where she argued for equal opportunity for women based on a rational capacity common to both sexes, expressing 'the wild wish to see the sex distinction confounded in society'. Her feminist aspiration is sex equality in the family and society at large.

Among the social and cultural revolutions of the twentieth century, feminism was the greatest decisive revolution of modernity. Feminism is a movement which demands for emancipation, equality and liberation of women and stresses the need for a social transformation of law, culture and social patterns which release women's potential. Feminism can be defined as the self-conscious creation and vindication of representations of feminine and the position of women in social reality by women themselves—in contrast to the accepted 'common sense' or 'everyday' notions which are taken as imbued with masculine conceptions—and which are aimed at the emancipation of women. According to Clare Dalton, (1987) feminism is a "range of committed inquiry and activity dedicated first, to describe women's subordination—exploring its nature and extent; dedicated second, to asking both how—through what mechanisms, and why—for what complex and interwoven reasons—women continue to occupy that position; and dedicated third to change."

ORIGINS OF FEMINIST JURISPRUDENCE

Although feminist jurisprudence can be traced back into nineteenth century, it has only from seventies of twentieth century, emerged as legal theory. Feminist jurisprudence is a development from the women's movement more generally. This emerged in the late 1960 and early 1970s with writings of Simone de Beauvoir (The Second Sex 1949), Betty Freidman (The Feminine Mystique 1963), Germaine Greek (Sexual Politics 1970), Kate Millet, (Patriarchal Attitude 1970), etc. Feminist Jurisprudence is stronger in North America and Australia than in Britain.

The large number of women studying law 1960s onwards began to question a curriculum which neglected issues of central concern to women; rape, domestic violence, reproduction, unequal pay, sex discrimination, sexual harassment. Most of the leading writers in feminist jurisprudence were studying law at this time or later, (i.e. 1960s or later).

Many feminist legal theorists subscribed to the 'basic critique of the inherent logic of the law', the basic principle of the Critical Legal Studies (CLS) movement. Women at CLS conferences were 'ghettoised'. In 1983 the CLS Conference devoted a section of the conference to feminism specifically. A caucus of 'Fem-Critis' emerged at that conference.

The term 'feminist jurisprudence' can be traced from an intervention of Ann Scales at a Harvard Conference in 1978. Her article "Towards a Feminist Jurisprudence" was published in 1981. And, Catherine Mackinnon's influential article "Feminism, Marxism, Method and the State: Towards Feminist Jurisprudence" first appeared in 1983. 'Scientific feminism seeks to analyse the contribution of law in constructing, maintaining, reinforcing and perpetuating patriarchy and it looks at ways in which this patriarchy can be undermined and ultimately eliminated.

Dealing with the Basic Issues of Feminist Jurisprudence: The problems that feminist jurisprudence is called to address are:

(1) The first is the concrete reality of oppression repeatedly legitimated by legal regulations;
(2) The second is the issue of patriarchy, or the system of male authority which structures the institutions and organisational rationality which constitute the oppressive and exploitative relations which affect women; and
(3) The third is the question of women's sense of justice, or what sort of 'truth' is involved in the traditional male argument that women are different from men and have an undeveloped sense of the abstract and impartial objectivity that justice requires.

To address the above issues, the supporters of feminist jurisprudence should:

(i)hi ghlight areas where the law either legitimates oppression or the operation of the law effectively treats men and women differently;
(ii) study the epistemology of traditional jurisprudence and try to change the traditional views;

(iii) undercut the structure of abstract masculinity which is depicted as the organising force of a great deal of social, moral and political thought;

(iv) bring women's experiences directly into both theorising and the practice of understanding law in reality;

(v) seek to illuminate and define the wrongs done to women neglected by traditional perspectives;

(vi) resist commonplace perceptions of the normality of standards, such as in the conception of equality, or the recognition of problems as domestic violence, since these may be standards created under patriarchy;

(vii) try to understand the dichotomies imposed by theory on the analysis of life and to reject as artificial those which claim a naturalness or universality which are based on masculine perspectives and argue that the feminine modes of thought are superior; and so on;

(viii) research what happens to women in the world shaped by patriarchal law; and

(ix) challenge the structure of legal thought as contingent and in some culturally specific sense 'male', implying the need for some radical changes and revisions than the ameliorative amendations.

Heather Wishik suggested the following seven questions that feminist jurisprudence poses for the feminist inquiry into law:

(1) What have been and what are now all women's experiences of the life situation' addressed by the doctrine, process or area of law under examination?

(2) What assumptions, descriptions, assertions and/or definitions of experience—male, female or ostensibly gender neutral—does the law make in this area?

(3) What is the area of mismatch, distortions or denial created by the differences between women's life experiences and the law's assumptions or imposed structures?

(4) What patriarchal interests are served by the mismatch?

(5) What reforms have been proposed in this area of law or women's life situation? How will these reform proposals, if adopted, affect women both practically and ideologically?

(6) In an ideal world, what would this woman's life situation look like, and what relationship, if any, would the law have to this future life situation?

(7) How do we get there from here?

FEMINIST METHODOLOGY

Feminist theory challenges the positivist—empirical tradition, the assumption that through observation and measurement by an objective observer the truth about reality will emerge. Feminist legal methods are influenced by the imperative or hermeneutic tradition and by the methods of critical theory. The hermeneutics' goal is to understand, and the critical theorists' approach is to emancipate—that is, to uncover aspects of society, especially ideologies, that maintain the *status quo* by restricting or limiting different groups' access to the means of gaining knowledge.

In 'Feminist Legal Methods', Katharine Bartlett analyses three methods. Notably:

(i) 'asking the women question', or identifying and challenging those elements of existing legal doctrine that leave out or disadvantage women and members of other excluded groups;

(ii) 'Feminist practical reasoning', or reasoning from an ideal in which legal resolutions are pragmatic responses to concrete dilemmas rather than static choices between opposing often mismatched perspectives; and

(iii) 'consciousness-raising', or seeking insights and enhanced perspectives through collaborative or interactive engagement with others based upon personal experience and narrative.

As the themes of traditional jurisprudence essentially derive from the masculine experience of life, feminist writers offer counter-descriptions of life. Women experience perceive the world in a different way to men. The distinct form of feminist reasoning arises from this different experiential existence and the claims of feminist jurisprudence may be based on this foundation.

SCHOOLS OF FEMINIST JURISPRUDENCE

Cain offers a useful categorisation of feminist theories into four schools of thought: liberal, radical, cultural and post-modern. For liberals equality under law amounts to equal opportunity. Radicals focus on differences between women and men and support affirmative measures to challenge inequalities. Cultural feminists also emphasise difference and use the rhetoric of equality to advocate change that supports the values of the differences and, post-modern feminism sees equality as a social construct and, since it is a product of patriarchy, one in need of feminist reconstruction, but it warns against searching for a new truth to replace an old one. It denies there is a single theory of equality that will benefit all women.

(I) The School of Liberal Feminism

The first wave of feminism argued for equality of treatment for both men and women. Liberal feminist jurisprudential aim was to attain equal legal subjectivity for women as with male citizens. The legal liberal philosophy of the 18th and 19th centuries provided the intellectual foundational structure for the first wave of feminist writing, such as Mary Wallstonecraft (1789), William Thompson (1825), John Stuart Mill ['The subjection of women' (1869)] and Harriet Taylor (1851).

Under the banner of liberal feminism women won most of their legislative and judicial victories, including the suffrage, equal pay benefits, access to employment and education, the right to serve on juries, and the limited right to choose to terminate a pregnancy. In U.S.A. the liberal feminists are Wendy Williams, Herma Hill Kay, and Nadine Taub and the most prominent representative is Justice Ruth Bader Ginsburg; Key notions of legal liberalism are those of neutrality, impartiality and universality, arguments and legislative provisions had to be framed in such a way as not to contradict these ideals. For example, the 1975 Sex Discrimination Act in the U.K. prohibits discrimination on the basis of sex, rather than prohibiting discrimination against women. Most of the victories made for women's rights have been made by proponents of legal liberalism.

According to Scales, feminism proceeds from the principle that objective reality is a myth, with patriarchal myths as projections of the male psyche. She is critical of the U.S. Supreme Court's equal protection approach to sex discrimination because it makes maleness the norm of what is human, the goal being neutrality. She argues that it is necessary to reconstruct the legal system. Scales looks to a feminist jurisprudence which will focus on domination, disadvantage and disempowerment rather than one which examines differences between men and women.

According to Robin West, the failure of modern legal theory lies in its understanding of what it is to be a human being. Such theory is male because it assumes that individuals are essentially separate from one another. She argues, to the contrary, that women are connected to other human beings, especially through the biologically based activities of pregnancy, breast feeding, etc. West argues for a feminist jurisprudence that reconstructs legal concepts to take account of the realities of women's experiences. Thus Wests' 'connectedness' thesis is essentialist.

Windy Williams (1984), a liberal feminist argued that feminists have only two choices: either equality on the basis of similarities between the sexes or special treatment on the basis of sexual differences. She favoured the former, since difference always means women's difference, and this provides the basis for treating women worse as well as better than men.

Legal liberalism presupposes autonomous individualism and takes as its central value the notions of separation and freedom; freedom is defined as distance from the 'other' and the social space for the individual to pursue her/his own ends. Freedom and autonomy is the official value of liberalism, is hope; the fear lies in the vulnerability of the human condition and the danger that the discrete, separate 'other' may annihilate you. To protect themselves from this 'other', human beings create and respect the state. The foundational supposition of liberal legalism is that human being experience the world as separate individuals, unconnected to others unless they so choose; as a result, the value that is put forward above all else is the right to pursue our lives relatively free of outside control.

Legal liberalism, however, offers little help in understanding the nature and causes of women's oppression and may appear to downplay the real policy struggles which daily take place. Legal liberalism is charged with ignoring the reality of male power and domination in formulating the seemingly neutral principles of liberalisms agenda of sexual equality. The victories of liberal feminists are viewed as something weakening the potentiality of feminism and allowing women success in professional occupations only if these women 'become as men'. Thus an equal treatment approach only benefits women who meet male norms and not those who engage in female activities, child bearing and rearing most notably.

(2) The School of Radical Feminism

Radical feminists view the existing cultural, social, economic and legal differences between men and women as a product of male domination. Catherine Mackinnon is probably the most influential of feminist legal scholars. In the extract from 'Feminism Unmodified' (1989) she argues that feminists should concentrate on identifying dominance. This treats gender equality issue as question about the distribution of power, about male supremacy and female subordination. It is dominance, not difference, that is central to Mackinnon. This conceptualisation enables Mackinnon to broaden the focus of inquiry beyond the orthodox terrian of work conditions to take in violence, prostitution and pornography (treatment of obscene subjects, especially sexual perversions in writing, pictures, etc.). She claims that the dominance approach is the authentic feminist voice:

> "The difference approach", she argues, "adopts the view point of male supremacy on the status of the sexes; the dominance approach sees social inequalities from the standpoint of the subordination of women to men".

Catherine Mackinnon works through a neo-Marxist perspective with its themes of power, domination, alienation and the pursuit of an emancipated future state of social relations. In an early article (1982) Mackinnon says, "Sexuality is to feminism what work is to Marxism; that which is most one's own, yet most taken away." The first site of domination lies in the male appropriation of women's pre-social natural sexuality, an appropriation which constitutes woman as the object of male desire. Thus, women's sexuality in society is structured into an objectification of the male gaze rather than a consequence of natural or true form. Gender formations are structured on the basis of male supremacy. The process that gives sexuality its male supremacist meaning is therefore the process through which gender inequality becomes socially real.

The consequences of the pervasive male domination leads to conclude that women cannot trust the state. The state is male in the feminist sense; the law sees and treats women the way men see and treat women. The liberal state coercively and authoritatively constitutes the social order in the interest of men as a gender—through its legitimating norms, forms, relation to society, and substantive policies. The liberal rule of law state is the rule of men under the guise of the rule of law—its power intensified through the hegemony of subterfuge.

Not only is the state not to be trusted but the very notion of equality is suspect. If women want to claim equal rights, they claim only the right to be viewed as men under the gaze of the male state which adopts the standpoint of male power on the relation between law and society. Mackinnon's argument is at the level of hegemonic understandings, the social inequality which existed in the traditional patriarchical social order has not been destroyed by the legal rights offered by liberalism; such inequality is harder to see and to fight because it is the role of the state not to intervene in the reformation of the social order. The liberty is legitimate if it were true that the genders were actually equal before the law, if the liberties of the social body were evenly distributed; but they are not. The real harm of various assaults on women is the depiction of subordination and objectification.

Mackinnon's style can be seen from two issues; abortion and pornography. The preachers of liberal thought fail to understand the fact that multitude of factors including social pressure, learning, economic disadvantage, sexual force, inadequate contraception, and weak laws against sexual assault impact so that women do not control the circumstances under which they become pregnant. This structurally forced maternity is a perpetuation of economic, domestic and sexual inequality; abortion is needed to redress a woman's basic lack of control over the process of reproduction. Similarly, Mackinnon sees pornography as dehumanising traffic in women that sets the standard for the mistreatment of women, engendering rape, sexual abuse of children, battery, forced prostitution, and sexual murder and she does not position the pornography in the context of freedom of speech and individual autonomy. The very nature of pornography contributes to, and defines, women's social and legal inequality.

Mackinnon's feminism can join with radical criminologists in seeking to redefine 'harm'. In the criminological arena of victimology.

recent attempts have focussed upon defining certain types of 'harms' beyond those normally recognised. Similarly, feminist writers have focussed on the maleness of legal proceedings, specifically the trial of sexual crimes such as rape. Simply put, in the rape trial the procedure is designed to break down the story of the woman complainant both by subjecting it to vigorous doubt and by implicitly sexualising it. The victim becomes an object of the male gaze and forced to relive her ordeal. Mackinnon argues that the domination of maleness places severe handicaps on women understanding the 'truth' of their own lives; feminist theory is an agent of liberation.

If Mackinnon is correct on the power of ideology and hegemony there is no secure way for women to think out their positions and strategy. Mackinnon solves this by granting men some privileged status as 'reality'. "The feminist point is simple. Men are women's material conditions. If it happens to women, it happens. Not only, however, does this deny the maleness must also be socially constructed, but this dooms women to know only by resistance, to know only that they ought to assert the non-male, rather than the (fe)male.

Littleton is another radical feminist. Her critique of equality is based on its 'phallocentrism'. She calls for a reconstruction of thinking about equality to transcend its enmeshment within the very gender system that feminists are resisting. She labels her model "equality as acceptance"; to 'accept' women's difference, society must do more than merely accommodate the difference. Littleton requires of 'women' (her identity, her specificity, her difference from men) in normative debates about how the world ought to be structured". Equality as acceptance focuses not on sources of differences, but on their consequences, the differences that difference makes. To show how the acceptance model would work, Littleton constructs "gender complements" by matching a female-gendered difference to its male complement and then treating them equally in terms of compensation, status and opportunity for promotion into decision-making positions. It is the claim of Littleton that the values upheld by phallocentrism will be chállenged and changed as women achieve equal decision-making opportunities.

(3) The School of Cultural Feminism

For cultural feminism, male domination is based on the grounding of the modern structure of thought (reason) on the male experience and the force of violence, but many things of value are lost to humanity by the downgrading of the experiences and perspectives of women. Cultural feminism endeavours to present the reasoning of the feminine 'other'.

Carol Gilligan, an American educational psychologist is the prominent cultural feminist and she developed a thesis on a woman's voice and an ethic of care in her, 'In a Different Voice: Psychological Theory and Women's Development' (1982). Gilligan's work argued that women's moral reasoning was not inferior, it was simply different, emphasising contrasting values. Women's judgment reaches the stage of development, where goodness was equated with pleasing and helping others. This is the result of the life experiences 'allowed' to women and implied that if women had a greater role in the public sphere they would move onto the higher stages that typify men's judgment. Her empirical research reveals 'a woman's voice', a different voice, not necessarily inferior to the man's voice.

Gilligan conducted interviews with college students on identity and moral development in their early adult years, carried out an abnormal decision-making study on the relation between experience and thought and the role of conflict in development and rights and responsibilities, a study on conception of self-morality, experiences of moral conflict and choice, and judgments of hypothetical moral dilemmas. The study revealed the following:

(1) Women conceive relationships in a different mode from men. While men see relationships as a hierarchy, which is unstable. Women conceive them as a web which is stable; the desire is to be at the centre and the fear is being too far out on the edge.
(2) The abortion study had revealed a distinct moral language for women of selfishness and responsibility, which defines the moral problem as one of obligation to exercise care and avoid hurt.
(3) Women give a distinctive construction to moral problems, seeing moral dilemmas in terms of conflicting responsibilities. Women have an ethic of care or responsibility and men have an ethic of rights or justice.
(4) The conception of self and world is thus one of relationship rather than domination and separation. Self-description reveals women's identity and is defined in the context of relationships and judged by a standard of responsibility and care.
(5) One of her subjects describes being alone or unconnected as 'like the sound of one hand clapping there is something lacking'. In contrast, the male self-descriptions, while speaking of attachments, were characterised by adjectives of separation.

For Gilligan true maturity for both sexes would be to move away from the absolutes with which they are associated. That is, men must move away from the absolutes of rights, truth and fairness, to a realisation of differences between other and self and a recognition that multiple truths exist. Similarly, women must move away from the absolute of care and recognise a claim for equality and rights that transforms their understanding of relationships and their definition of care. Gilligan looks forward to a 'more generative view of human life'. For her the ethic of justice (that everyone should be treated the same) should be added to the ethic of caring (that no one should be hurt) to produce a better outcome. Her conclusion is thus not to produce a separatist system of justice for women, not to replace the ethic of justice with the ethic of caring. Gilligan never suggested that women's voices were biologically determined or even that they are only found in women.

For Mackinnon, Gilligan does not describe what women actually are, but what women have been socialised to be. Gilligan therefore describes and then reifies gender oppression. Viewed in this light Gilligan's work is regressive.

Robin West (1988) claimed that male legal theorists exhibit a specific form of reasoning because they experience the world firstly and fundamentally as separate autonomous individuals; the foundation of both traditional and 'critical' masculine jurisprudence is a 'separation' thesis. Conversely, women are not essentially separate from the human beings. They are 'connected' life and to other human beings during pregnancy, the monthly experience of menstruation and breast feeding. Women reason out of a 'connectedness' which men cannot experience. This counter experience of women provides the basis of an alternative to legal theory which, through the presuppositions of the separation thesis, has become 'essentially and irrevocably masculine.'

In seeking a positive mode of thought and morality in the experiences that women endure, cultural feminism develops the connection thesis, but closes off analysing the material conditions in which this development takes place. Its essential truth lies in connection, a truth which 'ought' to be universal.

Cultural feminism is humanism. According to Drucilla Cornell, "Ethical feminism 'envisions' not only a world in which the view point of the feminine is appreciated; ethical feminism also 'sees' a world 'peopled' by individuals, 'sexed' differently, a world beyond contraction. Through our 'visions we affirm the 'should be' of a different way of being human. The 'goal' of ethical feminism, which 'sees' the 'should be' inherent in the feminine viewpoint, is not just power for women, but the redefinition of all our fundamental concepts, including power. Feminine power should not, in other words, be separated from the different, ethical vision of human 'beings' sought after in the feminine, understood as a redemptive process."

A self-conscious black feminism is relatively recent. Frances Beale (1970) coined the term 'double jeopardy' to characterize the condition of being both female and black. Alice Walker prefers terminology of 'womanism' defined as a commitment to the survival and wholeness of entire people, male and female. 'Womenist' is preferred by some women of colour who feel that 'feminist' is too one-dimensional and who want to indicate solidarity with men of colour as well as with women. The term 'Womenist' has perspective regarding the relationship among class, sex and race.

A black feminist ideology declares the visibility of black women. Second, black feminism asserts self-determination is essential. Black women are empowered with the right to interpret our reality and define our objectives. Third, a black feminist ideology fundamentally challenges the interstructure of the oppressions of racism, sexism, and classicism both in the dominant society and within movements of liberation. Finally, a black feminist ideology presumes an image of black women as powerful, independent subjects. Today black feminists consciously take up the narrative tradition while demarcating themselves from 'feminism' in general. Black feminists reclaim a self from the structures of slavery and multiple oppression.

(4) The School of Post-Modern Feminism

In part, post-modernism is the difficulty of accepting any settled position. The feminism movements have not given rise to a dominant perspective and there are many diverse interpretations. In part feminists have reproduced the universalising tendencies they abhor in the traditional. Post-modernity encourages one to think in terms of varied social rations and of a multiplicity of social sphere where there are many obstacles and opportunities for advancing liberty and the treatment of self and others as equals. The post-modern condition demands that women abandon any supposed unity and homogeneity in answering the 'woman question' and look to analyse and intervene in a multiplicity of relations of subordination, transforming oppression into an affirmation of life's possibilities and opportunities.

Post-modern feminists ended up arguing from very anti-theoretical positions. Their emphasis on the local and particular, their attack on what they call 'totalizing narratives' on the very notion of truth and casualty, were deeply discouraging to feminists trying to develop a coherent and systematic theory of women's oppression. The insight associated with post-modernism that social and political power influence science, led many to scepticism. Also despite the inconsistency, it led many to claim that everything is socially constructed thereby eliminating the distinction between sex and gender that had been so central to feminist critiques of gender relations. But if the body disappears in significations, what is the basis for arguing for reproductive rights? Given that some of post-modernism builds on insights associated with feminism and presents itself radical, its effect was disorienting to say the least.

THE SCHOOL OF SOCIALIST FEMINISM

Nancy Holmstrom of Rutgers University in Newark, New Jursey explained another school of feminism, 'socialist feminism'. It is called as 'material feminism' or 'feminist materialism' in 1990s by Martha Gimenez.

Women within the women's liberation movement found themselves dissatisfied with the prevailing of women's oppression. Liberalism was not radical enough, and radical feminism ignored economic realities. Seeking to combine the best of Marxism and radical feminism, these women developed a theory they called 'socialist feminism'.

Nancy Holmstrom says, "Socialist feminism is an attempt to understand women's subordination in a coherent and systematic way that integrates class and sex, as well as other aspects of identity such as race/ethnicity or sexual orientation, with the aim of using this analysis to help liberate women". Barbara Ehrenreich says, "Socialist feminism is really socialist, internationalist, antiracist, anti-theterosexist feminism."

The socialist feminists observe that the present day globalisation affect women disproportionately. Displaced by rapid economic changes, women bear a greater burden of labour throughout the world as social services have been cut, whether in response to structural adjustment plans in the third world or to so called welfare reform in the United States of America. Women have been forced to migrate, are subject to trafficking, and are the proletarians of the newly industrialising countries.

On top of all this, women continue to be subject to sexual violence and in much of the world are not allowed to control their own processes of reproduction. Socialist feminism is the approach with the greatest capacity to illuminate the exploitation and oppression of most of the women.

Socialist feminism sees class as central to women's lives, yet at the same time none would reduce sex or race oppression to economic exploitation and class is always gendered and raced. Socialist feminist perspective informs what activism there is, including most significantly, labour activism.

What is now called 'intersectionality'—that is, the recognition that a woman's position is always a function of her class, ethnicity, and so on, as well as her sex—is paid attention by most feminists.

Those who call themselves 'multicultural' or 'global' feminists who foresee the evils of 'globalisation' and 'sex industry' would be considered as 'socialist feminists' in broader sense.

CRITICISM OF FEMINIST JURISPRUDENCE

West distinguishes the contracts in fears and hopes. Each perspective fixes upon one or other tendency in the human condition at the expense of others. Andrea Dworkin identifies feminism's official value (intimacy) as a cover for harm. Radical feminists are torn between denying the inhumanity and alienation of individualism and claiming that because intimacy constitutes a harm, women long for individualisation. Conversely, they wish to free women of the colonisation of their minds by the hegemony of patriarchy. The dominant culture tells women that they value intimacy and dependency to make them more easily governed by men; separation and independence are what they actually need, but this risks returning the liberalism.

Most feminists would accept that unwanted intercourse, rape, is a harm and that to some women unwanted pregnancy is a harm, but radical feminists push their argument much farther than this, often presenting the idea that pregnancy and motherhood constitute harms *per se*, because the foetus and the child are intrusive. For radical feminists, intercourse, including voluntary intercourse, is a harm since it 'divides a woman internally'—it pre-empts, challenges, negates, and renders impossible the maintenance of physical integrity and the formation of a unified self. Such extreme fears of radical feminists are considered as utopian as voluntary in the course is the result of natural sex instinct. According to Wayne Morrison, feminists have to recognise their own embeddedness; their complexity. Feminists have to think in terms of varied social relations and of a multiplicity of social spheres where there are many obstacles and opportunities for advancing liberty and the treatment of self and others as equals.

15

POST-MODERNIST JURISPRUDENCE

Critical legal studies movement and feminist jurisprudence both had by the end of the 1980s become submerged into post-modernism.

MEANING OF POST-MODERNISM

Categorisations of periodisations may be made as 'pre-modern', 'modern' and 'post-modern' in time space. Pre-modern is an ancient one and is traditionally derived with orthodox reasoning with tribalist characteristics. Modern is a system of thought and regime of knowledge. Modernity refers back and claims to overcome a historical period. Modernity was an attempt to create a just society of organised and transparent structure - a world of coherent practices organised around rules, where the rules themselves took their legitimation from a belief in some underlying structure or their inherent functionality, or in terms of their purity. Modernism is a cultural and artistic movement. Modernism is a rage against existing order. It is said to exalt 'the attack on form, the belief that an ability to go beyond, to transcend, to break through, is the *raison d'etre* of art and perhaps of life'.

Since Post-modernism is post-modern, it seems it comes after the modern, but it is a culmination of modernity. Post-modernism is the realisation that there is 'no beyond', no place 'outside of the forms'. And modernism can be celebrated as an 'exhilarating moment' of rapture for it defies the system, suspects all total single thought and homogeneity and opens space for the marginal, the different and the 'other'. It stands for 'flux, dispersal, plurality and localism'. There is a cluster of styles, strategies, preoccupations, texts, readings, objects and performances.

The post-modern condition is ushered in with the growing realisation of the lack of deep structure. The main stream of politics in the post-modern condition sees the desperate attempt to avoid ideas and return political speech to common sense.

Radical changes have occurred in social order over the last thirty years. These changes are labeled as 'the post-industrial society', 'the globalised society', 'the post-capitalist information order', 'the society of advanced world capitalism', 'the consumer society' and lately, 'post-modernism'. Jean Francois Lyotard (1984) in his book 'The Post-Modern Condition' coined the term 'post-modern'. According to him it reflects changes in the level of science and technology, in particular the development of computers, mass communication and increasing emphasis upon language in social and cultural studies. For others, post-modernity is characterised by a feeling of extreme ambivalence to the hopes and social structures of the last two hundred years: a mood of nostalgia; cultural relativism; moral conventionalism, scepticism and pragmatism; a dialectic of localism amidst globalism ambivalence towards organised, principled political activity; and a distrust of all strong forms of ethical or anthropological foundations. But according to Eagleton (1996), post-modern is the feeling of failure and deep confusion where next to go, either personally, or in terms of striving to create projects aiming at a just society.

The terms 'modem' and 'post-modern' were first used in the world of art and architecture, only later influencing philosophy, social theory, history politics and ethics. Post-modernist jurisprudent, however, used in late 1980s.

Post-modernism can be seen as a strategy for liberating suppressed narratives and voices drowned out by uni-vocal projections of master narratives. A major theme in post-modernism is subversion, the commitment to undermine dominant discourse. Post-modernists believe that the potential for subversive struggle is particularly propitious given the discrediting of Marxism, the instabilities of late capitalism and the contradictions of the bureaucratic welfare state. These faults and fissures are seen as a source of resistance and freedom. Post-modernists look to new forms of politics that go beyond emancipation because if they exist at all, are no longer the bourgeoisie or the boss so much as the bureaucracy, centralized government and 'democratically elected' representatives.

POST-MODERN STATE AND LAW

Post-modernism is a response to the 'legitimate crisis' of the society. It is argued that the modern bureaucratic state has become dysfunctional, either because it has 'colonized other life-worlds', or because it has inappropriately interfered with the functioning of other subsystems. The result has been inefficiencies in managing economic and social problems and the distortion of human relations.

By way of contrast, the post-modern state is minimalist because radical democracy depends on the proliferation of public spaces where social agents become increasingly capable of self-management.

One important post-modernist theme invokes the instability or indeterminateness of the 'subject'. First, traditional social categories (women, gays, blacks, etc.) live in different worlds simultaneously, and the social identity is fractured—there is no scope for reconciliation. Secondly, there is differences of psyche of the individual. Thus there is fragmentation and differences rather than unity and university. The one is, however, clearly in tension with the other.

The result of post-modernist jurisprudence is to shift the focus of jurisprudence from a study of the legal system and its properties (order, coherence, determinancy, etc.) to the 'nature of the legal subject' who apprehends the legal system and judges it to have these properties. Thus, 'the nature of legal understanding' becomes central to 'jurisprudential enquiry'. Since the legal subject is socially constructed, the ways this social construction has led the legal subject to understand the legal system also becomes crucial. And equally, jurisprudence makes 'the subjects' contribution to the legal system invisible.

Balkin points to three dimensions of jurisprudence. First, subjects bring 'purposes' to their understanding of law. Legal understanding is a purposive activity of subjects. Secondly, judgments about the law rest on the 'nature of the self and thirdly, subjectivity is important to the study of law because 'legal understanding' is also a source of power over the legal subject. Legal understanding thus makes the legal subject a locus of ideological power.

The post-modern alternative converts the state into an 'absent structure' and makes possible "the autonomy of law as a system of social regulation". There is a new emphasis on legal pluralism. The state is not the only source of rules of law. We live in families, we work in offices and factories, we buy goods as consumers in the market, we may accept religious affiliations.

The considerations of law reflect the ambiguities, hopes, confusions and fear of the post-modern condition. Santos argues that the modern idea of global rationality has disintegrated into a multitude of uncontrollable, irrational mini-rationalities. What is required is to reinvent these mini-rationalities so that they form a new totality. Politics and the law in the post-modern transition is 'the emergence of a new legal minimalism and of micro-revolutionary practices.'

The political agenda will emphasise redistribution of economic resources, as well as the distribution 'post-material goods' such as a better environment and peace and greater democratisation. It will lead to the empowering of victmised groups. And law will be 'decanalized' as it proves ineffective, opening a gap in social imagination. Social change will follow as 'autonomous subjectivities, free themselves from the prejudices of legal fetishism'.

As James Boyd White, a prominent of an emerging 'law and humanities movement', states that law cannot help but partake of the radical uncertainty of post-modern life, and its multivocal structure renders it implicated in many contrasting accounts and languages. Law's flexibility ensures it in the post-modern dialectic. of multi-directionality against directionless preformivity.

ELEMENTS OF POST-MODERNITY
(Temptations for Jurisprudence in Post-modernity)

Law is the sword of the sovereign who is to watch over the subjects and within whose dominion the subjects can pursue their legitimate desires. In time, the idea of social progress was joined with law so that law was seen as an instrument to guide us to that land and time of their happiness. Law was to be the guarantor of modernity, the instrument of rational power. In post-modernity many carry swords, but only to brandish them; law seemed to have lost its rationality. The coherence be created through historical struggles and the granting of legal rights, of a modern subject which was being incorporated—by a process of assimilation— into the modernity. Instead, however, of contentment and reasoned satisfaction relates feelings of personal suspension and ambiguity. In post-modernism the subject is forced to live a situation of contingency and choice, longing for a life of relative peace and contentment within a socially just and acceptable social order, the subject finds only a rapidly moving where there are few places to rest and insufficient time to attain certainty. The subjects become increasingly con-fused as they attempt to ascertain the truth of their social context and the essence of the institutions. In this uncertain world, neither the law nor their cultural heritage offer certainty. The following temptations arise to face such post-modernism.

(1) To Accept Radical Relativism

The modern person has to assume, or has to be told, that perfection—truth—is a realistic, albeit futurist, possibility. In that way the struggle for justice, the political commitment to justice, the march into the future and out of the past, is provided with some sort of meaning and purpose. By contrast, post-modernity is the growing awareness that that linkage is absurd. Thus, post-modernism is the realisation that there can be no utopia of the just society—the voyage is doomed—and, by implication, we are at the destination, the problem is that the destination is no conclusion. There is no end.

(2) Abandoning the Search for the Wisdom of Law in Favour of Preformivity

The Critical Legal Studies Movement wished to return social organisation to human concerns, to less alienated forms of social life and human interaction. Conversely, proponents of law and economics tend to ask jurisprudence to speak only in the language understood by economic power—money. Economics is the language most computer friendly, most minimalist in its claims concerning human nature. The discourse of the law and economics movement speaks a post-modern language.

Scientific knowledge is not however self-sustainable. It exists in competition and conflict with other forms of knowledge which Lyotard labels as narrative and which dominated in traditional societies. While modernity waged war on narratives, narrative survived bestowing legitimacy upon the social institutions and providing positive and negative forms of integration into the established institutions. Thus we witness the growing law and humanities movements and the narrative style of feminism—but their power base is ambiguous.

(3) To Abandon Modernity for a Dialectic of Tribalism and Rampant Subjectivity

Social and cultural modernism has come under attack from diverse quarters throughout the developed world. From the fight, conservatives argue that modernism has undercut the values of every day life and common sense. Hedonism, lack of social identification, lack of obedience, self-love, the withdrawal of defence from authority, are seen not as features of successful modernisation, but of a social and cultural modernity which has lost its way. Conversely, for those on the left, the post-modern problem, is that of the incomplete modernisation of the world. When Lyotard claims that in post-modern condition the grand narratives have lost their credibility at the same time as we keep on playing the games that were formerly legitimated by those grand narratives, and do so at a greater level of proformivity.

Jamerson defines post-modernism as a nostalgia for the past where, at the same time, we seem to lose our ability to locate ourselves historically. We became incapable of embedding ourselves in a time-space contingent that makes sense. Post-modernity denotes a feeling of loss, in that we can no longer grasp what is going on in society, or indeed the globe as a whole, yet at the same time we need to know what is going on at this level of totality in order that we can say that it is no longer possible to say what is going on. Thus whilst it is fashionable to say that there is no single theoretical discourse, which is going to offer us explanations of all forms of social relations and make possible legitimate modes of political practice and legal intervention, this itself is, reflexively, a theoretical understanding of totality.

(4) To Misunderstand the Nature of Deconstruction

Along with the realisation of contingency and the dreams of dynamic flexibility, the post-modern cultural consciousness is obsessed with the process of deconstruction. Deconstruction enters jurisprudence first through the law's textual nature, and, secondly, through the modernist (functional) linkage of Schools of Jurisprudence law with social structure. By asking a continual series of questions, deconstruction seeks to sap the strength of a social structure whose substance lies in the prohibition of asking.

For Derrida (1992) deconstruction is a form of humanism, deconstruction's uncovering of the infinite regress of truth's being is not a denial of the task of enlightenment, but a call to remember that the task of philosophy is not to capture truth but to enable us to live in the spirit of truth. To live amidst the process of deconstruction is the fate of the modern person who retains both a critical distance from acquiescing in the power of the sword of law and who seeks to unpack the normalising process of everyday discipline.

(5) To Refuse the Burden of Deconstruction by Retreating into Gamesmanship

In post-modernism where everything can be doubted, where justice is authenticity—rather than guarantee—the burden of existence moves, inescapably upon our shoulders. Post-modern life is a life on the run in conditions of great preformability.

Though everyday academic and professional legal practitioners play the game of rational reconstruction—doctrine is developed, sometimes new kinds of law are won —such as 'Restitution Law'—out of the battles of legal language games. The games of life, the games of law respond to the need for recognition. Jurisprudence as the search for the truth of law, is the desire for wisdom. That humanities follow desire, rather than instinct, is the source both of our power and our existential problems. Through speech, desires one articulates the ideas of dignity and the sacred. The language-games of contemporary jurisprudence speak to the multi-focused nature and sources of these desires. Desire becomes mobile, transitory, unfocussed or, to put it more correctly, moves in a continual state of focusing.

The games of the post-modern are not self-sustaining or a historical. In the games of post-modernity, it matters what the position of the game in the social order is. In the post-modern condition, we must acknowledge the impossibility of escaping from our existential inadequacy. The challenge of the post-modern is to continually ask the meaning of being human, in full consciousness of the fact that any answer offered, and any social order thereby constructed, is only a temporary respite, an embodiment of some of our desires, solace to our fears.

16

CURRENT TRENDS IN JURISPRUDENCE

THE THEORY OF ADJUDICATION: ANDREA DWORKIN

Modern legal theory has been much concerned to explore the inner working of the judicial system. To engage in judging is to represent the role of the judge. The judging individual (i.e. the judge) is not acting 'on his own' but qua judge. The role of judge stands in relationship to other roles, the totality of which comprises the institutions of law. Ideally, rules enable society to function smoothly and efficiently. There are, however, conflicts. The society expects the judges to solve disputes in a rational way. The paradigm of a rational decision is one reached according to rules, principles or standards. Adjudication according to rules means that an *ad hoc* decision-making process is deprecated. It posits that judges must conform to established rules.

Judges and Discretion

Judges fill in the gap left by rules by using their discretion. Positivists from Austin to Hart placed emphasis on the part played by judicial discretion. The Realists emphasised the paramountcy of the judge's discretion. It is the thesis of Dworkin that judicial discretion in what Dworkin calls its strong sense does not exist.

For Dworkin, judges are always constrained by the law. There is no law beyond the law. The cases may be 'hard' or 'clear'. Cases are hard where arguments exist as to what is the best understanding of the law; clear cases are those where no such doubts exist. The division of hard case and clear case is only of secondary importance to Dworkin and nearly all cases that reach the stage of argument in court are hard cases. According to Dworkin, in every adjudication there are controlling standards which the judge is obliged to follow. Judicial decisions are 'characteristically generated by principle' and 'enforce existing political rights', so that litigants are 'entitled' to the judge's 'best judgement about what their rights are'. Dworkin agrees that different judges can come to different conclusions because a constitutional theory requires judgements about political and moral philosophy. But according to him, judges may not rely on their own political views but only on their beliefs in the 'soundness of those convictions'.

Dworkin says that judges should not act as 'deputy legislators' for two reasons. First, they are not elected officials answerable to the electorate and secondly, the losing party will be punished, not because he has violated some duty he had, but rather a new duty created after the event.

Dworkin distinguishes three senses of discretion, two 'weak' and one 'strong'. Discretion in a strong sense occurs where a person 'is simply not bound by the standards set by the authority in question'. Judges do not have freedom to choose. Judges have 'weak' discretion if they have come to a wrong decision by exercising his judgement inappropriately. There is another sense also in which discretion may be said to be weak. It exists where an official has the authority to make a decision. Greenawalt argues that the line between unacceptable strong discretion and its weak acceptable sense is elusive. He claims that strong discretion exists if more than one decision is considered proper "by those to whom the decision-maker is responsible and whatever standards may be applicable either cannot be discovered by the decision-maker or do not yield clear answers to the questions that must be decided

Interpretation

Dworkin states "Judges who accept the interpretative ideal of integrity decide hard eases by trying to find, in some coherent set of principles about peoples' rights and duties, the best 'constructive interpretation' of the political structure and legal doctrine of their community. They try to make that complex structure and record the best there can be."

'Constructive interpretation' is a methodology for interpreting social practices like courtesy, texts and works of art. Dworkin employs this method to interpret legal practice. The distinctive feature of this is that it is 'argumentative'. Dworkin distinguishes two ways of the argumentative aspect of legal practice. There is the 'external point of view of the sociologist or historian' and 'the internal point of view of those who make the claims'. To understand legal practice the internal participants' view must be embraced. In his 'Law's Empire', he tries to grasp the argumentative character of our legal practice by joining that practice and struggling with the issues of soundness and truths participants face. The distinctive feature of the internal participants point of view is that one can take an interpretive attitude to a practice.

The process of constructive interpretation is made up of three analytical stages: the pre-interpretative stage, the interpretive stage and the post-interpretive stage. At the pre-interpretive stage, the participant identifies the rules and standards that tentatively constitute the practice. At the interpretive stage, the interpreter 'settles on some general justification for the main elements of the practice identified at the first analytical stage. Finally, there is a post-interpretive stage at which the 'participant' adjusts his sense of what the practice 'really' requires so as better to serve the justification he accepts at the interpretative stage'. At the interpretative stage, the participant postulates the value of the practice.

Dworkin works through this interpretive process with the social practice of courtesy. He says, 'Law is an interpretive concept like courtesy' What the law requires in a particular case thus rests ultimately on a constructive interpretation of legal practice.

Law as Integrity

Dworkin constructs three theories of law -conventionalism, pragmatism and law as integrity. Out of these, he argues, law as integrity shows legal practice in its best light. Key to Dworkins constructive interpretation of legal practice is his concept of law as integrity. Law as integrity directs judges to decide cases by using the same methodology from which integrity was derived. Dworkin says, "The adjudication principle of integrity instructs judges to identify legal rights and duties. . . . on the assumption that they were all created by a single author—the community personified—expressing a coherent conception of justice and fairness". A judge committed to integrity is required to decide particular cases by seeking a principle that "both fits and justifies some complex part of the legal practices, that provides an attractive way to see, in the structure of that practice, the consistency of principle integrity requires". For Dworkin the 'historical' legal record must constitute the source of legal interpretation. This interpretation must fit into the existing body of legal materials. Dworkin tries to propose a set of principles he can offer to integrity, a scheme for transforming the varied links in the chain of law into a revision of government now speaking with one voice, even if this a very different from the voices of leaders past. Dworkin is compelled to conclude that what constrains interpretation is not historical legal material in some objective sense, but the judges' 'convictions' about fit.

Dworkin says that the constraint upon judges arises from their personal need as individuals to integrate their convictions about 'fit' with their convictions about whether their interpretation shows the interpreted practice in its best light. He says, "It is not the constraint of external hard fact or of interpersonal consensus. But rather the structural constraint of different kinds of principle within a system of principle, and it is none the less genuine for that". Dworkin maintains that the process of adjudication inherent in the theory of 'law as integrity' yields right answer to question of law. At the same time he admits the possibility of disagreements amongst the judges as to what those right answers are.

Integrity and Legitimacy

Dworkin says that integrity is that it captures our intuitions about checkboard statutes. He argues that 'a political society that accepts integrity as a political virtue thereby becomes a special form of community, special in a way that promotes its moral authority to assume and deploy a monopoly of coercive force. A state that accepts integrity as a political ideal has a better case for legitimacy than one which does not. Integrity insists that 'each citizen must accept demands on him, and may make demands on others, that share and extend the moral dimension of any explicit political decisions'.

Dworkin says that any argument for legitimacy must be able to account for the fact that political obligations are not consensual, and, further, to explain that such obligation is special. He argues that political obligation is a type of 'associative obligation'. Associative obligations are an important part of the moral landscape. Associative obligations are defined by social practices which attach special obligations to membership within a particular social group. A community's social practices give rise to 'genuine' obligations only when the community is a true one.

Dworkin argues that political obligation is an example of associative obligation. In his view political practice is a 'bare' community which defines a nation state and imposes upon members of it obligations, including the obligation to obey the law, by virtue of membership of the nation 'group'. But to give rise to genuine obligations, a political, community must be a 'true' community. Only a community that endorses the 'ideal of integrity'—'a community of principle'—can claim the authority of genuine associative community and therefore claim moral legitimacy, 'that its collective decisions are matters of obligation and not bare power in the name of fraternity'. Dworkin's account of associative obligation may be convincing in the context of family or friendship, its place in explaining political obligation has not been made out. The obligation of community rests upon coercion but the obligation of family and friendship do not. It would seem that a state who had to enforce laws by means of coercion was undercutting its own foundation which rests on a relationship where there is obligation.

To Dworkin, the ideal in judging is to find the best justification for each statute and, in so doing, to enable the polity to become a community of principle, not just a 'rulebook community'. Interpretation is central to the project realise the ideals of 'political integrity and fairness and procedural due process as they apply specifically to legislation in a bureaucracy'. Judges are to collaborate, to be coauthors in the 'chain novel' that is the law-making process.

INDEX

Accept Radical Relativism, 334
Ajangar, Prof. Rangaswamy, 253
Allen, Prof. C.K., 239
American Civil War, 124
American Dilemma:
Negro Problem and Modern Democracy, 42
American Realists, 182
Analytical Theory, 65
Ancient Hindu Law, 250
Anglo-American Jurisprudence, 306
Anthopological Approach, 122
Applied Comparative Law, 285
Aquinas, St. Thomas, 206
Arabic Society, 278
Aristotle, 6
Aristotle's Contribution to Legal Theory, 8
Associative Obligation, 340
Athenian Democracy, 5
Austin, John, 69, 78
Ayer, A.J., 28

Barlett, Katharine, 321
Banoick, Sir Garfield, 67
Beneke, Edward, 164
Bentham, Jeremy, 69, 162
Biological Interpretation, 120
Boulding, Kenneth E., 45
Brhaspati, 245, 255
Briand Kellogg Pact, 1928, 106
British Commonwealth, 47
British Homocide Act, 1957, 48
Buchanan Committee, 44
Byrne, Hedley, 88

Categorical Imparative, 19
Character of Commentaries and the Digests, 251
Civil War, 212
Classical Roman Law, 197
Coarse Allusion, 75
Common Law Tradition, 193
Comparative Jurisprudence, 283
Comparison and Contrast between East and the West, 295
Computer Prediction, 195
Concept of Legal System, 13
Concept of Law, 12
Conceptual Institution, 179
Constructive Skeptics, 182
Critical Legal Studies and Legal Practice, 308, 315
Criticism of Feminist Jurisprudence, 329
Current Trends in Jurisprudence, 337

Dabin, Jean, 214
Dah Samaskar, 272
Darwin, 119
Das Recht des Bestzes, 110
Date and Character of the Three Smritis, 252
Decretum Gratianum, 207
Denning, J., 57
Dewey, James, 24
Descriptive Comparative Law, 285
Dharmasutra, 247
Dialectic Interpretation, 118
Difference between Realism and the CLS Movement, 309
Dike, 5
Dissolution of Marriage Act, 1939, 280
Distinction between Roman Jurisprudence and Islamic Jurisprudence, 303
Divine Right of Kingship, 247
Doctrine of the Class Character of Law, 132
Doctrine of the Economic Determination of Law, 132
Doctrine of the Identity of Law and State, 133
Doctrine of the Withering Away of Law and State, 133
Double Jeopardy, 327
Dutch Reformed Church, 176

Economic Approach, 129
Elements of Post-Modernity, 334
Empirical Theories, 22
Engels, Friedrich, 130
English Common Law, 55

Essential Targets for CLS Movements, 310
Ethical and Legal Theories, 22
Ethical Theories and Solution of Legal Problem, 30
Ethical Theories and Valuations, 21
Ethics and Social Morality, 20
European Communities Treaties, 59
Everett, Professor C.W., 70

Facts, Values and Judgment in the Social Sciences, 41
Father of English Jurisprudence, 69
Father of Modern Sociological Jurisprudence, 159
Feminist Jurisprudence, 318
Force of a Law, Sanctional or Incitative Part, 73
Formal Style, 194
Frank Jerome, 182
Freedom of Contract, 27
From Homer to Pericles, 5
Fuller, Professor Lon L., 225, 238

Gandhi, Mahatma, 297
General Jurisprudence, 85
Genetic and Responsibility, 51
German Civil Code, 113
German Historical School, 122
Gierke, 112
Gilligan, Mackinnon, 327
Grand Style, 194
Gray, 184
Greek Philosophy, 3
Ground for CLS Movement, 310
Group Approach, 195
Groups and Institutions, 175
Groups and Values, 176
Groups as Institutions, 178

Habitual Obedience. 13
Hagerstrom, 197
Hart, Prof. H.L.A., 14, 30, 86, 240
Hegel, 8, 118
Heisenburg, Feedback Effect, 196
Hesiod, 5
Hindu Succession Act, 1956, 276
Historical and Anthropological Approaches, 108
Historical School, 108
History of Roman Law, 111
Holmstrom, Nancy, 329
Human Condition, 240
Hume, 212
Huxley's Brave New World, 32

Impact of Laws on Society, 160
Implications of a Temporal Approach, 227
Independent Imperative, 201
Indian Evidence Act, 268
Indian Limitation Act, 268
Individuality of a Law, 75
Industrial Self-management, 143
Integrity and Legitimacy, 340
International Declaration of Human Rights, 150
International Labour Conventions, 59
Islamic Jurisprudence, 277

James, William, 24
Jerome Hall, 222
John Rawls, 217
Judges and Discretion, 337
Judicial Committee, 251
Judicial Committee of the Privy Council, 100
Judicial Procedure, 261
Justice Holmes, 121, 184, 186

Kene, Dr. P.V., 253
Kaut, 8
Katyayana, 245
Katyayanasmrti, 258
Kay, Herma Hill, 322
Kelson, Hans, 22, 91
Kennedy, Duncan, 310
Kentucky State Court, 185
King Asoka, 297
Knowledge and Politics, 313
Kohler, 8
Krabbe, H., 239
Kriyapada, 262

Lauterpacht, Sir Hersch, 105
Law and Social Change, 53
Law and the Enforcement of Morals, 34
Law as Integrity, 339
Law, Justice, Ethics and Social Morality, 12
Law, Morality and Social Change, 33
Law of Compatability, 194
Law of Singing Reason, 194
Legal Idealism and the Sociological Approach to Law, 56
Legal Sociologist, 157
Legal Theories based on Objective Ethical Criteria, 23
Legal Theory and Social Evolution, 57
Legal Theory and Social Theory, 315
Liberalism's Contradictions and Critical Legal Studies, 312
Living Law, 12
Llewellyn, Karl N., 191
Logic of Enquiry, 29
Logical Positivism, 23

Lord Buddha, 297
Lord Devlin, 35
Lord Macmillan, 287
Lord Simmonds, 35
Lundstedt, Vilhelm, 198

Mackinnon, Catherine, 323
Maine, Sir Henery, 122, 244, 248
Managerial Revolution, 135
Manu and Yajnavalkya, 249
Marriage:
- Nature, 291
- Conditions of Marriage, 291
- Number of Wives, 291
- Divorce, 291
- Maintenance of Husband, 292
- Right to Dower, 292
- Waiting for Re-marriage, 292
- Individuality of Wife, 292
- Custody of Children, 292
- Adoption, 293
- Pre-emption, 294
- Succession, 294

Marx, Karl, 130
Mayne, J.D., 244
Methods of Inquiry, 38
Mill, John Stuart, 8, 322
Millet, Kate, 319
Minimum of Effectiveness, 98
Misunderstand the Nature of Deconstruction, 335
Mixed State, 10
Model Penal Code of the American Law, 47
Modern Theories, 212
Montesquieu, 155
Moore, G.E., 21
Moral Guilt, Determinism and Legal Responsibility, 48
Morris, Clarence, 220
Mosaic Law, 197

Nagel, Ernest, 41
Narada, Brhaspati and Katyayana, 245, 249
Naradasmrti, 253
Naradiya Manusamhita, 252
National Socialist Germany, 47
Natural Law, 226
Neo-Thomism, 214
New Economic Policy, 130
Non-cognitivist Ethical Theories, 28

Olivecrona, 198
Oriental and Continental Approaches, 244
Origin of Feminist Jurisprudence, 318
Orthodox Church, 149
Ownership and Property in Eastern and Western Jurisprudence, 299

Participation in Institutional Procedures, 16
Pashukanis, 141
Pericles' Funeral Oration, 5
Period from 1921-1937, 140
Period from 1938 to the Present, 143
Period from Marx to 1920, 130
Personal Laws:
- Family Relations, 301

Philosophical and Natural Law Theories, 205
Plaint and Reply, 265
Plato, 7
Plato's Approach to Law, 6
Poincare, Henri, 38
Policy Decisions and the Art of Judgment, 43
Political Community, 71
Political Society, 71
Positivism-Naturalist Debate, 232
Post-Modernist Jurisprudence, 331
Post-Modern State and Law, 332
Post-Rgvedic Period, 246
Pragmatism in Ethics and Law, 24
Primarily an English Criminal Statue, 80
Primay Rules of Obligation, 14
Primary Social Goods, 218
Principia Ethica, 21
Principle of Analogy, 134
Principle of Indeterminancy, 93
Principles of Morals and Legislation, 69
Probable Law, 190
Problem of International Law, 229
Professor Dwaokin, 89
Professor Olivecrona, 200
Psychology and Criminal Responsibility, 46
Pure Theory, 91
Punishment, 302
Pure Comparative Law, 286

Racial Theory of Law, 121
Radbruch, Gustav, 18
Railway and Factories Accident Law, 1871, 114
Rangaswamy, Prof. K.V., 256
Realism, 182
Recognized Agents or Pleaders, 264
Relation of Justice to Law and Ethics, 57
Relativism in Ethics and Legal Philosophy, 25
Remedial Appendages, 74
Restitution Law, 336
Revolutionary Legality, 140

Rgveda Period, 245
Roby, H.J., 298
Roman-Dutch Law, 113
Roscoe Pound, 165
Ross, A.L.F., 203
Royal Commission on Capital Punishment, 47
Rulebook Community, 340
Rules and Reasoning, 314
Russian Marxists, 137

Scandinavian Realists, 196
School of Culture Feminism, 325
School of Feminist Jurisprudence, 321
School of Radical Feminism, 323
School of Socialist Feminism, 328
Science and Legal Theory, 37
Scientific Socialism, 131
Scope of the Present Book, 260
Second World War, 30, 150
Secondary Rule of Recognition, 87
Sen, Dr. P.N., 271, 289
Sicilian Tyraut Dionysius, 7
Sidewick, Henery, 26
Social and Legal Responsibility, 46
Social Criterion of the Validity of Law, 172
Social Interest in General Morals, 167
Social Interest in the General Security, 167
Social Interest in Individual Life, 169
Social Morality and the Legal Order, 32
Socialist Consciousness of Justice, 134, 140
Sociological Approaches, 154
Soloon, 5
Sovereignty of the People, 173
Soviet Communist Party, 137
Spencer, Herbert, 8, 120
Stammler, 215
Stevenson, Charles, 28
Stone, Julius, 183
Stufen Theories, 13

Tantamount to Surrender, 223
Task of Laws in Society, 162
Temporal Approach to Natural Law, 234
Theory of Adjudication, 337
Theory of Apurva or Invisible Force, 288
Theory of Interpretation, 97
Thompson, William, 322
Transcendental Idealism, 211
Toulmin, S.E., 26
Tubingen School, 164

Under, Roberto, 313
United Nations Charter, 59
United Nations Organisation, 230
Utopian Socialism, 131

Valid Law, 203
Value Judgment, 43
Vashistha Dharmasutra, 271
Veechio, Del, 8
Veid of Ignorance, 219
Vickers, Sir Geoffrey, 44
Vindication of the Rights of Women, 318
Volksgeist, 112

Wallstonecraft, Mary, 322
War Communism, 130
Weber, Max, 18
What is CLS?, 308
Wild, John, 224, 237
Williams, Professor G.L., 49, 229
Wishik, Heather, 320
Wolfenden Committee, 34
World's Legal Philosophies, 245
World War II, 78

Yajnavalkyasmrti, 249

Zeyd, 293
Zweek, Der, 158